Christmas 1961

To The Padre

With love

and best wishes

Betsy

NATURE, MAN AND GOD

NATURE, MAN AND GOD

BEING THE GIFFORD LECTURES
DELIVERED IN THE UNIVERSITY OF GLASGOW
IN THE ACADEMICAL YEARS 1932–1933 AND 1933–1934

BY

WILLIAM TEMPLE

LONDON
MACMILLAN & CO LTD
NEW YORK · ST MARTIN'S PRESS
1960

First Edition October 1934
Reprinted January and May 1935, 1940, 1949, 1951, 1953, 1956, 1960

MACMILLAN AND COMPANY LIMITED
London Bombay Calcutta Madras Melbourne

THE MACMILLAN COMPANY OF CANADA LIMITED
Toronto

ST MARTIN'S PRESS INC
New York

PRINTED IN GREAT BRITAIN

TO THE MEMORY OF

EDWARD CAIRD

PREFACE

THE most agreeable experiences in life are those which are marked by a coincidence of duty and pleasure. I have that happiness as I express my thanks to the Principal and the Senatus of Glasgow University for the honour which they did me in the invitation to deliver Gifford Lectures, and the abundant kindness which they showed me during my visits to Glasgow for that purpose. I have especially to express my gratitude to Sir Robert and Lady Rait, and to Professor Paton, for their delightful hospitality.

I must also here record my obligation to Canon Quick, the Rev. Lancelot Mason, and Mr. T. Hodgkin, who read the whole book in galley-proof and made very numerous suggestions for the clarification of statement and, in some material instances, of thought. I wish I could honestly suppose my work to deserve the labour that they have expended on it. I also cordially thank the Rev. A. E. Baker for his kindness in reading the page-proofs; and I am specially indebted to my friend and chaplain, the Rev. H. C. Warner, Vicar of Bishopthorpe, for the compilation of the Index.

One serious omission among authorities mentioned seems to call for explanation. I have nowhere referred to Dr. Tennant's great book *Philosophical Theology*. But his method of approach is so different from mine that I thought it would be more misleading than illuminative to draw attention to the many points on which I am happy to find myself in agreement with his conclusions. The difference is fundamentally one of epistemology;

but this difference leads to another affecting the use of religious experience as part of the data to be handled in the enquiry.

My purpose has not been to construct, stage by stage, a philosophical fabric where each conclusion becomes the basis of the next advance. I fully recognise the value of that method of thought, though I believe it to be more fruitful in exposition than in enquiry. For I am persuaded that the initial "certainties" of that method are bound to be abstractions, so that the cogency and clarity of the argument is purchased at the cost of detachment from actuality. My own endeavour is rather to provide a coherent articulation of an experience which has found some measure of co-ordination through adherence to certain principles. The endeavour is exposed to perils of its own, because the experience may contain illusions, and the analysis can never be carried to an ideal limit; but so far as it is successful it has the advantage of contact with actuality at every stage. I do not claim that my method is the best, or only really sound, method of philosophical thought. But I claim that it is legitimate and that it has certain merits of its own.

Men seem to differ very profoundly in the fashion of their thinking. If two men are presented with a novel suggestion and both exclaim "I must think about that", one will begin by putting together what he knows with reference to the subject, his former opinions based upon that knowledge, his general theories concerning that department of enquiry, and so forth; piece by piece he will work out his conclusion with regard to the suggestion made to him. The other will find that his mind goes blank; he will stare into the fire or walk about the room or otherwise keep conscious attention diverted from the problem. Then abruptly he will find that he has a question to ask, or a counter-suggestion to make, after which the mental blank returns. At last he is aware, once more abruptly, what is his judgement on the suggestion, and subsequently, though sometimes very rapidly, he also becomes aware of the reasons which support or necessitate it.

My own mind is of the latter sort. All my decisive thinking goes on behind the scenes; I seldom know when it takes place—much of it certainly on walks or during sleep—and I never know the processes which it has followed. Often when teaching I have found myself expressing rooted convictions which until that moment I had no notion that I held. Yet they are genuinely rooted convictions—the response, not of my ratiocinative intellect, but of my whole being, to certain theoretical or practical propositions.

This characteristic must needs affect the philosophical method of him who suffers (or gains) from it. In discussion with others I frequently find myself eager to know to which of the two types described—are they the Aristotelian and Platonic, the Pauline and Johannine, respectively?—my interlocutor belongs. So, following the Golden Rule, I expose myself to the contempt of whoso may think my own type to be contemptible.

At one time I thought of giving to these Lectures a descriptive sub-title: *A Study in Dialectical Realism*. But that might suggest an ambition to inaugurate a philosophical tradition suitably so designated. I have no such desire. But I believe that the Dialectical Materialism of Marx, Engels and Lenin has so strong an appeal to the minds of many of our contemporaries, and has so strong a foundation in contemporary experience, that only a Dialectic more comprehensive in its range of apprehension and more thorough in its appreciation of the inter-play of factors in the real world, can overthrow it or seriously modify it as a guide to action. I certainly have not supplied that more comprehensive and more thorough Dialectic; but I have sought to make a contribution towards it.

Such method in thought as I possess, and especially such grasp of the principles of Dialectic as I have acquired, I believe myself to owe to my Master at Balliol, Edward Caird. His name is venerated in Glasgow no less than in Oxford, and I have therefore ventured to confer upon my book at least this measure of distinction, that it is dedicated to his memory.

WILLIAM EBOR:

BISHOPTHORPE,
June 1934

INTRODUCTORY NOTE

It may assist the reader if the stages of the argument are set out as follows:

I. Lectures I and II. An outline statement of the field of enquiry, with some of the elements of the main problem.

II. Lectures III and IV. A clearing away of the débris *of past controversies.*

III. Lecture V. The main problem stated. A start is made from the picture of the world offered by science. The recollection that Mind is a factor in that world leads to a re-consideration of the picture. This is the first dialectical transition.

IV. Lectures VI to IX describe certain characteristic activities of Mind, or characteristics of mental activity.

V. Lecture X. Consideration of what has been set forth concerning Mind and its activity leads from a doctrine of Immanence to one of Transcendence. This is the second dialectical transition.

VI. Lectures XI to XIII set out some of the ways in which the Transcendent Mind, by its immanent operation in the world, makes itself known to finite minds.

VII. Lectures XIV and XV introduce consideration of the Evil attendant upon finite minds and the resultant conception of the relation between these and the Transcendent Mind. This is the third dialectical transition.

VIII. Lectures XVI to XVIII set out the significance of the finite in the scheme of the whole.

IX. Lecture XIX aspires towards some apprehension of the meaning of the world as so far understood for that Transcendent Mind in which it is grounded.

X. Lecture XX surveys the entire argument and concludes that Natural Theology culminates in a demand for the specific Revelation which its principles forbid it to include in its own province. This is the fourth and last dialectical transition; because of its nature, a study in Natural Theology can only indicate, not expound, the theme to which this transition leads.

Ἐμοὶ γὰρ δοκεῖ περὶ τῶν τοιούτων τὸ μὲν σαφὲς εἰδέναι ἐν τῷ νῦν βίῳ ἢ ἀδύνατον εἶναι ἢ παγχαλεπόν τι, τὸ μέντοι αὖ τὰ λεγόμενα περὶ αὐτῶν μὴ οὐχὶ παντὶ τρόπῳ ἐλέγχειν καὶ μὴ προαφίστασθαι πρὶν ἂν πανταχῇ σκοπῶν ἀπείπῃ τις, πάνυ μαλθακοῦ εἶναι ἀνδρός· δεῖν γὰρ περὶ αὐτὰ ἕν γέ τι τούτων διαπράξασθαι, ἢ μαθεῖν ὅπῃ ἔχει ἢ εὑρεῖν ἤ, εἰ ταῦτα ἀδύνατον, τὸν γοῦν βέλτιστον τῶν ἀνθρωπίνων λόγων λαβόντα καὶ δυσεξελεγκτότατον ἐπὶ τούτου ὀχούμενον ὥσπερ ἐπὶ σχεδίας κινδυνεύοντα διαπλεῦσαι τὸν βίον, εἰ μή τις δύναιτο ἀσφαλέστερον καὶ ἀκινδυνότερον ἐπὶ βεβαιοτέρου ὀχήματος, λόγου θείου τινός, διαπορευθῆναι.

Simmias in Plato's *Phaedo*

Ἐν ἀρχῇ ἦν ὁ λόγος, καὶ ὁ λόγος ἦν πρὸς τὸν θεόν, καὶ θεὸς ἦν ὁ λόγος. . . . καὶ ὁ λόγος σὰρξ ἐγένετο, καὶ ἐσκήνωσεν ἐν ἡμῖν, καὶ ἐθεασάμεθα τὴν δόξαν αὐτοῦ.

St. John's Gospel

CONTENTS

PART I

THE TRANSCENDENCE OF THE IMMANENT

LECTURE I

A great change has come over men's habit of thought concerning the distinction between Natural and Revealed Religion since Lord Gifford founded this Lectureship on Natural Theology. The distinction was originally drawn by Christian theologians, not by scientists or philosophers. What was believed on the authority of the Bible and the Church was revealed; natural theology was such thought about God as could be conducted without reference to Church or Bible. But the Bible is, amongst other things, a record of religious experience; and as such it falls within the sphere of natural theology, which may claim, and if it is thoroughly scientific must claim, to take all such experience as part of its data. Recognition of this leads to the conclusion that the distinction between Natural and Revealed Theology is not really concerned with the subject-matter discussed, but with the method of discussion. So far as a doctrine is accepted on authority only, such acceptance lies beyond the sphere of Natural Theology; but the fact that a doctrine is so accepted by some people cannot hinder Natural Theology from examining it by its own methods.

This does not mean that to accept religious doctrine on authority alone is unreasonable; it may be the most reasonable course available. And all that has made religion a power in the world has first been accepted on authority. The tendency to regard the distinction of Natural and Revealed as concerned with subject-matter and not only with method of treatment, has suggested that Revealed Religion is essentially non-rational, and has excluded from scientific Philosophy of Religion all that makes Religion worthy of philosophic consideration: thus it appeared that Religion must be either insecure or uninteresting.

The change here, as in most departments of modern thought, is due to the adoption in this field of the historical method—which is indeed the only characteristic or distinctively modern feature of contemporary thought. The chief influences at work in giving a new direction to enquiry are Psychology, Anthropology and the Comparative Study of Religions. But the new method of approach inevitably finds itself embarrassed by the fact that actual human religion is authoritative through and through, not indeed in the sense that it can only be received on the authority of other persons but that it presents itself as entitled to homage. The worshipper can no more treat his God with detached criticism than the scientist can enquire whether Truth is worth finding. It is hard to combine the attitude of worship with the intellectual integrity of scientific investigation.

LECTURE II

The first lecture led to a closer association between Natural Theology and the actual religions of men. But closer intercourse may be an occasion of greater friction no less than of greater friendliness. In spite of the present cordiality between philosophy and religion, at any rate in Great Britain, close intercourse between them is bound to result at least in tension. Throughout the nineteenth century there was an anxiety (or in some quarters hope) that science was supplanting religion; there were those who said confidently "Science does not deny God; she does better, she makes Him unnecessary".

Philosophy and Religion both claim a universal sphere, and supremacy throughout it. Here at once is material for tension if not for conflict. It is not only, or chiefly, in relation to miracles that difficulty arises; it concerns our whole mental attitude towards life and the world. The primary assurances of Religion are the ultimate questions of Philosophy. The divergence of view is specially evident in relation to three religious convictions: (1) that Spirit is the true source of initiation of processes; (2) that all existence finds its source in a Supreme Reality of which the nature is Spirit; (3) that between that Spirit and ourselves there can be, and to some extent already is, true fellowship.

Religious faith, when confronted with the problem of evil, does not prompt men to a dispassionate survey of the facts which may lead to a general view that does justice to them all; rather it inspires a passionate search for an explanation which may bring vindication of faith without denying the actuality of the evil. It finds its most searching trial in Psychology, which may suggest not only that it is incompatible with other elements in experience, but that it is in itself a fraud—a mere project of automatic processes in ourselves.

Religion starts from the Supreme Spirit and explains the world by reference to Him. Philosophy starts from the detailed experience of men, and seeks to build up its understanding of that experience by reference to that experience alone. It is worthy of notice that Christ taught men to trace the activity of God especially in the normal and calculable processes of nature, not chiefly in the astonishing and unpredictable. Much actual trouble would have been avoided if men had followed His guidance. Yet that would not remove the tension which is due to the essential character of Religion and Philosophy; but it never need be more than tension if adherents of each will remember the true character of their own pursuit. Anyhow, the heart of Religion is not an opinion about God, such as Philosophy might reach as its conclusion; it is a personal relationship with God.

LECTURE III

Perhaps the most disastrous moment in the History of Europe was the period of leisure when René Descartes, having no claims to meet, remained for a whole day "shut up in a stove". In that period he made his celebrated attempt to doubt all things: and found that he could doubt all else, but not that he was doubting; that remained certain; hence the declaration *Cogito, ergo sum*—I think, therefore I am. From this pivotal assurance of his own existence he sought to build up again this fabric

PAGE

of knowledge. This retreat upon individual self-consciousness as the one secure starting-point is the philosophical counterpart of Luther's *Hier steh' ich, ich kann nichts anders*—Here I stand, I can naught else—in the sphere of religion. Both represent the collapse of the old tradition and the need for a new start. But that could only be from the self-consciousness of the individual. This would not involve self-assertion, but it would involve self-centredness. A man would submit to the authority of conscience, but it must be his own conscience, or to the Voice of God as he heard it, but only as *he* heard it.

By reducing the initial certainty to thought which is thought of nothing, he involved himself in the necessity of holding that the mind knows only its own ideas. But some of these are clear and distinct, and the veracity of God (whose existence is supposed to be established by the Ontological Argument) guarantees that these give real knowledge of the extended world. So Descartes at last has three real entities—the mind, God, the extended world—God being the link between the other two. On the Continent the rationalist elements in Descartes were worked out, on the assumption that clear and distinct ideas give knowledge of reality. This led through Spinoza and Leibnitz to the ludicrous dogmatism of Wolf. In England another stream was set flowing which applied to the Cartesian scheme an empirical criticism, so that Locke denied the objective reality of secondary qualities, Berkeley also of primary qualities, and Hume of the mind itself—so that there was nothing left but ideas or impressions caused by nothing and held by nothing. Here Kant took up the tale and sought to unite the English and Continental lines of thought; but even for him that task was impossible so long as Descartes' statement of the problem held the field.

We are now escaping from the Cartesian entanglement. But this does not imply a return to mediaeval habits of thought. As we try to reconstruct a view of the world more consonant with actual experience and with common sense, we carry with us the emphasis on intellectual integrity which is the great merit of the Cartesian period.

LECTURE IV

MATHEMATICS, LOGIC AND HISTORY 82

Descartes' adoption of the isolated individual consciousness as his starting-point made logical certainty the only justifiable form of assurance. It is of great importance to distinguish between assurance which is logically well grounded and assurance which is not. But the most important of mental disciplines is not that which distinguishes certainty from probability, but that which leads to discrimination between the degrees of justification attaching to unproved assurances. Descartes could not help with this. But he did effect a welcome simplification. He swept aside the intricacies of Scholastic Logic, and substituted principles which provide a complete programme for the scientific era. In effect those principles recognised in mathematics a supremacy which that science had often been allowed to exercise without this formal recognition.

The connexion between traditional Logic and Mathematics is very close. The syllogism turns upon the Universal; and if its conclusion is applicable to experience, the Universal must be understood as the essence of a Real Kind. But the Real Kind with its changeless Essence does not exist. What does exist is the evolutionary Species. Logicians have not yet recognised the importance of Evolution in its bearing on their science regarded as a study of the grounds of Knowledge. The developing race has the advantage of being at once a Universal and a particular. Here the

sharp distinction commonly drawn between sense and thought breaks down, and with it must go much of traditional Logic.

But there is still need of a discipline which may produce accurate and valid thought. This must in our day be concerned with process, whereas the traditional Logic was concerned with unchanging Forms and Kinds. The modern view of the world supplies nothing more abstract or generalised than mathematics, with which a science of pure thought can concern itself. The study of all existing things must consist partly in a study of their history. The understanding and consequent evaluation of thought is to be reached by a study of the history of thought. Logic will come to be used in such phrases as "the logic of the situation". It is not a special and independent science, but the science or art of dealing appropriately with the subject-matter of the various subjects of study; for thought itself is an extension of the organic process of adjustment to environment.

LECTURE V

The Cartesian epoch put in the forefront of all philosophy the question, How is knowledge possible? Science, which could not wait for an answer to this before setting out on its actual quest of Knowledge, tended to drift away from philosophy. This was increased when science led its votaries to a belief in the late appearance of mind in the story of evolution, while philosophers made it the presupposition of all existence. But the scientific view has established itself. The world which we apprehend is apprehended as having been extant before any one apprehended it: apprehension takes place within the world, not the world within apprehension.

When further we study the history of organic life, and the appearance of consciousness in connexion with it, we must agree with Whitehead that "consciousness presupposes experience, not experience consciousness". Consciousness arises within the process of which it is conscious; it is of process, and itself is process. There is here no problem for the unsophisticated mind. We all progressively apprehend processes every day without bewilderment. But our conceptual thinking lags behind; for it the datum is not the passing present, but the past, which, as past, is fixed and no longer actual process. The place of conceptual thinking in our complete apprehension of the world is that of critical analysis in our appreciation of a work of art; it is an interim process which heightens appreciation when we return direct to apprehension.

Consciousness is generally assumed to arise concomitantly with the power of locomotion; we attribute it to the animal, but not to the plant. Similarly self-consciousness arises with the passage from instinct to intelligence as Bergson describes them, that is, from adaptation of the organism to its environment to adaptation of the environment to the organism.

But the earliest form of consciousness or self-consciousness is not cognition. It is emotional; it is sympathy and antipathy. The self does not infer the existence of other selves by observing the conduct of their bodies; it comes into consciousness as one term in relation to another self—the mother. The child is not immediately conscious of himself and inferentially of his mother; he is conscious of himself and his mother together as related terms in a single apprehension.

Mind "emerges" as an episode in the process which it apprehends. But this implies a character in that process. That the world should give rise to minds which know the world involves a good deal concerning the nature of the world. If Mind is part of Nature, Nature must be grounded in Mind. The more we identify ourselves with the natural order, the

PAGE

more we shall be compelled to assert the reality of a supernatural Creator; but for the full justification of this proposition we must wait until the whole position is more completely stated.

LECTURE VI

TRUTH AND BEAUTY 135

Hitherto we have considered the special activity of Mind and the general character of the World Process. From this point onwards we shall be concerned with the interaction of Mind and the environment which the World Process supplies for it. In this interplay Value and the apprehension of it reside. It has been customary to speak of three "absolute Values"—Truth, Beauty and Goodness; these three terms denote three forms of excellence—Intellectual, Aesthetic and Ethical. It quickly becomes apparent, however, that Truth and Beauty are not, strictly speaking, absolute Values; it is true that they have their Value in themselves, and are not to be judged by criteria other than their own; but they are not absolute, for there are circumstances in which it is better not to know the Truth, and there are instances of Beauty which in some circumstances had better not be apprehended. But Goodness is truly absolute; it could never be better that a man should be a worse man than he is.

The pursuit of knowledge derives its impulse, like any other pursuit, from desire. This should ideally be no other than desire for truth or knowledge; but in fact that is inadequate to direct the pursuit, for it will not help us to determine what part of truth to pursue, and it is impracticable to pursue it all at once. Desire is concerned with generalities, and from this fact the scientific concern for Laws and Types arises. But akin to desire, and actually prior to it in experience, is affection, which is always for individuals; and out of its concern for the individual Art arises.

What mind apprehends, even when it apprehends mistakenly, is reality; but the true apprehension of reality is gained at the end, not at the beginning, of the mental process. Mind finds reality to be such as to vindicate its own proper activity. In that mutuality of Mind and its environment is the essence of truth; and this correspondence of Mind with Reality is the essence of Value or Good. The intrinsic good or value in the attainment of truth is the discovery or recognition by mind of itself in its object.

The same must be said concerning Beauty. It is true that there is no actual good in instances of Beauty which no one at all perceives; yet when Beauty is perceived, the percipient mind finds the good in the object. It enjoys its own apprehension; but it admires the work of art. In that perception the mind finds in the object what is akin to itself: it finds itself in its other. And the mind that it finds expressed as Truth and Beauty is such as to claim reverence.

APPENDIX A: AMBIGUITIES IN THE TERMS BEAUTY AND VALUE . 162

LECTURE VII

MORAL GOODNESS 166

In the consideration of Truth and Beauty we found that Value consists in Mind's discovery of itself in its object. This, however, can only occur in full measure when the object not only represents or expresses, but

PAGE

actually is, another mind. Value or Good is therefore present in absolute form only in personal relationships. From this fact arises the uncompromising quality of obligation. This has sometimes been obscured by the recognition that different acts are regarded as obligatory in different parts of the world. That difficulty is removed when we ask what is the proper sphere of obligation. No act is universally obligatory; nor is any action, unless the motive of duty is treated as part of the action. It is always obligatory to do one's duty, but that does not determine what duty is. The only available principle here is Dr. G. E. Moore's "optimific" doctrine: our duty is to secure that the difference made by our action is the best possible, with the understanding that personal relationships are the sphere of the highest good.

This involves the result that some uncertainty attaches to many moral judgements including those by which we guide our own conduct. The only absolute obligation is the obligation to will the right so far as it can be ascertained, and, as a part of this, to take every possible step to ascertain it. But the moral life is an adventure not only in detail but in principle.

From birth we find ourselves living as members of a society with one weal and woe. By the constitution of our nature we are bound up with one another. This is the root of consciousness of obligation; though that quality in our consciousness is usually only brought into distinct apprehension when obligation clashes with supposed interest. Moral progress consists largely in the widening of the area in which the obligations of membership are recognised. Different codes of conduct are appropriate to the successive stages of this process, so that the content of duty varies from one civilisation to another; but this does not affect the nature of obligation itself, or the inherent logic which makes it a principle of progress.

Because duty is concerned with all varieties of persons it calls for infinitely delicate adjustments that can only be reached by sympathy. When we combine this with the recognition that what is obligatory is not a code of conduct but the conscientious will, we see that the only satisfactory form of the moral law is "Thou shalt love thy neighbour as thyself". But if man is made to live by love, then in the ground of that natural order from which he springs there must be the source of love.

APPENDIX B: THE MORAL PROBLEM PRESENTED BY A CONFLICT OF OBLIGATIONS 196

LECTURE VIII

PROCESS, MIND AND VALUE 198

We take our start from the picture which Science gives us of a world undergoing modifications through the interaction of its parts, while as yet there is, apparently, no mind to observe its process; within that process mind appears, and it first appears as an aid towards making effective the reactions of the organism. This "emergence" of consciousness must be due either to non-conscious causes, or to a fresh creative act of a divine mind, or to the presence of rudimentary mind in the earlier stages of evolution. The first may be dismissed as a manifest absurdity; between the other two it is not necessary for our purpose to choose; each of them makes mind integral to the world-process itself.

Mind having appeared as an aid to the life of the organism proceeds to develop a life of its own through its capacity to form "free ideas", or ideas which can be contemplated even though the reality to which they refer is not present. By this means mind acquires a certain emancipation

PAGE

from time. In any case, the "present" is not the mere meeting-point of past and future, but is so much of the process as is directly apprehensible. Mind, which arises out of flux, and is in origin an episode of the flux out of which it arises, declares its own nature by demanding permanence. It is able to hold together a whole stretch of time, and actually to apprehend the present both as the result of the past and as the cause of the future.

The relation of Process to Value is specially important. The past as fact is fixed; but the value of the past is alterable. It is even true that what was bad when it occurred may come to be rightly judged good. Thus Christians regard the Crucifixion as, in itself, the worst thing that ever happened, yet, taken in conjunction with its consequences, the best.

If we start from the physical end, we cannot account for mind; if we start from mind, can we account for physical existence? That way of putting the question is misleading. What we may reasonably ask is whether either of the two elements in the datum of actual experience is capable of accounting finally for that experience. In principle mind has this capacity. For reality comes before us as Process; mind expressed in process is purpose; and purpose is a self-explanatory principle, in the sense that when we have traced an occurrence to intelligent purpose we are satisfied. To regard the world as so explained is Theism. This involves the view that the world as created is "very good". But inasmuch as Value is alterable, that may be true even though some goods do not now exist and some evils do. The reasonable attitude is not that which says "This is good, therefore it must be real" or "This is evil; how can it be explained?" but that which asks concerning every situation that arises how good may be won out of it, and how even what is now evil in it may be made subservient to good.

APPENDIX C: AN ILLUSTRATION FROM DANTE 221

LECTURE IX

FREEDOM AND DETERMINISM 223

The problem of freedom has been confused by the tradition of associating it specially with the will and with the acts that make up conduct. This has been due to its close, but by no means simple, connexion with the idea of responsibility. An extreme doctrine of free-will is even more fatal to the idea of responsibility than is Determinism. But in fact all reasonable doctrines of freedom assert, no less than Determinism, the continuity of character. What is amiss, from the ethical standpoint, in thoroughgoing Determinism is its implied insult to personality. But the popular judgement, by associating freedom with actions, has become hopelessly entangled. For this results in presenting the question as though it raised a doubt of any real causality in moral actions; but the only alternative to causality is chance—if indeed that be anything but a name for blind causality.

Stark Determinism is stark nonsense, for if everything is completely determined by everything else, the process of mutual determination can never start. Each term must be something in itself in order either to determine others or to be determined by them. There has been some excitement in theological circles over the supposed discovery of indeterminacy at the basis of the physical world. This is misplaced. The whole contrast of freedom and determinism is due to the false supposition that freedom is chiefly shown in moments of action. But Freedom is not absence of determination; it is spiritual as distinct from mechanical determination.

or in other words, determination by what seems good as contrasted with irresistible compulsion.

The clue to the problem is in the freedom of Thought, which is possible though the capacity of the mind to form free ideas, to which it can give its attention even though the external environment does not at the time present any corresponding objects. Will, properly speaking, is the whole nature organised into effective unity; the character of this will, or organised personality, depends on its initial elements, on its social environment, and on its habitual direction of attention. Inasmuch as a personality is a largely self-organising system, it has real control over the habitual direction of attention and thus a real choice of the influences which shall determine it further.

But if the will—or habitual direction of attention—is wrong, it cannot change itself. It is free, because its direction is expressive of itself and is not forced upon it; but it is also fettered because from itself it cannot escape. It is at this level that freedom of choice exists; and so much freedom is necessary to morality; but it is not yet spiritual freedom, which is only found when choice is transcended and the personality acts by its own necessity alone. To reach that we need, not moral effort but conversion; self-determination only becomes true freedom when it fulfils itself in self-surrender to that which is entitled to receive its submission.

LECTURE X

Our survey hitherto has given us ground for such a belief in a divine Immanence as would encourage a certain religiousness of outlook but no definite religious faith. We have now to follow more carefully the line of enquiry suggested by the note of authority which is present in all experience. Experience commands our judgement rather than submits to it. The growing mind, in proportion as it is emancipated from the authority of other human minds, comes under the authority of Truth itself; and it recognises in Truth a proper object of reverence quite other than is appropriate as part of the mind's apprehension of bare fact. The sense of moral obligation towards Truth is of that quality which is only appropriate in connexion with personal claims.

The same is true concerning Beauty. The whole aesthetic experience is unintelligible unless there comes through it a revelation of spirit to spirit. There is more in Beauty than Beauty alone. There is communication from, and communion with, personal Spirit. Still more evidently are we led to this result by the claim of Goodness. The reverence which ethically sensitive persons find themselves impelled to pay to the Moral Law implies a personal righteousness expressed in that Law; for the reverence of persons can be appropriately given only to that which itself is at least personal.

If it be true that Mind is capable of initiating activity, which includes physical movements, then the physical universe is not a closed system governed only by its own laws. Further any account of the World Process as a whole must account for the occurrence of Mind as an element within it. And whatever is to account for the universe as a whole must be such as itself to require no further explanation.

Only Mind itself—of entities known to us—satisfies these conditions. But the hypothesis that the process of nature in all its range is to be accounted for by intelligent purpose is Theism. We still have to ask, however, if the Divine Mind has its whole being in the World Process or is something over and above this. Here we part company with Dr. Whitehead, with whom we have been in general agreement hitherto. If God and

PAGE

World are correlated terms, so that each explains the other, then the totality God plus World is unexplained.

Personality is always transcendent in relation to Process; it acts within it, yet stands apart from it; and this is alone adequate to the need. Personality expresses its own constancy in the infinitely delicate adjustments by which it pursues one purpose in varying conditions. As immanent it is a principle of variety; as transcendent it is (in proportion as it is perfectly integrated) unchanging. It is the transcendent personality of God which gives their quality as awe-inspiring to the Values in which He is immanent and through which He is known.

APPENDIX D: SOME QUOTATIONS FROM DR. WHITEHEAD . 270

PART II

THE IMMANENCE OF THE TRANSCENDENT

LECTURE XI

THE IMMANENCE OF THE TRANSCENDENT 277

The argument of the former series of lectures led to the conclusion that there is at work within and throughout the cosmic process a spirit which also transcends it. Moreover, there was discovered ground for the conviction that this spirit is good, as fulfilling all ideals, both intellectual, aesthetic and ethical, that claim the homage of our minds, and in relation to each of these it was found that the Spirit apprehended in and through them, is transcendent as well as immanent.

But these terms require further consideration. It appears that what is immanent is always a principle, never a person; and that what is transcendent is always a person. The principle is not actual apart from the occasions which illustrate it; personality is. Further, personality discloses its continuous identity, not in unvarying constancy of action but in infinitely delicate adjustments whereby a constant purpose may be fulfilled in varying circumstances. What a true doctrine of transcendence will assert is not a reservoir of normally unutilised energy but a volitional as contrasted with a mechanical direction of the energy utilised.

It has been commonly suggested that immanent Deity may be conceived not only as a constant principle of action but as a principle of constant action, while transcendent Deity possesses reserves of power which may be exercised by way of miracle. But personality, whether human or Divine, is, in so far as it is immanent, a principle of variability. There is in the world an immanent Reason—a Logos. If this is impersonal it may be only a principle of logical coherence.

If it is personal it must be a principle of perpetual adjustment according to "sufficient reason". But behind, or above, the successive movements of conduct in which personality is immanent there is the personality itself, transcendent and, in proportion to its completeness of integration, unchangeable. God immanent is a principle or energy of adjustment, and therefore of variation; God transcendent is the eternally self-identical —the I AM.

But if the immanent principle of the universe is personal, we must not only see the whole universe as the expression and utterance of His activity, but must expect to find in its course special characteristic and

PAGE

revealing acts, which are no more truly His than the rest, but do more fully express Him than the rest. If God is personal, Revelation is probable.

LECTURE XII

Revelation and its Mode 301

We have found reason to assert without mitigation the full personality of that ultimate Reality in which the whole universe is grounded. This is another way of asserting the doctrine of Creation. The essence of that doctrine is not that God inaugurated the existence of the world at a particular moment of time, but that it owes its existence—not only its beginning—to His volitional act.

This carries with it the possibility of unusual action where there is sufficient occasion, and such unusual action will be in the specialised sense of the word a Revelation. But we must not draw any sharp distinction between the works of God so as to regard some of these as constituting His self-revelation and the others as offering no such revelation. Either all occurrences are in some degree revelation of God or else there is no such revelation at all.

But if all existence is a revelation of God, as it must be if He is the ground of its existence, and if the God thus revealed is personal, then there is more ground in reason for expecting particular revelations than for denying them. What is the mode of such revelations? Not the dictation or suggestion of infallible oracles to the minds of individuals, but the coincidence of divinely guided events and minds divinely illuminated to interpret those events. Revelation so conceived is the full actuality of the relationship between Nature, Man and God.

Here we have at its fullest development that living intercourse of mind and world process which is the true life of thought, for here the mind, which arises within and out of the process, apprehends the process for what it truly is—the self-expression of that creator-mind in the kinship of which created minds are fashioned. The essence of revelation is the intercourse of mind and event, not the communication of doctrine distilled from that intercourse. From all this it follows that there is no such thing as revealed truth. There are truths of Revelation, that is to say, propositions which express the results of correct thinking concerning revelation; but they are not themselves directly revealed.

The event in which the fullness of Revelation is given must be the life of a person; for the revelation consists in the unveiling of a person to persons. And the marks of a true revelation are these: a union of holiness and power, before which our spirits bow in awe, and which authenticates itself by continuous development to some focal point wherein all preparatory revelation finds fulfilment and from which illumination radiates into every department of life and being.

Appendix E: A Reply to Professor Pringle-Pattison . . 325

LECTURE XIII

Spiritual Authority and Religious Experience . . 328

The supposed conflict between Authority and Experience in religion is really a tension between two indispensable elements. For the individual.

PAGE

Authority, whether as tribal custom or as alleged revelation, is prior to Experience ; in the race as a whole Experience is prior to Authority.

The authoritative quality of tradition is at its maximum where the tradition is taken to be, or to contain, a specific Revelation. This authority may stimulate an experience responsive to itself, or give to an already existing experience deeper intensity. But a particular mind may be more sensitive to other claims, and may then regard tradition with its authority as a barrier hindering the free movement of the Spirit.

Where several influences of diverse origins are at work, the current orthodoxy is commonly felt to be a restraining rather than a stimulating factor; and orthodoxy itself is constantly re-fashioned so that its permanent essence may be synthesised with an ever growing range of experience.

While in the individual this experience very largely depends on belief, and this again on tradition, it is none the less true that in the totality of religious history tradition and belief depend on experience. It is experience which gives rise to religion itself in all its aspects and also carries it forward to fresh apprehensions; and this experience in its fullest developments is always Revelation.

It is clear that Revelation, for those who accept it as such, carries overwhelming authority. But it is easy to seek this wrongly through confusing the revelation with its medium. The essence of spirituality is freedom; spirit is controlled, not by force or physical causation, but by the Good in one or other of its forms. This control only becomes operative through appreciation on the part of the spirit subject to it. Consequently the essential principle of spiritual authority is the evocation by good of appreciation of itself. Holiness, therefore, not omnipotence, is the spring of the spiritual authority of God.

Because Revelation comes in spiritual experience, that is the apprehension by divinely illuminated minds of divinely guided events, it follows that, in the reception of it, "private judgement" plays an essential part. In whatever degree reliance on infallible direction comes in, spirituality goes out. Yet this judgement is exercised in response to what claims authority. It is impossible to have knowledge of God as we have knowledge of things, because God is not a thing. We know persons only in the communion of sympathetic intercourse; and God is personal.

But besides this He is Creator, so that the communion of man with God is that of creature with Creator ; it is worship and obedience or else it does not exist.

LECTURE XIV

FINITUDE AND EVIL 356

The problem of evil only exists for those who believe that the world is created and governed by God. If there is nothing but a series of happenings guided by no purpose, there is no reason to expect it to conform to our ideals; the fact that Evil perplexes even atheists is evidence of the deep tendency of men to believe in God.

It is to be observed that while Evil can never make Moral Good contributory to itself, Good has this power in respect of Evil. Moreover, much that seems evil—such as accidents causing great sorrow—are found to be incidental to what is certainly good. The crucial part of the problem is that which concerns moral evil or sin.

Life, in the process of evolution, is found to develop minds which become subjects of value-judgements. The presence of imagination in man gives to the life of desire an unlimited expansion, because it enables the mind to present to itself the objects of desire when they are not present

to the senses. So far as Evil is a product of exaggerated or misdirected desire, the condition of its occurrence is identical with that which makes possible all the higher ranges of human life. But this does not take us far. The root trouble is in the character which determines for a man what shall appear good to him; for this will both attract his attention and control his conduct. Why are men such that what appears to them good is other than the real good?

The human mind is a focus of appreciation. It has knowledge of good and evil. The winning of that knowledge is called the Fall of Man, because acts, which before he won it were merely instinctive reactions to environment, became through that knowledge sins against the light. Again, because they are done against the light they are done with a new degree of self-assertion. And, once again, because imagination is so potent to stimulate desire, there is an additional impulse to those acts. Man in so far as he is evil is worse than any animal; and in every man there is the bias or tendency to evil.

The human mind is finite; its range is very limited. It naturally attaches more importance to values that are actual to itself; each cares more about what seems to be good for him than about goods which he does not expect to enjoy. So a man becomes not only the subject of his own value-judgements, which he can never cease to be, but also the centre and criterion of his own system of values, which he is quite unfit to be. It was not necessary that this should be so, and therefore it is not true to say that God predestined man to sin; but that it should be so was "too probable not to happen", and therefore sin must be regarded as falling within the divine purpose.

We are in part mutually determining and determined. Consequently the self-centredness of each makes others more self-centred. So the force of selfishness accumulates to the devastation of the world. And this self-centredness corrupts personality as a whole. The trouble is not fundamentally that of unruly desires as yet uncontrolled by righteous spirit; it is spirit itself which is corrupt.

Yet selfhood itself is not evil, but self-centredness. This is a spatial metaphor and therefore misleading. In a life not wholly integrated there are several centres; as integration advances these are reduced in number; but for the most devout who still falls short of perfection, there are still two: God and Self.

Enlightened self-interest may carry a man far; but only by truly disinterested love does man enter into completeness of fellowship with God.

LECTURE XV

Belief in Predestination affords the clearest illustration of the principle that an article of faith has quite different effects when it becomes matter of experience from what is expected by observers. It is commonly supposed that this belief must lead to moral and spiritual torpor; history shows on the contrary that it induces activity of peculiar energy.

The divine control is exercised at various levels from the purely physical to the purely spiritual. But our special concern is with spiritual control or control of the will. This cannot be by any system of rewards and punishments. Are we to say that God only becomes sovereign over the spiritual world by the self-initiated movement of the finite will towards submission to him? That would make His sovereignty very precarious; and such self-initiation of volition is very hard to understand. Then does all depend on the action of God in making to the soul the

PAGE

appeal which for it is irresistible? If so, why does He not at once make the appropriate appeal to every soul?

The will chooses freely; in other words it is determined by its own apparent good, and itself, by its actual constitution in each self, determines what shall be its apparent good. Hence it has, or rather is, the freedom which is perfect bondage. It is free, for the origin of its actions is itself; it is bound, for from itself there is no escape. Partial escape is indeed possible in the pursuit of truth, beauty and goodness, just because that pursuit is not self-initiated but is a response to a call from without. For the need of the self is to escape from self-centredness and this it can never do by its own effort.

The escape, when effected, always involves, at first or at last, the sharp break which is called conversion or the new birth. We see how radical this must be when we consider the implications of spiritual pride, where the self finds a self-centred satisfaction in its own state of deliverance from self-centredness.

The true aim of the soul is not its own salvation; to make that its chief aim is to ensure its perdition, for it is to fix the soul on itself as centre. The true aim of the soul is to glorify God; in pursuing that aim it will attain to salvation unawares.

The self is not wholly contaminated; every part of it is tainted, but as a rule no part is utterly corrupt. So response is possible to a divine claim; but it is not a complete response. Advance which comes as continuous progress is an expansion of the circle of which the self is still the centre.

This may theoretically be so expanded as to include all mankind, even all spiritual beings. But self is still the centre, and if God Himself be included in the circle, He is peripheral and not central. He is, for me, my God, not God whose I am.

What is quite certain is that the self cannot by its own effort lift itself off its own self as centre and re-systematise itself about God as centre. The one hope of bringing human selves into right relationship to God is that God should declare His love in an act, or acts, of sheer self-sacrifice, thereby winning their freely offered love. Then all is of God; the only thing of my very own to which I can contribute to my own redemption is the sin from which I need to be redeemed. We are clay in the hands of the Potter and our welfare is to know it.

LECTURE XVI

THE COMMONWEALTH OF VALUE 404

The bewilderment of our epoch is due to the fact that the period hitherto called Modern, as distinct from Ancient or Mediaeval, is manifestly coming to its end. Its fundamental characteristic has been re-action against the mediaeval unification, the attempt to account for experience in mechanical terms, and above all the assertion of the independence of the individual consciousness. All this has worked out in a departmentalism now run to chaos.

But we cannot go back to mediaevalism, or abandon the positive principles of the Renaissance and the Reformation. Individualism and Nationalism, the autonomy of art and science in their own sphere, are principles capable of disproportionate assertion but intrinsically sound.

We most easily begin with the moral problem of the individual. His duty is to do the greatest good that he can; but how is he to find out what that is? Above all, how is he to estimate the comparative values of two goods between which he has to choose—as, for example, whether he

PAGE

shall produce an artistic masterpiece or abandon art in order to do works of "social service". We have found reason to hold that the Good of personal relationships is the highest form of Good; ethics alone would carry us no further.

But if the Theistic position be accepted, it is apparent that the Divine Will is the source of world order, and also the determinant for every finite mind of its special place within that order and of the appropriate contribution of each such mind to the life of the whole. Consequently, the solution of the outstanding problems of Ethics is to be sought in terms neither of Utilitarianism, nor of Intuitionism, but of Vocation.

Inasmuch as some Goods only become actual as good when appreciated —Beauty being conspicuous among these—there are some that wait for appreciation as the condition of their actualisation. The Divine Mind, which cannot experience error or sin within itself, is also disabled by its very infinity from experiencing the appreciation won by courage and toil. The Harmony, which is characteristic of the world order as divinely planned, requires all the varieties of finite minds, each fulfilling its own vocation.

This Harmony of Minds and Values is the condition of eternal life. Mere everlastingness of the isolated finite mind would be intolerable. But for the self in fellowship everlasting existence is desirable and for the ideal perfection of the fellowship is necessary. As this condition is approached, the everlasting is transformed into the eternal, by perpetual approximation even if the process be never completed. But the Harmony or Commonwealth finds its centre and ground in God, who claims for the fullness of His own joy in His creation the special excellence that resides in each finite spirit as it both achieves and appreciates the values that are proper to it alone.

LECTURE XVII

THE MEANING OF HISTORY 427

History, as we now understand it, is a comparatively recent achievement of the human mind. There have been chroniclers, and real historians of contemporary events like Thucydides. But the effort to treat a great stretch of past time as Thucydides treated his own life-time seems to begin with Gibbon. The acceptance of evolution as a biological, and then as a cosmological, hypothesis, led to the use of the historical method in every branch of enquiry. This has created a frame of mind for which the passing event is alone indubitably real, while the very existence of any eternal object is matter for debate. But exclusive concern for the temporal makes it as meaningless as does the exclusive concern for the eternal which is characteristic of Oriental philosophies; for the successive, as such, cannot display meaning.

There are three main ways in which the relation of History to Eternity has been conceived. First there is the Platonic doctrine that Time is the moving image of Eternity; secondly, there is the view that eternity is the sum-total of the temporal; the third view is that the eternal is in itself constant and is the initiating cause of the temporal, and that into it the temporal in some way returns. There is also a fourth view which seeks to combine these three in such a way as to let each correct the deficiencies of the others.

The Platonic view makes History meaningless. Though the Eternal is the ground of the Temporal, it remains unaffected by it. God eternally abides, and History occurs because of Him but makes no difference to

PAGE

Him. The ethical struggle is thus reduced to insignificance. For Christianity such a view is completely unacceptable.

This difficulty is avoided by the second view, for which the Eternal is the sum of the Temporal. History and the moral struggle are thus invested with a capital importance. But this view is confronted with an uncertainty about the course of History and consequently about the character of the Eternal. And if, to avoid this, it be held that God so controls History as to guide it to the end that justifies it, once again it is become purely episodic, and God is wholly aloof from it except as its controller.

The third view, which is the naïve religious view, frankly accepts this. It does not start with either term and then effect a transition to the other; it starts with both as postulates. Thus it preserves alike the supremacy of the Eternal and the importance of the Temporal. But it leaves the connexion between them external, and supplies no reason why the Eternal ever called into being the Temporal.

In framing the fourth and synthetic theory we must first agree with the first view that History does not make a difference to the Eternal in the sense of changing it; that would indeed be a contradictory notion. But we go on to agree with the second view that History makes a great difference to the Eternal in the sense that if there were no History, or a different History, it would argue a different Eternal. The Eternal is the ground of the Historical, and not *vice versa*; but the relation is necessary, not contingent—essential, not incidental.

The end of History is not predictable from the beginning; and the beginning can only be understood in the light of the end. Consequently our apprehension of the Meaning of History is very meagre. But we apprehend these two points. It can only have meaning at all if Eternal Life is a reality; and the meaning then is one which we do not so much discover as actually make.

LECTURE XVIII

MORAL AND RELIGIOUS CONDITIONS OF ETERNAL LIFE . . 452

The possibility, at least, of eternal life is indispensable to every higher interest of man. Yet in our time there is an unparalleled absence of concern with the whole subject. This is due to the fact that in this, as in our whole outlook, we have come to the end of the Modern or Reformation period; all existing presentations of the theme are unsatisfactory. There is need to re-think the whole topic.

The hope of eternal life properly springs from faith in God. To invert this order of priority is disastrous. The chief aim of religion is to transfer the centre of interest and concern from self to God. If assurance of immortality comes before assurance of God, it may hinder that process. Except as implied in the righteousness and love of God, immortality is not a religious interest at all; it is therefore positively undesirable that there should be experimental proof of man's survival of death.

The relation of Immortality to Ethics is similar. The ethical utility of Heaven and Hell, conceived as reward and punishment, is that of a preparatory discipline from which we must escape if our actions or characters are to be truly moral. And the utility of Hell, so conceived, is very early exhausted, even if not from the outset over-weighed by disadvantages. For fear is the most self-centred of all emotions. The hope of Heaven may have a high value as implied in an independently established morality, but only in that subordination.

The authentic Christian doctrine has three special characteristics. (*a*) It

PAGE

is a doctrine, not of Immortality, but of Resurrection; (*b*) it regards this as a gift of God, not a property of the soul; (*c*) it is not so much a doctrine of rewards and punishments as the proclamation of the inherent joy of love and the inherent misery of selfishness. The stress in the New Testament is upon the quality of the life to come and the conditions of inheriting it; and the quality of that life is determined by the doctrine of God.

The possibility of man's survival of physical death is grounded in the essential quality of mind as a capacity for "free ideas". The mind increasingly organises itself and its own world apart from the processes which, for the most part, control the body as whose function the mind first came into being. As mind increasingly takes control of the organism, so it becomes increasingly independent of the organism as physiologically conceived. Man is not by nature immortal, but capable of immortality.

Here we confront a dilemma. Man's freedom seems to involve the possibility of a final repudiation of God which is for him perdition; but then God's love has failed, "which must not be". But since God is love, and love controls men through their freedom, the opposition of these two considerations is not absolute in principle. Yet a "universalism" accepted on such grounds must be true also to the principle of "abiding consequences". Thus we may avoid the demoralising influence both of the shallow optimism which says "Never mind, it will all come right in the end", and of the terrorism which stereotypes self-centredness by undue excitation of fear.

LECTURE XIX

The Sacramental Universe 473

The modern scientific view affords an apprehension of the world as existing in a series of *strata*, such that the lower is necessary to the actuality of the higher but only finds its fullness of being when used by the higher as its means of self-actualisation. Such a scheme can be regarded from either end of the series; but whichever view-point is adopted, care must be taken to avoid obliterating what is evident from the other. We must not assume that, because the actions and re-actions studied in physics and chemistry are real, therefore those studied in biology, aesthetics, ethics, or theology, are either unreal or only complicated forms of the other group; nor that, because the actuality of the spiritual is assumed, the equal actuality of the physical is doubtful. Spirit arises within and as part of an organism which is also material and expresses its spirituality not by ignoring matter but by controlling it.

In any organism the distinctive principle of unity is the highest and latest evolved. Man is both a chemical compound, a biological organism, a living mind and a spirit. But the distinctive principle which also gives unity to the whole is spirit. So too in the universe itself, if it is a single system at all, its "highest principle of unity" must be sought in spirit. When we combine this conviction with what has already been said concerning the relation of History to Eternity, we find that we are trying to conceive this relation in a new way. It is not simply the relation of ground and consequence, nor of cause and effect, nor of thought and expression, nor of purpose and instrument, nor of end and means. It finds its closest parallel in a certain element of religious tradition, so that we may best describe this conception of the relation of the eternal to history, of spirit to matter, as sacramental.

Alike from the physical and from the spiritual side there is pressure to keep matter and spirit apart from one another in our thought. Physicists rightly object to the introduction of teleology into the subject-matter of their enquiry when regarded as such. Religious people fear to contaminate

the spiritual if it is too closely associated with the material. But unless it is recognised that spirit is most of all itself in exercising control over matter, the vaunted exaltation of spirit has its counterpart in bodily immorality. It is in the sacramental view of the universe, both of its material and of its spiritual elements, that there is given hope of making human both politics and economics and of making actual both faith and love. And to such a view our whole enquiry has been leading us. For my consciousness is not something within my organism, taking note of the relations of that organism to its environment; my consciousness is itself the relation of that organism which I am to its environment.

If our whole course of argument is reliable, we reach a conviction of the independence and the supremacy of mind or spirit; we do not reach a conviction of the non-existence of matter. On the contrary, it is from an assertion of the reality of matter that we reach our conviction of the supremacy of spirit. In our final view, matter exists in full reality but at a secondary level. It is created by spirit—the Divine Spirit—to be the vehicle of spirit; and the sphere of spirit's self-realisation is the activity of controlling it.

LECTURE XX

Our survey has led us to a conception of the world as grounded in the creative purpose of the living God who "fulfils Himself" in the fulfilment of that purpose. For such a view the difficulty created by the problem of evil is especially acute. That problem, at the level of human experience, we found to be due to the extremely restricted range of minds which control their respective organisms by reference to their own apparent good. From the self-centredness so arising, and the interaction of many self-centred minds in many generations, the familiar complexity of evil arises, and even the best in man's experience is, in part, vitiated.

This corruption has its seat in the highest part of man's nature, the "principle of unity" in his organism. The source of evil is also the only source in man of his highest hope; consequently he can never grow, or lift himself, out of this entanglement of sin. Man may, indeed, by the exercise of "free ideas" conceive a world better than that which he knows; then he must work upon the actual in the light of his ideal according to the capacity of the actual to respond. But he is himself a product of the actuality which he would transform, and if he forgets this is likely to become, through his reforming efforts, more deeply self-centred than those whom he is seeking to transform.

The apparent hopelessness of the practical problem is vitally relevant to the theoretical enquiry. For if in practice evil must remain unconquered, then in theory theism is refuted.

Evil as suffering is the occasion of fortitude, and natural admiration declares that a world with both of these is better, because nobler, than a world with neither. Evil as sin is self-centredness; where love by its own sacrifice has converted self-centredness into love, there is excellence, alike in the process and in the result, so great as to justify the self-centredness and all the welter of evil flowing from it. Thus evil may be justified. But nothing meets the theoretical need of our position, except a demonstration that evil not only can be but actually is justified. Evil is actual, and only an actual justification is relevant. And this man cannot supply. He cannot meet his own deepest need, or find for himself

PAGE

release from his profoundest trouble. What he needs is not progress but redemption.

We pass here beyond the frontiers of Natural Religion or Natural Theology. From these a man may learn that worship is the fulfilment of his being exactly because its essence is that the worshipper is drawn out of himself and wholly given to the Object of worship. But Natural Religion knows no object worthy of such worship, and Natural Theology cannot supply one. Thus Natural Religion ends in a hunger for what would transform it into something other than itself—a specific Revelation.

Subject Index 521

Index of Proper Names 528

PART I

THE TRANSCENDENCE OF THE IMMANENT

LECTURE I

THE DISTINCTION BETWEEN NATURAL AND REVEALED RELIGION

Those upon whom Lord Gifford laid the responsibility of selecting lecturers on his foundation have adopted the practice of mixing among thinkers who have given their main effort to the study of philosophy or science, some whose primary avocations are in other spheres, and for whom philosophy is not a business but a recreation. In this I think they have been wise; though my evidence must be discounted as that of a biassed witness, for it is only in virtue of this practice that the great honour could ever have come to me of occupying a place in the distinguished series of Gifford Lecturers. The wisdom of the electors in taking this course is grounded in the fact that every form of mental activity tends to affect the method of approach to ultimate questions; and concern (for example) with political or administrative problems produces its effect in this matter as surely as concern with a departmental science or with metaphysic itself. I should expect to find some valuable diversity of colour and emphasis in the metaphysical constructions of a scientist, a politician and a professional metaphysician. If that expectation is well founded, then philosophy requires, for the full manifestation of its riches, the contribution of those who are not professional philosophers as well as of those who are; and one of the special contributions of this kind, particularly to the study of Natural Religion, should come from persons whose main concern is with the promotion of the specifically religious interest of mankind, unless indeed it be held that this interest is essentially spurious and delusive.

But for one whose mental habit is inevitably influenced by such an occupation there is a special need to be clear about the real scope of Lord Gifford's intention. The Lectures are to deal with Natural Theology, and are not to rely in any way on a divine Revelation accepted as such. Lord Gifford's words are these:

"I wish the Lecturers to treat their subject as a strictly natural science, the greatest of all possible sciences, indeed, in one sense, the only science, that of Infinite Being, without reference to or reliance upon any supposed special exceptional or so-called miraculous revelation. I wish it considered just as astronomy or chemistry is. . . . The Lecturers shall be under no restraint whatever in their treatment of their theme; for example, they may freely discuss (and it may be well to do so) all questions about man's conception of God or the Infinite, their origin, nature and truth, whether he can have any such conceptions, whether God is under any or what limitations, and so on, as I am persuaded that nothing but good can result from free discussion."

These words refer to the handling of the subject, which is itself described as follows:

"The Knowledge of God, the Infinite, the All, the First and Only Cause, the One and the Sole Substance, the Sole Being, the Sole Reality and the Sole Existence, the Knowledge of His Nature and Attributes, the Knowledge of the Relations which men and the whole universe bear to Him, the Knowledge of the Nature and Foundation of Ethics or Morals and of all Obligations and Duties thence arising."

At the time when Lord Gifford wrote those words the distinction between Natural and Revealed Religion was much clearer in most men's minds than it is to-day. It is important to realise that this distinction was drawn by Christian theologians, not by scientists or philosophers as distinct from theologians. During several centuries the authority of the Bible was, with whatever qualifying considerations, accepted in Europe as final. It was the vehicle of a divine self-disclosure. Natural Theology was then such thought about God—the grounds for belief in His existence, the evidence of His character, and so forth—as might be conducted without reference to the Bible. Revealed Religion was man's response in thought and feeling and purpose to the self-disclosure held to be contained in the Bible. Doubtful inferences were drawn from these assumptions and universally accepted. Thus it was the general scholastic doctrine that the existence of God is a truth of Reason, attainable without supernatural aid, while the doctrines of the Incarnation and of the Trinity are truths of Revelation, which Reason could never reach without such aid. But there have been doctrines of a divine Trinity quite apart from Christianity—in some versions of Hinduism, for example, and in Neo-Platonism. And if it be said that these are not the Christian doctrine, it must be replied that, while that is true, it is also true that there is no one complete doctrine of the Trinity accepted by all orthodox Christians. There is an orthodox formula, which excludes certain conceptions of the Divine Nature; but that formula is itself capable of many interpretations, from the approximation to Tritheism found in the Cappadocian Fathers to the approximation to Unitarianism (in this respect) of St. Augustine and St. Thomas. And in our own time men discuss whether the Hegelian doctrine of the Trinity is compatible with Christianity or not.

The supposed clearness, then, of the distinction between Natural and Revealed Religion, as it existed in the minds of our grandfathers, was partly illusory. For us it has, in that form,[1] been completely destroyed by recent study of what was taken to be the main source of Revealed Religion—the Bible. In the eighteenth century, and for much of the nineteenth, the theologian believed himself to draw his principles from the lively oracles of God contained in Holy Scripture, and developed his theology as a deductive science. The critical philosopher, on the other hand, left the Bible altogether

[1] What I conceive to be the true distinction between Natural and Revealed Religion will appear in Lecture XII.

on one side. The former was engaged in systematising Revealed Religion; the latter was exploring Natural Religion.

But we are now vividly conscious that whatever the Bible may contain of divine self-disclosure, it is also the record of a very rich and significant human experience. And while modern Biblical scholarship has made that record vivid and full of suggestion for us, the Comparative Study of Religions has set it side by side with other records of religious experience, tracing out points alike of resemblance and of contrast. There is here a whole mass of data for the Natural Theologian which was not available until recent times.

Whenever there is doubt about the precise point at which the line should be drawn between two terms which are undoubtedly distinct, but which either overlap or else possess a common frontier, it is well to employ the method known in naval gunnery as bracketing; first a shot is fired well beyond the target, then another well short of it, after which the interval is narrowed down until the target is found. Now no one disputes the right of the Natural Theologian as such to include among the facts, which he seeks to correlate and from which he seeks to draw his conclusions, the religious beliefs and practices of primitive races as described for us by anthropologists. On the other hand no one would give the name of Natural Theology to a process of thought which began by accepting as infallible the utterances of some religious leader—Buddha or Mohammed or Christ—and aimed at setting forth the experience or the duty of mankind in the light of these.

But if the religious beliefs and practices of primitive races may be included, there can be no ground in principle for excluding those of races more advanced. And in fact references to the beliefs and practices of ancient Greeks and Romans, of Moslems, Hindus and Confucians, have been frequent in Gifford Lectures: and recently Professor Pringle Pattison published a volume based on his Gifford Lectures delivered in Edinburgh during the year 1923, which deals almost exclusively with the development of religious experience and doctrine recorded in the Bible.[1]

The truth quite plainly is that the distinction between Natural and Revealed Religion or Theology is in no way directly concerned with the content of the beliefs examined, but solely with the principle determining the method of examination. So far as any doctrine is accepted on authority only, such acceptance lies beyond the frontier of Natural Theology, and all conclusions drawn from the belief so accepted must be excluded from its sphere. But the fact that a doctrine forms part of a dogmatic system, which is itself based on utterances regarded in some quarters as beyond all criticism, cannot exclude that doctrine from the purview of the Natural Theologian, provided that he considers it, or proposes it for acceptance, independently of such authority.

This is not to say that the acceptance of articles of belief on authority is in any way unreasonable. Not every man can give much time to the study of Natural Theology, and yet every man must adopt some attitude towards God; for indifference and neglect are, after all, an attitude. In view of the place which Religion has held in the experience of mankind, it is no more reasonable for any individual to adopt in practice a negative attitude towards religion on the ground that he has not proved for himself the reality of its object, than it is to adopt a positive attitude because he has not disproved it. It is a perfectly reasonable, if provisional, judgement, which declares that what has been so great a power in human life cannot be altogether illusory. It is not the beneficence of religion that is here in question; about that there is much more to be said. Our question concerns its manifest potency, for evil as for good. It

[1] *Studies in the Philosophy of Religion.*

is not inconceivable that so great a force is grounded solely in the psychological vagaries of the human mind; but it is not unreasonable to prefer the alternative hypothesis and, merely on a broad survey of human history, to adopt the view that man's religion is a movement within him of some great force which it behoves him to appreciate, or his response to some object of supreme import which it behoves him to understand, or both of these at once.

It is worth while to insist on the reasonableness of such an almost unreasoned acceptance of religion as we embark upon the enterprise of Natural Theology, for this enterprise easily leads those engaged in it to the unfounded belief that only by its means can men win the right to believe in or to worship God. But this conclusion would not only reduce to negligible proportions the number of those who are to be regarded as possessing that right; it would also destroy a great part of the evidence which Natural Theology itself is called upon to consider and to evaluate.

We are here dealing with a kind of back-wash from the excessive emphasis put upon authority in an earlier period, and the consequent false division which allocated some whole departments of belief to Revelation, leaving others as the proper sphere of Natural Theology. Here as so often the Liberalism of the eighteenth and nineteenth centuries failed through lack of thoroughness in the application of its own principles. Confronted with an apparently accepted division of religious beliefs into truths of revelation and truths of reason, it did not take the truly radical course of denying the distinction and insisting on the universal supremacy of reason; on the contrary, it accepted the distinction, and confined its attention to the truths (so-called) of reason. Its intention was to dub the other beliefs irrational, and so to divert attention from them as subjects of possible intellectual concern. It failed to observe that in this way it retained for its sphere of study themes whose living interest sprang solely from that treatment of them which it excluded. For the question whether there is a God derives all its interest from the question what manner of Being He is; and the question whether God can work miracles, or what evidence would be necessary to convince us that He has done so, is very defective in emotional thrill as compared with the asseveration that He raised Jesus Christ from the dead. Thus it could come about that David Hume should compose his *Dialogues on Natural Religion*, so cogent in argumentation, so urbane, so devastatingly polite, at a moment when John Wesley was altering the characters of thousands and the course of English History by preaching salvation through the precious Blood—a theme which one suspects that Hume and his friends would have thought ill-suited for refined conversation. If Natural Theology is restricted, or restricts itself, to the study of what has never been part of a supposed revelation, then it is concerned with what is very unimportant alike to its own students and to all mankind.

"But surely", it will be objected, "the three great notions styled by Kant 'Ideas of Reason'—God, Freedom and Immortality—are of supreme and transcendent importance to every child of man; and these are the traditional concern of Natural Theology." To which I answer that no one of these ideas is of any importance at all until it has received some measure of determination. To prove that the world is a rational whole in such sense as to make scientific procedure possible, and then to call its attribute of rationality by the name of God, is a course of argumentation in which much dialectical skill may be displayed, but it does not establish the existence of such a Being as can satisfy man's age-long search for God. Freedom, again, is a word used in many senses; there is a conception of Free Will more ruinously destructive of morality than the crudest type of Determinism; and if Immortality is the doom of the soul in virtue of its own nature to continue for ever in unending successiveness, it corresponds to no deep spiritual need, and can even become an object of truly spiritual abhorrence, as the great religions of India tragically testify.

Of these three famous terms the first and the last—God and Immortality—derive their actual content from the historical religions, not from any such Natural Theology as has excluded the content of the actual religions from the scope of its enquiry. For many generations this was concealed alike from philosophers and from the public by the tacit assumption that the meaning of the great religious terms is fixed independently of the historical religions. But this is not so; and when Kant spoke of God, he had in mind the somewhat deistic object of contemporary Lutheran faith and worship. It is only after criticising these three terms that Natural Theology has the right to use them; and when it undertakes that criticism it finds that it can give no content to these terms which will justify the expenditure of time and thought in the discussion of them, except what is drawn from the actual religion of men, which is never based on Natural Theology alone.

The source of trouble is the uncritical acceptance by Natural Theologians of that distinction of the two spheres—Natural and Revealed Religion—which was itself drawn by the exponents of Revealed Theology. What I am now contending is that the true distinction is one not of spheres but of method. And this contention would scarcely need to be advanced in these days, if the influence of the old habit of thought were not so persistent and so pervasive. For in effect that false distinction of spheres involved the exclusion from Natural Theology of all consideration of Religion itself as it has historically existed among men; it limited it to the philosophical introduction to Religion, and even then condemned it to ignorance of the subject introduced. Like Laplace, it scanned the heavens with its telescope, and either found, or did not find, that it had need of the hypothesis of God. If of late it has been less concerned with the celestial mechanism and more with conceptions drawn from biology, it is still true that for it God is too often a hypothesis, to be accepted or repudiated independently of and previously to any examination of the forms which faith and worship have taken among men. The question is whether Faith is justified; and philosophers have set themselves to answer this by considering the universal cogency of established yet ever advancing mathematics, the presuppositions of triumphant physics, the new demands of self-confident though still speculative biology—anything and everything in fact except Faith itself. Before a man says his prayers he is to gain permission to do so from a philosophy which, in deciding whether to grant such permission or not, considers everything except those same prayers. What wonder that Faith and Philosophy have tended to drift apart! There is enough in their own proper natures to make them suspicious of each other, as we shall see more fully in the next lecture, without such artificial inducements to antagonism.

No doubt the Philosophy of Religion must set Religion in the context of man's general knowledge as that has been established at any period when this enterprise of philosophy is undertaken. But this must not mean that only the context is studied, and never the subject itself. It may be that in the practice of religion men have real evidence of the Being of God. If that is so, it is merely fallacious to refuse consideration of this evidence because no similar evidence is forthcoming from the study of physics, astronomy or biology. Sir James Jeans says in his justly famous book, *The Mysterious Universe*:

"We discover that the universe shews evidence of a designing or controlling power that has something in common with our own individual minds—not, so far as we have discovered, emotion, morality, or aesthetic appreciation, but the tendency to think in a way which, for want of a better word, we may call mathematical."[1]

But his meaning is unfortunately obscure. If he means that in the course of his personally and brilliantly conducted tour of the stellar system we have found no evidence of a God who cares for our ethical and emotional interests, the answer is that no religious person, and perhaps even no sensible person, would think of looking for such evidence in that quarter, though if he has come on other grounds to faith in God as Christians believe that they know Him, he will gladly link together the declaration of God's glory by the heavens and the purity of His law which converts the soul.[2] If, however, Sir James Jeans intended his words to be taken more absolutely, and to convey an actual denial of evidence for the moral character of God, we must assert very plainly that he has no right to draw that conclusion from any premises which he has put before his readers.

The fact that astronomy reveals God only as mathematician is not surprising, for astronomy is a mathematical science studying the mathematical aspects or functions of the objects under review. If we attend to no other aspects, it may leave us gazing spellbound but fundamentally hopeless into the depths of

> The everlasting taciturnity—
> The august, inhospitable, inhuman night
> Glittering magnificently unperturbed.[3]

So a great poet interprets for us one mood—a legitimate but not a necessary mood. Another poet, who is himself, in the words of a third, "gold dusty with tumbling amidst the stars",[4] will see the moon as an "orbed maiden with white fire laden", round whom may be perceived, through a cloud-rent, the peeping and peering stars as they "whirl and flee like a swarm of golden

[1] *Op. cit.* p. 149. [2] As is done in the nineteenth Psalm.
[3] William Watson, *Melancholia*.
[4] Francis Thompson, *Shelley*, p. 18, in vol. iii. of his *Works*.

bees", and the depths of heaven's vault becomes the "star-inwoven tapestry" that curtains the sleeping sun.[1]

The plain and crude fact is that you can get out of philosophy just what you put in—rearranged no doubt, set in order and rendered comprehensible; but while the machine may determine the size and shape of the emergent sausage, it cannot determine the ingredients.

Surprise has lately been expressed that mathematics appears to be the only fully surviving science, for all others are passing into mathematics. It would not have surprised our forefathers: *Optime autem cedit inquisitio naturalis, quando physicum terminatur in mathematico.*[2] But this is due to the acceptance of a mathematical ideal for science, which we must discuss on a later occasion. For the present it is sufficient to observe that *if you begin by attending to objects only in so far as they are measurable, you are likely to end by having only their measurements before your attention.*

The argument, however, is carrying us beyond the province of this introductory discussion. Enough has been said to expose the futility of the method to which, until lately, Natural Theology condemned itself. But it is fair that we should remind ourselves how deep a separation from established tradition would have been involved in any avoidance of this course. The historical method and historical habit of mind are novelties in this realm of thought; indeed they are the great distinguishing characteristics of the "modern thought" of our era. It was not open to theologians or philosophers of an earlier period to make use of them. Consequently our forefathers were precluded from tracing out the process, so familiar to us, whereby an initial act of divine revelation, or what was taken for such, has led to fresh forms of religious experience or to new exploration of divine mysteries, and has thus issued in an accepted formulation, which itself becomes the starting-

[1] Shelley, *The Cloud* and *Hymn of Apollo.*

[2] Bacon, *Novum Organum*, ii. 8.

point of further novelties in experience and in doctrine as these interact upon one another. For those to whom such an enquiry was almost impracticable, there was no escape from the dilemma which offered either Reason or Revelation as the source of any religious conviction, with no third alternative and no recognition of any serious intermixture. No doubt it was always recognised that Reason may work upon the content of Revelation; but this was to explicate it, not to affect it in any essential way. And, as has been already said, it was the exponents of Revealed Religion who, for very good reasons as will shortly appear, insisted on the non-rational or supra-rational origin of the "truths of revelation". It is true that for them God was the source of Reason, and that there was therefore nothing intentionally irrational in their view of either the method or the content of Revelation. But such doctrines as those of the Trinity or the Incarnation or the Atonement could never have been reached, it was held, by any process of human reasoning, though reason had had its part in formulating them for presentation to men's understanding.

When, in the sixteenth century, philosophy began its course afresh in independence of an avowedly accepted theology, it was almost inevitable that it should at first accept this situation. It had no desire to break with the accepted theology, if only it were left free to follow its own methods for its own purposes. It had no interest in attacking (for example) the Church's Trinitarian doctrine. That lay off its track. It was a truth of Revelation; no one was supposed to be able, still less to be required, to reach it by scientific enquiry into men's normal experience of the natural universe. The philosopher himself could quite well accept it on the authority of Revelation, and neither cause nor feel anxiety on the ground that his philosophy did not actually lead him to it.

But this frame of mind could not be permanent. As

soon as the spirit of independent enquiry was established, it vindicated itself in ways that were bound to have reactions in all departments of thought. More particularly the theories resulting from independent enquiry offered themselves for verification. The desire to test all propositions by actual experience became dominant. Doctrines which relied for their commendation on the august character of the authority promulgating them began to be at a disadvantage. A distinction which had once protected the truths of Revelation now tended to involve them in contempt. Natural Theology no longer suggested that beyond its reach lay truths which the soul could embrace with an assurance never due to its own conclusions, but rather suggested that it alone offered the grounds of certitude, which are to be found in the realm of possible experiment, while beyond lay flights of fancy on which whoso would might embark provided he did so as a private venture at his own risk.

Thus was reached the situation which has been described, in which it appeared that the method which had some promise of cogency could only achieve what has little interest, while all that gives interest and power to Religion has its source in spheres that are not open to criticism and are therefore ignored or reverenced with equal intellectual right. Religion, it appeared, must be either insecure or else uninteresting.

From that situation we have been making our escape, though the deliverance is still incomplete. It is largely the work of three allied sciences—Psychology, Anthropology and the Comparative Study of Religions. For these have undertaken to treat as the subject of scientific enquiry exactly those traditions, beliefs and practices which were previously regarded as lying beyond the scope of such enquiry. At first this new development only brought under examination the cults of primitive races or the beliefs of religions other than that familiar among ourselves. The scientific investigation of the Bible led to much alarm and indignation while it was still an innovation, and the psychological treatment of prayer and worship and conversion is still an occasion of apprehension in many quarters. This is partly due to the survival of a sense that what springs from divine revelation should be accepted without criticism, partly also to the fact that the scientific tradition has not in the past made its count with the possibility of Revelation, which *ex hypothesi* lay beyond its sphere, with the result that many scientific enquirers approach their subject with a strong presupposition that no such thing exists.

What is needed, and what is plainly coming to pass before our eyes, is the deliberate and total repudiation of any distinction of spheres as belonging respectively to Natural and Revealed Religion or Theology. It is abundantly clear that a great deal, at least, of the actual religion of mankind is traced by its adherents to a supposed act of Revelation or to a tradition so deeply rooted as to have the equivalent of divine authority. In Hinduism the system of Caste is not accepted as being a valid generalisation from human experience. The position of Buddha among his followers does not depend on the cogency of the reasoning by which Buddhist philosophers may seek to justify it. The Koran claims its authority on the strength of its alleged divine origin. No doubt it is true that in the very long run a failure to produce any rational defence of these positions may make them untenable. What is contended is that as a matter of historic fact the Hindu or the Buddhist or the Moslem holds his belief independently of any rational justification of it. But this fact, and the various beliefs thus held, are themselves the proper subject of scientific enquiry, and that enquiry is now well established. In just the same way the beliefs and practices of Christians have been increasingly made the theme of such enquiry, to the great advantage, as I am persuaded, of those beliefs and practices themselves, and to the vastly increased interest of Natural Theology.

Let it then be frankly and fully recognised that there neither is, nor can be, any element in human experience which may claim exemption from examination at the bar of reason. If reason's attitude to the arcana of Religion has sometimes seemed truculent and unsympathetic, that is largely because Religion has tried to exclude reason altogether from investigation of its treasures. This was natural enough, but unwise; and in our days, when the authority of science is a far more potent force among men than the authority of religious tradition, the unwisdom is apparent in the disaster to which it has led.

One lamentable result of that false division of spheres which we have been considering is traceable in the habit of mind with which the study of religion has been approached. Few whole-hearted believers in any of the great religions have attempted the most difficult task of a dispassionate examination of their convictions. The task has thus been in great measure left to those who study all religions from outside. These may be reverent; they may be sympathetic; yet even so, if they are not worshippers of God, they cannot speak of worship with real knowledge. A man who is colour-blind may master the science of optics, he may be as competent as any one else to follow discussions of rival theories of light, but he will never see a sunset as others see it, and his appreciation of a poetic description of it is bound to be sadly limited. So the man, who studies the worship of others but is not himself a worshipper, may discuss with clarity and insight the grounds which prompt men to worship, or which lead them to a sense of sin and its forgiveness; but what those things are in themselves and in their pervasive influence on experience as a whole, he can never know unless he learns to worship. The problem thus created will concern us in the next lecture.

But the undertaking to examine scientifically the living content of actual religions has difficulties of its own. These are not only due to the general and almost diametrical opposition between the intellectual habit natural to Religion and that appropriate to Science; to the consideration of that opposition we must return.[1] But there is a special difficulty arising from an element in Religion so universal as to be apparently essential. This is precisely that note of Authority which led to the division of spheres about which so much has been already said.

The plea was made earlier that there is nothing unreasonable in the acceptance by any individual of a religious creed on the basis of what seems to him adequate authority, if only because not every one has time to examine the arguments that may be adduced for or against the principle of religious faith in general or any given religious creed in particular. But that is a very small part of the relevant truth. Far more important is the consideration that almost every one who has any religious belief at all forms it in the first instance on the basis of authority, and, even though he may find reason for it as years go by, this process does not weaken the authoritative element in his creed but rather strengthens it. This is a point so frequently misconceived, so essential to the life of Religion, and so important, even if also very awkward, for the study of Natural Theology as we now understand it, that some time must be spent in its elucidation. With its significance we shall be concerned throughout these lectures.

For we understand by Natural Theology the scientific study of Religion, as it exists among men, in relation to the general interpretation of man's experience as a whole within which religion is a part. Religion claims indeed to be not only one part along with others, but the dominant element, exercising over all the rest a certain judgement and control. The investigation of that claim is one of the functions of Natural Theology; it may have to declare it invalid and presumptuous;

[1] See Lecture II.

certainly it cannot admit it without criticism, for to do that is to go over to the other theological method with which Natural Theology is contrasted; but while it cannot admit this claim at the outset, it must observe as part of the subject under review the fact that the claim is certainly made. And in just the same way Natural Theology must recognise that actual human Religion is authoritative through and through, and that this characteristic becomes more, not less, conspicuous as the religious life matures. No doubt this fact is the explanation of the false distinction between Natural and Revealed Religion or Theology, which bases the contrast on their contents instead of on the method of handling those contents.

Now it is universally recognised that religious belief, like all other, rests at first on authority.[1] There is here no relevant difference between a child brought up by religious parents and a full-grown unbeliever converted by the appeal of a preacher. In the latter case the act of surrender is more conscious, and it is also more conspicuous because surrender is a less frequent occurrence in the life of an adult than in that of a child. But it is still, in both cases, surrender. The number of instances in which a man becomes in a living sense religious because he has been convinced by argumentation must be extremely small.

The child accepts what he is told concerning God as he accepts all else that he is told by those in trust upon whom he lives, according to his capacity to receive it. In the same way he accepts the dogmatic assertion that $7 \times 7 = 49$ without working it out for himself. But in most departments of life the basis of belief is gradually shifted from the authority of parents and teachers

[1] It is important to remember that there is no contrast between Reason and Authority. It is impossible to accept a belief on Authority except so far as the Authority is accepted by Reason. In so far as a child's acceptance of what he is told is *totally* uncritical, that is not acceptance on Authority, but on the causal action of impressions received. His belief rests on Authority only when his acceptance of what he is told is due to trust in those who tell.

to his own experience and his own reflection upon this. And so far as this happens, his belief becomes more autonomous. It is his own; he has verified and vindicated it. He is still grateful to parents and teachers—more grateful now than ever. But his belief no longer rests on their authority. He has put it to the proof himself; very likely in so doing he has modified it; but in any case it is now his own, not something which he has borrowed from others.

The process is familiar also in religious growth. But here there is a difference. The believer who finds that experience and reflection confirm his belief is also in the position of having changed a faith rooted in the authority of teachers to one based on and vindicated by his own experience and criticism. In that sense he too is translated from dependence on authority to a real autonomy. Yet that is not the feature in the situation which is most conspicuous to himself. No doubt, if challenged, he is ready to assert the immediacy of assurance with which he now holds his faith. But it requires a challenge to bring that aspect of the matter into prominence. What he realises day by day is that his growth in personal certitude, in detachment from any human authority, has brought him into ever closer relations with a Being who claims the allegiance of his entire nature—desire and thought, conscience and will. He is delivered, not from, but to, authority, though to authority of a new kind; for the point on which he has reached personal conviction is the existence of a God entitled to exercise authority over him, and of his own consequent obligation to serve and obey that God. He does not find here any conflict with reason; nothing can be so reasonable as total submission to the God with whom he has to do. It is not unreasonable for the ignorant man to trust and implicitly to follow the expert; on the contrary, it is unreasonable for him to set up an ill-formed judgement in opposition to real knowledge; he may begin to study the subject so that he may understand the expert, but till his understanding is equal he will defer in judgement. So to the devout man it would seem the height of unreason that he should set up his judgement against that of his God. He, too, will try to understand the mind of God, but he will not expect to reach the end of that enterprise, and as he looks back upon his philosophisings in the light of his vision of God he will exclaim with Job:

"Who is this that hideth counsel without knowledge? Therefore have I uttered that I understood not, things too wonderful for me, which I knew not. I had heard of thee by the hearing of the ear, but now mine eye seeth thee; wherefore I loathe my words and repent in dust and ashes."[1]

"Yes", it may be urged, "that is the character of Religion, and so much the worse for Religion. It is at root a fanatical devotion to uncriticised oracles. It flourishes in every sort of Infallibilism—it may be of the Pope, it may be of the Bible, it may be of the Koran, it may be of individually accepted Guidance. It can give no justification for its initial act of surrender, and it instinctively makes war upon all criticism because it knows that in the end it cannot sustain itself by reason; therefore it will admit reason only as exponent of its fundamental dogma, whatever that may be, but never as its judge."

That contention is not without truth, and it is well, at the outset of an attempt to set forth a rational view of Religion, to recognise that the various irrationalities which have attended its whole history are not mere accretions. If they are perversions, they are what may be called true perversions; that is to say, they are not imported from without, but are developments of such a kind as to be quite inevitable if the purely religious interest is not balanced by and harmonised with others.

It is a modern, and already happily vanishing, delusion to suppose that in the eyes of religious people all Religion is invariably good. The truth is that Religion

[1] Job xlii. 3, 5, 6.

is a very great power for good or evil, and it is therefore supremely important to secure that its power is for good. The highly developed religions do not look upon their rivals as essentially colleagues in a conflict with irreligion. There is a great danger as well as a deep truth in the contemporary realisation that all religions have a common cause against secularism. For while it is certainly true that all religions posit a spiritual interpretation of the universe, and must all alike perish if that is discarded, it is by no means true that any religion is better than none. A strong case could be made for the contention that on the whole Religion, up to date, had done more harm than good. Nor is this a purely modern conception based on standards supplied by humanitarian ethics. "*Tantum religio potuit suadere malorum*," is the cry of the greatest of Latin poets.[1] There was indeed in the ancient world little possibility of atheism; there was for most men only a choice between one deity and another. But this did not make the adherents of one creed tolerant of those of others. The Biblical writers of the Old Testament have as a rule no doubt that the worshippers of the ethnic deities are better destroyed; and the prominence given to Idolatry as the greatest of sins is hardly compatible with a modern tolerance which might say, "Well, of course you ought to worship Yahweh; but if you cannot bring yourself to do that, at least become a worshipper of Moloch". We have come falsely to suppose that the essence of Idolatry is found in the worship of material images; but that kind of idolatry comes second in the Decalogue. The first commandment is: "Thou shalt have none other gods but Me"; and the same is reiterated to-day in the cry of the Moslem muezzin. Religion itself, when developed to real maturity, knows quite well that the first object of its condemnation is bad Religion, which is a totally different thing from irreligion, and can be a very much worse thing.

[1] Lucretius, *De Rerum Natura*, i. 101.

If that is so, we are not censuring the inner principle of Religion when we say that some natural developments of that principle are false and bad. We have indeed as yet found no criterion for distinguishing these from developments which are true and good. We have only found that the distinction must be drawn and the criterion discovered.

The recognition of the indestructible note of authority—not in human teachers but in the object of religious faith itself—has lately been brought home to European readers by Rudolph Otto in his well-known book *Das Heilige*,[1] and also by theologians of the school of Barth and Brunner. What Otto speaks of as the "*Mysterium tremendum*", the quality in the object of religion which he describes as "Numinous", is just that before which we do not reason but bow. He recognises that the perception of this needs to be educated, and that in the end the most rational faith is also the most religious. But this does not mean that there is any assertion of independence or autonomy in the believer. The sense of "creatureliness", to use Von Hügel's favourite expression, remains and is intensified; for all the elements of human nature, including sovereign reason itself, are united in our acknowledgement of the transcendent Majesty of God and of our creaturely insignificance in face of it.

To reach that point a man must, like Job, retain his integrity; he must not consent to lie on behalf of God,[2] for that involves attributing to God something less than perfect goodness and truth. Yet the end is total surrender.[3] And even if the Voice of the Almighty says to the prostrate worshipper, "Stand upon thy feet, and I will speak with thee", yet it must be the Spirit of the Almighty which strengthens him to stand in that Presence.[4]

Now the first thing to recognise about this charac-

[1] *The Idea of the Holy.*
[2] Job xiii. 7, 8, 15; xlii. 7.
[3] Job xlii. 5.
[4] Ezekiel ii. 2.

teristic of religious development is that it is by no means without parallel, and the parallels may suggest the direction in which we are to look for the criterion that will help us to distinguish between true and false developments of the essential principle. The transition from the child's belief that God exists, which is based on the teaching and practice of others, to the man's belief, which is expressed in the same words but is based on his own experience and reflection, has been so far compared to a similar transition in relation to any particular proposition, such as that $7 \times 7 = 49$. But this is not the right comparison. *A belief in God based on experience and reflection is not one particular apprehension among others, but an apprehension of universal import. It corresponds, not with the scientist's apprehension of some one Law of Nature, but with his conviction of the supreme claim of Truth.* If the scientist were asked to explain why he must give loyalty to Truth precedence over all other considerations, he would find it hard to comply. It does not seem to him unreasonable, but he cannot give a reason for it, because it is the rational presupposition of all particular "reasons".

Scientists do not often give accounts of their conversion or vocation. But there have been scientists who suffered persecution for their loyalty to truth, and it must be often that a clash occurs between that loyalty and various enticements of personal or worldly interest. Now this loyalty to truth is inculcated in childhood as surely as faith in God, and there is a transition from the child's apprehension of it at second-hand to the scientist's independent grasp of it. But when he grasps it, it is not something which he masters; it is something which masters him. And here too, arising out of this loyalty to Truth, there may be perversions in either direction; there may be obscurantism, such as Mr. Bernard Shaw claims to find in the General Medical Council, or there may be fanaticism such as many Christians think they see in the so-called rationalism of the Rationalist Press Association. And we must recognise that these, if perversions at all, are true perversions—that is to say, they spring from real loyalty to Truth, though the conception of Truth which gives rise to them is narrow and one-sided. And the way of remedy is the way of ever closer adherence to the central core of the fundamental principle of Truth in its purity but also in its fullness.

Scientists seldom give accounts of their conversion or vocation. Poets are less reticent. This is partly because the poetic temperament is naturally given to self-expression, partly because devotion to Beauty is less often inculcated in childhood than devotion to Truth or faith in God, so that its emergence, if it ever emerges at all, is more prominent in consciousness. Among many expressions of this sense of vocation to a conscious loyalty Shelley's is perhaps the most explicit:[1]

Spirit of Beauty, that dost consecrate
  With thine own hues all thou dost shine upon
  Of human thought or form,—where art thou gone?
. . . .
  Man were immortal and omnipotent,
Didst thou, unknown and awful as thou art,
Keep with thy glorious train firm state within his heart.
    Thou messenger of sympathies,
    That wax and wane in lovers' eyes—
Thou—that to human thought art nourishment,
    Like darkness to a dying flame!
    Depart not as thy shadow came,
    Depart not—lest the grave should be,
Like life and fear, a dark reality.

While yet a boy I sought for ghosts, and sped
  Thro' many a listening chamber, cave and ruin,
  And starlight wood, with fearful steps pursuing
Hopes of high talk with the departed dead.
I called on poisonous names with which our youth is fed;
    I was not heard—I saw them not—
    When musing deeply on the lot

[1] Shelley, *Hymn to Intellectual Beauty*

Of life, at the sweet time when winds are wooing
All vital things that wake to bring
News of birds and blossoming,—
Sudden, thy shadow fell on me;
I shrieked, and clasped my hands in ecstasy!

I vowed that I would dedicate my powers
To thee and thine—have I not kept the vow?

It is not always easy for the artist to keep that vow. If in Shelley's case the difficulty came as much from his loyalty to Truth and Right, as he understood them, as from loyalty to Beauty, yet there are many artists in words, in line, and in colour, in bronze or marble, in tone and rhythm, who have had to choose between the gains of popularity and loyalty to the Beauty they had apprehended. Art and Science have their martyrs equally with Religion. And we do despite to their experience if we say that they suffer for fidelity to their own ideals and therefore, indirectly, to themselves. "To thine own self be true" is a piece of high-class ethical futility which Shakespeare appropriately puts into the mouth of his own most priceless old dotard.[1] The first condition of attainment in Science or Art or Religion is not loyalty to self, but forgetfulness of self in concentration on the Object; it is most truly the meek who possess the earth.[2] But that Object is not a passive recipient of recognition or of homage. To perceive it is to be conscious of its prehensive grasp, not only calling but drawing the percipient into its allegiance and service.

We have here the clue, only to be followed with diligence and pain—or at least the readiness to suffer pain—by which we may learn to distinguish true from false developments of the central principle in Art or Science or Religion. For despite the intense objectivity

[1] *Sc.* Polonius. See *Hamlet*, Act I. Sc. 3. Shelley's vision of Beauty taught him "to fear himself and love all humankind". For the truth that is distorted by Polonius see below, p. 195.

[2] St. Matthew v. 5.

of each of these in its own essence, yet of necessity the apprehension of the Object is subjective, and the selfhood of the perceiving subject must introduce limitations, and may introduce distortions, into the perception. Criticism must be sympathetic, or it will completely miss the mark; but it must also be dispassionate and relentless, and nothing whatever must be allowed to escape its universal inquisition. In the sciences this criticism is part of the scientific process itself; in the aesthetic sphere it has the name of criticism as used in the specialised sense; in relation to Religion the task of criticism is discharged by Natural Theology. Natural Theology should be the criticism of actual Religion and of actual religious beliefs, irrespective of their supposed origin and therefore independently of any supposed act or word of Divine Revelation, conducted with full understanding of what is criticised, yet with the complete relentlessness of scientific enquiry.

LECTURE II

THE TENSION BETWEEN PHILOSOPHY AND RELIGION

We have been led to conceive Natural Theology as that philosophical discipline which pursues enquiries into the true nature and general validity of Religion, making use of the actual religions of mankind to assist it in this enquiry, and setting Religion as a whole, and therefore also each religion in particular, in the context of our knowledge and understanding of the universe. The changed mental attitude which has been noticed and commended only affects this conception so far as it envisages Natural Theology as drawing on the contents of what purports to be Revealed Religion, and regarding these as an important part of the data into which enquiry must be made. There is no doubt, for example, that millions of human beings have believed the creed: "There is no God but God, and Mohammed is the prophet of God". Natural Theology does not say that this creed must therefore be accepted as true, or the whole fabric of philosophy so schemed as to include it and to be in harmony with it. But Natural Theology must say that here is one of the major facts in the actual religious history of mankind, and an enquiry into the nature of religion must take account of it, and of other similar beliefs.

But this closer relationship between Natural Theology and the actual religions of men does not of necessity lead to a greater friendliness. Closer intercourse may be a cause of greater friction. While actual Religion needs the services of Natural Theology for its purgation, it can hardly be expected to welcome them with cordiality.

So long as Natural Theology was concerned mainly

with proofs of the Being of God, the devotees of Religion in its various forms could afford to pay scanty attention. The traditional proofs might be declared valid: well and good; Religion welcomed a new support. Or they might be declared invalid; less well, no doubt, but still well enough; for worshippers were not led to their belief or practice by any of those proofs. Nothing would be serious except a formal disproof of the Being of God, and that was not forthcoming. To deny the validity of an argument does not trouble any man unless in fact he had relied upon that argument.

But when secular thought began to offer an alternative account of facts for which any religion was supposed to offer an account of its own, a conflict between that religion and the secular thought of the day was inevitable. Thus it came about that Darwin's alternative explanation of the Origin of Species stirred up a great deal of excitement in the religious world, while Hume's fundamental scepticism had stirred but little. Darwin's hypothesis was in fact compatible with all that is of religious importance in the Biblical account of Creation and of the Fall, whereas Hume's philosophy is not compatible with any rational faith of any kind. But Hume's scepticism touched faith at a point where faith knew that it was in origin non-rational, and it confined itself to agnosticism; it did not positively invade the sphere of faith, except so far as Miracles are within that sphere; and by a curious paradox the discounting of Hume on account of his general scepticism seems also to have been taken as discrediting his very formidable argument against Miracle. Darwin's version of evolution, on the other hand, invaded a province which faith had until that time regarded as its own.

The same point may be made with reference to the recent developments of Psychology and of the Comparative Study of Religions. Here the beliefs and practices of the adherents of a particular religion, who hold those beliefs and follow those practices in obedience to a supposed Revelation, are accounted for by reference to general tendencies of the human mind and are set side by side with the beliefs and practices of others who have not received, or even have repudiated, that supposed Revelation. This at first is very disconcerting, and certainly calls for a rather fundamental readjustment of mental attitude. The impression is created that what had been regarded as the foundation of religious life was after all an unnecessary hypothesis. The attitude of non-religious thought ceases to be hostile to religion, and becomes contemptuously indifferent—a more insidious form of attack. The declaration of the young free-thinkers of the Congress of Liège in 1865 went to the heart of the matter: "Science does not deny God; she goes one better, she makes Him unnecessary."[1]

Throughout the latter half of the nineteenth century religious people in Western Europe had the feeling that this was happening over the whole area of religious interest. There had been no occasion to determine the proper relations between Religion and Science, and Science seemed to occupy one region after another. Was there any place left for God?

Now though the tension and friction arose through the impingement of particular sciences upon particular religious beliefs, yet the real ground for it lay in the very nature of Religion and Science themselves. It is necessary therefore to go back to those more general considerations about which there was less bitterness of controversy, because they underlie the questions on which bitter controversy has occurred.

There are two main factors in the tension between Philosophy and Religion: the first is the identity of the province in which each claims supremacy; the second is the complete opposition in their method of dealing with it resulting from a difference of aim. For Philosophy seeks knowledge for the sake of understanding, while Religion seeks knowledge for the sake of wor-

[1] See René Arnaud, *The Second Empire and Napoleon III.*, p. 328.

ship. The province claimed by both is the entire field of human experience. No one doubts this in the case of Philosophy; its attention may be directed at any one time to some one department of experience; but it always holds itself free to follow the argument into any other department where matter relevant to its enquiry may be found. And so far as philosophers aim at constructing philosophic systems, their aim is to include the governing principles of every department in one coherent synthesis.

In the case of Religion, universality of scope is not always recognised. This is due to the fact that the concern of Religion is different with different departments of experience, not because there are some with which it has no concern at all. No one in the modern western world disputes the proposition that Religion is concerned with Ethics. Here its concern is practical as well as, perhaps more than, theoretical. It sometimes purports to give direction to ethics; sometimes it provides added inducements for ethical behaviour; sometimes it offers actual power to respond to ethical obligation; or it may do all of these at once. The relation of Religion to Physics is totally different. Here it certainly does not offer direction or inducements, and can only be said to offer power so far as the peace of mind which it occasions may facilitate concentration and integrity of thought. Yet it insists that the Laws which physical science discovers are expressions of the mind of God, and is ready to offer resistance at once if, on the basis of Physics, a proposal is made to dispense with all reference to God in what claims to be a complete interpretation of the universe.

Between these two limiting instances fall various grades of concern on the part of Religion with aspects of the world as they are studied by the different sciences. Biology comes nearer to Religion than Physics comes; and there are ideas easily suggested by some biological theories which Religion would be bound to resist. But these do not lie within the field of Biology itself; they may be illustrated by a familiar version of Determinism often associated with the doctrine of Natural Selection in that neo-Darwinian form of it which is supported by Weissmann and his school. That, as a complete account of human nature, Religion would be bound to resist. Such resistance involves no claim to dictate conclusions to the science of Biology, for Determinism is a theory outside the limits of that science. Broadly speaking, the attitude of Religion to Biology is the same as to Physics. It has nothing to say to Biology that can affect the methods or conclusions of that science, but claims any established biological conclusions as added knowledge concerning the works of God. This is true also of its relation to Physiology.

When we pass to Psychology the question is complicated by the fact that the province of this science is not as yet clearly delimited. Sometimes it is treated as if it were identical with general Philosophy; in that case Religion has a great deal to say to it. If, for example, Psychology presumes to account for all experience in such a way as to class its religious content under the heading Illusory, it is clear that every form of Religion must resist. Again if Psychology be so reduced as to be almost indistinguishable from Physiology, with the strong implication that the material body as known to Physiology is the sole constituent of personality, Religion must insist that its own life is a denial of any such doctrine. If, however, Psychology takes for its field of study the actual processes of the human mind in its impulses, sentiments and emotions, its habits of thought, feeling and volition, then Religion has only to claim that the experience of devout persons shall be treated with as much seriousness as that of others. To do this will of itself prevent the psychologist from affirming (to take the same example again) any of the spiritually objectionable forms of Determinism. But here the contact is closer than in the case of Physics or Biology, just because Religion must demand of Psychology the serious study of its own manifestations, whereas it has no such demand to make of the physical sciences.

No doubt Psychology is liable to aberrations from which the physical sciences are safe; their dangers lie in other directions. Because Psychology studies mental processes, it is very liable to behave as if Logic (the study of the validity of mental processes) were one of its own subdivisions. But in fact Psychology, like every other science, must presuppose the autonomy of Logic; otherwise the writings of psychologists could be no more than their own autobiographies—not nearly so interesting or important as the autobiographies of statesmen, soldiers or artists. The interest which a psychologist claims for his theory is not that he happens to hold it, but that it is a true account of your experience and mine as well as of his own. But in this case he must have something to say in support of his theory over and above its psychological history. For every theory ever held has a psychological history. A theory which teaches that this is all that can be said about theories, condemns itself to the same futility as the rest. Psychology, like Physics or any other science, presupposes the existence, and some criterion, of truth: but that belongs to Logic.[1] And the failure of many psychologists to do justice to Religion is rooted in their neglect, or inadequate comprehension, of Logic. To what is involved in an adequate comprehension of Logic we must return.

With Politics and Economics there is much dispute whether Religion has any direct concern or not. But this dispute really turns on the relation of these two sciences to Ethics, with which admittedly Religion has direct concern. If Economics is an "exact science" like Geometry or Physics, then the relation to it of both Ethics and Religion is limited to an exhortation that men should acknowledge its "laws" in their plans for society.

[1] See the discussion of the nature and province of Logic below, pp. 103-108.

If on the other hand Economics is the study of a certain department of human conduct, which is itself at once dependent on, and productive of, moral character, then Ethics and Religion may have a far more extensive and penetrating relation to it. We are not now concerned with the definition of Economic Science, and it is sufficient for our purpose to observe the nature and source of the controversy concerning its relation to Religion. That Religion and Ethics are closely related is, as has been said, not open to dispute, at any rate in the Western world. But it is not here that any serious tension arises between Religion and Philosophy, so that we may conveniently leave the nature of their relationship to be discussed separately.

The rapid survey just completed has had only one aim in view, and, cursory as it has been, that aim is now achieved; for it is apparent that, so far as there is tension between Religion and either Science or Philosophy, this cannot be due to any of the actual conclusions reached by the several sciences within their own spheres. Some religions, and, most conspicuously among the great religions, Christianity, make assertions which deal with events apparently falling within the sphere of particular sciences; but those are hardly points for the consideration of Natural Theology, even as we have conceived it, except so far as Natural Theology takes note of the particular assertions and considers the principles involved both in the fact that they are put forward, and in their admissibility or inadmissibility. Professor A. E. Taylor has followed this method with great effectiveness in his most admirable Gifford Lectures, *The Faith of a Moralist*. But with the truth or falsity of the actual assertions now in question Natural Theology is not concerned.

The main type of that tension, then, which we have now to consider, is not caused by particular doctrines either of Religion or of Philosophy, but consists in a sharp difference in mental habit and outlook with reference to the same objects of attention. This may be briefly expressed by saying that *the primary assurances of Religion are the ultimate questions of Philosophy*. Religion finds its fullest expression in absolute surrender to the Object of its worship. But the very existence of that Object is a main theme of philosophical disputation. It is not possible to surrender one's self to what is felt to be an unverified hypothesis; it is not possible to discuss impartially the existence of a Being to whom one is utterly self-surrendered. How then can a religious person be a true philosopher? Or how can a philosopher who has not yet solved the problems of existence permit himself the exercise of religion? And if he do not permit himself this exercise, how can he know Religion from within in such a fashion as to qualify himself to pronounce upon its validity and to place it rightly within, or exclude it justly from, his ultimate construction?

That these are grave questions no one who has seriously attempted to combine the two activities is likely to deny. Yet the difficulties are not insuperable in principle, and it seems to be the special duty of some persons at least to engage in the hazardous enterprise of overcoming them.

The divergence of view is specially evident in relation to three central convictions of Religion in its higher forms. These are perhaps different expressions of one truth, but as expressions of it they differ, and it is well to state them separately:

First is the conviction that Spirit is a true source of initiation of processes—a real ἀρχή, a *vera causa*;

Second is the conviction that all existence finds its source (ἀρχή, *vera causa*) in a Supreme Reality of which the nature is Spirit;

Third is the conviction that between that Spirit and ourselves there can be, and to some extent already is, true fellowship, at least such as is involved in our conscious dependence on that Spirit.

The first of these convictions is, as stated, little more than the denial of materialism; but this denial carries positive implications of momentous import. The true nature of spiritual freedom must occupy our attention later; but some aspects of it concern us now. If it were true that by inspection of the Nebula, from which our solar system formed itself, an intelligence of sufficient scope could have predicted all the acts of moral choice that would ever be made by human beings living on this planet, then the whole aspiration and endeavour of Religion would be dismissible as part of the phantasmagoria of a consciousness which emerged only to take note of, never to direct, the process in which it was a transient and ineffectual episode.

Now the sense of the inherent determinism of the physical system, including our bodily organisms, is so strong that some great religions have to a certain extent made terms with it. The Hindu doctrine of Maya is such a compromise. It expresses despair of the spiritual domination of matter; but in order to safeguard both the reality and the supremacy of spirit, it dismisses the material as illusory; the great aim of life which it proposes, is to be delivered from the Wheel of Change (the figure of materialistic Determinism) so that the spiritual reality may exist in its own freedom. This attempt altogether to exclude matter from reality issues in a curiously uncontrolled empire of matter, so that Hinduism, which finds expression in some of the loftiest spiritual philosophy of the world, also makes room for obscenity in connexion with worship itself. You cannot regulate what you do not recognise. If matter is so unreal that spirit, which is real, has neither need for it nor control of it, then in its own sphere it will make havoc. The way to be spiritually effective is not to ignore matter but to use it.

Yet to deny the reality of matter in order to assert that of spirit is less disastrous to Religion than to let the spiritual be swallowed up in the material, as the

West is always liable to do. The assertion of the reality and independence of Spirit in the Universe and in Man is a primary necessity for Religion. In the case of Man we may, for the moment, put this at the very lowest and be content to say that the causal process, as it affects human conduct, passes through consciousness and is modified by this passage. If preferred, the same thought may be expressed by saying that, attention having been attracted to the causal process, volition intervenes as an additional determinant of the result The main point is that consciousness does affect the result, but this does not make the process leading to it other than causal, so that human beings act differently because they are conscious and self-conscious from the way in which they (or rather their bodies) would act if they had no consciousness and self-consciousness.

But while this alone is enough to break the chain of sheer materialistic Determinism, much more is required for the assertion that the Ultimate Ground of the Universe and all things in it is spiritual. This is a claim, not only for the independence of Spirit, but for the universal supremacy of Spirit. It is the claim that Spirit is not only *a* source of initiation, one ἀρχή among others, but is the only ultimate source of the whole World-process. All the more developed religions, which do not deny the reality of matter, have advanced this claim. It is the doctrine of Creation. It is not of direct importance to Religion to assert a date for the act of Creation, or even to assert that it is an act having any date at all; it may be a never-beginning and never-ending activity. But it is of vital importance to Religion to assert that the existence of the world is due to the Will of God. This is the essential notion of Creation, and Religion dare not let it go, unless it is prepared to deny the real existence of the material world. For the only remaining alternative is the acceptance of limitation in the conception of the Supreme Spirit, not only in the sense of an actual finitude which none the less includes or controls all existence, but in the sense of leaving some part of existence outside its control. Such a dualism would be repudiated by Philosophy, which cannot rest in a multiplicity or duality of ultimate principles; and it is entirely fatal to Religion, because to a limited authority only a limited allegiance is due, and absoluteness of allegiance is the very life-breath of Religion.[1]

But this claim to absolute allegiance is one which Philosophy must investigate. Enquiry must be made into its precise meaning, and then into the relation of the claim so interpreted to the facts of common experience. If, for example, it is meant that all things exist only in dependence upon the Will of a Spiritual Being who is good and wise in the ordinary sense of those words, then there is a great deal of experience which cannot be treated as unreal and yet is very hard to appreciate as illustrating the goodness and wisdom of its Author. This is, of course, the familiar problem of Evil, which becomes acute in exact correspondence with the moral sensitiveness of the mind reflecting on it. A mind of low moral sensitiveness may be little troubled by this problem, for it will have a less exalted conception of the divine goodness, and will also be less afflicted by the evil elements in experience. As sensitiveness to moral issues develops, bewilderment before the problem of Evil deepens. It has found no more passionate expression than that given to it in many of the Hebrew Psalms.

That fact alone is sufficient evidence that this problem is not the creation of an alien criticism, but arises out of the heart of religious faith itself. Yet it is inevitable that when rationalising criticism sets to work, it should intensify the perplexity of religious people by seeming to exploit it in a hostile manner.

[1] Of course this does not mean that no one may properly be called religious who has not in practice attained to this absoluteness of allegiance; but it is essential to Religion in all its higher phases that the worshipper should regard his Deity as entitled to such allegiance and himself as under obligation to render it.

For the aim of the religious person is to stabilise and deepen his faith; the aim of the philosopher is to understand, to "follow the argument wherever it leads", and to regard nothing as assured which is not supported by sufficient evidence. Between these two there is manifest tension; but no one is so intimately aware of that tension as a person who tries whole-heartedly to play both rôles at once.

We have been considering the first two of those three central convictions of Religion which were mentioned a little earlier—the independent initiative of Spirit, and the spiritual nature of the ultimate initiative of the Universe. It is doubtful whether it would be possible in the long run to hold these two convictions with any assurance apart from the third, which presents itself rather as matter of direct experience than as an intellectual conviction; this is the reality of intercourse and fellowship between the spirit of Man and the supreme Spirit. Not once nor twice, but many times over has the assurance of the reality of that fellowship revived faith in the reality of the God who is one of the partners to the fellowship. One of the best expressions of this sequence of thought and moods is to be found in the Seventy-third Psalm.[1] Here is a man who has just recovered his faith; he records, first the recovery:

> Truly God is loving unto Israel,
> Even to such as are of a clean heart; (v. 1)

then the nearness of the disaster escaped:

> Nevertheless my feet were almost gone,
> My treadings had well nigh slipped; (v. 2)

then what led him to the edge of the precipice—the problem of Evil in its familiar form of social injustice:

> And why? I was grieved at the wicked,
> I do also see the ungodly in such prosperity;

[1] I follow the Prayer Book rendering because of its familiarity to English readers.

For they are in no peril of death
But are lusty and strong;
They come in no misfortune like other folk,
Neither are they plagued like other men; (vv. 3-5)

these wicked folk think they can presume on at least the indifference of the Almighty:

Tush! say they, how should God perceive it;
Is there knowledge in the Most High? (v. 11)

and experience seems to support them; and if so, what is the value of self-control and restraint or of respect for the requirements of morality:

Lo, these are the ungodly,
These prosper in the world and these have riches in possession;
And I said 'Then have I cleansed my heart in vain
And washed my hands in innocency;
All the day long have I been punished
And chastened every morning. (vv. 12, 13)

So the Psalmist himself nearly took their side, but something stopped him; he remembered those who were loyal and he could not condemn their lives as based on a delusion:

Yea, and I had almost said even as they;
But lo, then I should have condemned the generation of thy
children; (v. 14)

this leads him to reflect, and he finds his solution of the problem in two forms; the first is theoretical and false:

Then thought I to understand this,
But it was too hard for me
Until I went into the sanctuary of God;
Then understood I the end of these men—
Namely how thou dost set them in slippery places,
And castest them down and destroyest them.
O how suddenly do they consume,
Perish and come to a fearful end! (vv. 15-18)

the other is empirical and unassailable.

Whom have I in heaven but thee?
And there is none upon earth that I desire in comparison of
thee;
My flesh and my heart faileth,
But God is the strength of my heart and my portion for ever.
(vv. 24-25)

What is the attitude of the critical philosopher to such a record of experience? He will acknowledge the reality of the problem; he will recognise the cogency of the consideration which checked the writer's progress towards infidelity, for saintliness exists and is itself an impressive phenomenon demanding both recognition and explanation; he will at once repudiate the first solution, termed above theoretic, for it is directly contrary to a large amount of experience; and he will recognise the final solution as something which commands his respect, but also as something which he cannot accept solely on the assurance of the writer. There are psychological processes for which allowance must first be made; the reality of this experience of assurance will not be questioned; but its interpretation will be regarded as doubtful until many questions have been asked and answered.

We have here a useful illustration of that tension which it is our present aim to appreciate and understand. If we take the Psalmist as representative of the religious attitude of mind and our imagined critic as representative of the philosophic, we find them agreed as regards the main fact under consideration, agreed again as to the reality and nature of the problem, disagreeing as regards one projected solution, differing with the difference between passionate assurance and detached suspense of judgement as regards the other. It is the closeness of their companionship which makes the tension so evident.

Even where there is agreement, the tension is already apparent. For to the believer, stating with passion a difficulty which threatens ruin to his faith, the calm observation of the philosopher, even if what he observes is identical, or perhaps all the more on that account, is offensive. The believer is not interested in solving a problem; he is interested in the reality and goodness of God; to agree with him dispassionately is to exhibit a greater divergence than hotly to deny his statement of the facts. If any one said to him, following the line of Job's comforters, "The wicked do not flourish for long; your trouble is due to the shortness of your view", he might have pointed to contrary instances, but would not have been conscious of alienation; indeed, after his recovery he relapses himself into precisely this form of dogmatism. But if any one said, "Your statement of the facts is quite correct, and we must take care that our general philosophy does justice to them", he would feel that his fundamental concern was being ignored. For him the facts of observation derive their importance from a conviction which was formed apart from them and is now threatened by them; he does not want to frame a theory which does justice to them; he wants to re-establish in face of them the faith which they threaten.

When we come to the disagreements between the believer (as represented by the Psalmist) and the philosopher, we find illustrations both of the service which Philosophy may render to Religion and of the injury it may inflict upon it. For it was necessary that Religion should be purged of that easy dogmatism concerning observable facts which appears in what we have called the theoretical solution of the Psalmist. He here meets the challenge of social injustice and says that in the long run it does not exist; poetic justice ultimately appears, at least in the destruction of the wicked, if not in the prosperity of the righteous. The writer is not thinking of a rectification effected in another world than this; even if he were, it would be no solution of the real problem, as we shall see later;[1] but as his reference is certainly to this world, we must say that he is dogma-

[1] Cf. Lecture XX. pp. 507-511.

tising, from the vantage ground of his religious experience, about facts of common observation, and that his dogma is both false and even reprehensible. At a higher stage in the religious development of Israel the author of the Book of Job represents the Almighty Himself as pronouncing censure upon the three friends of Job for enunciating precisely this dogma.

Yet in that extremely human document which we are considering as an illustration of the main thesis, the enunciation of this dogma is dramatically in place. Psychologically regarded, it is seen to be merely a way of saying that the initial problem is solved; as the writer can only conceive one possible solution, he states that solution; but this is comparatively unimportant. What is important is the reality of the solution which he has found, not in any doctrine or generalisation, but in his own experience. In his fellowship with God he has found that nothing matters in comparison with that fellowship. He had been perplexed that the ungodly should prosper, and almost thought of throwing in his lot with them. But now he knows that, however great their possessions, they are truly destitute, while the man who has found fellowship with God is rich though he possesses nothing. That is the real solution—not an answer to the riddle, but the attainment of a state of mind in which there is no desire to ask it.

And here the influence of a critical philosophy may be truly injurious, at least for a time. It is, indeed, not likely that such assurance as the Psalmist expresses would be disturbed by any amount of rationalistic questioning; the believer would merely say, if Christian language were his medium of expression,

Expertus potest credere
Quid sit Jesum diligere.[1]

[1] S. Bernard. Caswall's mistranslation of these lines in the well-known English hymn is most unfortunate. Jesus loves all men; but not all men love Him. The true rendering, however awkward in English, is:

"The love of Jesus, what it is,
None but who love Him know."

But religious conviction may exist in varying degrees of intensity; and while it can, where it exists at all, carry the believer past doubts arising from extraneous causes, it needs to be very strong in its own nature if it is to resist doubts raised concerning its own validity. For this reason the psychological line of enquiry presents a more insidious peril to Religion than any other.

This reflection leads to a new consideration. The difference between Religion and scientific Philosophy[1] in relation to the Object of attention is not only one of temper but also one of method. The latter results from the former. In temper the attitude of Religion is that of assurance; the attitude of Philosophy is that of enquiry. It is hard enough to combine these, and probably it can only be done by deliberate alternation. But to combine the resultant methods is harder still. Religion, of which the essence is assurance of fellowship with, or at least of dependence on, the Supreme Spirit, and therefore also of the existence of that Supreme Spirit, necessarily makes its start from that point, and, so far as it enters on the field of Philosophy, seeks to offer explanations of the facts of experience by reference to the character of the Supreme Spirit. This is Theological Philosophy, and I had better here confess my belief that it is in the end the only Philosophy which has any hope of being altogether satisfactory. But it is also most hazardous, and is certain to lead the mind that follows it into all manner of fantasies unless it is constantly checked by a purely critical Philosophy which makes its approach from the other end. In the Middle Ages the course was clear for Theological Philosophy, and the wonder is that it avoided the fantastic as much as it did; yet that element is present in it in sufficient quantity to show the danger.

[1] By the phrase "scientific Philosophy" I mean any philosophy which takes its start from the departmental sciences, ranging from Physics to Epistemology or Ethics, as distinct from a philosophy which takes its start from the deliverances of religious experience as formulated by Theology. Wherever I speak of "Philosophy" without any epithet it is to be understood as "scientific Philosophy" in this sense. Of course Theological Philosophy is no less scientific than this in its own procedure.

Theology, which is the science of Religion, starts from the Supreme Spirit and explains the world by reference to Him. Philosophy starts from the detailed experience of men, and seeks to build up its understanding of that experience by reference to that experience alone. Its inevitable and wholesome kinship to Science inclines it to account for everything by the "lowest" category that will in fact account for it; Theology begins with the "highest" category of all and fits in the "lower" categories in the most orderly hierarchy that it can devise in subordination to that "highest" principle. And this difference is inevitable, though it has been exaggerated by the dominant tendencies of European thought from the time of Descartes onwards. With that exaggeration, its causes, and the way to correct it, we shall be concerned in later lectures. Our present concern is with the difference itself, which would still exist if there were no exaggeration at all. The source of the method of Theological Philosophy in the nature of Religion itself has already been made clear. But the method of critical Philosophy is equally inevitable.

This can perhaps be made plain by some reference to its early history. Its recent triumphs date from the sixteenth century and the subsequent period. Science was born long before that; yet till then its life was hardly vigorous; the general conditions were too unfavourable. In the ancient world, as among primitive races to-day, all change or motion was accounted for by direct reference to the principles of Life and Will. The sun rose and set because it was, or was indwelt by, a god. The fact that Apollo was endowed by the Greek imagination with attributes so glorious, seems to separate him by a great gulf from the crude conceptions of Animism; but behind that great poetic creation the principle of Animism is found to be at work. Part of the accusation for impiety which led to the banishment of Anaxagoras was that he declared the sun to be really a red-hot stone.

The fact is that the religious impulse, having its ultimate explanation always ready, is impatient of that search for proximate causes in which Science has its being. Science could hardly flourish, for example, among people like the ancient Hebrews, who were prepared to refer all occurrences not due to human volition to the direct action of Yahweh. Thus Meteorology would hardly thrive among people whose natural comment on a great storm was, "It is the glorious God that maketh the thunder", however true that comment may be in itself. That, no doubt, is merely an instance of human frailty, and is not due to the essential principle of either Science or Religion. But it is in fact certain that Religion will, until challenged, apply its ultimate category to all phenomena calling for explanation in such a way as to make the reference of occurrences to "natural" causes have the appearance of impiety, and the challenge when presented will itself at first seem impious.

It is most worthy of notice that by the Teacher whom multitudes have acclaimed as supreme in the religious sphere, one special source of difficulty is avoided. It has ever been the common tendency of mankind to trace the activity of God in the unexpected or astonishing. It was not that other explanations of the normal were accepted, but that no explanation was sought at all. The normal was taken for granted; the astonishing and unpredictable was regarded as the act of God. The result of this has been that every new triumph of Science in accounting for phenomena has seemed to involve a curtailment of the sphere of God's activity. But Jesus of Nazareth taught men to see the operation of God in the regular and normal—in the rising of the sun, the falling of the rain, the growth of the seed into the plant. If men had been ready to follow Him in this, much of the actual conflict between Religion and Science would have been avoided. But His wisdom remained high out of reach till Science itself supplied the ladder, and led us to see God at work, if at all, not only now and then, but everywhere and always.

Inasmuch as men could not rise to the level to which Christ had called them, but still let their minds be governed by the childish notions of the race's infancy, Science has been bound for its very life's sake to keep closely to its principle of employing always the lowest categories that are truly applicable. Nor is this only a principle of expediency in view of the opposing tendency of Theological Philosophy; it is the only way of establishing securely each advance as it is made. For progress in scientific knowledge it has been, and still is, necessary to refuse admittance to each "higher" category until it is really proved that the "lower" categories are inadequate. It is possible that on these grounds even the Pythagorean notion that the explanation of all things is to be found in Number can be justified as a necessary episode in the progress of Science. Number is applicable to all things; if they exist at all they can be counted. *Nos numerus sumus*,[1] says Horace when he wishes to express the futility of the human race; we are only good for counting. This is the "lowest" of categories, and its capacity had to be tried out, though the effort to use it as a universal principle of explanation led to the wildest fantasies, and the end of the test could be expressed in Edward Caird's dictum that "Number tells us something about everything, but very little about anything".

The enormous influence of Mathematics (about which more must be said later) led to a desire at least to limit the area of scientific enquiry to what was Measurable. If Number or Measure itself was not the explanation of all things, let enquiry be made whether all things be not explicable in terms of what can be counted or measured. Thus arose the long endeavour to confine scientific procedure to the study of Mass and Motion—the "mechanical" era. And we must recog-

[1] Horace, *Epistles*, i. 2. 27.

nise how great was the success attained by this method. Physiology is a science well established and far advanced towards mastery of its subject; but it is only in very recent times that any general readiness has been apparent to recognise other than physical and chemical processes at work in the animal organism, even if it can be said to be general to-day. But at least in many quarters there is a conviction that the organic principle is itself incapable of exposition in physical or chemical terms; this principle may be roughly stated as the predominance of the unity of the organism such that the action and reaction of every part is controlled by that unity. And we are now witnessing the interesting endeavour to read back this principle from the sphere hitherto marked off as organic into the realm of Physics and into the very constitution of matter. The question then arises how far Life, and Mind, and the spiritual activities of Religion, Morality, Art and Science itself can be regarded as manifestations of the organic principle.

Now so long as scientific enquiry is limited to the physical, the physiological, and even the biological sphere, Religion has in principle no concern with it except to claim its results as added knowledge of the works of God; and no quarrel arises. There may be incidental friction, either because in the sacred books of a particular religion expression is given to the purely religious interest of such a kind as involves statements within the sphere of a departmental science, or else because scientists deny on purely scientific grounds facts which some religion asserts on grounds which are beyond the cognisance of Science. An illustration of the former is provided by the trouble about Darwinism in the third quarter of the nineteenth century. Biology, advancing a theory of the *Origin of Species*, found the ground occupied by the first chapter of Genesis. But it did not take competent theologians long to appreciate the fact that the spiritual interest in the doctrine of

Creation lies solely in the assertion of the dependence of all existence upon the Will of God,[1] and that the first chapter of Genesis is a magnificent presentation of that truth; indeed the wonder is that the picture should be so close to the scientific account of the process,[2] though this fact is of very small importance. An illustration of the latter type of friction would be a denial on physiological grounds alone of the Christian doctrine that Christ was born of a Virgin; for the Christian contention is that there was operative in that instance a cause with which the science of Physiology is not concerned. I have been told that some physiological-psychologists are of opinion that a singularly intense religious experience, such as is recorded in the story of the Annunciation, might of itself initiate conception.

[1] Cf. the following passages in the Bampton Lectures delivered by my father, Archbishop Frederick Temple, then Bishop of Exeter, on *The Relations between Religion and Science*, in 1884:

"We all distinguish between the original creation of the material world and the history of it ever since. And we have, nay all men have, been accustomed to assign to the original creation a great deal that Science is now disposed to assign to the history. But the distinction between the original creation and the subsequent history would still remain and for ever remain, although the portion assigned to the one may be less, and that assigned to the other larger, than was formerly supposed. However far back Science may be able to push its beginning, there still must be behind that beginning the original act of creation" (pp. 106-107).

"Whatever may be said of the relation of the doctrine of Evolution to Revelation, it cannot be said that this doctrine is antagonistic to Religion in its essence. The progress of Science in this direction will assuredly end in helping men to believe with more assurance than ever that the Lord by wisdom hath founded the earth, by understanding hath He established the heavens" (p. 123).

"We cannot find that Science, in teaching Evolution, has yet asserted anything that is inconsistent with Revelation, unless we assume that Revelation was intended not to teach spiritual truth only, but physical truth also. Here as in all similar cases, we find that the writer of the Book of Genesis, like all the other writers in the Bible, took nature as he saw it, and expressed his teaching in language corresponding to what he saw. And the doctrine of Evolution, in so far as it has been shewn to be true, does but fill out in detail the declaration that we are 'fearfully and wonderfully made; marvellous are Thy works, and that my soul knoweth right well' " (p. 188).

[2] *Sc.* in presenting Light as the first form of physical existence; in the order of advance from inorganic, through vegetable and animal forms of life to Man; in the use of the word "created" (as distinct from "made") at just those points where Science still fails to trace the transition from earlier and lower to later and higher—the beginning of all things, the appearance of Life, and the arrival of Man. It is worth while to remember that the treatment of this chapter as pictorial Myth is not a device of modern theologians due to a desire to escape from difficulties raised by Science, but was familiar to the ancient Church. St. Augustine regards it as ridiculous to think of the Days of Creation as periods of actual time, whether of twenty-four hours or of any other length.

If so, it is open to the Christian to suppose that God made use of such a psycho-physical means to effect His purpose. But I cannot become greatly interested in reconciliations of Science and Religion along those lines. Such a reconciliation itself seems to me unimportant, and any emphasis upon it tends to obscure what is important. The harmonising of Science and Religion must be achieved, if at all, in principle and not piecemeal.

Apart from such relatively accidental occasions of friction it is not until the sphere of human conduct is reached that the tension develops on any considerable scale. But here the effort of Science to account for events by the "lowest" category must involve very serious tension, unless or until either Science admits the principle of free spiritual initiative or Religion surrenders its citadel. Yet Science is right to make the effort, provided it is true also to its other principle of recognising facts for what they are and never refusing evidence only because it conflicts with current theory. And it is right to carry this process forward into the region of religious experience itself. The phenomena of religious mania are a reminder of the need for a criterion external to religious experience by which its authenticity may be tested. While this scientific enquiry into Religion is going on, many theories will be propounded that are entirely fatal to Religion. It must be a long time yet before Psychology, as a science, can be so sure of having exhausted the possibilities of a purely psychological origin of religious convictions, that it can safely admit the hypothesis that they are due to the action of God (a Being necessarily unknown to Psychology) upon the human mind. Of course the man who is conducting the psychological enquiry may believe a great deal which lies outside the scope of that enquiry; and he may conciliate the feelings of religious people by adding an appendix to his exposition to say that in his private capacity he is of their number. But he must not admit into his scientific procedure the hypothesis of direct divine action until he has exhausted all other possibilities.

This must not be understood as suggesting that support for religion is to be drawn from the failure of scientific explanation. As we shall see more fully later, the religious explanation is equally necessary and satisfying when the scientific account, on its own plane, is also complete.[1] But the method and aim are different; and this difference appears in the fact that Religion refers all things to God from the outset, while Science, including Psychology, only refers to Him at all if driven to desert its own method by failure to follow it to a satisfactory issue.

The inevitability of tension between Religion and Science or the Philosophy which is in line with the scientific impulse is now clear. The method of Natural Theology no doubt requires ideally that the validity of Religion itself should be established before we consider, even cursorily, how this tension may be relieved. For if one of the two parties to it has no real right to exist, the tension is only to be properly relieved by the abolition of that party. Yet for purposes of exposition it is convenient to deal with this whole question of tension together, and the principles to be observed with a view to reconciliation are easily stated, though their detailed application is difficult enough.

First, then, the adherents of Religion must be ready to distinguish between the elements or expressions of their faith which are of real spiritual importance, and those which have come to have sentimental value through association with the former. They will not be agreed among themselves about this distinction with regard to any point which is newly called in question. Some will be specially eager to say the point does not matter, so as to avoid the spiritual loss always involved in the tension between Religion and Science; these will be called

[1] See Lecture XI.

Latitudinarians or Modernists, according to the fashion of the day; they will usually have intellectual clarity but little spiritual *élan*. Others will hold on till the last possible minute to every questioned phrase, lest what is lost be not only of sentimental but also of spiritual value. These will be called Traditionalists or Obscurantists; they will often have great spiritual force, and often, too, great learning, but as a rule, little intellectual enterprise. Between these two there will be others representing every possible gradation. But all may be loyal to the principle just stated, and may fulfil various necessary parts in winning for it a justly discriminating application. What must be excluded, and is very hard to exclude, is the element of purely personal sentiment. To cling to some belief, when it appears to have no inherent spiritual value and to be discredited by scientific advance, on the ground that it is bound up with what has spiritual value by ties of mere association, is a form of self-assertion which must be condemned by Science and Religion alike. But the nature of spiritual value is such that it is very hard to distinguish between it and personal attachment so that great sympathy is due to those who are perplexed by the need of making such a distinction at all.

The requirements to be made of scientific enquirers are different, though these too are largely various forms of the demand to avoid all self-assertion. Two are perhaps the most important. First it is to be remembered that Science, in following its method of using the "lowest" category applicable, is not entitled to deny the applicability of "higher" categories but is only seeing how far it can go without them. Even if it can cover all the facts and hold them together by means of "lower", as for instance mechanical, categories, it does not necessarily follow that the "higher" categories, such as purpose, have no rightful application at all. Indeed, while an actual machine is an entity of which the unifying principle is mechanical, the natural inference from its existence is that a living intelligence designed and constructed it.[1] And if that is true of a steam-engine, it is hard to see why it should not be true of the stellar system or of the cosmos generally. It would be hard to refute the argument which urges that the more perfect the universe is in itself as mechanism, the more forcibly does it suggest an intelligent Creator as its cause. But this carries us past the main point, which is that the positive work of Science, in giving an account of observable facts by its own method, never justifies Science in proceeding to negative inferences concerning other methods of interpretation, provided that these in their turn do not exclude the method of Science.

Secondly, it is to be remembered that there are spheres in which the most characteristic methods of Science are inapplicable. This is true in varying degrees of Ethics and of Art. Our appreciation of Right and Good is independent of argument and experiment. These may certainly affect our estimate of various actions or relationships; we may be persuaded that an action or a social order which we had thought good was in truth bad. But this never touches the ultimate objects of moral judgement. If a man tells me that he finds indulgence in cruelty one of the best things in life, I may try to make him contradict himself, as Socrates did with Callicles in a similar connexion,[2] and so show that he did not really mean what he was saying; or I may try to have him shut up in a prison or an asylum; but I cannot directly attack his proposition by argument. "Our sense of value, and in the end for every man his own sense of value, is ultimate and final".[3]

The realm of Art offers an illustration as clear as that

[1] *I.e.* "living" when it so designed and constructed. All arguments of this type are open to Hume's devastating suggestions in the *Dialogue* of which the following may be quoted: "This world, for aught (any man) knows, is very faulty and imperfect compared to a superior standard; and was only the first rude essay of some infant deity, who afterwards abandoned it, ashamed of his lame performance".

[2] Plato, *Gorgias*, 494-495.

[3] F. H. Bradley, *Essays on Truth and Reality*, p. 132.

of Ethics. In these days when our minds are chiefly influenced by scientific activity people are often inclined to say that they cannot believe where they have no proof; or at least they demand a balance of probability calculated by formulable laws of evidence. Yet they will without hesitation affirm and even passionately insist on (say) the superiority of Schubert to Mendelssohn, though it would puzzle them to prove it or show it to be manifestly probable.

But it is in personal relationships that the inadequacy of Science is most manifest. We should not recommend a pair of lovers to test the advisability of marriage by making each a psychological analysis of the other. We even use the word "understand" with a different sense in relation to other persons from that which it bears in relation to impersonal objects. To "understand" a person is to have that insight into his character and motives which is another aspect of what is also called sympathy. A wise scientist does not follow only scientific methods, as these are commonly understood, in choosing his wife or expressing his affection for his children.

The heart of Religion is not an opinion about God, such as Philosophy might reach as the conclusion of its argument; it is a personal relationship with God. Its closest analogy is not found in our study of astronomy or any other science, but in our relation to a person whom we trust and love. If Science is not the best of aids in helping the child to determine his relation to his father, no more is it—still less is it—the best of aids in determining the relation of a man to his God.

We have seen that tension between Philosophy and Religion is inevitable; and as both are here assumed to have a rightful place in life, this tension must even be regarded as good. We have seen ways in which it may be alleviated, through the recollection by the adherents of each, what is the real nature and concern of that activity to which they are committed. We may reasonably hope to find here the grounds for an ultimate reconciliation in principle; but that can only be when each is perfect in its own kind. Till then the tension will remain, to the special bewilderment of those who are conscious of an obligation to be loyal to both at once. Yet these may hope that through their travail the progress towards ultimate reconciliation is being made.

Prof. A. Wolf ends his admirable chapter on "Recent and Contemporary Philosophy" in *An Outline of Modern Knowledge* with a warning against the dangers involved in "the unusually friendly relationship which is loudly proclaimed to exist now between science and the Churches"; and he adds this paragraph:

> "Contemporary philosophy likewise seems to stand in need of an analogous warning. Considering the fact that so many philosophers were formerly students of theology, the relations between philosophy and theology are naturally expected to be friendly. Among British philosophers, indeed, the number of defenders of the faith seems to be abnormally large. It may be that academic conditions, and institutions like the Gifford Trust, either encourage this tendency or give undue prominence to those who follow it. But philosophy will be in a healthier condition when it has entirely ceased to be a handmaid to theology, and pursues its cosmic problems as independently as possible of vested interests."[1]

Prof. Wolf is more concerned with the welfare of Philosophy; I am, no doubt, more concerned with the welfare of Religion. Consequently my phraseology would differ from his. Yet I agree with him in substance. There not only is, but there ought to be, a tension between Philosophy and Religion. That tension is only relaxed when one of the two assimilates itself excessively to the other. The present atmosphere of friendliness may blunt the edge of philosophic criticism because there is an unwillingness to wound the feelings of religious people; it may also lead Religion to tone down its note of Authority because it does not wish to antagonise its philosophic friends. But the tension is

[1] *Op. cit.* p. 592.

not to be regretted; it is right in principle and stimulating in effect. And it can be delivered from the danger of doing harm if both parties respect the principle of Justice—τὸ τὰ αὑτοῦ πράττειν. But let no one suppose that this principle is as easy to practice as it is to enunciate.

LECTURE III

THE CARTESIAN FAUX-PAS

If I were asked what was the most disastrous moment in the history of Europe I should be strongly tempted to answer that it was that period of leisure when René Descartes, having no claims to meet, remained for a whole day "shut up alone in a stove". But no doubt that is a jaundiced view of a necessary movement of thought, and any bitterness of feeling with regard to it is due to the fact that we are only now emerging from the movement then initiated, so that we regard it with some aversion, but have not achieved complete deliverance, and our aversion cannot yet be dispassionate. That many of our worst troubles, not only in philosophy but also in politics and economics, with all that this means for human happiness or misery, are closely associated with the habit of thought then established I cannot doubt. But many gains are associated with it also; and we have already passed out of the tunnel into which Descartes led us, even if our eyes are as yet too unaccustomed to the daylight of common sense to perceive clearly the landscape that meets our gaze as we emerge into it.

The time is come, I am convinced, when we should learn to see the course of "modern thought" up to date —that is, its course from about A.D. 1500 till near our own time—as one phase in what Hegelians call a "dialectical movement of thought". The great principle of the Hegelian dialectic has fallen into some discredit, partly because Hegel himself attributed to it a more universal applicability than it possesses, but mainly I think because it has been supposed that it ought to supply a guide for the actual thinking of individual philosophers. A theme, other than a stretch of past history, to which an individual philosopher could apply the dialectic method would have to be either very highly abstract, like Hegel's own transition from *Sein* through *Nicht sein* to *Werden*, or else so limited in scope as hardly to be a topic for philosophic discussion. As a loyal pupil of Edward Caird I find the phrase "a dialectical movement of thought" always suggestive of something that occupies several centuries, though no doubt lesser illustrations are discoverable.

In such a movement it is natural that the second phase—the "antithesis"—should be briefer than the other two. The "thesis" formulates a *prima facie* view, which, because it is taken *prima facie*, has much of the quality of "common sense". It has that kind of guarantee that is provided by absence of sophistication. It is like the wisdom of the uneducated rustic—a wisdom which is the direct deposit of actual experience in a mind of which the balance has never been distorted. This wisdom has great limitations, but it is real wisdom, not cleverness.

The "antithesis" is born of the limitations of the "thesis". The "thesis" is never a complete statement; there are aspects of the problem which it ignores. As men become conscious of these, they feel the need to assert them. There is, as a rule, no room for them within the accepted formulation of the "thesis", so it becomes necessary to make a new start from the assertion of these hitherto neglected aspects, or from a deliberate questioning of what has hitherto been unquestioned. So the "antithesis" receives statement. As compared with the "thesis" it is artificial, a thing consciously constructed; it may be defended with conspicuous ingenuity, but is not likely to be a fount of wisdom.

When the "antithesis" has been worked out, and its shortcomings also have become apparent, the time is come for the "synthesis". This is not a mere average struck between the two. It is always a reassertion of the "thesis" with all that has proved valuable in the "antithesis" digested into it.

A vivid, though crude, illustration of this triadic process is afforded by the parliamentary history of Great Britain under the two-party system. The Conservative party, at its best, is expressive of the "thesis", the actual situation as it has historically developed; this party does not stand for stagnation, but it repudiates all general theories concerning the kind of change that should be made, believing that action on each occasion should be dictated, not by general theory but, by the exigencies of the actual situation at any moment. The Liberal party has in the past represented the "antithesis" in the form of an attack on various forms of privilege or of restrictions upon individual liberty. Perhaps it may be said that the Labour Party is essentially an extension of this, with more intimate knowledge of and concern for the wage-earning classes, for its action has as yet been comparatively little affected by doctrinaire Socialism. But at any given moment the Conservative party itself represents the "synthesis" of the "thesis" and "antithesis" of the last generation. This is recognised in the principle avowed by some detached Radicals that while they are eager for drastic reforms they wish to see these enacted by a Conservative Government, because that will secure that the country is really ready for them.

It is, of course, well known that Karl Marx applied the Hegelian dialectic in the economic field, and presented Communism as the "synthesis" which was to solve all problems, the "dictatorship of the proletariat", now established to some extent in Russia, being the necessary "antithesis" to the "thesis" of Capitalism. But it is hazardous to construct the "synthesis" in advance, and almost equally hazardous to apply with any thoroughness in practice an artificially constructed "antithesis". Human thinking is sure to omit some of the relevant facts; often it has not even the opportunity of becoming aware of them. But unknown facts produce their consequences equally with known, and in practice opportunism is itself a sacred principle, though when followed alone it degenerates into cynicism if not into downright immorality.

In the field with which we are now concerned the "thesis" finds expression in various forms in the whole of ancient and of mediaeval thought; its principle is that in experience we are directly aware of real objects. This was held—sometimes as an uncriticised assumption, sometimes (as by Plato) with vivid realisation of some of the difficulties involved—from Thales to William of Occam. Sophists, like Protagoras, might apply a thorough-going humanism to the problems of philosophy, or like Gorgias, a thorough-going scepticism to the bare possibility of metaphysic; but they represent eddies, "dialectical" eddies it may be, each setting up a little "antithesis" within the main stream which proceeded to swallow it in the original "thesis". The very form and terminology of the mediaeval controversies illustrate this point. "Realism" as applied to mediaeval controversies is concerned with Universals only; its rivals are—not Idealism, or the assertion that we know only our own ideas but—Nominalism and Conceptualism. In other words the controversy was not concerned with the general question of the relation of Mind to real objects, but merely with the departmental question whether certain ideas are ideas of objects existing in their own right. That, broadly speaking, we have knowledge of real objects was not disputed.

During the fifteenth century many things were happening which tended to arouse the critical spirit. All tradition and the assurance associated with it was bound up with the Church. There was a scheme of thought embracing Theology, Metaphysic, Logic, Politics, Ethics and Economics. It was in itself coherent and close-knit; but Theology was the keystone of its arch, and the guardian of theological doctrine was the

Church. The Church itself was Catholic or Universal, and while it had learnt to unite men of different regions and races in its system, it had not learnt how to recognise at all fully within that system different nations as self-conscious communities. Meanwhile the spirit of Nationalism was developing, perhaps finding its first quite clear expression in Joan of Arc. A clash between the new Nationalism and the old Catholicism was inevitable. The problem of doing justice to both was not insoluble, and if the Church had been universally recognised as the repository of spiritual power which it existed to be, the problem might have been solved. But just when the Church needed its spiritual resources in a very special degree, they were found to be at a very low ebb. Moreover the new Greek learning had suggested another method of thought, and, more important still, another intellectual temper than that of the Aristotelianism which the great Schoolmen had employed to construct their magnificently, but excessively because prematurely, coherent scheme. Thus the authority of the current theological tradition was weakened among those who, because of their learning, might have been its most effectual champions. The readjustment called for in this department also might have been effected if the Church had been before all else dedicated to its spiritual vocation. Whether the worldliness of the Church as an ecclesiastical organisation in the fifteenth century would of itself have led to a break-up of the mediaeval system it is impossible to say; what is certain is that it deprived the Church of the moral authority required for guiding the new forces into harmonious co-operation with the old.

It was in the sphere of Politics that the breach with the old order was first openly proclaimed. Its herald was Machiavelli, a very penetrating thinker who has brought upon himself the execration of mankind by stating with a lucidity that seemed indecent the principles upon which men were often already acting in his day and have consistently acted ever since. What was new was not the treatment of the political State as its own end, so that its isolated interest becomes the fundamental principle of political morality, but the unremorseful announcement of this as a commonplace, and the unashamed deduction of the conduct conformable thereto, not in action (every one was used to that) but in words. And after all if "hypocrisy is the homage which vice pays to virtue" it may be better to be a hypocrite than to pay no homage to virtue at all.

But Machiavelli could not, if he would, break up the theoretical unity of Christendom, just because the theory had already long outlived the slender influence that it ever enjoyed in political practice. The first actual breach came, as was natural and almost necessary, in the religious sphere itself. Europe was living by a system of tradition too narrow for it; the keystone of that system was the theology of a Church now seen to be corrupt. A breach was bound to come. But if the Church and its system were repudiated, what could take its place. If a man's thoughts and purposes were no longer to take their start from the only tradition available, where could they begin? And the only possible answer was "with himself". If a man was not going to start as a member of a system, accepting that system and his own place in it, then he must start with his isolated self. Of course he would submit to the authority of conscience, but it would be *his* conscience. He would submit to the Voice of God as he heard it, but it would be as *he* heard it. So the modern movement was bound to be a movement of individualism. We owe to it the distinctive blessings of modern life, but also its distinctive ills.

This strong assertion of the individual as the source or medium of the authority to which he must bow found its spiritual expression when Martin Luther, standing alone for truth as he knew it before the Diet of Worms, declared *Hier steh' ich; ich kann nichts anders.*

It found its intellectual expression in the course of meditation with which René Descartes occupied his leisure in that stove which is the birthplace of modern philosophy. The moment is so important that it seems worth while to let him tell the story once more in his own words:

"J'étois alors en Allemagne, où l'occasion des guerres qui n'y sont pas encore finies m'avoit appelé; et, comme je retournois du couronnement de l'empereur vers l'armée, le commencement de l'hiver m'arrêta en un quartier où, ne trouvant aucune conversation qui me divertit, et n'ayant d'ailleurs, par bonheur, aucuns soins ni passions qui me troublassent, je demeurois tout le jour enfermé seul dans un poêle, où j'avois tout le loisir de m'entretenir de mes pensées.[1]

"Je ne sais si je dois vous entretenir des premières méditations que j'y ai faites; car elles sont si métaphysiques et peu communes, qu'elles ne seront peut-être pas au goût de tout le monde; et, toute fois, afin qu'on puisse juger si les fondements que j'ai pris sont assez fermes, je me trouve en quelque façon contraint d'en parler. J'avois dès longtemps remarqué que pour les mœurs il est besoin quelquefois de suivre des opinions qu'on sait être fort incertaines, tout de même que si elles étoient indubitables . . .; mais pour ce qu'alors je désirois vaguer seulement à la recherche de la vérité, je pensai qu'il falloit que je fisse tout le contraire, et que je rejetasse comme absolument faux tout ce en quoi je pourrois imaginer le moindre doute, afin de voir s'il ne resteroit point après cela quelque chose en ma créance qui fût entièrement indubitable. Ainsi, à cause que nos sens nous trompent quelquefois je voulus supposer qu'il n'y avoit aucune chose qui fût telle qu'ils la font imaginer; et, parce qu'il y a des hommes qui se méprennent en raisonant même touchant les plus simples matières de géométrie, et y font des paralogismes, jugeant que j'étois sujet à faillir autant qu'aucun autre, je rejetai comme fausses toutes les raisons que j'avois prises auparavant pour démonstrations; et enfin, considérant que toutes les mêmes pensées que nous avons étant éveillés nous peuvent aussi venir quand nous dormons sans qu'il y en ait aucune pour lors qui soit vraie, je me résolus de feindre que toutes les choses qui m'étoient jamais entrées en esprit n'étoient non plus vraies que les illusions de mes songes. Mais aussitôt après je pris garde que, pendant que je voulois ainsi penser que tout étoit faux, il falloit nécessairement que moi

[1] *Discours de la Méthode: Deuxième Partie.*

qui le pensois fusse quelque chose; et remarquant que cette vérité: *je pense, donc je suis*, étoit si ferme et si assurée que toutes les plus extravagantes suppositions des sceptiques n'étoient pas capables de l'ébranler, je jugeai que je pouvois le recevoir sans scrupule pour le premier principe de la philosophie que je cherchois."[1]

It is no main part of my purpose to criticise the logical validity of this procedure on its own ground and within its own limits. I do, in fact, regard it as invalid; and I am disposed to think that the bare possibility of doing so is as fatal to the argument as a formal refutation would be. Of course I share the conviction at which Descartes arrived; when I doubt, I cannot doubt that I doubt; even though I should doubt all else, I could not doubt myself as the subject of that doubt; that, as a matter of psychology, is true. But to me it seems that in fact I cannot really doubt all else except myself; I cannot really doubt the earth, or the stars, or (above all) my friends; so that I cannot find in fact any greater psychological assurance about the existence of myself than about the existence of a great deal else. And there seems no reason to regard the assurance at which Descartes arrived as more than psychological. There is at first sight a certain logical cogency about it; for as Mr. Boyce Gibson puts it, "that which is thought is always exposed to metaphysical doubt; but that which thinks is the condition of metaphysical doubt itself".[2] But this does not really carry us far, for it is impossible to think without thinking something. The subjective function of thought can be properly and usefully distinguished from every object of thought taken separately; but it cannot be isolated from all objects of thought whatsoever without ceasing to exist. And it is on the possibility of such isolation that Descartes' argument turns. The appearance of logical cogency is illusory; the assurance to which Descartes clings is psychological

[1] *Discours de la Méthode:* Quatrième Partie.
[2] A. Boyce Gibson, *The Philosophy of Descartes*, p. 83.

only. Now if it be suggested that he and I are both of us figures in the dream of a Demiurge, as Tweedledum suggested that Alice and Tweedledee and he himself were all figures in the Red King's dream, there is no way of refuting such a suggestion. If the Red King dreamt that Alice was sure of her own existence, she would be sure of it; but that would not prevent her going out like a candle when the Red King woke up. She would indeed never know that she did not exist, for so long as she knew anything she would have all the existence possible for her—that of a figure in a dream. Whatever she knew, she would know because the Red King dreamt her as knowing it. Now I do not *feel* as if I were only a figure in some one else's dream; but neither do I *feel* as if I had more grounds for assurance of my own existence than for assurance of the existence of other things; these assurances arise together—or rather are different elements in the initial fact of consciousness. Personally I find it not at all impossible to entertain the fancy that *all* our experience, that of self included, is part of the dream of a Demiurge, that all of it

> shall dissolve
> And, like this insubstantial pageant faded,
> Leave not a rack behind. We are such stuff
> As dreams are made on, and our little life
> Is rounded with a sleep [1]

—not our sleep, but that of the Demiurge. I cannot refute that hypothesis, and I find it possible to contemplate it without intellectual turmoil. I am equally unable, no doubt, to refute the notion that my primary assurance is of myself, and that my awareness of the world about me is secondary and derivative. But I cannot contemplate that hypothesis without intellectual perturbation of the profoundest kind—a perturbation which is the deposit of all the acrobatic feats by which philosophers from Descartes to Kant have worked out

[1] Shakespeare, *The Tempest*, Act IV. Sc. 1.

the implications of that hypothesis and tried to avoid becoming entangled by it in manifest nonsense.

I believe, then, that Descartes' method is, even on its own ground, invalid. I believe that when once he started his process of purely artificial doubt, he had as good ground for doubting everything as anything. Doubt, as an active movement of the mind, does not commonly arise through our looking for reasons to believe in this or that; it arises from an apparent collision between one actual element in experience and another—it may be of fact with theory, or of theory with theory, or of fact (as observed) with fact (as observed).[1] What Descartes indulged in his stove was purely academic doubt; he was really as sure of the stove as of himself. If it be urged that this academic doubt was not an empirical absence of assurance but an "ideal supposal", I must reply that this method is permissible enough, but that Descartes found the wrong residuum. What he ought to have reached as the irreducible basis of all thought, including doubt, was the subject-object relationship. Then all the subsequent trouble would have been avoided. But academic doubt is in itself only an extension of nursery make-believe—"Let us pretend that we do not know that there is a Sun, or that Napoleon existed, or that selfishness is bad, and see if we can prove any of these things". Such an intellectual pastime would never occupy men's thoughts and direct their enterprises unless it represented something much deeper than itself.

What it represented when Descartes embarked upon it was the total collapse of the authority of mediaeval tradition. There was urgent need to find some new foundation on which the habitation of the spirit of man could be securely built. If the individual could not find it in the whole scheme of things in which he was placed, he must find it in his own integrity. That which

[1] Of course this is rough and ready. I do not wish to suggest an ultimate distinction between "fact" and "theory"; but there is a clear provisional distinction; *e.g.* there was a "theory" that all swans are white until some one came across the "fact" of black swans.

was true to him he would assert before Emperor and Princes: *Hier steh' ich, ich kann nichts anders*. He would stand by his own thought and reach such truth as he might: *Cogito, ergo sum.*

The difficulties with which Descartes found himself confronted in trying to advance from his initial certainty of self are familiar; but it is relevant to our main purpose to outline them once more. Having no initial certainty except that of thought which is yet thought of nothing, he could not avoid holding that the mind knows nothing directly except its own ideas. It has reached its certainty of itself by the process of doubting the very existence of all else. Descartes, then, found himself possessing many ideas, some vague and confused, some clear and distinct. He found that the latter impressed the mind with their reliability. But why should he trust that impression? By reviving the Ontological Argument he established to his satisfaction the reality of God as a Being perfect in Goodness, Wisdom and Power. Such a Being would not have created us with an irresistible impulse towards the acceptance of certain ideas unless those ideas were in fact true. Thus the existence and character of God are the guarantee of the veridicity of clear and distinct ideas; relying upon God's veracity I may believe that in such ideas I have true apprehensions of the real world.

Of course the argument is circular in a vicious manner.[1] The Ontological Argument depends for its validity upon that reliability of clear and distinct ideas which is only established by means of it. Even if it is valid in itself, which in the Cartesian form it manifestly is not, its inner validity would supply no reason for accepting its conclusion as an apprehension of reality apart from the actual content of that conclusion itself. The plain fact is that Descartes, having confined himself to self-consciousness as the only immediate datum, has, and can have, no right to believe in the

[1] Not all circular argument is vicious. Cf. *Mens Creatrix*, pp. 15-23.

existence of anything else at all except his self and its states. Solipsism is the only logical issue of his initial procedure. But being not only an intellect of consummate power but also, which is a greater thing, a sane man, he would not accept Solipsism. He had to break out somehow, just as he had some day to get out of his stove. And he did it this way.

Thus he was left with three accepted realities: his mind with its ideas; God; and the real world of which his ideas were apprehensions. Among these ideas those that are clear and distinct are reliable. Now in this respect mathematical ideas are pre-eminent. Thus apart from deliberate intention (though Descartes was a supremely great mathematician) a bias was given in favour of those aspects of reality that are susceptible of mathematical treatment—that is, its measurable aspects.

This position was worked out through two streams of thought, one flowing on the Continent and one in England. On the Continent the rationalist element in Descartes prevailed—the insistence that clear and distinct ideas give secure knowledge, so that reality is regarded as subject to the laws of our thinking. In England the Cartesian scheme provided the occasion for empirical criticism. In the Continental stream the moments of consequence are Spinoza and Leibniz; in the English stream Locke, Berkeley and Hume. Every one of these is something much more than a link in a chain or a phase in a continuous transition; but it is as links in the chain that we are now concerned with them.

Spinoza is a name that has won a universal and well-merited veneration. It is tempting to pause in contemplation of his mighty structure of thought, but that would only postpone our effort to outline a scheme that may adumbrate a reconstruction of his own on different foundations. Spinoza could not be satisfied with the three distinct and very loosely related entities which constituted the foci of Descartes' thought. He took that which was always the bond of unity—God—and treated the others as modes of its being. Thus the one Substance—God—whose Attributes are infinite, is known to us under two Attributes only, Thought and Extension. And the fact that both were attributes of one Substance guaranteed a correspondence between the two. This raises the problem of Error in a specially awkward form. If Thought and Extension (where the latter term includes all spatial objects) always corresponded, well and good. Spinoza discusses the question how Error actually arises and how it may be cured; but he never answers the question how it can be possible at all, or how the one Substance is affected by the failure of correspondence between its attributes while Error lasts.

The preference of Descartes for clear and distinct ideas led Spinoza to conceive his fundamental Substance in those elementary terms of which alone we have such ideas. The religious passion of the Fifth Book of his *Ethics* is therefore found to have no place within the framework of his scheme. The essential incoherence of Spinoza is one of the first warning signs of the false lead given to "modern thought" by its founder.

Leibniz dealt with the supposed parallelism of ideas and actualities by the famous hypothesis of the pre-established harmony imposed upon the whole system of "monads" by the Creator. But this is not a harmony of "thoughts" and "objects"; for in his view material objects are appearances within the experience of minds. Each mind is a "monad", a self-contained unit; and the "harmony" is of monad with monad. God has so made them that in fact their activities harmonise. This was to take refuge in dogmatism in the bad sense of the word. From Leibniz sprang the so-called dogmatic school which reached its ludicrous apogee in Wolf.

The avoidance of similar dogmatism in the English school led to the complete break-down of the whole scheme. Locke, who was more wise than clever, and both in Politics and in Epistemology frequently saved himself from absurdity at the cost of sacrificing consistency with his main theory, is chiefly of importance here because he began the curtailment of Descartes' three entities. He perceived that the mind gets all its material from sensations; if only clear and distinct ideas are reliable witnesses of the real, then only extension is altogether real, because this alone submits to exact measurement. So what we now tend to call objective reality was reduced to the "Primary Qualities"—that is to the measurable. These are the same for all; but the "Secondary Qualities" vary according to the receptivity of the percipient and are both vague and confused. These Locke held to be subjective only. Berkeley followed and showed that there was no more reason to predicate independent existence of the "Primary" than of the "Secondary Qualities" which Locke had regarded as effects produced on the mind by the "Primary Qualities". Thus Berkeley abolished independent objective existence altogether apart from spiritual entities and left only God and the mind with its ideas. Hume followed, and showed that on the now accepted basis of philosophic enquiry there was no ground for believing in the mind itself, so that nothing at all was left except a flux of ideas—caused by nothing and held by nothing, but just happening.

At this point Kant took up the story. According to his own account he tried to read Leibniz through the eyes of Hume and Hume through the eyes of Leibniz. He sought to reach truth by a method that should reconcile the widely divergent streams that traced their source to Descartes. The enterprise resulted in a new epoch of philosophy, and Kant is entitled to the honour justly due to a courageous pioneer. But he did not effect the reconciliation which he sought. As Edward Caird used to say, "He started from both ends of the road at once, but he never met himself". In fact it was impossible that he ever should; for he never discarded the fatal Cartesian hypothesis that the mind deals directly not with objects known throughout as objects, but with its own ideas which have to be related to the real world by a special act. When as a boy I read the *Critique of Pure Reason*, having then never heard of Descartes or of Berkeley, I got the impression that Kant meant what I afterwards learnt to have been the meaning of Berkeley. Later I tried to adjust my mind to the fact that Kant supposed himself, not to have established this position, but to have refuted it. Later still I have returned to the conviction that, though this was not his intention, the real upshot of the argument of that *Critique* is Berkeleyan Idealism, with the Thing-in-Itself attached as an illogical appendage.

One of the "Ifs" on which it is interesting to speculate is this: "If Biology had reached the point of development represented by Darwin before the time of Kant——" But Science for Kant meant Mathematics and Mathematical Physics. He was himself a considerable astronomer. So it was natural that when he thought of Knowledge, the clear and distinct ideas of Descartes should still preoccupy his attention. His scheme of Categories makes it clear that the whole habit of thought associated with Biology and still more with History was not his. In the *Critique of Practical Reason* he released Ethics from the *impasse* in which he found, and left, Epistemology engulfed, though even here his position could only be squared with his general theory by making the Autonomous Will, on which all depends, a Thing-in-Itself which never operates in the phenomenal world. In the *Critique of Judgment* he moves to still greater freedom of mind at a still greater sacrifice of consistency with his initial doctrine.

Various schools of post-Kantian philosophy have attempted to assert the primary unity which Kant failed to construct. In particular the English Hegelians laid reiterated emphasis on the fact that the distinction between Self and Not-Self is drawn within the given unity of experience. But in them still the old tradition sufficiently prevailed to lead to an assumption of an epistemological and thus (for this philosophy) a metaphysical priority of the Subject in the Subject-Object relation of Knowledge. For this there is no foundation if once the Cartesian starting-point has been discarded. There is, as we shall see, a real priority of Spirit, but not in its function as Subject of Knowledge.[1] And until this is fully recognised there is insuperable difficulty in the mere notion of man's knowledge of God. For if there is an inherent priority in the subject, then in man as knowing God there is a priority towards God. It is partly in the endeavour to avoid such an absurdity that some philosophers tend to substitute for man's knowledge of God his absorption in an Absolute conceived primarily as experience perfected in all-embracing knowledge.

It may well be held that an apology is required for introducing into the august series of Gifford Lectures a summary of modern philosophical development which is commonplace, even where disputable, to every novice in philosophy, and which may suggest to others that the great names of the past are not worthy of the veneration which has been paid to them. Certainly nothing could be further from my own desire than to give any support to that suggestion; every name that I have mentioned is truly honourable; some represent an integrity as pure, an insight as penetrating, and an organising ability as thorough as was ever displayed by the human mind. But we are not now directly concerned with the development of modern philosophy. For our purposes there is illumination in the outline of its development, but the outline is all that we require. And

[1] "This presupposition that what is known exists independently of being known is quite general. . . . It is, therefore, unnecessary to consider whether idealism is assisted by the supposition of a non-finite knowing mind, correlated with reality as a whole. For reality must be equally independent of it. Consequently, if the issue between idealism and realism is whether the physical world is or is not dependent on the mind, it cannot turn upon a dependence in respect of Knowledge."—Prichard, *Kant's Theory of Knowledge*, pp. 118, 119.

if this, as I have sketched it, is commonplace, that is, I suggest, because substantially it is true. And what it everywhere illustrates is *the inherent error of its initial assumption that in knowledge the mind begins with itself and proceeds to the apprehension of the external world by way of construction and inference.*

This is nowhere clearer than in Kant, where the development reaches its true completion and new tendencies begin to appear, though they cannot at first shake themselves quite free of what had become the traditional presupposition. Kant "started from both ends of the road at once, but he never met himself". He held fast to the line of development which followed the way of "clear and distinct ideas"; and he also started from Hume's doctrine of "impressions", each one of which is unitary. He accepted this notion of discrete or atomic sensations, which is the inevitable upshot of the process starting from the Cartesian dichotomy of Mind and Extension. Mind, examining, not the world as it finds it, but its own impressions of the world, can only discover first one and then another. How from these can it build up that continuous and coherent world of which it is in fact conscious? Hume with relentless self-consistency declared that this occurred through the association of impressions, which occurred according to discoverable laws of association of impressions. This led in due course to Bain's associative Psychology and Bradley's annihilation thereof by ridicule. But Kant could only answer Hume by transferring the principles of association from the impressions themselves to the mind which received them. In the very act of perception, according to Kant, the mind organises its inherently discrete or atomic sensations by means of its own Forms of Space and Time and of its own Categories of Quantity, Quality, Causality and Modality. But the sensations so organised are set up in the mind by Things in Themselves which do not come under this organising control of Mind and its furniture. Knowledge therefore is of phenomena only, that is, of sensations or impressions as organised by Understanding in the very act of perception. Its relation to Things-in-Themselves remains wholly indeterminate, and they remain wholly unknowable. The Mind is also possessed of certain Ideas which refer to what lies beyond actual or possible human experience. These are called Ideas of Reason, and they have a certain regulative value but they are not principles of knowledge. Hume stated that he could not be consistent with his sceptical philosophy in practice; Kant required belief in God, Freedom and Immortality as "postulates of Practical Reason". Is there not substantial truth in the epigram that "what Hume gave to Kant as a problem Kant handed back unchanged as the solution"? And as it was more a problem than a solution, Hume's position is more defensible than Kant's.

More defensible; but not more tolerable. For though Kant accepted the false starting-point, and tried to solve the problem by setting out from both ends of the road at once instead of standing in the middle and setting out in both directions from there, yet by devising the critical method he gave us the instrument we need. For so soon as he has left behind the attempt actually to construct a continuous world out of atomic sensations, and is busy with the principles on which the continuous world is actually constructed—even though it be in his view a world of mere phenomena—he breaks new ground not only, and indeed not so much, in his conclusions, but in the more fundamental and fruitful realm of method. He does not proceed either deductively or inductively, but critically; that is to say, he interrogates the conditions of experience in general to ascertain the principles presupposed in its possibility. The universality of causation is not, for him, an inductive inference from the frequent observance of causal sequence; it is found to be the presupposition of all rational experience. It is ascertained by the process called transcendental deduction. This is not in the least like deduction of the syllogistic type; yet it is deduction, because it makes the object of enquiry dependent on something wider, and in that sense more universal, than itself, namely, rational experience. Kant knew that he was introducing a novelty; how new, or how deeply significant it was, he could not know. But in the critical method of Kant was supplied the true substitute for that scholastic Logic which had both guided and cramped thought for centuries, and which the Cartesian philosophers had discarded without providing any substitute.

The question of Logic and its claims will occupy us in the next Lecture. Before we leave the consideration of the Lutheran and Cartesian "antithesis" we must try to appreciate its merits so that these may be incorporated into the "synthesis" which we must endeavour to construct. We have already associated the names of Luther and Descartes, and that association is neither superficial nor accidental. Both express one great principle—the principle of "Private Judgement". This is the essential principle in that movement of the spirit in a great section of mankind which is generally referred to as the Reformation. It was preceded and accompanied by the Renaissance, which displayed the same temper of individualism, but never grasped this as a principle. The men of the Renaissance behaved individualistically; but they were not sufficiently in earnest, nor did they meet with sufficient resistance, to feel the necessity of bringing out into clear light the principle of their action. That came first when Luther set his conscience against the whole authority of the organised Catholic Church in one of the most splendid and decisive moments of history.

It is always to be remembered that what the Reformers taught was not so much the Right, but rather the Duty, of Private Judgement. Certainly it is true that no seriously minded person can suppose that all individuals are in every sense at liberty to think what they like. What this great principle affirms is the obligation upon every rational intelligence to master his own experience as fully as he can. This may lead to some harmonious unity at the end of a long process; but it is inevitably productive of disruption and division by the way. And the chief characteristic of the modern or post-Reformation period has been departmentalisation. The great enterprise of all-inclusive unity, which was characteristic of the Middle Ages, was progressively abandoned. Machiavelli, as has already been mentioned, proclaimed the independence of Politics; the hope of unity was most easily abandoned in that sphere because it had been so little fulfilled. The declaration of independence was next issued in the name of religion. Art was increasingly emancipating itself by the setting of mythology alongside of Scripture as a store-house of themes. Shakespeare, the culmination of the English Renaissance, is scarcely touched in his artistic apprehension of the world by any religious dogma. Science was breaking loose and in Francis Bacon found an influential if not very profound apologist. And Philosophy in Descartes attempted to reach certainty by an all-embracing experiment in doubt. What has been the result for mankind?

In the sphere of Politics the unmitigated assertion of national independence led to the fuller development of the various national types, with consequent enrichment of the art and literature of the world, and to local experiments of universal value in the making of constitutions and in the relations between political and social life. But it also led through various instances of national self-assertion to the international Hell or Bedlam of the years 1914 to 1918 from which we are now struggling to emerge. The check which it might have been hoped that Religion would exercise could not be applied, for Religion also had become departmentalised, and was by most people regarded as a "private affair between a man and his Maker", so that its main if not its only concern was with personal piety. But in reaching this position it laid a new emphasis on the personal element in all true religion, and while it cannot be said to have initiated a deeper devotion than had already been attained by innumerable saints, yet it occasioned a far more widespread appreciation of personal devotion as the heart and mainspring of religion. The characteristic Evangelical doctrines and modes of apprehension were not new in themselves, but they were new as widely pervasive forces in popular religion. Art in like manner became incapable of permeating life with Beauty because it had adopted the principle of "Art for Art's sake". This is, perhaps, the most refined form of the principle of departmentalism which finds its grossest expression in the formula "Business is business" and its most immoral in "My country, right or wrong". It was proclaimed as a real emancipation, and asserted the truth that Beauty is an ultimate, and that neither theological, nor political, nor ethical canons are relevant to purely aesthetic questions. This needed to be established. And the enrichment of art in all its forms resulting from this emancipation is unquestionable. But the formula "Art for Art's sake", in which the movement of emancipation ultimately found expression, is an exaggeration as false and pernicious as the contrary error. It expresses a complete detachment of Art from all other interests or modes of experience so that artists, under its impulse, are liable to become engrossed in self-expression without any enquiry whether they have a self which is worthy, or even fit, to be expressed.

Philosophy meanwhile has been involved in the same process. Inasmuch as every particular study or pursuit of knowledge is the subject of a special science, Philosophy has been left with the study of knowledge in general, and has been in preposterous disproportion occupied with the enquiry whether and how Knowledge may be possible at all.[1] Mankind, being quite well aware that it possesses some fragments of what is Knowledge if such a thing exists and must pass for Knowledge if it does not, leaves Philosophy to spin its cobwebs and gets on with the business of the world as best it may.

Philosophy also has long ago set about its escape from the sterility of departmentalism, and the series of Gifford Lectures is evidence that the deliverance has been effected. Yet, though the repudiation of the Lutheran and Cartesian standpoint has often been vigorously expressed, this has seldom carried with it the clear consciousness that this repudiation marks the close of a philosophic epoch. This consciousness is vividly present, however, in Baron von Hügel, and especially in *The Reality of God*, a volume which consists in its first half of *disjecta membra* of the Gifford Lectures that he did not live to complete. There is evidence that von Hügel meant this repudiation to be his starting-point, for in commenting on Spinoza he writes as follows:

> "There never was, and I cannot think there ever will be again, a more detestably inappropriate form for what Spinoza meant to say, indeed for what at its best he really says, than all that mathematical, indeed geometrical form and procedure which masks the actual facts for all concerned. This perverse choice of his is, nevertheless, most natural, and most legitimate if clear chains of reasoning are held to be our only means of knowledge: and this is, of course, his fundamental assumption—the outlook tends to be Cartesian from beginning to end, and suffers from all the incompleteness and lop-sidedness of Descartes' own outlook as we found this outlook to be in our first section."[2]

That "first section" does not appear among these *disjecta membra*. In the second section of the same

[1] "It was the most unfortunate error of the Scottish philosophers that they identified the epistemological with the metaphysical problem."—A. S. Pringle Pattison, *The Balfour Lectures on Realism*, 1933, p. 256.

[2] *Op. cit.* p. 100.

volume, however, we find a passage which shows what the course of its argument would have been:

"Modern philosophy started with a strong emphasis upon the subject, and this starting-point was first impressively articulated in Descartes' famous (but, alas, dangerously inadequate) fundamental formula—his one axiom—'*cogito, ergo sum*'. We thus take for granted, as rock-certain, what is demonstrably non-existent: 'I think' instead of 'I think such and such realities', or at least, 'I think such and such objects'. The subject and object, always interconnected in man's actual experience and hence to be assumed in this their interconnexion, were thus severed from each other, in the very starting-point of philosophy; and then this severance and quite artificial separateness could hardly any more be bridged over—the object could hardly be recovered, since man (after all) is in fact restricted, and is here rightly recognised as restricted, to the analysis of what actually exists, and to what he really experiences. The appeal here to its experience and to its analysis was, then, right; what was wrong was the exclusion, before any and all investigation, and without any justification, of one entire third of every living experience. For all experience is always threefold: it is always simultaneously experience of the subject, of the object, and of the overbridging thought; indeed, clear consciousness always first concerns the object, and only much later on the subject. And thus, through that artificial abstraction, there promptly arose such sheer figments of the brain as knowledge, not of objects at all, but of subjective states alone; and (stranger still) knowledge that objects exist, and that they all have an inside, but an inside which is never actually revealed to us by the qualities of those objects; and (culminating miracle of strangeness) that this inside abides ever essentially unknowable by us, and yet, all the same, we absolutely know that it contradicts all these appearances. Man thus, though well within the universe, isolates himself from it; he imprisons himself in his own faculties, and, as to anything further, knows only that objects exist as to which these faculties essentially and inevitably mislead him.

"Here no criticism of the logic of the position is sufficient; indeed, such criticisms mostly end by bearing unwilling, or even unwitting, testimony to the general self-consistency of this subjectivism. Only a criticism, not of the conclusions as consistent or not with their premises, but of these premises as adequate or not to real experience, is sufficient."[1]

[1] *Op. cit.* pp. 188, 189.

Return to the concrete richness and bewildering variety and still more bewildering interconnexion of actual experience must be the mode of deliverance from that false scent on which Descartes set the modern mind in its search for truth. It is not a return to the Middle Ages that we want. It is not desirable any more than it is possible to put back the clock. Those are not wise guides, I am very sure, who wish to cultivate a mediaeval mentality on the ground that we need to recover the mediaeval sense alike of objectivity and of unity. It is our task consciously and deliberately to construct a "synthesis" of the classical and mediaeval "thesis" with the modern "antithesis", and this in some fundamental respects will resemble the "thesis" more closely than the "antithesis". But it will not leave the "antithesis" unexpressed; we cannot go behind the Reformation—that great *bouleversement* of human thinking, wherein it was for the first time fully recognised that each man is by nature the centre of his own universe, however true it be that his most urgent need is to discover that it does not revolve about him as its pivot. The "duty of private judgement", the autonomy of the individual conscience, the integrity of the individual mind—all these which find their basis in the proclamation of personal sincerity as the fundamental human excellence—not the highest but the most basic—are realities discovered in the period of departmentalism and never again to be forgotten.

The incorporation of all that men have learnt during the four centuries of the Reformation period into a reconstituted unity of articulated experience must be a task of many generations. There is hardly any department of human activity or thought which it will leave unaffected. But none is so deeply concerned as Religion; for, as has been said, the central element in any authentic religious experience is Authority, and at first sight there is a complete antagonism between the very principle of Authority and the principle of individual integrity and autonomy. With that problem we shall have to deal at length later on. But the clue to its solution will be found in a fresh recognition of the essential nature of Authority as distinct from either coercion or dictation,[1] and in the appreciation of man's ethical problem as primarily one of conversion and vocation.[2] In short the restoration of unity to man's experience depends mainly on securing at once the supremacy of Religion among human interests, and the true spirituality of Religion both in itself and in the mode of its supremacy.

[1] See Lecture XIII. [2] See Lectures XV. and XVI.

LECTURE IV

MATHEMATICS, LOGIC AND HISTORY

THE Cartesian movement had two main characteristics, which are closely interconnected. The first was the adoption of the individual consciousness as the starting-point of the whole process of thought, the other was the reliance upon "clear and distinct ideas". The latter was necessitated by the former, for if the individual mind is to start from its own ideas alone, it can have confidence in its conclusions only if it can perceive these as necessary implicates in what it cannot doubt. There was indeed, as will shortly become apparent, no very great novelty in the special reliance upon clear and distinct ideas; but through the thought of Descartes it became more explicit, and was then, so far as I know, for the first time formulated. But while it was scarcely novel in principle, it was a necessary postulate in the Cartesian scheme in an altogether new sense. For if the isolated individual consciousness is the starting-point, there can be no external reference and then logical certainty is the only justifiable form of assurance.

Of course it is true that all men have assurance on many subjects without reaching their conclusions by cogent inference from self-evident propositions. Such assurance mainly springs from sense-perception, or from tradition and the current opinions of our contemporaries. But these are both specifically mentioned by Descartes as unreliable. Descartes was fully aware of the necessity for accepting in practice much that he could not justify by his method. The second maxim of his "provisory code of Morals" was "to be as firm and resolute in my actions as I was able, and not to adhere less steadfastly to the most doubtful opinions, when once adopted, than if they had been highly certain".[1] But this maxim, difficult enough in any case, is not likely to be effectively obeyed if great emphasis is laid upon the exclusive right of "clear and distinct ideas" to be the objects or occasions of assurance. And it is significant that Descartes' profession of attachment to the Catholic Faith is conspicuously lukewarm. It is dictated by his first maxim, namely:

"to obey the laws and customs of my country, adhering firmly to the Faith in which, by the grace of God, I had been educated from my childhood, and regulating my conduct in every other matter according to the most moderate opinions, and the farthest removed from extremes, which should happen to be adopted in practice with general consent of the most judicious of those among whom I might be living. For, as I had from that time begun to hold my own opinions for nought because I wished to subject them all to examination, I was convinced that I could not do better than follow in the meantime the opinions of the most judicious; and although there are some perhaps among the Persians and Chinese as judicious as among ourselves, expediency seemed to dictate that I should regulate my practice conformably to the opinions of those with whom I should have to live."[2]

Now if a man's acceptance of Christianity in preference to Zoroastrianism, Mohammedanism or Confucianism is based on that consideration of expediency, it will be very hard for him to adhere to it as steadfastly as if it had been highly certain. He may on that basis practice mystical meditation and go very far in it, but he is not likely to come under the full force of definite religious faith. There can be no doubt about Descartes' sincerity in his religion as elsewhere, but the wonder suggests itself whether he had any notion whatever of the true nature of religious faith—such faith, for example, as that of Francis or Luther or Pascal. His intention of conformity is like the intention of most of us to use our knife and fork in the conventional way;

[1] *Discourse on Method* (Veitch's translation), p. 25.

[2] *Op. cit.* pp. 23, 24.

it has no suggestion of any submission to overwhelming Authority.[1]

Now it is certainly of great importance to distinguish between assurance which is logically well-grounded and assurance which is not thus grounded, and it may be necessary from time to time that this distinction should be enforced even at the cost of seeming to deprive of real justification all assurance which lacks proof. But that position has the value only of a temporary protest, for the area of experience in reference to which actual proof is possible is narrowly limited, and the most important of mental disciplines for almost all purposes is not that which distinguishes between certainty and probability, but that which leads to discrimination between the degrees of probability, and especially between degrees of justification attaching to unproved assurances. To such a discipline the Cartesian method contributes little or nothing. Having involved all convictions in artificial doubt, Descartes seeks a way of secure advance from his assurance of doubt to assurance of ascertained truth. There could be none such except the way of clear and distinct ideas. When the mind sees one idea to be essentially involved in another, it passes from the first to the second with absolute assurance. Even then its trust in the applicability of its conclusion to the real world reposes on faith in the veracity of God, who would be a deceiver if He had made our minds in such a way that they are bound to believe what may yet not be true. And if the veracity of God—or if God Himself—be not ascertainable by the way of clear and distinct ideas, these are

[1] Professor Boyce Gibson claims that Descartes was in fact a truly religious man; that may be true, but it does not make his philosophy religiously tolerable. It is urged that his philosophy also is religious, because God is the pivot of it, and apart from the reality of God it would fall to pieces. That also is true; yet it is still not a religious philosophy, for it sets no value on God in Himself, but only as the lynch-pin of its own mechanism. It does not interpret the world in the light of knowledge of God, but makes use of God to vindicate its own interpretation of the world, and constructs its concept of Him with that in view. He is to be used for our purpose, not we for His. This is the essential principle of magic, which is thus found as a canker at the heart of Rationalism.

themselves unreliable and we are left to choose between *petitio principii*, absolute scepticism and circularity. Thus European thought was launched on its labyrinthic course, which culminated in Kant's attribution of our right to certainty to the function of the Understanding as itself ordering the experience of which it thereafter understands the order.

Yet at the outset there was a most welcome and profitable simplification. Scholastic Logic, like Ptolemaic Astronomy, had become more and more complex, as the attempt was pursued to fit into its framework the infinite subtleties of living thought. Refinement was added to refinement, just as Astronomy, in order to keep pace with the observed movements of the heavenly bodies, added epicycle to epicycle. It was most welcome, then, when Descartes made a fresh start:

"Instead of the great number of precepts of which Logic is composed, I believed that the four following would prove perfectly sufficient for me, provided I took the firm and unwavering resolution never in a single instance to fail in observing them.

"The *first* was never to accept anything for true which I did not clearly know to be such; that is to say, carefully to avoid precipitancy and prejudice, and to comprise nothing more in my judgment than what was presented to my mind so clearly and distinctly as to exclude all ground of doubt.

"The *second*, to divide each of the difficulties under examination into as many parts as possible, and as might be necessarv for its adequate solution.

"The *third*, to conduct my thoughts in such order that, by commencing with objects the simplest and easiest to know, I might ascend by little and little, and, as it were, step by step, to the knowledge of the more complex; assigning in thought a certain order even to those objects which in their own nature do not stand in a relation of antecedence and sequence.

"And the *last*, in every case to make enumerations so complete, and reviews so general, that I might be assured that nothing was omitted."[1]

It would be hard to conceive a more complete programme for the scientific era. Descartes lays down all

[1] *Discourse on Method* (Veitch's translation), p. 19.

its leading principles: here is set out the method of analysis which has carried us through molecules to atoms, through atoms to protons, electrons, and neutrons, and now threatens to dissolve these in mere measurements which are measurements of nothing; here too is that conviction that the simple contains the explanation of the complex, which leads to the denial of objective reality to aesthetic and moral qualities because these only appear at a stage of high development and advanced complexity.[1]

But it is noticeable that the first precept is ambiguous. That it should be so was inevitable, but it is also fatal. Descartes will never accept as true what he does not clearly know to be such; and this he paraphrases as meaning that he will never include anything in his affirmations which is not presented to his mind so clearly and distinctly that he could have no occasion to doubt it. But does this include Isaiah's vision? or such a flaming apprehension of God as is recorded in Pascal's celebrated fragment? And if not, why not? To the subjects of these experiences there was nothing about them either confused or questionable. Why is my perception that $2 + 2 = 4$ to be regarded as either more clear and distinct, or more compelling of acceptance, than Isaiah's perception of the Holiness of God? The truth is that in order to make his method work at all, Descartes was obliged to state its first principle in terms which covered much more than he intended; for if he had limited his terms to the scope of his intention, he would have been driven to assert a unique claim to truth on behalf of mathematics, and would have drawn upon himself the contradiction of all who dispute that claim. His position has plausibility because his fundamental precept is so stated as to be unexceptionable, but is then without notice so restricted in interpreta-

[1] "The deliverances of clear and distinct consciousness require criticism by reference to elements in experience which are neither clear nor distinct."—Whitehead, *Adventures of Ideas*, p. 348.

tion and application as to make the second and third precepts appropriate successors to it.

If we consider the Cartesian revolution as a moment in the history of thought, it appears as at once the repudiation of scholastic or formal Logic and the substitution for it of its own unrecognised principle. For the connexion between mathematics and formal Logic is intimate.

The influence of mathematics upon philosophy has been very close and very formative. It supplied an ideal for the search after knowledge, because it moves by necessary steps to a conclusion as certain as its starting-point. It offers an example of perfect cogency in its process and perfect certainty in its result. It was natural that philosophers should see in it the type of true knowledge. Plato, himself a mathematician, followed its lead; for him Physics was a science as purely mathematical as it is for Whitehead or Jeans; Whitehead is fully conscious of the close similarity between his cosmogony and that outlined in the *Timaeus*.[1] But Plato's Metaphysic showed the marks of the same influence. All the "propaedeutic studies" outlined in Book VII. of the *Republic* as a fitting preparation for that Dialectic which leads to apprehension of the Idea of Good, are mathematical; and the schematisation of Ideas to which the whole process points has many of the characteristics of a geometrical pattern.

This mathematical ideal of knowledge has often been valued for precisely those qualities which constitute its fatal defects: these are its indifference to Time and its precision. There is, of course, a great intellectual satisfaction in the elaboration of a chain of thought where every term is precisely understood and every step in the argument is appreciated as both necessary and secure. The intensity of that satisfaction led men to regard what occasioned it as the true type of knowledge. If our apprehension of the phenomenal and historical

[1] Cf. *Process and Reality*, pp. 129-133, and many other passages.

world never corresponds to it, so much the worse for that apprehension; but also—so much the worse for the phenomenal and historical world. For it was perceived that in the study of that world it was not our faculties but the subject-matter itself which refused to correspond to the ideal of knowledge. So there had to be devised a realm of entities apprehensible only by the mind, without any interposition of sense, which should be the counterpart of a true knowledge; and this must be regarded as the real world, or realm of true Being; for what is altogether real is what answers to knowledge most perfectly; τὸ παντελῶς ὄν, παντελῶς γνωστόν.[1] This realm of reality is changeless, not only in the sense in which a Law of Nature is an unchanging principle governing a process of change, but in the sense of having no reference to change or process at all.

The objects of pure mathematical "knowledge" answer to these requirements. The triangle is unchangingly what it is defined to be, and possesses unchangingly the qualities which it is proved to possess. Here is the field of study in which every term is fully understood and every step can be both necessary and secure; hence its deep fascination for those who are skilled in it. Hence also its immense and pervasive influence on all reflection concerning the nature of knowledge and the way to reach it. For traditional Logic is in form, and largely in substance, applied mathematics.

It is not easy to be sure what Aristotle took to be the real function of the discipline set out in the *Prior Analytics*, in which are given the rules for the Syllogism. What is quite clear is that that treatise is not his account of the way in which knowledge is reached. It gives the rules, not for seeking truth but for conducting argument. Sometimes those two are combined in one intellectual activity; but not all argument is controlled by a desire for truth. Desire to refute an antagonist is a more frequent motive. Among the Greeks,

[1] Plato, *Republic*, 477 A.

Argument was a fashionable game; it was necessary to have rules about it and a means of deciding who had won. For such a purpose the *Prior Analytics* is admirably designed. But whether in earnest or in fun, cogency in the process is, when attainable, of vital moment in argument. And cogency belongs to the regions of thought where every term is fully understood and each step can be both necessary and secure.

The key to necessary inference is the Universal, and therefore the history of Logic is largely the record of controversies concerning the Universal, from Plato's Ideas and Aristotle's Forms, through the conflict of Realists, Nominalists and Conceptualists, down to discussions of the concrete Universal in our own day. For purposes of that truly necessary inference, of which the syllogism is the type, a universal proposition is necessary. How is it to be obtained? There are only two ways of gaining the initial security, without which the whole process is insecure. One of these is "complete enumeration" of all instances comprised in or under the Universal. But this is seldom applicable; and if it is, no inference is necessary, for the observation in which it consists can detect the fact stated in the conclusion without going through the inferential process at all. The other way of reaching a secure Universal is to treat it as a definition; but then it can only be referred to experience hypothetically. When once the term triangle has been defined, the equality of its interior angles to two right angles can be proved—provided, of course, that the Euclidean postulates and axioms are admitted. But it does not follow that the interior angles of any wooden object that appears triangular are equal to two right angles. We can only say "If this is a triangle, then its interior angles are equal to two right angles". As a matter of fact we know that it is not a triangle; for if it is made of wood, its sides are sure not to be geometrically straight, and if we really want to know the sum of the degrees of its interior angles—an unlikely yearning—there is nothing for it but to measure each and add up; and then, of course, the measurement will not be mathematically exact.

The familiar illustration is a syllogism opening with the proposition—All men are mortal. This certainly cannot be established by complete enumeration, for not all even of men already born have as yet died. If approached in that way, the proposition is a generalisation which has no irresistible claim to universality. It can only acquire universality by becoming a definition or part of one—Man is mortal. That could be justified if it could be shown that essential elements in human nature include or supply the causes of mortality. But even so we should not have certainty that any particular man now living is mortal, for it always might be that in him evolution had produced a specimen of a new species in which the cause of mortality is automatically counteracted by new organic adjustments. If it be urged that he would not be a man, I must reply that this is to save logical consistency by the sacrifice of rational interest.

And if these methods fail to give us secure knowledge, certainly Induction is no better. No one ever supposes that the rules of inductive inference as formulated by Mill or by anyone else can give us certainty. Mill indeed has the distinction of having affirmed that essentially real inference is from particulars to particulars; and Bosanquet echoes this in his famous definition: "Inference is the indirect reference to reality of differences within a universal by means of the exhibition of this universal in differences directly referred to reality".[1] But Bosanquet's "universal" is not a term or proposition at all; it is a systematised apprehension of a group of interrelated facts. We need have no hesitation in assenting to the summary criticism of traditional Logic which declares that Deduction has no right to its starting-point and Induction has no right to its conclusion.

[1] Bosanquet, *Logic*, vol. ii. p. 4.

But of course this only holds if we suppose that knowledge is concerned with the world of actual experience. And we find ourselves confronted with this paradox: if knowledge is of actual experience it lacks cogency; if it has cogency it is not concerned with actual experience.

In the traditional Logic there is much which is of permanent value concerning Terms and Judgements. For here we are in the realm of direct apprehension, and the manifold variety of this apprehension is recognised and articulated by the traditional Logic, as, for example, most conspicuously by Aristotle in his doctrine of Categories. But when the traditional Logic deals with inference, its concern for cogency leads it to treat all inference according to the mathematical model, and in effect to reduce all thinking to mathematics. For its laws of inference take terms (to use its own language) in extension only. Its laws with regard to Excluded Middle, Illicit Major, Illicit Minor, all deal with extension only. The fact that such a heresy as Hamilton's Quantification of the Predicate was even possible goes far to prove this contention. These rules treat a Universal as a class or an area, within which or without which the particular instances in question fall. In its essence it is either arithmetical or geometrical. It is obscurely yet truly an application of the science of Quantity; and the name of that science is Mathematics.

That this was bound to be so we may perceive by approaching the matter from another side. As we study Greek philosophy and the continuation of one strand in it into Scholasticism, we become aware that, except in relation to Ethics and Politics, it is all in fact, though not in intention, more intimately a study of cogent mental process than of empirical reality. The Astronomy which Plato includes among the propaedeutic studies is to dispense with all reference to the observed movements of the heavenly bodies; it is a purely notional discipline. And if it be true that transcendent entities were conceived by Plato to exist in correspondence with the perfectly pure notions thus studied, this was not because they were actually experienced,[1] but because "what is perfectly real is perfectly knowable", and the counterpart of perfect intellection is perfect reality.

Aristotle did not accept the doctrine of self-existent Ideas. But he did believe in Real Kinds—*γένη*—and this belief persisted into the Scholastic period. There is very much in Aristotle himself which represents another line of thought, and to these elements in his whole body of teaching we must give attention shortly. But the notion of Real Kinds, finding their common characteristic in a Universal, held the field for centuries, so that the great logical controversies concerned the nature of Universals. And here the traditional Realism of the Church was indispensable to any belief in the validity of thought. The test of a doctrine was not that it should be authenticated by experience, but that it should be established by inevitable process from unquestioned premises. That was part of the trouble about Copernicus and Galileo. The dispute arose because the conclusion reached was novel; but in the background of thought was the apprehension that this novel conclusion represented a new mentality—a mentality that would discard the whole established apparatus of thought, as it did when Descartes induced in himself a doubt of all but his doubt.

Now all this, as we said, was inevitable, because the human mental capacity was fully developed, but its store of systematised observation was very scanty. The great strength of Greek thought is in the realms of Politics and Ethics—or in other words in the study of the field of human action; if to this is added Logic, that is still a study of a sphere of human activity. Physics and

[1] As a matter of fact I think Plato was predisposed to believe in the reality of his Ideas by an experience which he interpreted as an actual apprehension of the Idea of Beauty: see my article on "Plato's Vision of the Ideas" in *Mind*, N.S. 68. But this is at most the psychological predisposition, not the philosophical ground, of the belief.

astronomy were in a rudimentary state, so that Mathematics had not its point of contact with sense-experience which has in our time enabled it to appear as the master-science of reality. In other words, the available material on which the human mind had to work consisted mainly of the processes and activities of the human mind itself. It was this part of the tradition which was able to establish itself. And inasmuch as in other departments there was no possibility of testing thought to any great extent by external reference, it was inevitable that it should be tested by its own standard of internal coherence. The result of its processes was transferred to the external world by means of the dogma which correlated perfect reality with perfect intellection.

That was not the whole, nor the profoundest element, of Greek philosophy. Plato's combination of wide range and penetrating insight cannot be summarised in terms of scholastic or formal Logic; but still more important is the fact that Aristotle added to the treatise in which he laid the foundations of that Logic another in which he set forth the proper procedure for a mind bent on the acquisition of knowledge. The *Posterior Analytics* is a far more difficult work than the *Prior Analytics* and exerted far less influence. But whereas the easier work is mainly concerned to give rules for conducting a process of inference from established or assumed knowledge, the harder work is concerned with the more vitally important stage of attaining to the knowledge from which inferences could be drawn. It would be out of place to discuss here the Aristotelian scheme; it is enough for our purpose to call attention to the stages by which such knowledge is to be reached. They are five: Sensation, Memory, Experience, "Induction", Reason: *αἴσθησις, μνήμη, ἐμπειρία, ἐπαγώγη, νοῦς*.[1]

Plainly this is not a technical analysis of inductive inference such as we find in Mill's celebrated Methods.

[1] *Posterior Analytics, ad finem.*

It is in fact something much more valuable, and the vagueness of some of its terms is part of its merit; for what it describes is not a cut-and-dried procedure according to rule, but the activity of living thought with all the elasticity and delicate adjustment of response which is characteristic of life. The process begins with sense-perception—the mind's first apprehension of its data. But these must be stored in the mind. If the mind is only conscious of them as they pass, they may initiate processes of association but not of reflection or scientific ratiocination. So in addition to sensation there must be Memory. But this again will only clog the mind if it is unsystematic; here, therefore, Aristotle introduces an element vital to such thought as he is describing but quite incapable of direction by precise formulae; this is "experience" or, to give the suggestion of the word more fully, aptitude due to familiarity. By means of such aptitude the student is able to enter on "Induction", or, more closely, Adduction of Relevant Instances. And then Reason—by an unregulated intuition—universalises the result, or detects in the relevant instances the universal which is to be the mainspring of subsequent deduction. The apprehension of principles by Reason is always intuitive.

How modern that is! It is hardly distinguishable from the method of scientific advance outlined by Poincaré in his *Science and Hypothesis*. The three last stages are specially significant. Experience: it is only the man familiar with the subject who is qualified to judge the instances provided by Sense-Perception and stored in Memory, and to say which are relevant and worthy of consideration. Only the Historian can securely estimate historical evidence; only the lover of Art can select the pictures on which may fairly be founded a generalisation concerning Italian or Flemish painters; only the wise man—Aristotle's φρόνιμος—can say what is the rule by which action in given circumstances should be regulated or judged. And then, when Experience has facilitated Adduction of Relevant Instances, Reason attains to the comprehension of the Essence of what is under consideration by right of its own inherent faculty for universalisation. So Knowledge (ἐπιστήμη) is reached; what it apprehends is Essence (οὐσία); the formulation of the essence so apprehended is a Definition (ὁρισμός); and from the definition Demonstration (ἀπόδειξις) may proceed. And so the merry game of the *Prior Analytics* and of Scholastic Logic is set agoing.

Now Aristotle does not seem ever to have decided clearly what is the relation of the Essence apprehended by Reason to the initial data of sense-perception. He rejected the doctrine that the Essence is a transcendent entity apprehensible by pure mind; yet he certainly did not regard it is an adjectival quality of the objects of sensation. Perhaps it would not be unfair to say that having refused to exalt the Essence as a transcendent entity, he reached the same result by depressing that in which it is found as a mere substrate—ὑποκείμενον. He did once at least offer the suggestion that knowledge (ἐπιστήμη) is a potentiality of which the realised activity is contemplation (θεωρία)[1]—a doctrine which anticipates Spinoza's *cognitio tertii generis* which is *scientia intuitiva*.[2] But he did not follow this through to the thought of the apprehension of the sensible world in all its manifold particularity by an intelligence able to grasp all the universal principles which that would illustrate. On the contrary the perfect intelligence of God was supposed to have no apprehension of the material world just because this will not perfectly fit into intellectual forms; this world is not a proper object of knowledge; God, being perfect intellection, therefore knows nothing about it, and has for His occupation the thinking of thought.[3] Thus at the critical

[1] *Metaphysics*, 1087 a 10-25; cf. *De Anima*, 417 a 21-29.
[2] *Ethics*, Part II. Props. XL.-XLII.; Part V. Props. XXV.-XXVII.
[3] *Metaphysics*, 1074 b 32-35.

points Aristotle dropped out of his pattern the thread that connects him most closely with modern science and philosophy. If experience is in any way recalcitrant to the forms of pure thought, it must be ignored, and pure thought is left in possession of the field.

But even pure thought is not thought about nothing at all. It is thought about the aspects, functions, elements of reality which are intellectually apprehensible with perfect clearness and are capable of definition. Experience presents us with a multitude of men and another multitude of dogs. It is evident that these have something in common with each other, which may be called Animal Life; it is also evident that the members of each multitude have something in common with one another which they do not share with members of the other multitude—human nature in the one case, canine nature in the other. There is therefore ground for setting up two Real Kinds—Man and Dog—and considering the characteristics of these. But whereas the definition of a Triangle states the whole nature of Triangle as such, no definition of Man states the whole nature of Humanity as such. A doctrine of Real Kinds, with definition of essences by *genus* and *differentia*, is not going to help living thought to make much reliable progress with regard to such a Kind as mankind.

And yet the Universal is the key to cogent reasoning. Can we get further if we pick up the thread that Aristotle dropped and follow that? This will be in effect the method of the Concrete Universal, which has often been described as the distinctive contribution of modern thought to Logic. But at once a distinction must be made. For the unfortunate modern philosopher can never for a moment ignore the problem of Time or Process. The Scholastic, having distinguished his Real Kind by definition of its Essence, treated it as one of the unchanging constituents of eternal reality. Though there was a process by which he reached his knowledge there was none within that knowledge itself and none within the subject-matter of that knowledge. Mathematics supplied the norm. There is process in the discovery that equilateral triangles are equiangular: but there is no process in the triangle, and when once the discovery is made there is no process in the knowledge of it. That knowledge is secure and static. Its only defect is in relevance to anything besides its own regulations.

But the Cartesians altered all that. For them the natural world was the centre of interest. For them Geometry was no longer a study of figures precisely corresponding to their definitions, but the articulation of the spatiality of the world as apprehended in experience. And the scientific process which has its very life in this constant reference to experience has led us to conceive the world as perpetually changing. Even in Physics, the object studied is a process; Space is no longer considered in isolation from Time, for Motion, which involves them both, is the initial fact. Pure Mathematics alone is occupied with the Timeless. Elsewhere the Real Kind with its changeless Essence is gone, and its place is taken by the evolutionary Species.

As far as I know, the momentous consequences for Logic which are implicit in the idea of Evolution were never appreciated until attention was called to them by Mr. Michael Foster in an article contributed by him to *Mind* in January 1931.[1] Mr. Foster begins by pointing out that the Universal as conceived by Aristotle determines its own particularisation. Thus it is inherent in the general notion of Triangle that triangles should be distinguished as equilateral, isosceles and scalene; for if there are three sides, then all three may be equal, or two may be equal, or none may be equal. But this illustration of the principle illustrates also its difficulty; for this differentiation does not carry us over from the Universal to the Particular of actual experi-

[1] Dr. Schiller had opened up the subject in *Formal Logic*: see pp. 55-57 and 333. But he did not develop the argument with the thoroughness which is found in Mr. Foster's treatment of it.

ence. Rather it illustrates Plato's demand for the insertion of the How Many (ὅποσα) between the One and the Many, while we leave the multitude of particulars to "go to infinity".[1] But that is to throw up the game, for the crux of the problem is the relation, not of *genus* to *species*, but of both *genus* and *species* to individuals.

Plato and Aristotle were, both of them, vividly aware of the problem. The Ideal Theory of Plato, with its difficult appendix concerning a realm that lies between Being and Not-Being—the realm of phenomena—is an explicit recognition of it. Aristotle's difficulties with Matter—the substrate of the correlate of definitions—are in like manner a recognition of it. But the scholastic philosophers tended to forget it, and to pass, by an unrecognised and uncriticised form of the Ontological Argument, from the completeness of the intellectual system to an affirmation of its existential reality. Thus when modern science began its enquiry into efficient as distinct from formal causation, as the way to an explanation of the existence of actual things, it was following a method so diverse from that of the accepted Logic that Science and Logic tended to part company, to the serious injury of both. And the only method of reconciliation is by the discovery of some form of Universal which "can be shown to include the residual element" —the individuality of the extant thing—"within the scope of its determination".[2] Bosanquet, who treated Logic as the "Morphology of Knowledge", was conscious of the problem and attempted to solve it by means of reflections drawn from the "comparative" sciences; but the attempt is only successful in relation to the field of those sciences. Here I quote Mr. Foster's comment in full:

"Scholasticism had declared that the whole being of a substance was determined by its character (substantial form). The new philosophy based on Galilean physics had retorted that everything was determined to be what it was by its causal relation to

[1] *Philebus*, 16 c. [2] Foster. *Mind*, N.S. 157, p. 7.

the infinite system of everything else, and that its character or form was wholly inoperative. Bosanquet, basing himself upon the 'comparative sciences', cries in re-action against the physicists, 'Form *is* operative'. He forgets that the physical sciences continue to exist none the less because the comparative sciences have arisen by their side, and that his results can claim an application at least no more extended than the sphere of observation from which they were derived.

"The understanding of Bosanquet's *Logic* becomes suddenly illuminated by the recognition that it is derived almost exclusively from reflection upon the 'comparative' sciences (Botany, Zoology, Anthropology) and its conclusions then applied uncritically to the whole of knowledge. The comparative sciences are, roughly, the sciences of Life; and to them Bosanquet's conception of 'individual system' is, as we shall see, genuinely adequate. But below them exist the sciences of matter, which work with the conception of causal law; and above them exist the sciences of spirit (the historical sciences) which work with the notion of the individual. Since system is intermediate between (causal) law and individual, it was inevitable that an attempt to extend this conception beyond its proper sphere into the spheres both above and below it should lead to that confusion of thought and terminology in which Bosanquet's doctrine is in fact obscured."[1]

But this is not the end of the trouble, nor the worst of it. For, as Mr. Foster goes on to show, Bosanquet's doctrine requires, not only that "there must be a systematic articulation in the world of universals", but that "this articulated system must have an historical existence in space and time"; and the arguments (so far as he offers any) by which Bosanquet accomplishes the transition "are in essence the ontological argument from the organised complexity of a system to the necessity of its real existence".[2] And this is a mere postulate of which the legitimacy is by no means apparent.

[1] *L.c.* pp. 13, 14. Mr. Foster, in a footnote, supplies the qualification of his remarks about the sciences of matter which recent physical theories may be held to require.

[2] *L.c.* p. 15, with quotations from Bosanquet's *Logic* there given: *Logic*, i. pp. 225 and 230. The difference between development and mere change consists, I take it, in the fact that development is change *either* in the direction of a fixed form in attaining to which the development culminates and ceases, *or* in the ever fuller articulation or application of a principle which is dominant throughout the process.

Logicians had continued to insist upon the doctrine of the "determining activity of the generic concept" in protest against "the opposite doctrine that physical causation is the only active determinant".[1] And philosophers who based themselves primarily on the scientific investigation of phenomena in the causal series retaliated by adopting a short way with Logic. It was perhaps impossible to do justice to both claims until the idea of Evolution had taken possession of men's minds; but when once that had happened, it was possible to put in place of "the activity of the universal in determining its own specific determinations", "the development of the species through actual generations. The race which develops is the concrete universal which needs no ontological argument to add concreteness to it."[2]

It is certainly true that the "race which develops" is different from the Universal as commonly understood, for it is itself, from one point of view, a Particular; but from another point of view it is not a Particular, because it is certainly not apprehensible by sense. The fact is that here the sharp division between thought and sense is already broken down; but the generic character of the race does not completely pervade and interpenetrate its members; each has many characteristics which cannot be regarded as determined by it. It is only when we come to "the historical individual" that we return to that synthesis of sense and thought with which all intelligent experience begins. For this "historical individual"—by which is meant not a person but such an entity as the British Empire or such an occurrence as the Renaissance or the Reformation—is a Universal which profoundly penetrates its constituent elements and points to that ideal wherein the distinction between accidental and essential qualities is eliminated. It is true that Bosanquet glanced at the "historical individual" as a possible solution of his

[1] *L.c.* p. 16. [2] *L.c.* p. 17.

problem, and explicitly rejected it.[1] His reason for doing so is to be found in his dependence upon the "comparative sciences".[2]

All modern thought and science is historical in method. Whatever is studied is considered not only as it is now observed to be, but in the light of the process by which it has come to be. Natural History, until recently, was the classification of existing species; now it is quite equally concerned with the origin of species. Geology is not only a study of the crust of the earth but an examination of the question how that crust has been formed. Astronomy aspires to give us a history of the heavens. Similarly in the Humanities we no longer treat the utterances of prophets or philosophers as oracles to be accepted or rejected, but seek to understand them in relation to their historical context, reconstructed as fully as possible, and to evaluate them in the light of that understanding. This use of the historical method is the main distinguishing characteristic of our own modern thought as compared with the thought of all former ages; and it coheres closely with the notion of Evolution as a general term for the process whereby things not only are but come to be, and indeed have their being in the process of coming to be.

Now of such a process there cannot be exact analytical knowledge of the mathematical type. The Greeks sharply distinguished the realm of Being from the realm of Becoming. Knowledge, and accordingly Logic, were concerned with the former; the latter was the sphere of Opinion or Belief, and of Art or Skill, and the study of the process by which this was reached was, as it still is, Psychology. Knowledge was concerned with the unchanging Forms, the Ideas, the Kinds of Being (γένη τῶν ὄντων). The particulars of our actual experience might "go to infinity"; science was not concerned with them. This inevitably, though undesignedly,

[1] Cf. *The Principle of Individuality and Value*, pp. 77-81.
[2] Cf. p. 99 *supra*.

involved the elaboration of an *a priori* science, which was imposed dogmatically on a more or less recalcitrant experience. The heart of this method was the conception of static Real Kinds, of which the Form or Essence could be defined, so that from the definition valid inferences could be drawn by deduction and the volume of ascertained truth thus be increased. This coheres closely with such a conception of the act of Creation as is formed by an acceptance of the first chapter of Genesis as literal historical truth. Perhaps that is part of the reason why Darwin's success in making the popular mind aware of the implications of Evolution provoked so great an uproar; it not only set aside the literal and (at that time, though not always) traditional interpretation of a passage in the Bible, but it assaulted the doctrine of Real Kinds which was the central position of the traditional Aristotelian logic in its conflict with Empiricism.

The philosophers of the post-Reformation period started from the science, specially the physical science, which was entering then on its independent career.[1] Two novelties in their equipment and method call for special notice. One is that Mathematics was regarded as supplying an account of the physical world. To Plato its great value was that it effected a transition away from the physical world,[2] which by its help we might learn to leave behind; it was the science of extended form as apprehended by the pure intellect. But for the Cartesians Mathematics is a study of the extended world. An independent science of Arithmetic, and (still more influential) of Algebra, was growing up side by side with Geometry, and this made possible the universal application of numeration as distinct from measurement throughout the natural world, whereby modern Mathematics obtained its distinguishing characteristic

[1] Throughout this section I am indebted to suggestions made to me in private correspondence by Mr. Michael Foster. But he is not responsible for the use I make of his suggestions.

[2] *Republic*, 521 D.

of being applicable to nature; and besides this, Geometry itself was treated as thus applicable. Einstein is reported as having said,[1] that the great distinction between Euclidean and Cartesian Geometry was that the Greeks lacked the conception of space as a single continuum. From this it would follow that the Greeks studied geometrical figures as species of an Idea, conceiving them as related to one another not physically at all, but only intelligibly or logically. But if every geometrical figure is a part of one single space, it follows that geometrical knowledge is knowledge of that single spatial system which comprises (or even which *is*) the physical universe.

The Cartesians discarded Logic. They did not need it as a criterion of truth, because the guarantee of truth was found in the perception of clear and distinct ideas; the power by which the mind could judge the principles of Logic to be valid enabled it also to grasp the truth of propositions or arguments without reference to those principles. As a normative science telling us how to think correctly it was otiose. As a basis for physical science it was even misleading; for it led men to seek for the explanation of things in the self-differentiation of a generic concept and not in the actual process of efficient causation. Some philosophers, indeed, among whom Malebranche is the most conspicuous, retained the Intelligible Forms of Greek and Scholastic Logic as objects of the Divine Thought informing the Divine Purpose, which was itself the sole cause of actual occurrences. But this, though sound in itself as I believe, is to abandon the notion of the Form as itself determining events. Formal causation, as such, had disappeared. What Malebranche represents is an attempt to salvage Final Causation and what had been serviceable in Formal Causation from the floodtide of Cartesian Rationalism and pure Empiricism, which were alike in treating Efficient Causation as alone truly causative and

[1] In a lecture delivered at Oxford.

were thus sweeping human thought into the abyss of mechanical determinism.

The Cartesians were right to repudiate Scholastic Logic as a discipline of universal applicability. They were not right in discarding the requirement of a discipline which should result in accurate and valid thought. They trusted to a "natural light"—the philosophic counterpart of the "inner light" of the Quakers; they spoke of Reason as "the eye" of the mind. We must accept their ultimate appeal on each occasion to the apprehensions of the individual mind. But this need not involve acquiescence in the notion that all men have, by natural endowment, a faculty of "seeing" that a proposition is self-evidently true or that an action is self-evidently right. Such intuitions are only reliable when they are the apprehensions of trained minds. The Middle Ages had supplied the apprenticeship for that Conscience and Reason to which Luther and Descartes and Locke appealed. Such insight as is a guarantee of truth only comes at the end of a long process of training alike in the individual and in the race. But if we have understood this, we must realise that the end of our discipline is the escape from our temporal and personal contingency, not into a timeless realm of static Truth, Beauty and Goodness, but into the full historic process wherein both we and those sublimities have actual being.

Now the discipline which is aiming at this result must be itself concerned with process, whereas the traditional Logic was concerned with the unchanging Forms and Kinds. Kant perceived that the mental act which is the ground of the validity of a conclusion is not immediate (as the Cartesian language implied) but conditioned—it is true that he says "transcendentally conditioned", and the value of his argument is diminished by the presence of that perplexing adverb. The conditions in question are discovered by critical reflection, which resolves the act of knowing into its constituent elements. Unfortunately by the introduction of the term "transcendental" Kant lifts the process of conditioning or mediation out of the time process, and though the object of "Transcendental Logic" is a "process" it is declared to be a "timeless process". Yet still he does recognise, in opposition to traditional Logic, that the study of a *process* may still be a study of the grounds of *validity*—not only a study of how men come to hold conclusions, which is Psychology, but a study of their justification in holding conclusions, which is Logic. Hegel seized upon this and developed it, so that for him Logic is the science of the Dialectical Process; but he still regards this as timeless, and so makes it after all only a variant of the self-differentiation of the Intelligible Form.

But what is there, in fact, of which Logic so conceived can be the study? As we descend through the scale of categories from the more concrete—such as Life or Personality—to the more abstract, we arrive at Mathematics, the science of Quantity, which "tells us something about everything, but very little about anything". Logic, if it is to be the universal science of the validity of thought, must be more abstract still. Can it be occupied with Being as such? But that, as Hegel showed, is indistinguishable from Not-Being. To Be is to be Something. The study of existence apart from all study of what exists is the study of sheer vacuity. Or perhaps Logic is the study of thought, not as an actual psychological process but as the pure activity of Mind acting according to its true nature. But then we have no data. Such thought may exist in God; in us it certainly does not, and so far as we have need of Logic as a discipline, we need it to aid our estimate of our approximations to valid thought or true knowledge, in an experience where these exist side by side with, and at first undistinguishable from, prejudices, casual opinions, and products of mere self-assertiveness.

The fact is that the Logic of Inference as traditionally conceived has no object or sphere of its own at all. There is a certain application of mathematical principles which gives rise to Formal Logic, and this has complete validity in relation to certain types of argument, and a certain very real value for all types as supplying a norm of cogency, but provides no criterion of the subject-matter to which it is properly applicable. We now recognise that the understanding of all other existing things is to be reached in part by study of the historical process which has led to their being what they are; is it not probable that in like manner the understanding and consequent evaluation of thought is to be reached by a study of the history of thought? At any rate that is the study which is chiefly offered in our Universities as the required discipline of the mind. No one now teaches Philosophy otherwise than by teaching the History of Philosophy; and though this would not be everywhere avowed as a principle in relation to Logic, yet in practice that subject too is largely taught by reference to the theories of Logic set forth by various thinkers in different ages, and to the process by which one of these gave rise to another either through the interplay among themselves of the notions expounded, or through the reaction upon these of processes in vogue in various branches of scientific enquiry. The conclusion we reach is this: that the discipline required to perform the function traditionally ascribed to Logic is the History of Thought, and especially the History of Philosophy.

Especially—but not only: for we have returned to the doctrine of Aristotle at the close of the *Posterior Analytics*. Understanding, Appreciation, Knowledge come by the process of Sensation, Memory, Training by Experience, Adduction of Relevant Instances, Rational Intuition. The last is the "natural light", the "eye of the soul" relied on by the Cartesians. But it only deserves such reliance when the stages of the process have been thoroughly traversed; and of these the most determinant is Training by Experience. For thinking, as will later appear more clearly, is grounded in, and is an extension of, the adjustment of organism to environment or *vice versa*. Therefore the experience must be relevant, or else the aptitude developed by it will not be relevant. Thus, for example, experience of engineering does not train a man to appreciate Flemish painting. For this reason there is a different discipline for the mind in every department of enquiry, and only the mind trained in relation to any department is capable of secure judgements with regard to it. Lawyers are as a rule not good judges of historical evidence; mathematicians are not qualified as such to pronounce upon questions calling for spiritual perception. There is a different discipline for every department. The traditional Logic has a certain value as a standard of reference and norm of procedure. It is, as has been said, a special application of the principle of Mathematics, and has that degree of universal relevance which is involved in the truth that "Mathematics tells us something about everything", but only that degree which is compatible with the further truth that "Mathematics tells us very little about anything". It is all extremely useful preparatory discipline, but it is not a universal guide to valid thinking.

It is important to determine our use of terms. We might decide, as the upshot of this discussion, to confine the term Logic to what is recognised to be a very subsidiary discipline; or we might keep it with a modified significance to represent the discipline that results in accurate and adequate thinking. What always leads to dangerous confusion is to use it with an undefined significance, as is commonly done by persons who say that Life is wider or richer than Logic. If they mean that Life is too rich to be articulated in the forms of Deductive or Subsumptive Logic, that is true and may be important. But there is usually in the minds of those who use such expressions a sense that Logic covers the field of intelligence, and their meaning is that we often get on better if we stop trying to think accurately. Well, *we* may; but if so that is because we think badly, not because good thinking can ever be misleading. And there is a wider use of the term in vogue, as when we speak of "the Logic of facts" or "the Logic of the situation". It would be well to adopt such a use of terms that these phrases would not be metaphors, but would point to the only Logic that has any bearing on the occasion. With such a use of the term Bosanquet says that "freedom is the logic of individuality".[1] And he adopts as a synonym of Logic "the spirit of totality".[2] With the same conception in mind he declares that "love is the mainspring of Logic",[3] for "by Logic we understand, with Plato and Hegel, the supreme Law or nature of experience, the impulse towards unity and coherence (the positive spirit of non-contradiction) by which every fragment yearns towards the whole to which it belongs".[4] "All logical activity is a world of content reshaping itself by its own spirit and laws in presence of new suggestions; a syllogism is in principle nothing less, and a Parthenon or *Paradise Lost* is in principle nothing more."

This use of the word is fully justified, and it seems better to retain the word with this use than to abandon it. For this self-shaping of our experience is apprehensible by mind and follows principles which mind recognises as its own, while mind fulfils its functions precisely in that apprehension and that recognition.

[1] *Principle of Individuality and Value*, p. 80.
[2] *Ibid.* p. 23.
[3] *Ibid.* p. 341.
[4] *Ibid.* p. 340. Cf. also the eloquent exposition of the Logic in Great Art, pp. 332, 333, of which the closing sentence is quoted above.

LECTURE V

THE WORLD AS APPREHENDED

It has been the habit, and, if the contention of these Lectures is justified, the besetting sin, of philosophy to take cognition as the initial form of apprehension, and to seek, by such expedients as may be available, to evolve the other forms of apprehension, such as appreciation, from this. That is the source of the Cartesian error, though indeed it is much older than Descartes. For it is this assumption of the priority of intellection that gives such plausibility as it possesses to the notion that we begin with our mind and its ideas and then from these advance to knowledge of the external world by inference. Hence comes the whole farrago of Subjective Idealism, Pre-established Harmony, Psycho-physical Parallelism, and other outrages upon common sense. Indeed from these or other equally outrageous alternatives there is no escape when once the priority of intellection or cognition has been assumed; for some one is then bound to ask the questions which in fact were put to himself by Descartes, and the questioner or others must try to answer them.

That philosophy should fall into this error was natural enough. For it is an intellectual process; and to it the intellectual apprehension of the world was nearest to hand. The intellect was almost bound to see first how far it could advance by consideration of its own processes and of their results. But by degrees the results of the process itself compelled the intellect to recognise that its apprehension is not primary but derivative. For the scientific study of the world began to present a picture of the world as existing long before the human intellect existed to apprehend it, and human thought as appearing in the course of the world's development. At first it seemed that this difficulty could be met by postulating a Divine Intelligence as thinking the universe into existence, so that as we study the universe we are entering into the thoughts of that Intelligence. There is real ground for that postulate, and in other connexions it becomes important. But in this connexion it is easily seen to be called for only in order to preserve the initial assumption of the priority of intellect; and for that purpose it could not satisfactorily maintain itself in face of the fuller detail which science began to give to its picture of the world. For science now went on to show intelligence itself developing from most rudimentary beginnings in which it was scarcely distinguishable from instinct or even from unconscious organic reaction. So soon as that idea had gripped the mind, it became more natural to conceive the intellect as a function of the organism, which apprehended reality with approximate accuracy because it was evolved in interaction with it, rather than as a regal faculty whose principles are valid of reality because reality itself is governed by the "Royal Mind of Zeus".[1] We shall come back to a position very similar to that, but the difference of approach is vital.

For some time there existed an almost complete alienation between scientists and philosophers, because scientists were content to present the picture of the late evolution of mind on the earth, without raising the question what may be implied in the fact that the earth is such as to be intelligible to mind when mind appears, while philosophers continued to occupy themselves chiefly with this question without relating their answers at all closely to the increasingly authenticated picture of the world which science was offering. In recent years that alienation has been diminishing through the perpetual increase of attention on each side to the preoccupation of the other. The great series of Gifford

[1] Plato, *Philebus*, 30 D.

Lectures delivered by Bernard Bosanquet were marked by a specially full appreciation of the significance of organic evolution, though he was in certain respects deeply infected with Intellectualism; Professor Pringle-Pattison carried still further the movement towards a synthesis; while Professors Eddington and Whitehead, starting from the side of science, and even of the physical sciences, have taken up the specifically philosophical enquiry. And these, of course, are no isolated pioneers, but are outstanding representatives of a world-wide movement of thought.

The dominating fact in the new situation may be stated thus: the world as apprehended is now something which antedates apprehension. The world which we apprehend is apprehended as having been extant historically before any one apprehended it. So far as our experience is concerned, *Apprehension takes place within the world, not the world within apprehension.*

If the postulate of continuity, which science commonly makes, is allowed to stand, this will mean either that we shall try to account for all apprehension, including the scientist's grasp of the world, in terms of the action and reaction of atoms, or electrons, or whatever else is at the moment presented as the ultimate product of the analysis of matter; or else we shall interpret those actions and reactions as embryonic apprehensions. The former is a plain *reductio ad absurdum*; the latter must therefore be preferred. It is the adoption of this method which (if I understand him rightly) constitutes the special suggestiveness and also the special difficulty of Professor Whitehead's *Process and Reality*. Reason will be given later[1] for holding that this doctrine of continuity is itself, if not misleading, at any rate irrelevant to Natural Theology; and there are other strands in Professor Whitehead's thought which suggest that it is not indispensable. But when he adopts it, as for the most part he does, it leads him to speak of

[1] See Lecture X.

purely physical relations as prehensions and feelings. This is very awkward as a matter of language, but for that Professor Whitehead is not responsible. Whatever words he uses will either connote consciousness or will not. If they do not, there will be a suggestion of discontinuity when the account reaches the level of consciousness; if they do, they will convey an unintended suggestion of consciousness at the lower level; that Professor Whitehead's terminology should be confusing to the reader is no cause for wonder. He develops his own view by means of comparison and contrast with the philosophy of Descartes, Locke and Hume, especially Hume. He speaks of "the disastrous confusion, more especially by Hume, of conceptual feelings with perceptual feelings";[1] and with reiterated emphasis insists upon the fact that for Hume the primary data are percepts, while for himself they are "prehensions" which may be non-conscious. Thus he writes:

"Hume and Locke, with the over-intellectualist bias prevalent among philosophers, assume that emotional feelings are necessarily derivative from sensations. This is conspicuously not the case; the correlation between such feelings and sensations is on the whole a secondary effect. . . . The confinement of our prehension of other actual entities to the mediation of private sensations is pure myth."[2]

This position is for Whitehead fundamental. He says:

"The principle that I am adopting is that consciousness presupposes experience and not experience consciousness. It is a special element in the subjective form of some feelings. Thus an actual entity may, or may not be, conscious of some parts of its experience. Its experience is its complete formal constitution."[3]

Here is still the awkwardness of language. For the terms

[1] *Process and Reality*, p. 324. [2] *Op. cit.* p. 197.

[3] *Op. cit.* p. 72. In this quotation, whenever I refer to it, I presume the word "presupposes" to mean "supposes as its historical condition", not "supposes as its logical ground". It is with the historical order only that I am concerned at this stage. Towards the end of this Lecture an enquiry is initiated which, especially as developed in Lectures VIII, IX, and X, effects a transition to the logical order of such sort as to lead to an account, in the closing Lectures, of the relation of these two orders to one another.

"feeling", "subject" and even "experience" have commonly been taken as connoting consciousness. But in the case of "experience" the developments of Psychology have brought assistance, for we are all familiar with the notion of elements in experience which lie on the margin of consciousness or altogether beyond it. In any case, that awkwardness of language is, as has been said, inevitable for one who accepts the doctrine of continuity, and is easily overcome by the exercise of a little special attention. Whatever we may have to say later concerning the doctrine of continuity, as for example from the inorganic level to the organic, and from the organic to the personal, the principle stated above must, I submit, be accepted as manifestly true at least as far as human consciousness is concerned.

As we consider the picture presented by scientific study of the world we see that the earliest traceable form of existence is that of physical entities related to one another in the ways which the science of Physics describes. Admittedly that science is more conscious now than it was a short time ago of the provisional character of its results. Thus for example it works alternately with the corpuscular and the undulatory theories of light, though both cannot be true together in the form at present given them.[1] But it is not necessary for our purposes to enquire further into the nature of the physical structure of reality. Either it is itself rudimentarily organic, as Whitehead urges, or else it supplies to the organic world as known to us its substratum, and is so ordered as to supply in the instance of our planet the necessary conditions for life as we know it.[2] That purely physical realm may consist of

[1] Cf. Whitehead, *Science and the Modern World*, p. 264.

[2] "As we know it" because there is no reason to suppose that there may not be very different forms of life. It is sometimes urged that this must be the only inhabited planet, because this alone provides the necessary conditions of physiological life. But if "inhabited" means "dwelt in by rational beings" this is a *non sequitur*. The Jewish conception of a Seraph was that of a being made of fire. Such beings may not exist; but science cannot prove that they do not. If they do, they presumably require physical conditions quite different from ours.

protons and electrons and the rest moving in paths and at velocities which can be calculated; and that may be all that can be fairly said about it. Or again all that is said about these may be, as some scientists suggest, not a description of facts but a diagram by the help of which we can calculate future events from present observations, as sociologists may make a "graph" of seasonal or cyclical unemployment, and use it for the suggestion of policy without suggesting that it is a picture of the concrete fact of unemployment. Or yet again it may be that even at this level the principle of the organism finds illustration. What is entirely beyond dispute is that this principle finds illustration long before consciousness appears on the scene; and whether or not all existence is organic, yet it is by the organic principle in the first instance that we must seek to understand our apprehension of the world and the place of our apprehension itself in the world that we apprehend.

The flower turns its face to the sun, and closes its petals to protect itself from the damp night; the dog hurries to the place where he is fed when it is time for feeding; the child runs to his mother when he is hurt; the sinner, when he becomes aware of his sin, humbles himself in penitence before his God. Any one can see differences in these different activities, and with them we shall be concerned later. But it seems quite arbitrary to draw a sharp line at any point or totally to deny continuity of principle. Our inherited habit of thinking by means of supposed Real Kinds makes difficult for us the intellectual appreciation of continuity of growth, however eager the intellect may be to trace continuity in the world wherever it can. But all of us who are grown up have lived through many stages of the continuous process, and a man is no less a responsible citizen because he was once a semiconscious infant and cannot draw any sharp lines between his infancy, his childhood, his adolescence, and his manhood. But the assertion of continuity in growth is neither the assertion that there is no more in the mature development than in the germ, nor the assertion that the germ actually contains what appears in the mature development. The desire for heads of classification here perverts an apprehension which the unsophisticated mind achieves every day and every moment without either difficulty or perplexity. Continuous becoming is the most familiar fact of experience. Coleridge solved the problem of Achilles and the tortoise by saying that Zeno, who propounded it, was postulating the infinite divisibility of space without allowing also for the infinite divisibility of time. That may have been, as one of his circle exclaimed, "a lightning-flash illuminating a darkness that had existed for centuries". But the darkness was highly artificial. To this, as to the parallel demonstration that motion is impossible, the truly rational answer is that of the Cynic: *solvitur ambulando*. For the initial error is the treatment of continuous change as if it consisted of a series of stages, each of which has its own fixed position or character. That is as false as to treat a circle as an indefinitely many-sided polygon. The line that bounds the circle never moves in any direction at all; there is no extent in the point at which the tangent touches it, but position only. So the boy who is growing to manhood changes his character while we observe and note it. Our recorded apprehension of the world is always out of date; but the apprehension itself is not out of date, unless it is perverted by the record or memory of previous apprehensions.

As we pass from actual observation or enjoyment to any form of reflection upon them, we fall behind the flow of facts. For the reflective mind, the datum is the record or the memory; and this fixes as an unchanging object of attention an experience in which movement was an essential characteristic. We may consider the evolution of a species, or a period of human history; and even if we are careful to recall in recollection the actual process, yet inevitably we ignore the previous and succeeding process, and thus tend to treat our section as if it were capable of isolation and, when thus isolated, had some characteristic which is not only distinctive but peculiar. There is real truth in saying that the Dark Ages present one distinctive character, the Middle Ages another, the modern period yet another. But each has the elements of what becomes the distinctive character of another. There are real turning points in Evolution and in History, but they are not points of transition from one strictly definable type to another strictly definable type. Whatever we define, or fix in a concept, is always thereby removed in some degree from fact.

Yet the conceptual treatment of reality vindicates itself in practice, and thereby proves that, even though not in immediate touch with fact, it is not wholly alien from it. A wholly conceptual geometry gives results which are verified in experience. But here a new complication intrudes itself. For the degree to which the conceptual treatment of experience is adequate or inadequate varies with the importance of the principle of individuality in the given field of study. It is at least broadly true that in those fields of study where we are concerned with what is most primitive and elemental in the evolutionary series individuality counts for least, while as the evolutionary process advances it counts for more and more, so that conceptual thinking comes nearest to adequacy in relation to what is least developed and loses adequacy as we follow the advance of evolution to more complex forms of being.[1]

For the moment, however, our concern is with the reality of our apprehension of process or growth as such. The trouble only arises if, having resorted to conceptual thinking, we stop there. The real value of conceptual thinking is found when, bringing its results

[1] That is why the Laws or Canons of a spiritual society ought to be as elastic as regard for the solidarity of the society will allow.

with us, we return to the actual living experience.[1] A man listens, let us say, to a symphony by Beethoven; there is a direct impact made by the symphony as a whole upon his entire being. Some elements he at once grasps in consciousness. It is hardly conceivable, for example, that any man should hear the Fifth Symphony without distinct apprehension and retention of the opening phrase, of the melody of the second movement, or the rhythm of the *scherzo*; or again, that he should hear the Ninth Symphony without distinct apprehension and retention of the startlingly simple melody in which the intricate pattern of themes and rhythms finally issues. But beyond this there is a vague feeling of balance in tone and rhythm and contrapuntal scheme. We may have no words to express all this, but it will be there. Mr. J. B. Priestley has given an admirable picture of this stage of musical apprehension in the effect which Brahms' First Symphony had upon Mr. Smeath.[2] But this is a rudimentary stage of appreciation. If the listener now studies the composition scientifically with the guidance of a competent critic, he will grasp far more fully than before the principles of its construction; he will make vivid to himself very many "themes" and "subjects" which he had previously heard without heeding. But if he stops there, he has got further from the reality of the music, not nearer to it. At the end of all his study, and having its results available, he should now hear the work itself again. It will be in one sense the same experience as before, but richer and fuller because so much more of it is now distinct to consciousness.[3] But in both actual experiences of the music, it is apprehended as a process. The listener is not in the least perplexed by paradoxes about the nature of Time.

[1] "The nature of reflective knowledge is such that it is always incomplete until we have returned from the reflective process to the concreteness of immediate experience."—Professor John Macmurray, *Interpreting the Universe*, p. 74.

[2] *Angel Pavement*, pp. 288-290.

[3] Thus he turns from ἐπιστήμη, the potentiality, to θεωρία, its energising actuality. See p. 90.

He does not find himself unable to relate the notes that are sounding to their predecessors on the ground that these are now not extant. Normal experience is of process, and the mind is wholly free from embarrassment in face of that fact unless or until it begins to treat conceptual thinking, not as the interim procedure that it is qualified to be, but as itself the real life and characteristic activity of a living and self-conscious organism.

This becomes fully apparent when we turn from the "bewildering entanglement of eventualities" which constitutes the process of the real world, and consider processes deliberately constructed to be comprehensible by the minds of men. Such processes we find in those works of art in which process is an essential element—music, poetry, drama and their fellows. From consideration of these processes and of the relation to them of our minds there is much to be learnt. For the moment our concern is with the unquestionable fact that in the apprehension of such a successive unity as a poem or a fugue the mind experiences a joy which springs from unimpeded exercise of its energies. Action is required of it, but it is the action proper to it. The accompanying emotion is not the depression of perplexity but the exhilaration of mastery.

We are familiar with the conundrums that can be asked as soon as we analyse Time into its parts and discuss their relation to one another, as though those parts had independent real existence. Past and Future must then be defined by reference to the Present; but the Present is no more than a cross-section between Past and Future, and even so is not the same for two seconds, or even for two infinitesimal particles of time, together. So there is no "clear and distinct idea" of Time; the concept is riddled with contradiction; consequently it must be regarded as unreal. Yes, certainly Time the abstraction is unreal; but so is Euclid's triangle, of which we have a perfectly clear and distinct idea. On the other hand successive objects or occasions are not unreal, and their successiveness is part—not indeed of their reality if this is thought to be something other than themselves—but of their existent selves.

The amount of succession that is apprehended by different minds may vary indefinitely, and also the amount that is apprehended by the same mind at different times. But always real apprehension is of process. What has been called "the specious present" is the true present. Every momentary perception both occupies time and is a perception of what changes in time. The apprehending mind is living in and through time, as truly as the objects which it apprehends. Many of those objects maintain their identity through time, as a picture seems to do; many again are of such a nature that their identity actually consists of a process of change, as a poem or a piece of music. The mind which apprehends shares in that kind of identity which is characteristic of the object apprehended, though to some extent the quality of the successive type is always discernible. If I stand gazing at a picture, the picture remains and my mind remains. The process of the universe goes on around us; other spectators come and go, men are born and die, planets revolve—about the picture and myself enthralled by it all this goes on; but the picture and I stand fixed. Yet that is not quite true. Subtle changes are in process in the picture, which produce in sufficient course of time perceptible modifications, and my mind is not quite static, for at every moment its apprehension is richer through the cumulative effect of long attention. When, to turn to the successive type, the mind is held by the occurrence before it of a great tragedy or symphony, the work of art has its own unity, but it is a unity which actually consists of a temporal process, and the persisting identity of the receptive mind has the same quality. At every stage the mind understands what has happened more thoroughly because in a fuller context. The Greek custom of choosing for Tragedy themes known to the audience beforehand secured that each action was appreciated in the light of its known result; [1] yet inasmuch as the colour to be given to that result by the poet was still unknown until the episode upon the stage disclosed it, that appreciation grew from moment to moment, and might at the conclusion be scarcely recognisable as that which had arisen in connexion with the opening scene.

Apprehension of process, then, may securely be said to present no difficulties of its own in principle. The difficulties only arise when we try to achieve a timeless understanding of it. So long as mind and occasion move together all is straightforward. And this is natural; for we have now to notice that our apprehension of the process of reality includes the very dawn of that apprehension as occurring at a moment in that process. Whatever it may become necessary to add concerning the spiritual nature of the ground of existence, it is impossible to deny, and vitally important to recognise, that within the historical process, mind is a late arrival. Within the ever-changing process of reality there appears, as one of its constituent elements, the capacity for observing it. The process becomes conscious, and then self-conscious, in some of its own parts. Historically regarded, mind is itself a process, and is part of the universal process. I refer here, of course, to mind as a mode of existence and activity within the historical process. The question whether there is a Divine Mind has not yet been raised. The actual emergence in the process of evolution is of particular minds; but here, as elsewhere, I use the generic term "mind" when the subject of interest is not the particular minds as such but the mode of being and activity in virtue of which each is entitled to be called a mind. That is, at a certain stage of the evolutionary process, a new mode of being and activity. It is true that as soon as reflection is directed upon that particular part of the universal pro-

[1] This is the basic principle of Tragic Irony.

cess, it reveals itself as something other and more than process is commonly understood to be; and then the question arises whether this is something altogether peculiar to mind, or something in which a characteristic of the whole process becomes for the first time manifest. To those points we must return at a later stage.[1]

Whether or not the actions and reactions of physical entities can properly be called "experience", the modern account of the evolution of the world makes it necessary to assent to Whitehead's proposition, already quoted, "that consciousness presupposes experience and not experience consciousness". Vegetable life exhibits much adjustment of the organism to its environment; the organism "responds" in various ways; but it is not capable of self-motion. There is, apparently, a transitional kind of vegetable-animal, which grows as a vegetable, but is capable of detaching itself from the soil and exercising self-movement. Where there is no self-movement we generally assume that there is no sensation, in the sense of a modification of consciousness; but no one can prove that the daisy does not "feel" the warmth of the sun to which it responds by opening its petals. Where there is self-motion, we assume that consciousness to direct such motion exists; though it is not clear why it should be needed to direct the motion of the whole organism, and not needed for the direction of its parts. Where the structure of the organism resembles that of our own bodies, we assume that its reactions are accompanied by sensations similar to those which accompany similar reactions in ourselves; but we only begin to have clear evidence of this where there is not only a physiological reaction appropriate to its stimulus, but some capacity to learn by experience, such as a dog has and a plant (I suppose) has not.[2]

[1] See Lecture X.

[2] I assume that the adoption by a plant of the direction in which its stems are trained is due to a purely physical hardening of the fibres in the appropriate shape and not to its giving up the effort to thrust them in some other direction; but I am not quite sure that this distinction is a real one.

Certainly it would seem natural that the power of self-motion should accompany, and even stimulate, a clearer differentiation of the organism from its environment, and thus encourage the development of any rudimentary consciousness that exists.

Bergson suggested that the clearest available distinction between instinct and intelligence is that drawn between the adjustment by the organism of itself to its environment and its adjustment of the environment to itself; thus he says that when nature produced a creature who needed clothes to maintain himself in life, it gave the *congé* to instinct.[1] Without going into the precise question thus raised, which does not concern us here, we may safely say that the activity of adjusting the environment to the organism is one which is likely to minister to the development of self-consciousness in the organism as surely as self-motion is likely to minister to the development of consciousness; but it can no more actually give birth to self-consciousness than self-motion can give birth to consciousness.

When we consider the development of full self-conscious apprehension as we find it in ourselves, we must begin with the reactions of the embryo in the ante-natal stage. It is then adjusting itself to its environment, and receiving from its environment what it transmutes into the substance of its own organic life. When the new-born child first opens his eyes upon the world, he is already well established in this habit of organic adjustment. The pressures and impacts of various sorts to which his system makes response are different in many ways from those to which it was responding in the earlier phase; but the habit of organic self-adjustment, and of using the environment for self-maintenance, is already well established. The rudimentary consciousness is not of objects as such, but of this actual process of responsive adjustment.

[1] *L'Évolution créatrice*, pp. 152, 155

Gradually the two main factors in that process distinguish themselves—not yet as subject and object but as self and not-self. It is found in experience that there is one entity which moves at desire, and which is a *locus* of sensation in the sense that when other entities impinge upon it sensation results. So the child comes to recognise his body as for him different from all other objects, and it becomes the basis of his notion of himself. Later on, though germinally from the first, self-consciousness is found to accompany consciousness of the reactions between organism and environment. The child not only feels or desires, but is conscious of himself as feeling and desiring. Thus becomes possible the contrast between the self as it is and the self as it might be, from which arises in turn the possibility of moral character and moral action. Thus also becomes evident the distinction of subject and object in experience, and with it the possibility of both science and philosophy.

But these are very late arrivals; indeed cognition itself is a late and specialised form of consciousness. First there is the reaction of the organism to its environment; then this becomes conscious, and (in one act with the emergence of consciousness) more highly unified. "The feeler is the unity emergent from its own feelings; and feelings are the details of the process, intermediary between this unity and its many data."[1] Consciousness first arises in its emotional form—not as knowledge nor as purpose, but as organic reaction become aware of its significance in terms of pleasure and pain. "We prehend other actual entities more primitively by direct mediation of emotional tone, and only secondarily and waveringly by direct mediation of sense."[2] But even so, the primitive consciousness is primarily objective in its reference. "The primitive form of physical experience is emotional—blind emotion—received as felt in another occasion and conformally appropriated as a subjective passion. In the language

[1] Whitehead, *Process and Reality*, p. 123. [2] Whitehead, *op. cit.* p. 197.

appropriate to the higher stages of experience, the primitive element is sympathy, that is, feeling the feeling in another and feeling conformally with another."[1]

In other words, the earliest form of consciousness is awareness of feeling in some part of the environment and responsive feeling thereby evoked. How remote is this conception from any speculation how the mind can pass from its ideas to an external world! How remote from questions whether we can know the existence of other persons as persons except by analogical inference from the resemblance of their perceived physical actions to our own! From the beginning of intellectual life the mind lives and moves and has its being in an actual apprehension of a world which is first realised in consciousness through the emotional tone which that world elicits in response to its own. Such a view of the growth of mind is necessitated by the picture which modern science gives of its history and of the history of the organism in the development of which it is found to exist.

Each individual human mind attains to full consciousness and self-consciousness by this process. There is first the relation between the embryo and its environment in the ante-natal stage; after birth the new world on which the infant opens his eyes is still primarily the world made up of himself and his mother in their mutual relationship. Professor Grensted admirably summarises the upshot of psychological study and reflection on this point as follows:

"Behind even the most primitive forms of knowledge there lies what can be most simply called the ego-object relation, its duality still implicit. The child does not start out into life with an assured individuality from which it sets out to conquer an outer world. It starts rather from an unresolved confusion within which the ego and the other are at first undifferentiated, and out of which they are developed into the comparatively sharp distinctions of adult life. The child accepts what the mother says, not as some new and external addition to the structure of its

[1] Whitehead, *op. cit.* p. 227.

personality, but rather as something existent within that relationship to the mother which is prior, unanalysed and unquestioned. It is not even, in James' phrase, 'faith in some one else's faith'. That is a later and much more complex development. It would be more nearly true to call it simply 'faith in some one else' if even that phrase did not imply a consciousness of faith and of the other, which goes beyond the direct and unresolved unity of the relationship. This is not as yet love, or knowledge, or faith, but it is the basis of all three."[1]

"The belief that knowledge of things is in some way prior to the knowledge of persons is sheer delusion. In the analysis of life, we cannot start from the solid world about us, for both its solidity and its apparent self-existence are mere interpretations of our experience. And the experience from which we set out to interpret the world is not simply our own. It is, and was from the very first, a corporate existence, in which we are intimately interrelated with others like ourselves. The contact of spirit with matter constitutes a problem of apparently insoluble difficulty. The contact of spirit with spirit is a primary and incontrovertible datum. Here at least is something of which all are directly aware, even if they cannot state in clear terms exactly what they mean. Faith and love are simple and immediate facts, and, unlike our knowledge of the so-called external world, they carry with them a certainty and security of their own."[2]

All distinctions which the developed mind elaborates are found by analysis of what is at first given as an apparently undifferentiated continuum. We do not first know sensations, and then build these up into a system or order. We do not first realise the world as extended and then raise questions whether it is beautiful. The extension and the beauty of the world are there in the initial datum. If it is the mind that discovers beauty, it is equally the mind that discovers extension. And it discovers them because they are there. I must regard as completely fallacious all theories of Perception which start with a so-called *sensum* as the object of immediate apprehension, on occasion of which the mind, by use of memory and imagination, builds up a picture of the world which it then believes itself to apprehend. The

[1] *Psychology and God*, pp. 79, 80. [2] *Ibid.* pp. 81, 82.

initial and permanent fact is the organism in interaction with the environment, which, if the organism is mental, takes the form of apprehension among others. What it apprehends is the real world, and no limit can be set *a priori* to the extent in space or time of its potential apprehension. *Sensa* and the like are part of the organism's machinery of this apprehension; but they are not the objects apprehended. Of course I do not claim with "naïve realism" that an object is, apart from knowledge, exactly what it is for knowledge: to ask what we can know it to be apart from knowledge is like asking what it looks like to a blind man. My contention is that in cognition the subject-object relation is ultimate, and neither term is in any degree reducible to the other. Apprehension is of the object. Moreover apprehension is interpretative from the outset, and sensation is from the first indissolubly inter-penetrated by interpretation—which may of course be mis-interpretation. To argue this position here would involve disproportionate digression. I mention the whole matter only in order to make clear what is my angle of approach, and so perhaps avoid confusion.

Supremely false is any suggestion that the individual mind, starting as an already established unity and as such apprehending a world of multiple phenomena, argues from the behaviour of some of these phenomena that they must be animated by other minds similar to itself. The fact is that only by intercourse with other minds does any mind fully attain to its own unity. It has, no doubt, at all stages of its growth a numerical unity as subject of its experiences; it is one with itself, and other than all else. But this is no more than the necessary presupposition of that unity of manifold apprehension which is already apparent in principle in the earliest stages that we are able to study and describe; and this unity is developed through entry into the corporate experience and understanding of experience which has been built up through the ages, and by comparison and contrast of itself with other minds, and especially with the purposes of other minds.[1]

The fact of language is here of incalculable importance. For while it may be disputed whether thought can exist at all without language of some kind, it is certainly true that our actual thought is developed and sustained by use of language. Thought definitely requires some symbolism; pure thinking, without either percepts or imagery does not occur. But it is possible that the individual mind might construct its own set of images to serve as vehicles of its thought-processes, even though these were quite unintelligible to any one else. To some extent, perhaps, a baby does this. But thought would thus make little progress. Its actual advance is made by acceptance of that articulated apprehension of the world of experience which language enshrines. Language itself is of very slow growth; sometimes, we must presume, its inadequacy holds thought back; sometimes its slow development is a mark of thought's failure to press beyond the stage which it has already found means to express. But thought and language have taken many generations to reach the degree of development which we find even among primitive peoples. When the child begins to use ordinary words with their accepted meaning, his mind is appropriating the accumulated thought of centuries; and it is by this acceptance of the deposit of corporate thought that the child achieves such mastery over his experience as he actually reaches. It is through social contacts that the mind is enabled to unify its experience even as material of the understanding.

Far more evidently is this true in relation to experience regarded as giving rise to emotional or aesthetic or ethical reactions. In the primal sympathy, of which perhaps the imitative tendencies of the organism are

[1] "Personality is mutual in its very being. The self is one term in a relation between two selves. . . . The self exists only in the communion of selves."—Professor John Macmurray, *Interpreting the Universe*, p. 137.

the first occasion, the mind finds itself feeling this or that solely because some other person who bulks large in his experience feels this or that. The other person who plays far the largest part in the calling forth of this primal sympathy is the mother. That sympathy, like all else at the early undifferentiated stage, is rather a potentiality of understanding and of love than the actuality of either; but both grow out of it; and from his understanding of his mother's, and then of other people's, understanding of the world, the child wins his own understanding of it; from his love for his mother, and then for other people, he learns the meaning of human society and its obligations.

All this is given in the initial experience, though it is not all received. But the reception of all the richness of the gift is not achieved by inference from initial percepts, but rather by the direction of attention to the different elements in the initial datum as practical interest, and later theoretic interest also, may require. To call the process analytical would suggest that it is more purely intellectual than it actually is. But in the sense that it is the discovery of what is within the datum of primary experience and not an inference from it, it is analytical. All that scientists have learnt, all that artists have perceived, is there from the outset. We build up the fabric of our knowledge by taking to pieces the datum of experience.

Thus we are led to the view that *thinking is grounded in the process of adjustment between organism and environment and is indeed an extension of that process. Enrichment of thought is an entry into appropriate adjustment to a wider environment—for only that part of contemporaneous existence which is relevant to the organism can properly be called its environment. Intellectual growth is a perpetually fuller responsiveness to the truth of the environment; aesthetic growth to its beauty; moral growth to its goodness; religious growth to its spiritual character expressed in all of these. Extension of the apprehended environment and develop-*

ment of the apprehending mind are two ways of describing the same fact; and the organism, now more mental than physical,[1] *is scientific, artistic, moral and religious because in the mutual reaction between it and its environment it finds the environment to be possessed of the characters to which these activities are the appropriate response.*

The mind, which conducts this progressive apprehension, itself "emerges" in the midst of the process which it apprehends. That fact must engage our further attention shortly. Meanwhile, we have to notice the actual correlation of mind with the world it apprehends. This is so fundamental to all science, and indeed to all reflection, that we seldom pay attention to it. We are so impressed by the greatness and multiplicity of the world we know, that we seldom reflect upon the amazing fact of our knowing it. Some men have even been so overwhelmed by the greatness of the known world as to deny all significance to the knowing mind. *But this fact of knowledge is more remarkable than all the varieties of known objects put together. For the mind which knows is in a perfectly real sense equal to what it knows, and in another real sense transcends it, unless what it knows is another mind which also knows. The mind of the astronomer is equal to so much of the stellar system as he grasps, and transcends it in so far as he knows it while it does not know him. That there should "emerge" in the cosmic process a capacity to apprehend, even in a measure to comprehend, that process is the most remarkable characteristic of the process itself. For though minds emerge as episodes within the process, it is, as will appear, essential to their nature as minds that they are not mere episodes. Thus the cosmic process gives evidence that it is not only process, and history supplies the proof that reality is more than historical.*

The word "emerge" is commonly used in this connexion, as I understand, to indicate that the emergent entity is not to be accounted for in terms of the ante-

[1] Because in any organism wherein mind is an element, this is the "principle of unity".

cedent stages of the process, and yet is not due either to chance, or to any known principle of teleology. It represents a certain Agnosticism coupled with a strong preference for continuity as against catastrophic irruptions of novelty. But when the process as a whole is considered, it is to be presumed that either its first term or its entire totality supply a ground for its various phases; and either assumption will necessitate the inference from the mere fact of knowledge to a spiritual (or at least a "mental") interpretation of existence. *That the world should give rise to minds which know the world involves a good deal concerning the nature of the world.*

Once more, mind and the world are found to be akin in such a sense that valid mental processes lead to verifiable results. It may be urged that this is only natural, for the mind is a product of nature and has grown up in intercourse with nature in order to guide our handling of nature; consequently nature seems to correspond to mind because mind was actually constructed in correspondence to nature. Even if that be admitted—and it cannot be a complete account of mind, as we shall see—yet the actual kinship remains. We know some of the characteristics of the mind, however it may have acquired them; and its kinship with nature is a fact worthy of consideration, whichever is taken to be the senior partner.

Taking these two considerations together we get the following result: there is a kinship between Mind and the World, so that we can assert of the World a relation of correspondence to Mind as we know it in ourselves, and can affirm that our minds rightly find themselves at home in the world. Further, our minds discover themselves to be occurrences within, and forming part of, the process with which they recognise kinship, so that a full account of the process must account for them along with the rest, and a full explanation of the process must explain how they come to be part of it.

Now as far as our experience goes, matter does not

generate thought, nor does thought generate matter. But in the world of matter there is no known principle which is self-explanatory; of every principle or systematisation of experience it is possible to ask—Why is it thus and not otherwise? At one period a certain school of philosophers would have been content to answer that in infinite time every permutation and combination of the ultimate particles of matter is bound to occur, and this is the one that is occurring now. I am not satisfied that such a view expresses a sound logic of probability; but it is scarcely worth while to discuss that point, because the argument in question ignores and contradicts the essential principle of the organism. An organism is not a mere collection of juxtaposed particles or cells. Its nature is determined by its principle of unity; and this also determines the organisms that proceed from it. Consequently of the whole organic world—whether that be the entire universe or not—we are bound to say, with Whitehead,

> "The evolution of history can be rationalised by the consideration of the determination of successors by antecedents. But, on the other hand, the evolution of history is incapable of rationalisation (*by that means*), because it exhibits a selected flux of participating forms. No reason, internal to history, can be assigned why that flux of forms, rather than another flux, should have been illustrated."[1]

But when we turn from the World as apprehended by Mind to Mind which apprehends the World, we find among its functions a principle which is self-explanatory—the principle of Purpose or of Intelligent Choice.

This is an ultimate principle of explanation. When we

[1] *Process and Reality*, p. 64. Into this quotation I have inserted the phrase "by that means", which seems necessary to balance the phrase "internal to history" in the sentence which follows. It will become apparent later, specially in Lecture X., that nothing can in fact be "rationalised" only "by the consideration of the determination of successors by antecedents". Events can be rationalised or explained only by reasons, not by causes. But we must not beg the question of the possibility of this. We must first apprehend the facts in the order of their objective occurrence and then see if, so apprehended, they offer a clue to their own interpretation.

find that the position of a given set of material objects is due to their having been arranged with a view to facilitating the accomplishment of some intelligible purpose, our minds are satisfied. That a plank should lie across a stream may call for much explanation if no human beings have ever placed it there; but if men laid it across to form a bridge, so that they could cross over dry-shod, no further explanation is needed. Purpose is a self-explanatory principle: that it is also a true principle of origination we shall seek to show later; and if that can be shown, certain further results are obtainable.

The picture of the World-Process as existing for aeons before it contained minds to apprehend it suggests at first that its non-mental functions must contain the ground of its mental functions—both of their occurrence and of their nature. But in fact all attempts to trace in evolution an explanation of the emergence of mind have totally failed. And if this is not explained, the Process is not explained, for this is an element in the Process. On the other hand we find that the Process is akin to Mind, that Mind arises in the course of it, and that Mind does exhibit what is essentially the thing required—a self-explanatory principle of origination. It is then more reasonable to test the hypothesis that Mind contains the explanation of the World-Process than to refuse to test it. That is not an extravagant claim. The whole future course of these Lectures will be concerned with one very limited attempt to test that hypothesis and to develop its implications. From the first it is more than a hypothesis awaiting verification. The considerations which suggest it go far towards establishing it.

But here, before going further, we must notice that there are other methods of rationalising a process than "the consideration of the determination of successors by antecedents". A poem is a process or a history of a certain kind; if it is a good poem every word in it is strictly necessary; precisely that word must occur in precisely that place. But the necessity does not reside in the preceding words or lines. The words "To be or not to be" do not contain any necessity predetermining the occurrence of the words "Who would fardels bear?"—nor do all the intervening words in Hamlet's speech. The ground of necessity for each word is the meaning which finds expression in the whole speech. But the process is completely rationalised. The same is true in even higher degree of that unity which gives rational coherence to the life of a great man. Therefore there is no insuperable difficulty in the view that the history of the universe is rational, though the ground of its rationality is only fully disclosed in its entire course, and though the element within it which supplies the unifying influence only appears late in that course.

But if we take such a view, we must recognise that what thus appears late must truly have been active from the beginning. That late appearance must be the clear "emergence"—the word is more appropriate now—of what was all along an immanent principle. In other words, our hypothesis is so far that of Immanent Theism. Whether on examination it will remain a hypothesis of Immanence only our further consideration of this view must decide.

Meanwhile let us review our course up to date. We have followed the guidance of "modern knowledge" so as to see Mind first as something which occurs in, or emerges out of, the whole evolutionary process of the universe; and our willingness to see Mind as one element in Nature has led—not to Naturalism—but to a fresh perception that if Nature (containing Mind) is to be explained at all, it is Mind that can alone supply the explanation. *The more completely we include Mind within Nature, the more inexplicable must Nature become except by reference to Mind.* If Nature is only a whirling mass of protons and electrons, that gyration might intelligibly go on for ever, and at some point in its endless permutations would present us with the physical universe of contemporary experience. Such a universe might exist apart from any Immanent or Transcendent Mind or Spirit. But if, as science has disclosed, Mind is part of Nature, then Nature (to contain such a part) must be grounded in Mind.

In short, the more we identify ourselves with the rest of the natural order, the more are we compelled to assert the reality of a supernatural Creator. But the justification of this proposition in precisely that form must wait for the further development of the argument.

LECTURE VI

TRUTH AND BEAUTY

Our course hitherto has led us to the conception of a World-Process in which are found, as episodes of the process, minds which apprehend the process. It has been argued that this occurrence of minds within the process is evidence that the process itself is grounded in Mind. That position will from this point onward be assumed, in order that it may be worked out and tested. We have now to notice that the life of mind as known to us has its being in the relationship both active and passive of mind to the process which supplies its environment. It is in that interplay of mind and environment that Value resides, as our further discussion will make clear; that discussion will be primarily concerned neither with the inner life of mind, conceived as separable from environment, nor with the object-world which mind apprehends and contemplates, but with the interrelation of these two. And it will be convenient to begin with certain accepted Values, which mind apprehends, but which come to full actuality as good or evil through such apprehension.

It has become customary of late for writers who maintain the existence of "absolute values" to present their case as if there were in fact three such values—Truth, Beauty and Goodness. It has then at once to be explained that Goodness here stands for Moral Goodness, or Goodness of Character, otherwise it might seem to be rather a synonym for Value than a department of it. The three terms then denote three forms of excellence—Intellectual, Aesthetic and Ethical. The trio could not have become so popular without much to recommend it. But it is in fact a very awkward classification, for it rests on a cross-division; and whereas Beauty and Goodness have at least a *prima facie* definiteness of character, Truth (if presented in alliance with them) seems to be ambiguous. For while Beauty is a quality of actual objects, and Goodness of actual characters, Truth is a quality of propositions—not of minds, nor of things. It is noticeable that Tennyson renamed this member of the trio when he shrewdly observed that

> Beauty, Good and Knowledge are three sisters
> . . . . .
> And never can be sundered without tears,[1]

and he may have had other reasons than those of metrical convenience for doing so.

But as soon as this change is made, a doubt arises concerning the "absoluteness" of the "value" in question. Is Knowledge unconditionally good? Is it good that every mind should acquire every fraction of Knowledge that it is able to acquire? We may all be ready to agree that Knowledge is a good in the sense that if in any case it is better avoided, that is due to defect elsewhere and not to any evil inherent in any form or instance of Knowledge. But "an absolute value" ought to be one which is good in all conditions whatsoever, not only a value which has in itself no negative element. Knowledge may be a pure or unmixed good; it is not self-evident that it is an absolute good. Indeed it is not easy to see how its claim in this respect is to be distinguished in principle from that of pleasure. It may be—no doubt it is—a higher good than pleasure, so that to sacrifice pleasure to attain it is noble, while to sacrifice knowledge in order to win pleasure is base. But many would say that to forgo the opportunity of acquiring some minute and probably unimportant fraction of knowledge in order to give pleasure to others might be permissible or even obligatory; and this would be an

[1] Tennyson, *Palace of Art* (introductory lines).

impossible judgement if Knowledge were an absolute good and Pleasure were not.

The change of Truth into Knowledge calls, however, for some further comment. For the opposite of Knowledge is either Ignorance—in its proper sense of mental vacuity in relation to any fact or group of facts, or Error —in the sense of false opinion. When it is said that certain persons had better be prevented from acquiring certain kinds of Knowledge, what is desired is usually that they may remain void of all information on that subject; it would at least require further justification to hold that it is better that they should receive false information than true. Yet if those moralists are right who hold that in certain circumstances it is a duty to tell a lie, it follows that it is better that the hearer of that lie should entertain a false conception than a true one. This is not to say that it is better for him to entertain a false conception than none at all; but it may be impossible that he should entertain none, and it may on that account be better to lie to him than to keep silence. The common instance of this paradox is the lie told to a sick person to maintain his spirits and therewith his vitality; other instances may easily be imagined.

The case of Beauty seems to be similar. Beauty is undoubtedly a good, and a perfect experience must contain fruition of Beauty. But it is not self-evident that to call an object beautiful is to give a final and all-sufficient vindication of its existence apart from all conditions. It may be doubted whether a picture (for example) of intrinsically immoral quality can be beautiful, for either the beauty will transmute the immorality or the immorality will contaminate the beauty. It is arguable, at least, that no true work of art is immoral. But it is indisputable that a truly consummate work of art may have demoralising influence upon those who are immature in aesthetic appreciation; and it is a tenable view that in such a case the beautiful thing had better not exist, despite its admitted beauty. Whether it can be truly said that in some circumstances, and (of course) for other than aesthetic reasons, what is ugly is to be preferred to what is beautiful, seems more doubtful. But what has been said is sufficient to dispose of the doctrine that Beauty, any more than Knowledge, is an "absolute value" in the only proper sense of that phrase. Beauty and Knowledge are both good *ceteris paribus*; but then, so is Pleasure; and it is in order to exalt them above Pleasure that philosophers have been interested to call them "absolute values".

These doubts do not arise concerning Goodness of Character. It would never be better that a man should be worse than he is. If sometimes we say, after the failure of a good man in some emergency, "a worse man would have done better", we do not, or should not, mean that virtue hindered him from doing what was right, but that his special virtue was irrelevant to that situation, and that another man, even though less virtuous on the whole, who possessed some appropriate quality, would have done better. There may indeed be occasions when the very stuff of a hero's virtue disqualifies him for the duty required of him by circumstance: that is the essence of true Tragedy; and no one who has appreciated the sublimity of Tragedy as the poets reveal it can ever say it would be better if the hero had less of the virtue that destroys him: more comfortable—yes; but better—no.[1]

This brief polemic against a conventional dogma has been interpolated here as an introduction to a consideration of Truth (or Knowledge) and Beauty more consonant with that understanding of the world and our place in it which hitherto we have been building up.

The basic fact is organic reaction to environment. It is in, and out of, the interaction between the organism and its environment that consciousness arises—and especially in and out of the interaction between it and

[1] See the chapter on "The Meaning of Tragedy" in my *Mens Creatrix*, specially pp. 132-142.

other organisms. The latter, it is natural to suppose, is specially potent in carrying the movement forward to self-consciousness; for the organism that is only conscious of its relation to an inorganic environment might rest at that stage, but it seems impossible that an organism conscious of relation to another organism should not become self-conscious at least to the extent of distinguishing itself consciously from that other. There might be interaction of organisms without any consciousness at all, but there could hardly be consciousness of such interaction which was not rudimentary self-consciousness.

In the mature human mind we have moved far beyond that; but we have not become independent of our origin. Mind does not know first itself and then the world; but it knows the world, and it knows itself—even itself knowing the world—as part of the world. We have said that the occurrence of mind as an element within the world-process throws a good deal of light on that process; and in elaboration of that thesis we have now to consider some of the manifestations or activities of mind in its varied yet always unitary apprehension of the process of which it is a part.

Rooted as it is in the life of the organism, mental activity begins as a means of satisfying more fully the need or appetition of the organism. In other words thought is at the outset closely linked to desire. Philosophers have commonly said that thought receives its material from sensation in the form of bare particulars; in whatever degree that is true, it is a reflection based on the behaviour of thought at an advanced stage of development. The thought of the scientist—thought of which the consciously accepted end is its own perfection—receives its material in the form of particulars supplied by sensation, and (perhaps) also from its own nature: *Nihil in intellectu quod non prius fuerit in sensu, nisi ipse intellectus*, the old scholastic formula, with Leibniz' revolutionary addition, is an accurate account of the scientific thought for which Kant was seeking a philosophical vindication. But thought in its rudimentary stages is highly selective as regards the elements in experience of which it takes note; indeed it remains selective to the end; and while the informing principle of its selection in the scientific student is love of truth, at the rudimentary stage its informing principle is concern for the needs of the organism itself; and this concern, as an element in consciousness, is desire.

Mr. Aldous Huxley has utilised this consideration to support his repudiation of the notion that reason or intelligence is identical in all men. Accepting the traditional account of its processes, he points out that the rules of the syllogism may indeed be the same for all men, but that does not lead to resemblance in their opinions, even when they exercise intelligence in forming them (which is rare), because they choose different major premises from which to start. "It is an important and significant fact", he says, "that there should be only one way of reaching a conclusion from a given major premise. But it is no less important and significant that there should be no single criterion for judging major premises, but that every man should select his own on personal and ultimately irrational grounds."[1] We shall consider later the implied denial of any universal truth, but the contention in itself is sound. Our thinking about the world at first derives alike its motive and its direction from desire.

By one process or another it is possible that this desire should be developed into the true scientific impulse, which is the desire or will to know; Bosanquet rightly resents "an intrusion of *choice*, which in science is chance, into the region of intelligible necessity, which ought only to be vitalised by a general *will to know*, not dominated by accidental interests."[2] But it is doubtful whether the finite mind ever perfectly attains that ideal,

[1] Aldous Huxley, *Proper Studies*, p. 37.
[2] Bosanquet, *Knowledge and Reality*, pp. 35, 36.

and certainly at the outset of its growth and discipline it is very far from it. Thought arises out of the life of the organism and is at first a servant of the organism. Science is the construction of thought; it may rise far above its origin, and the influence upon it of desire—other than that of the will to know—may become negligible. Yet its own advance imposes a necessity for specialisation. No one can in these days be a master in many branches of science; the range of each is so vast as to claim the study of a lifetime. Yet there does not seem to be a good scientific reason why a young student should select astronomy rather than biology, chemistry rather than anthropology, as the subject to which he will devote his time and energy. Inevitably he will determine this in accordance with his own aptitudes, or even by reference to something still more irrelevant to the will to know, such as a secure opening in a good commercial firm. He may eliminate from his scientific activities themselves all other impulse than the will to know, but the general will to know will not settle for him what in particular he shall wish to know, and his views on theology, politics, art and morals are likely to be influenced by the main occupation of his mind, so that a great deal of his thinking will continue to be dependent on the non-intellectual grounds determining its main direction. It is our duty to escape from such irrelevant influences as far as we may; but it is our wisdom to recognise that we are affected by them and that our escape is never complete.

Now so far as thought is thus correlated with desire—even when it is the desire to know—it is concerned with generalities. This very important point has been admirably brought out by Professor J. L. Stocks.[1] When we consider the growth of thought either historically or in relation to the organism, we find how very artificial was the whole setting of the problem which dominated European philosophy from Descartes

[1] See *The Limits of Purpose*, p. 40.

to Kant. For they all supposed thought to begin with the particulars supplied by sense, as apprehended in their particularity, so that the origin of general ideas was the occasion of much debate. But we find that, on the contrary, thought, for the most part, is first concerned with the particular data of experience precisely not in their particularity, but in their general character as capable or incapable of satisfying desires. For desire itself is never for the particular or individual; it is for the kind. The hungry man wants food—pleasant food, no doubt, for choice; but if his longing is for the cake of yester-year on account of its sentimental associations, it is some impulse other than hunger, or simple desire for food, which animates him. Hunger does not distinguish between this cake and that cake, if they are the same in feeding quality. Accordingly

> "the type of thought which is stimulated by desire and characteristic of a life organised in the service of desire is abstract and general, attentive not to the particulars themselves, but to them in respect only of certain general characters which they may exhibit. . . . The study of history and the comparison of different levels of culture show conclusively that the grasp of the individual is not the starting point but the goal of thought's journey."[1]

But there is also a relation of the organism to its environment, or at least to certain elements in its environment, which is akin to desire and yet differs from it fundamentally. For desire is a condition of tension. It arises from a failure in the environment to satisfy the organism, or a realisation that the environment is offering the means of satisfying a need till now unsatisfied; and so soon as under the impulse of desire the organism has found the satisfaction of its need, desire ceases; it exists in the tension which it seeks to relieve. But alongside of desire there is affection; indeed this is probably the most primitive and fundamental form of consciousness, though it embraces only a fraction of the whole

[1] J. L. Stocks, *loc. cit.*

environment. The first clear awareness of the young child is an awareness of the mother, both as a source from which desire may be satisfied and as an object of affection and trust, but the former is occasional, the latter permanent.[1] Affection may give rise to desire when its object is absent; but it does not cease when the object is once more present; its characteristic mode of being is the intimacy of comradeship. But the apprehension of affection is strongly individual. The lover resents the notion of classifying his beloved as one of a type; no doubt her appearance can be described in general terms for practical purposes, such as the obtaining of a passport; but the description is felt to be as false as it is true, for it is precisely what belongs to no class, what is unique, that affection makes its own. This is a relation of person to person, each whole and complete; and it is a relation of knowledge—not such knowledge as is in its own sphere final, such as $2 + 2 = 4$, but knowledge that is always growing not by extension but by deepening, while yet there are always depths unplumbed. To give this knowledge scientific expression is impossible; its only mode of expression is through art or through the service which love offers to the beloved.

It would not be true to say that Science and Art are no more than respectively the activities of intellect prompted by desire and of intellect prompted by affection; for when they have been launched upon their courses they become living interests in themselves. But it is true, I believe, that their origin is to be sought in those two conditions of the conscious organism, and even in their fullest development they retain the characteristics appropriate to their origin. For science is never concerned with the individual as such; it deals in laws and generalisations; it does not distinguish between one

[1] It is generally held that differential recognition first occurs at three months from birth, and distinguishable affection at six months; but each of these is grounded in a relationship which began before birth.

drop and another of the same acid in its laboratories, or between one instance and another of any instinct or sentiment in its psychological analysis. This is one main reason why a purely scientific education is liable to be a poor preparation for life, which always largely consists of human intercourse. There is indeed a certain knowledge of human nature which enables its possessor, up to a point, to use persons as his instruments; and this is the only use of them that finds a place in "a life organised in the service of desire"; it is a knowledge of their general characteristics. But for the life of fellowship, and even for the best utilisation of men's capacities, more than this is needed—a concern for the individual in his individuality. In common speech, to say that one understands a man is to say that one sympathises with him, or at least that one can imagine one's self acting as he has acted, or that one is sure of acting towards him in such a way as to produce in him the desired impression. Such understanding, especially of persons whose temperament is very different from one's own, may be facilitated by a knowledge of psychology, but in itself it is imaginative and emotional rather than purely intellectual, and it is always a direct apprehension of individual character, not only of general characteristics.

Now art, in distinction from science, is always thus concerned with the individual. The painter does not provide a diagram of the human body, to which all human bodies conform so far as they are normal; he gives a presentation of this normal human body or of that abnormal human body. He is not indifferent to universal significance; on the contrary, he presents universal significance in proportion as he succeeds in presenting the individual. The tree which the artist isolates for special attention represents the real meaning of trees far more fully than a botanical treatise, just because it actually is (pictorially) a tree. In the same way Othello represents the torture of a loving soul tormented by doubt of the fidelity of his beloved far more fully than the chapter on Jealousy in a text-book of psychology, just because he is (dramatically) an actual man "perplexed in the extreme".[1] The understanding which the dramatist both possesses and imparts is the understanding of sympathy.

Another aspect of the same distinction between science and art is brought into prominence when we consider their respective methods. Science has its life in mental restlessness; it asks of every fact the questions Why? or How? and of the answer it asks Why? or How? again. It seeks to understand the presented object by analysing it into its component parts or elements and by relating it to an ever-widening context. Art has its life in mental repose—not inactivity, but the activity of still contemplation. The frame round the picture, the curtain at the play's end, are symptomatic. The work of art is a world by itself, to be apprehended by a constant attention, wherein the mind becomes one with the thing it contemplates.

Now the conventional triad of alleged "absolute values" has this great merit, that it recognises truth as a value and sets it alongside beauty, thereby suggesting reflections of great importance. The first of these is that neither truth nor beauty is to be found by casual sensation. If a man travels by night to a region of noble scenery of a kind hitherto unfamiliar to him, having had no opportunity of studying geology or cultivating his aesthetic taste, he will not at once apprehend the truth or the beauty of that scenery by opening his eyes upon it when daylight has returned. He will receive impressions which are a rudimentary apprehension of both, but it may be so rudimentary as to seem to himself at a later stage to be almost utterly alien from the scientific and aesthetic apprehension which by then he

[1] *Othello*, Act V. Sc. 2. It is inevitable, though misleading, to speak of Othello as jealous, and he uses the word of himself in this closing speech. But it is not the jealousy which springs primarily from the possessive instinct. It is because his love for Desdemona is so intense that Iago's insinuations fascinate him with their horror. Then the fatal handkerchief turns "perplexity" into assurance.

has acquired. Our experience is always of the real world; and that world remains unchanged—at least sufficiently for us to study it in the experience of many years with a constantly growing understanding of it as one object. But our apprehension does not remain the same; even apart from conscious effort, its defects, and the suggestions due to the special angle of vision at earlier stages, are supplemented and corrected as time passes by later apprehensions of the same fact. A walker, who sees Great Gable from Wastdale only, may not recognise it if he sees it next from High Raise. Indeed of that one mountain there are five utterly distinct views—from Wastdale, from Sca Fell Pike, from High Raise, from Brandreth and from Kirk Fell. Between each of these are view-points which connect one with another because from them the outlines are seen which explain both of the other two; but there are five principal and distinct views of that one mountain, and all must be seen before either the truth or the beauty of the grandest of English mountains is grasped. Such progress towards full understanding may occur in great measure accidentally. To live at all is to acquire some wisdom as the days pass. But civilised man has long ago learnt that in the search for truth or beauty something far other is needed than the casual accumulation of impressions.

Mind is always apprehending reality, but it may misapprehend it. To suppose that mind knows only its own ideas is an error; its ideas are not some *tertium quid* mediating between mind and reality; they are the mind's apprehension of reality; and they may be in various ways inadequate. The mind always apprehends reality, but it may apprehend it amiss by wrong interpretation. In extreme cases, such as hallucination, it may interpret a nervous agitation as an external object. But the fact that men in *delirium tremens* see what they wrongly suppose to be snakes is no ground for doubting that visitors to the Zoological Gardens, being in sound health, really see real snakes—that is to say, apprehend real snakes by means of vision. Yet any first apprehension is always precarious, usually defective, and sometimes erroneous. "Seeing is believing", men say; but the proverb is in place only as supplying a criterion by which the work of mind upon experience may be tested, not as a defence of the credulity which trusts all deliverances of sensation apart from any intellectual criticism. We cannot begin with facts, and construct theories on them as on a foundation; it is only by means of much theorising that we truly apprehend the facts.

There is no such thing as an initial grasp of mere particulars, from which the mind may draw necessary or probable inferences by the way of generalisation. The mind interprets as it apprehends. And this is not due to an admixture of intelligence with sensation in such wise that sensation might exist without intelligence, and so existing might apprehend real particulars apart from all generalisation. For the basis of sensation and intelligence alike is in the reaction of the organism to its environment. As this becomes conscious, it appears as being essentially intellectualised sensation, for what is perceived is some element in the environment which has a meaning for the life of the organism as an object of desire or affection, or (negatively) of fear or dislike. If it is an object of desire, it is its generic quality which causes the selective attention of the organism to be directed towards it; its particularity is only perceived because of its general character; it is a universal first and a particular afterwards. Again, if it is an object of affection, it is a true individual—universal and particular in one; but it neither is, nor can be apprehended as, a bare particular.

These points are in substance very familiar and very elementary. But when we put together the two propositions in which they may be summarily expressed, very important results immediately emerge. Those propositions are: first, that what the mind apprehends, even when it apprehends mistakenly, is reality; secondly, that the true apprehension of reality is attained not at the beginning but at the end of the mental process. The result that seems unavoidable is the conviction of intimate kinship between mind and reality. When Sir James Jeans says of the impression created by modern science that "the universe begins to look more like a great thought than like a great machine"[1] he is giving vivid expression to just this conviction. Mind journeys through mazes of apparently abstract thought, and at the end finds that its conclusions are verified by observed occurrences in the physical world. It does not indeed follow that the physical world contains the counterpart of the successive stages in the abstract argument; what follows is that when Mind is true to itself it reaches its truest apprehension of reality; and that tells us a good deal about the nature of reality.

At an earlier stage we glanced at the objection that the kinship of mind with reality is of no ultimate importance because it is due to the fact that mind was "evolved", or "emerged", or "was secreted", or what not, out of the physical process as a part of it and as a means of enabling the organism to cope with its environment. The whole problem of the evolution or emergence of mind is still awaiting attention; but we can at once deal with this objection. A savage may be startled to find that a key, brought from a distance, fits the lock of a door through which he wishes to pass; and his surprise may be removed when he learns that lock and key were made by the same locksmith in order that one may fit the other. But the ending of his surprise will not end the effectiveness of the key. It may no longer seem odd that it fits the lock; but it does fit the lock, and it opens the door. In the same way if any one is astonished to find so close a correspondence between mind and the physical world that the most elaborate

[1] *The Mysterious Universe*, p. 148. But a machine is evidence of an intelligent designer. Cf. p. 53.

calculations receive vindication from the observed behaviour of the world, his surprise may be removed if he is persuaded that mind is bound to correspond to the world because it "emerged", irrupted, or otherwise appeared upon the scene, under pressure of the world, in order to assist its organism in its adaptation of itself to the world, and, still more, of the world to itself. But though the surprise might be removed, the correspondence would remain; and the importance of this correspondence between mind and the world is not its capacity to evoke amazement but its existence.

For *this correspondence of mind with reality is the essential condition of Value or Good.* No doubt that assertion calls for support, and our further examination of Truth and Beauty will offer such support. But for the moment it is convenient to notice *what follows if the discovery or recognition by Mind of itself in its object is the essential condition of Good, and if the presupposition of all science, which the progress of science daily vindicates, is the reality of correspondence between Mind and the World. For it follows that not only is it good to know the Real, but that the correlation of Reality with knowledge or appreciation is itself the essence of Good.* Having thus indicated the point to which the argument is leading us, we must return to the point that we had reached and make our way forward step by step.

When the incipient mind first confronts its environment, it finds itself at home with a small part of it, but the rest is strange. It sets itself to understand this strange part of its environment with a view to behaving wisely in relation to it; at this stage knowledge or truth has instrumental value only; it is not appreciated as in itself good, but only as useful for the establishing of satisfactory relations with the world as known. But in the process of this study of the world the mind becomes aware that it is discovering its own principles in the object of its study; indeed it usually becomes aware of its own principles at all, only in so far as it finds these exemplified in its study of the world. That is good Kantian doctrine; for Kant taught us to regard the causation traced in phenomena as really imposed upon the multiplicity of sense-perception by the understanding of which causality is an *a priori* principle; but also that this principle only becomes consciously apprehended through the mind's critical reflection on its own activity. This discovery by the mind of its own principles in the world of its environment, and that, too, in the "strange" portions of that world, at once invests knowledge with a value of its own. It is no longer good only because it enables us to act wisely; it is good in itself.

But this good that is in knowledge calls for further consideration, which will incidentally help us to understand why the term chosen for the familiar trio of Values has usually been, not Knowledge, but Truth; for Knowledge is an attribute of mind itself, whereas Truth, though properly a quality of propositions and therefore existent in mind rather than in its objects, is yet relatively objective when considered in relation to any particular mind. When the mind adequately grasps the objects of its experience it is said indifferently to know them or to know the truth about them; for the true propositions are conceived as at least possibly existing in some other mind before our own minds succeed in framing them. Yet the expression "know the truth", though natural and in many contexts appropriate, is not strictly accurate; the accurate expressions are "to have a true apprehension of reality", or "to apprehend reality truly"; for the object of apprehension or of knowledge is not a truth midway between the mind and reality, but is reality itself.

This may at first sight appear to be an erroneous view when the object of study is imperceptible from the point of space or time occupied by the person in question. It seems strange to say that I truly apprehend the Norman Conquest or the Spanish Armada. At an earlier date the Governor of Tilbury is presented as remarking to his daughter Tilburina:

> The Spanish fleet thou can'st not see, because
> It is not yet in sight.[1]

Can we be properly said to apprehend what is no longer, or not yet, perceptible by our senses? The common use of language would lead us to say that we do not apprehend these things themselves, but that we do apprehend the truth about them. No doubt the mode of apprehension is different; but if it be held that apprehension is only possible in the moment of sense-perception, it would appear that it is not possible at all; for if that line of argument is adopted, the "moment" of perception must be defined, and then, as we all know, it contracts to that meeting point of past and future in which nothing can happen at all. My apprehension of any object at twelve o'clock noon consists in part of my memory of it at 11.59 A.M., and often also of my anticipation of it at 12.1 P.M. The retentive and interpretative activities of mind are involved in every apprehension whatsoever. The proportions of sense-perception, memory, interpretation, explanation, may be indefinitely varied. All our apprehensions are associated with sense-perception, and none are limited to it. Certainly I apprehend the Norman Conquest in a way different from that in which a follower of Harold or William apprehended it; and if there were no records or narratives that I might see or hear, I could not apprehend it at all. But by the help of those records and narratives I do apprehend it—not only propositions about it, but the fact itself. That this should seem difficult or disputable is a result of that false start which has become traditional in epistemology, by which we assume that the immediate object of apprehension is a particular given in sensation. But this is not so. Apprehension is an awareness of our environment, or of some part of it that specially concerns

[1] Sheridan, *The Critic*, Act iii.

us, arising out of the relation and reaction to it of our psycho-physical organisms; in that relation and reaction the whole organism is involved, and it is often the general character rather than the particularity of the object which first claims attention.[1] The environment is itself in process of constant change, and the greater part of what is present in apprehension is no longer present in sensation—it is partly retained by memory pure and simple, and partly grasped by unconscious inference from what is still present in sensation or in actual memory.

The mind which has once found satisfaction in knowledge independently of any use to which it may be put, is eager to extend the span of its apprehension to the uttermost. It finds a perpetual exhilaration in the discovery or recognition of what is akin to itself in its world. But its joy is in that other which is akin—not in its discovery, but in what it discovers. That is why popular usage tends, as was observed above, to speak of Truth rather than of Knowledge as the intellectual form of ultimate Value; for though apprehension must be sure and adequate if mind is to find its counterpart in reality, yet it is in that counterpart when found and not in the apprehension that finds it, that mind takes delight. No one who has for a moment tasted the excellence of truth or knowledge can doubt that. We are false to the first quality of the fruition of truth if we suggest that the good of truth consists in our appreciation of it; the mind enjoys truth because it finds in it what is good; that good does not reside in, but occasions, the enjoyment. Moreover those in whom this experience is deepest and keenest are unwilling to speak of enjoyment or satisfaction. Truth to them appears as something august, making claim to their allegiance even while they do not as yet know what it is. The recognition by the finite mind of that which is akin to it in its world, is also a recognition that this which is akin is

[1] See above, p. 142.

yet remote, to be served rather than possessed. The man of science who has probed most deeply into the secrets of nature and stretched most widely the span of his apprehension does not speak lightly of possessing truth. Rather he feels that truth or reality possesses him, and there is more of awe than of boastfulness in his gratitude for the vision vouchsafed to him. In the progressive conquest of the unknown by the mind of man there is at every stage the satisfaction of success; but the great and lasting joy is not in the discovery of reality, it is in the reality discovered. The little mind of man increasingly perceives that it is tracing out the workings of mind mightier than itself. The intrinsic good or value in the attainment of truth is certainly actualised in the discovery or recognition by mind of itself in its object, and mind, which began as a consciousness of the environment enabling the organism more wisely to adapt its behaviour thereto with a view to its own comfort, finds that environment to be informed by mind, whose mighty workings it is imperiously called to trace out.

The same process and result is to be observed in mind's search for Beauty. Here, instead of perpetually widening the span of apprehension under an impulse that is in origin that of desire or appetite, mind fastens upon some one element in experience—or it may be on experience as a whole—with the fascinated concentration that is born of affection. Some objects naturally call forth affection, and these are the first subjects of artistic appreciation. But the history of art seems to show that everything is seen as beautiful if only attention can be concentrated upon it rightly. We are repelled by the ugliness of a modern industrial town, until some artist reveals the beauty of strong stark lines in factory chimneys, or of sweeping curves in a gasometer. This does not mean that what we had thought ugly is really beautiful, but rather that there is beauty present in it, and concealed in it until it is detected by a rightly directed and rightly concentrated attention. As in the ever-expanding field of scientific enquiry so in the deliberately and rigidly restricted field of aesthetic contemplation, the mind submits itself to its object and finds that the object is no stranger, but akin.

Here, too, as in the realm of Truth, the good or value is actualised in the process of apprehension, yet what is experienced as good is not the apprehension but the object apprehended. I can see no good in Beauty which no one at all perceives—neither man nor angel nor God. A beautiful object is only a potentiality of good until it is perceived and appreciated. But when it is appreciated, the percipient mind finds the good in the object; it *enjoys* the apprehension, but it *admires* the work of art or of nature. A man of untrained taste may go many times to see a great picture, and every time he sees the same lines and colours; at first he is unable to appreciate it; the picture is "no good" to him; gradually his sensibility is subdued to the proportions and colour-harmonies that are characteristic of the picture, and he begins to appreciate it; at last perhaps he is even fascinated by it. The picture has not changed; the change is in the man; and the new fact is the new mode of apprehension whereby he now appreciates the picture. But while there had been "no good" for him in the picture and now there is great good, and while his enjoyment comes through his apprehension of the picture, yet he finds the beauty neither in his apprehension nor in his enjoyment, but in the picture which he now rightly apprehends. The beauty is objective, but its good or value as beauty is only actualised when it is subjectively appreciated; yet the beauty is in the object, not in the appreciating mind.

Were it otherwise, there could be no canons of beauty. If the good resided in the appreciation, the only proof of beauty in any object would be *de facto* enjoyment of it, and we should have to account most beautiful that picture, poem, piece of music, which occasioned the most intense enjoyment in the greatest number. And as with Hutcheson's hedonistic formula, "the greatest happiness of the greatest number", we should have difficulty in determining the relation between the two superlatives; how is the keen enjoyment of a few to be compared and contrasted with the less keen enjoyment of a multitude? But this whole method of enquiry would be false to the essential nature of the aesthetic experience itself, for that is clearly and decisively experience of an object which is beautiful, and of which the perception causes enjoyment because the object itself is beautiful. If any one doubts or denies this, I do not know that there are any arguments by which he can be persuaded; I can only appeal to the actual experience of any one of aesthetic sensibility. But it is noteworthy that the testimony of language is unambiguous; according to the natural usage of all languages, it is the scene or the work of art that is beautiful, not our apprehension of it. We may see the beautiful object and not perceive its beauty, because our perceptive faculties are ill-developed; but when we perceive the beauty, we find it there in the object; we do not put it there.

In that perception, as in the apprehension of or attainment to truth, the mind finds in the object what is akin to itself; it finds itself in its other. It is not only the purely logical structure of mind that it now finds, but also its purposive and emotional qualities, though it is doubtful if there can be a real work of art in which there is not also discoverable a true logic. I would here once more associate myself with the passage in which Bosanquet expresses this view, and to which I have already referred:

"Not the invention of novelty, but the logic which lays bare the structure of things, and in doing so purifies and intensifies the feeling which current appearances are too confused and contradictory to evoke, is the true secret of art. No doubt we should fail to predict the incarnation which a painter's or a poet's thought will assume. . . . But this is not because we are too rational, but because we are not rational enough. The "fundamental brainwork" is lacking to us, as is a special capacity for the infinitely delicate logic of expression, by which the passionate thought, already in itself too great for us, is embodied in a million ramifications of detail, constituting a tissue of precise determination in which alone the thought in question with its passion could find utterance—could become itself."[1]

But while the mind which has attained to Truth or appreciated Beauty has found its own nature in its object, it has found it on such a scale as to feel the object to be more wholly Other even than when it seemed strange and alien. It is wonder that prompts the mind to examine its environment—and at first the elementary wonder how to make the best of it; but the enquiry ends in the wonder of awe, before that which, the more it is understood, by so much the more transcends our understanding. "*θαυμάζοντες φιλοσοφοῦμεν· φιλοσοφήσαντες θαμβοῦμεν.* In wonder (*τῷ θαυμάζειν*), says Aristotle, does philosophy begin; and in astoundment (*τῷ θαμβεῖν*) says Plato, does all true philosophy finish."[2] For what manner of mind is that of which our science forms but an inkling in its analysis and systematisation of the experienced world? From the play of minutest particles to the sweep of stars in their courses, the work of Mind is found—of a Mind so mighty in range and scope, so sure in adjustment of infinitesimal detail, that before it all our science is clumsy and precarious. Nothing merely strange or alien can seem so incomparably transcendent as that Mind in the likeness of which our own minds are fashioned yet before which they can only confess their impotence.

The search for Beauty leads to the same conclusion as the search for Truth. The artist is ever essaying to depict a human form more beautiful than any actual human form can ever be,[3] a landscape lit

[1] Bosanquet, *The Principle of Individuality and Value*, p. 332. See also *supra*, p. 108.

[2] S. T. Coleridge, *The Friend*, Section II. Essay XI.

[3] Cf. Plato, *Republic*, 472 D—a flash of intuition which shows that Plato really understood the nature of Art, though his formulated theories of it are so wide of the mark.

with an illumination such as never was seen by mortal eye:

> The light that never was by sea or land,
> The consecration and the poets' dream.[1]

Yet this is no emanation from the artist's brain; it is rather the attempt to catch and fix that Beauty of Reality, of which all beautiful things are momentary and partial manifestations. This true Beauty is apprehended, as it were, in fitful visions; but when apprehended, it is not as dream or hallucination, but as most real fact. Many artists have spoken of it—it suffices to refer to Shelley's *Hymn to Intellectual Beauty*, already quoted;[2] all artists have won some glimpse of it, and thereafter sought it diligently.

Just in the degree in which the artist—be his medium what it may—succeeds in winning from us that concentration of attention which is the essential condition of aesthetic experience, he makes a claim implicitly to satisfy the human soul. The beautiful object claims and holds our minds as nothing is entitled to claim and hold them which has not the promise at least of that which saints have called the Beatific Vision. In the moment of deep appreciation, all movement of thought is checked; in place of the movement of thought there is the activity of receptive rest; in place of the apprehended movement of time there is

> The moment eternal, just that and no more
> When ecstasy's utmost we catch at the core;[3]

for in that moment Beauty, whether of nature or of art,

> Here, for the sight of mortal man, has given
> To one brief moment caught from fleeting time
> The appropriate calm of blest eternity.[4]

Now there is a strong tendency in many quarters to

[1] Wordsworth, *Elegiac Stanzas suggested by a Picture of Peele Castle, in a Storm, painted by Sir George Beaumont.*

[2] Cf. *supra*, pp. 25-26.

[3] Browning, *Asolando: Now.*

[4] Wordsworth, *Upon the Sight of a Beautiful Picture.*

suppose that the search for Truth leads to contact with Reality in a sense in which the aspiration towards Beauty does not. It is urged that the processes of science have a certainty which is absent from those of art, and that all who follow its course must accept its conclusions, except so far as they are known among scientists themselves to be provisional, while many seem quite insensitive to Beauty, and those who value it dispute fiercely among themselves concerning their aesthetic judgements. In the one case, we are told, there is possible, and largely actual, agreement; in the other there is the chaos of opinion which suggests that the standards of judgement are purely subjective.

But the certainty of scientific processes is confined to the sphere of the measurable; and no one supposes that measurability is the only element in ultimate Reality. For even if it be admitted for the moment that the only world outside of consciousness is a world of measurables, yet these by their impact upon consciousness set up an experience of non-measurable qualities, and that experience with its content, being extant, is part of Ultimate Reality. But when all the facts are considered, it does not appear that science has the advantage over art which is alleged. It takes a considerable time for a secure aesthetic judgement to be formed, and with regard to contemporary art there is much debate. But when a common judgement is reached after long period of discussion, it is secure as scientific theories never are. Men may be uncertain in this second quarter of the twentieth century about the aesthetic rank of Epstein as a sculptor or of T. S. Eliot as a poet. But there is no serious dispute about Pheidias or Aeschylus, about Giotto, or Piero, or Botticelli, about Velasquez or Rembrandt, about Dante or Shakespeare. No doubt I "date" myself by the precise list which I select; there are some who put Euripides above Sophocles, some who prefer Beethoven to Bach; but every name thus mentioned is securely established in the list of Masters; and the

The only exception to this of which I can think is really an illustration of the principle. For though Lucretius set out to make poetry out of materialism, it is noteworthy that his most poetic passages are those in which he escapes from his own creed and finds the counterpart of human thought and feeling in his subject or directly expresses such thought and feeling.[1] And so far as there is beauty in the picture of the swirling atoms, it arises (as I think) from the thought of man's helplessness before the mighty force; it is beautiful by reason of its significance for mind.

When we combine with such reflections as these the consideration that mind historically appears as the flowering into consciousness of the organism's relation to its environment, there seems no valid reason for doubting the ultimate deliverances alike of the scientific and of the artistic consciousness. This testimony is an unambiguous affirmation of transcendent Mind apprehended by reason of its immanence in Nature physical and spiritual. The justification and closer determination of the term "transcendent" will appear more fully later, but already it is unavoidable. The apprehension of Truth is, after the manner of science, the more detached, yet even thus it moves to reverence. The apprehension of Beauty is the more intimate, and moves to such submission of the finite mind to its unmeasured counterpart as is properly called worship.

> What soul was his, when, from the naked top
> Of some bold headland, he beheld the sun
> Rise up and bathe the world in light! He looked—
> Ocean and earth, the solid frame of earth
> And ocean's liquid mass, in gladness lay
> Beneath him: far and wide the clouds were touched
> And in their silent faces could he read
> Unutterable love. Sound needed none,
> Nor any voice of joy; his spirit drank
> The spectacle: sensation, soul, and form,
> All melted into him; they swallowed up
> His animal being; in them did he live,

[1] E.g. *De Rerum Natura*, ii. 252-266; iii. 894-911.

And by them did he live; they were his life.
In such access of mind, in such high hour
Of visitation from the living God,
Thought was not; in enjoyment it expired.
No thanks he breathed, he proffered no request;
Rapt into still communion that transcends
The imperfect offices of prayer and praise,
His mind was a thanksgiving to the power
That made him; it was blessedness and love.[1]

APPENDIX A

AMBIGUITIES IN THE TERMS BEAUTY AND VALUE

THE recent emphasis on Value in philosophical discussions has led to much confusion of mind because of the different senses in which the leading terms are used. This is partly due to real differences of apprehension and interpretation, partly to differences of habit or convention in the use of language. Thus for Professor Whitehead (*Adventures of Ideas*, p. 324) "Beauty is the mutual adaptation of the several factors in an occasion of experience". This is not far from Professor Laird's theory of "natural election" (*The Idea of Value*, pp. 92-113), which is, as Professor Alexander says (*Beauty and Other Forms of Value*, p. 288), "the simple fact that one thing matters to another in an intimate manner". It is not surprising that Whitehead, having given so wide a definition of Beauty, treats it as the most fundamental form of Value.

But he recognises a more specialised meaning of the word Beauty. "There is the primary meaning which has been given in Section I. . . . This is Beauty realised in actual occasions which are the completely real things in the Universe. But in the analysis of an occasion, some parts of its objective content may be termed Beautiful by reason of their conformal contribution to

[1] Wordsworth, *The Excursion*, Book I.

the perfection of the subjective form of the complete occasion" (p. 328). Here he comes nearer to Alexander, who is concerned to specify the mode of this "conformal contribution". "Beauty", says Alexander, "is that which satisfies objectively the aesthetic impulse or sentiment, that is, the constructive impulse used contemplatively, and is beautiful or has value because it pleases us after the manner so described" (pp. 179, 180).

I am not concerned with the psychological question to which impulse of our nature, if any, the beautiful is specifically related as its satisfaction; I confess that I find it hard, and in some instances of undoubted beauty far-fetched, to establish connexion with the constructive impulse. The vital point, in my judgement, is that Beauty is apprehended by contemplation, and here I am at one with Professor Alexander. But I am not content with his correlation of the subjective and objective factors in the aesthetic experience. I welcome his contention that Beauty is neither a Primary nor a Secondary Quality (pp. 180-183); and I can assent to his description of it as a Tertiary Quality (p. 183), in a phrase borrowed from Bosanquet, if a clear priority is attributed to the objective factor. But this, as it seems to me, Alexander is unwilling to do.

> "In the total experience of the beautiful, in its relation to the appreciating mind, the pleasure belongs to the mind, the beauty is referred to the object which is said to have value in virtue of its relation to the mind, which relation is already embodied in its own form. Value is thus experienced as pleasure, as marking in the mind the satisfaction of the aesthetic impulse. The beautiful is said to possess value or to be a value, but value is not a quality of the beautiful but its relation to the mind, which is a partner in the total experience of beauty. Satisfactoriness in the object, satisfaction in the subject: this is the distribution of parts in the whole complicated situation" (p. 184).

This is not very remote from the phrase which I have borrowed from Professor Bowman—Beauty exists objectively but is subjectively conditioned. My difficulty with Alexander's language is in the balance of "satisfactoriness" and "satisfaction". For it appears, at least, as though "satisfactoriness" must be defined by reference to what it satisfies, and this seems to me false to the aesthetic experience as I know it in myself. Just when that experience is most unmistakeable, its mode is not that of an object adapted to me but of my adaptation to an object. The Beautiful does not submit itself to my contemplative attention, but claims it, and continues to hold it even when my adaptation to it is so slight that I find in it as yet no pleasure, nor what I can naturally describe as satisfaction, but rather an imperious spell. I have tried to set this out more fully in *Mens Creatrix*, pp. 125-128.

My own suggestion for the interpretation of Value may be set out in summary form as follows:

The essential condition for the actualisation of Value is the discovery by Mind of itself or its own principle in its object.

When Mind makes this discovery in the activity of contemplation, the form of Value actualised is Beauty.

When Mind makes this discovery in the activity of analysis and synthesis, the form of Value actualised is Truth.

When Mind makes this discovery in the activity of personal relationship the form of Value actualised is Goodness.

It will be noticed that I include positive Values only. The common usage of language encourages this. It is true that the term Value is also used in a neutral sense to cover Evil as well as Good, as in the phrase "Value-Judgements". Yet to speak of anything as having great value is always understood as attributing to it great good. Evil as Ugliness or Error or Sin—is primarily conditioned by alienation between Mind and its object, though it also appears in the form of what is akin but hostile.

No doubt the correlation of Mind and its environment is only one instance of the fitting-together-of-things; and we can call this fitting-together "value" if we like. But the fitting-together of Mind and environment is special, and a special term is needed for it. I think that the philosophic use of the term Value will be most consonant with its ordinary use if it is reserved for this relationship.

Thus I agree that actual Value is a relation to Mind. But the valuable character is primarily in the object. The object is not merely such as to occasion a valuable experience in the Mind; the Mind in experiencing it appreciates it as valuable. Only in and through the subjective appreciation does this value become actual, but when it thus becomes actual it is objective. A man may be of a loving disposition, but he actually loves only when another person exists to be the object of his love; and then the love is in him, not in the occasion of its actualisation; so, turning from active to passive, the picture is always admirable, but the value of this is actual only when it is admired.

I add here a note on the "kinship" of Mind and Reality which plays a great part in my argument. When I say that Mind finds itself or what is akin to itself in its object, I mean an experience which has two aspects: first, that it finds the counterpart of the principle of its own activities as for example the mathematical properties of mechanical combinations of forces or of aesthetic proportions; secondly, that with this discovery goes a feeling of being at home with the object, not lost or bewildered in presence of it. The latter aspect is not capable of definition, but seems to me to be easily recognisable and profoundly significant.

LECTURE VII

MORAL GOODNESS

WE have adopted for convenience, though with some reserve as regards its principle, the familiar classification of ultimate values as Truth or Knowledge, Beauty and Goodness. We have considered the first two, and have found among other things that their common characteristic and the source of the satisfaction which they occasion, is the mind's discovery or recognition in its object of what is akin to itself. When the mind, having apprehended the object in all its parts, so grasps these as to find the principles of its own nature exemplified in the object, it is in possession of truth concerning that object. In order to reach this attainment it must discipline itself so as to be secure against imperfect observation on the one hand, and premature systematisation on the other. And the informing principle of this discipline is subjection of the mind to the object, for there is no general scheme of universal truth, which the mind can first master *a priori*, and thereafter require that any theories which are to be admitted as true shall conform to this. Yet this does not mean that the mind has no standard of its own by which to guide its judgement. Its standard is that of totality—the embrace of all relevant reality in a comprehensive unity—and by this it must guard itself from prejudice, from inaccuracy, and from acquiescence in partial apprehension. The whole process of Science is the witness that mind is justified in its endeavour to reach totality; and experience is the witness to the satisfaction inherent in such attainment of it as has hitherto been achieved.

Our study of Beauty as an ultimate value led to the same result. For though the method of mind's activity in its search for and enjoyment of Beauty is the very antithesis of its method in the search for Truth, yet the result is the same. By becoming wholly receptive in its relation to the object, mind apprehends the object as corresponding to its own standard of totality. And here, as the self-surrender is greater, the emotional quality of the satisfaction in attainment is more intense. But also, by claiming an attitude of pure receptivity in the mind that would give itself to aesthetic contemplation, the object points to what alone can make that claim with full right, namely, such a counterpart of mind that in contemplation of it mind's satisfaction would be complete.

The same principles will emerge as we turn to the third member of the trio. But at once we are faced with the fact that the absolute character of the Value or Good inherent in Moral Goodness is far more widely recognised and more weightily attested than is the absolute character of the Good of Truth or Beauty. The use of language is itself *prima facie* evidence that the connexion here is specially close. For we do not call a man "good" without further qualification in respect of his scientific or aesthetic qualities; we do so describe him in respect of his character; and the fact that moral excellence is alone called "goodness" shows that in general estimation here is a good or value uniquely "absolute". It might be replied that this use of language implies no more than a recognition that moral goodness is the goodness proper to a man as such, while artistic skill is the goodness proper to him as an artist, or intellectual grasp the goodness proper to him as a scientist. But that reply seems to betray an insensitiveness to the tone or colour of language, which does not in fact use the word "good" with indiscriminate facility for all kinds of excellence, intrinsic or instrumental. There is a sense in which the word "good" belongs to the good character as it belongs to nothing else at all. This is in full harmony with our doctrine that the essence of value or good is found through Mind's discovery of itself in its object. Only in other minds can a mind thus find its counterpart completely; here therefore is the true norm of absolute good.

This has, of course, been the basic doctrine of many of the greatest philosophers, and was most fully expressed in Kant's declaration that nothing is good absolutely except the good will. But at this point a distressing paradox presents itself; for the philosophers who agree in this impressive affirmation are shortly found to be in conflict with one another, if not also with themselves, concerning the nature of the will that alone is good and even concerning the meaning of the word "good" as used of that will. Kant, for example, thinks of the will as pure autonomy; but this for him involves the conclusion that no particular action is directly attributable to the will. For all actual occurrences, being phenomenal, fall under the category of causation imposed upon the data of experience by the understanding. So the good will, which is perfectly free, is noumenal, and therefore, unknowable, and the best that Kant can do is, to admit that this freedom, together with its law which is the moral imperative, is incomprehensible, and to claim that we comprehend its incomprehensibility.[1] In the same way the principle of goodness appears as the empty form of universality; but every moral choice is this particular choice in these particular circumstances, and in the judgement of mankind generally, the particularity, though never alone decisive, is often highly relevant to the question whether a given act was right or wrong.

It would be disproportionate to review the various suggestions put forward by different philosophers for dealing with this problem. It is more germane to the course of our argument that we should follow our own enquiry, letting it lead us as it will. We find in our experience of the world that there is upon us in some

[1] *Metaphysic of Ethics, ad fin.*

situations an obligation to act, or not to act, in certain ways. When we try to understand this in relation to other features of experience we discover two things: first, we discover that wherever this sense of obligation is present, it is uncompromising; secondly, that the types of conduct to which it is attached are different in different regions or in the same region during different periods of history. This second fact—the variety in the things which men are conscious of an obligation to do or not to do—has been used to discredit the consciousness of obligation itself. Because this appears to have dictated monogamy in Europe and to have permitted polygamy in Arabia, it has been held that the obligation itself is purely contingent, and that the consciousness of it is nothing more than the reaction of a character trained in certain social institutions towards what conforms to or departs from the principle of those institutions. It must be admitted that the untutored conscience, and in a less degree the trained conscience also, derives much of its actual content from its social environment, which is itself the product of history. But this consideration is by no means able to account for the imperative note characteristic of the sense of obligation. We reach here a point on which debate is futile. If any man after reviewing his own moral experience and that of the men of strongest character, as recorded in their deeds and words, still thinks that the consciousness of obligation can be analysed without remainder into a spontaneous tendency to act in conformity with the customs of his social context, he must be left to think so; but it is hard on that hypothesis to understand why the most imperative demands of conscience are demands that the individual should defy his social context. Luther's declaration before the Diet of Worms has not the appearance of an overwhelming impulse to conform to social context.

Yet the varieties of moral convention remain; and the difficulty of determining the proper object or sphere of obligation remains. It may be that by considering the latter of these we may throw light on the former also. A convenient starting-point for this consideration is provided by two books lately issued from Oxford. Dr. W. D. Ross, in his essay on *The Right and the Good*, clarifies the issue by drawing a sharp distinction between *action* and *act*. If that at first appears over-subtle, it is seen to be justified as soon as we translate these two words into Latin; no one would dispute the distinction between *actio* and *actum*. He proceeds to follow this distinction by attaching the term *right* to *acts*, and *morally good* to *actions*.[1] So far he seems to me to have done much to elucidate the problem. If A owes B a sum of money, it is (apart from some special circumstances to be mentioned later) right that he should pay that money to B. This has nothing to do with his motive in paying it. If he has made up his mind to avoid payment, and then out of fear pays after all, the right act is still done, though there is no moral goodness in the action. Mr. Joseph, in *Some Problems in Ethics*, does not draw the distinction between *act* and *action*, and fails to find anything commendable in the payment of the money unless it is done from a good motive, and defends this by saying that an action done from one motive is different from an apparently identical action done from another.[2] Most of us will regard this as an unduly subjective treatment of the question. For whatever A's motive may be, if A pays, B gets his money, and not otherwise. Now if B's right to receive the money stands in any vital relation to A's duty to pay it, the distinction between *act* and *action* solves our problem. The *act* of payment which satisfies B's claim is right because it satisfies that well-founded claim; but it remains true that A's *action* is morally good only if he acts from a good motive.[3]

[1] *The Right and the Good*, p. 7. [2] *Some Problems in Ethics*, pp. 37-58.

[3] If the debt is repaid by accident (*e.g.* by the writing of a cheque drawn to the creditor by accident, when another name was intended) the right thing has happened, but this is not in the ethical sense an "act" at all. In order that there may be an "act" there must be the intention to do it. But the intention to do the right act may spring from bad motives as well as from good.

But Dr. Ross could not be content with this; for having attached moral good to the *action*, he refuses to attribute any good or value to the *act*. It is *right*, and that is all that can be said about it. He is very explicit about this:

"What are we to say of rightness? We must, I think, say that it is intrinsic, but that in so far as a right act has value, its value is not intrinsic. The rightness of an act . . . is intrinsic to the act, depending solely on its nature. But if we contemplate a right act alone, it is seen to have no intrinsic *value*. Suppose for instance that it is right for a man to pay a certain debt, and he pays it. This is in itself no addition to the sum of the values in the universe. If he does it from a good motive, *that* adds to the sum of values in the universe; if from a morally indifferent motive, *that* leaves the sum of values unchanged; if from a bad motive, *that* detracts from the balance of values in the universe. Whatever intrinsic value, positive or negative, the action may have, it owes to the nature of its motive and not to the act's being right or wrong, and whatever value it has independently of its motive is instrumental value, *i.e.* not goodness at all, but the property of producing something that is good."[1]

In all this the claim of the creditor is not mentioned. In this view the good which consists in the creditor's just satisfaction is not part of the act, but something which it is instrumental in producing; the act is the restoration of the money. This analysis leaves the act suspended between the action of the debtor and the satisfaction of the creditor; it leaves the rightness of the act unrelated, not only to the motive of the debtor but also to the claim of the creditor. In other words the act is totally detached from its social context. It is clear that in the act thus detached there is no *good*; but it seems to me equally clear that there is nothing to be meant by calling it *right*.

Actual obligation arises in actual social relationships. It cannot be said without qualification that rights and duties precisely correspond, so that A's rights constitute B's duties and *vice versa*; but it is a manifest and

[1] *The Right and the Good*, p. 46.

important fact that they are closely related. To take once more the payment of a debt, the creditor's right to receive the money is the correlate of the debtor's duty to pay. This is apparent when we consider the special circumstances in which it is not his duty to pay. If the creditor goes mad between the lending of the money and the repayment, the duty may cease. If what was lent was not a coin but a weapon, and if the lender, having developed homicidal mania, demands the weapon back in order to murder some one, it becomes a positive duty not to return it. In each case the duty lapses because the claim has ceased to exist. Dr. Ross appears to be in some difficulty here, as might indeed be expected; for it is the penalty of abstraction that it leaves us helpless before the complexities of the concrete. He can only say that acts conforming to the general principles of right are *prima facie* right.[1] This carries us very far from consciousness of obligation; and there is no method of determining which *prima facie* right should prevail, when two or more conflict, except the utilitarian method which Dr. Ross condemns.

Of course the problems with which Dr. Ross is dealing are very real problems. His position, however unsatisfactory, is one to which he is driven by difficulties crying aloud for solution. The suggestion which will here be offered is that there is no solution of the problems of Ethics on the level of ethical science, but that the moral consciousness, from which they arise, itself points towards an apprehension of the world which does full justice to the moral consciousness, but is more than moral as that word is commonly understood. For the problems of Ethics arise out of the relations of finite spirits to each other, but can only be rightly determined by reference to the relation of those finite spirits to the Infinite Spirit.

The greatest of all attempts to state the fundamental

[1] *The Right and the Good*, pp. 132, 133.

principles of Ethics in independence of what lies beyond Ethics is that of Kant. For him the Moral Law is the essence of Practical Reason. Thus morality is the expression of the autonomous reason, and its principle is the universality characteristic of reason; the will that is wholly conformed to this categorical imperative is the one and only absolute good. We have already referred to the defects of his view as a guide in the practical difficulties of life. The reason why a man must not lie is on the one side that the lie is only effective if it is accepted as true and is therefore a contradiction in its own nature, and on the other side that lying would be useless if every one did it; and this reason shows all lying to be wrong. So if a man intent on murder asks which way his victim has gone, I must not lie in order to send him down a wrong road and so save the victim. But here Practical Reason parts company with common sense and the common conscience. If we try to save the situation by saying that it is always right to lie in such circumstances, we do not really save the universality of the principle; for the identical circumstances are never repeated. Moreover, this is a different kind of universality from that which Kant sets up as a criterion. His concern is for the universality of the principle itself; the last suggestion only refers to the characteristics of a type of circumstance. Nor is relief to be found through attaching universality to the agent by a declaration that it is right for me to do that, and only that, which it would be right for any one else in these circumstances to do; for some acts are right when done by persons of a certain character or in virtue of a certain office, which are wrong if done by a person lacking those qualifications. Thus one man may freely forgive an offending brother without waiting for any previous repentance, and also without giving the impression that he condones the wrong, while another will give that impression and therefore can rightly forgive only when repentance precedes. Again, it is right for the King to enter or leave a room before his own guests; it would be wrong, because discourteous, for most of his subjects to do so. It may well have been right for Christ to cleanse the Temple; it would certainly have been wrong, because presumptuous, if some ordinary Galilean pilgrim had done it.

We seem to be getting back into the difficulties which earlier we hoped to solve by the distinction of the *action* from the *act*, for it appears either that the rightfulness of an act may depend, if not upon the motive, yet upon the character of the agent, or alternatively that there may be things which ought to be done (such as the cleansing of the Temple) which yet no one alive ought to do. Perhaps the latter is a true account of some moral situations. But let us seek further elucidation in further distinctions. There are two main questions to be considered: (1) What is meant by or involved in the consciousness of obligation itself? (2) To what is obligation properly attached? And of those the second divides itself into subordinate questions. It will be convenient to take it first, though it assumes that some rational answer can be given to the former. For obligation cannot rightly attach to anything, unless it has its own rightful place in the scheme of things. But it will be easier to determine its grounds and implications if we first consider its proper sphere of operation.

The first consciousness of obligation is undoubtedly concerned with possible action. A situation arises in which all considerations of pleasure and self-interest point one way, but the sense of obligation intervenes to forbid such action. In the early stages the sense of obligation is nearly always negative in its import. But positive commands of conscience appear early, such as the recognition of duty to save a child from burning or from drowning, at the cost of great risk and certain inconvenience. Often, of course, the distinction is hardly apparent, so that it is not clear whether the obligation felt is a positive one to tell the truth or a negative one not to tell lies. But whether positive or negative, in all such cases as we are now considering the consciousness of obligation takes the form of a direct moral perception. It may proceed from reason, but it is not a product of argument or reflection. The "moral sense" school of moral philosophy is on sure ground in insisting on this fact. And the moral judgement of those spectators who are aware of the alternatives open and the choice made, is as a rule equally unreflective and spontaneous. It is like the perception of beauty; it exists or not, and there is no more to be said.

This is fully compatible, of course, with the need of training and experience if it is to be reliable; for what has been said is also true of the aesthetic sense. But the method of training is different in the balance of its component elements. The aesthetic sense is trained by attention to admittedly beautiful works. By beginning with those which the immature mind already appreciates, and passing on to others as it is able in some degree to appreciate these also, any man may greatly extend the range and improve the precision of his aesthetic appreciation. Analysis of the works of art studied will also be useful in its place, but it is mainly by the direction of attention to what is excellent that progress is made. In the realm of moral judgement, deliberate attention to noble acts and noble characters may similarly quicken the moral perceptions, and for nine-tenths of actual conduct this is the surest way to right judgement; but there are difficult cases of ethical perplexity such as must be dealt with, not by a finely tempered discrimination, but by reflection upon the principle implicit in perceptions already trusted or judgements confidently given. There is a kinship between moral and aesthetic perception; otherwise the "moral sense" school of ethics could never have arisen. But whereas in aesthetic questions the last appeal is to perception—a rationalised perception no doubt—in ethical questions the last appeal is to reason, even if to a perceptive reason.

For when the conscience of the individual is in conflict with the conscience of his fellows, the only way to resolve the conflict is to find by critical analysis the principles on which both unwittingly rely. Moral progress has largely come through the perception by some members of any society that principles commonly accepted by that society condemn some action, or custom, or institution, to which hitherto the principles had not directly been applied. It was so that Wilberforce and his colleagues carried the abolition of the Slave Trade. They compelled their Christian fellow-countrymen to recognise that the principles of the religion which they professed were incompatible with acquiescence in the Slave Trade or in the Institution of Slavery. It is so with every prophet. His appeal is not to a new principle, but to a new application of an old principle, so that he often presents himself as urging a return to the better ways of past generations. Few radical reformers can hope for great success who are unable to present themselves with perfect honesty as the only true conservatives.

The individual confronted with a moral perplexity has in the same way to think the matter out. That process has two parts. He must bring into clear consciousness the principles involved; and he must become aware so far as possible of the whole nature of his act—that is, of the train of consequences which his action will bring about. It is this latter element in the determination of duty which provides a basis for the various forms of Utilitarianism. The Utilitarians rightly insisted that a man has no right to bring about all manner of evil which it is possible for him to foresee, by thoughtless conformity to some generally accepted rule of conduct. But they confused the issue by speaking so much of consequences as though these were detachable from the act, so that the act was to be justified or condemned by its consequences, and not by its own quality. This gives rise to an impression that results in the way of pleasure or happiness are the sole moral criterion, or (still worse) that such results may overbalance a purely moral quality recognised as residing in the action, so that it may sometimes be right to do evil that good may come. But in many cases it is impossible thus to distinguish between an act and its consequences. That distinction can perhaps be drawn if we confine our attention to very simple ethical relationships and the duties involved in them, such as the relationship of debtor and creditor, and the duty of the debtor to repay what he has borrowed. In those cases there is seldom any doubt where duty lies. But if two duties conflict, it is impossible to confine attention to the act so narrowly conceived. If a man who has promised to meet a friend in London, in order to spend a day with him in conversation of a purely friendly sort, hears that his wife has been taken ill in Scotland and desires his immediate presence lest she should die before he reaches her, most of us will agree without hesitation that the latter claim is the stronger, and that it is right to break the promise and disappoint the friend; and most of us would justify that view on two distinguishable but not wholly separable grounds, namely, first the special claim of a wife upon husband or husband upon wife, and secondly the consideration that a greater and more irreparable evil is likely to result from refusing the latter claim than from failing to meet the first; and this evil we should regard as being not so much a consequence of the act, but rather the act itself. For *a man's act is the difference that he makes; the whole train of consequences flowing from his action is his real act*. In most private relationships we do not need to extend so greatly the field of attention. Debts should be paid; promises should be kept; lies should not be told. But even in these relationships some elasticity is recognised as desirable. Courtesy and truthfulness are often hard to combine. And in political life, with its indefinitely complex ramifications, a man's act, conceived as the difference that he makes, may be so vast in its extent that it is very hard to estimate the value of its component elements and form a just appreciation of it as a whole. A statesman, let us say, sincerely believes that it is for the good of the country that his party should remain in power; but he disagrees with his colleagues about one point in their policy; he is questioned on that point by his constituents; if he states his whole mind, he will damage his party and perhaps, if the balance of parties is close, cause its fall from power; so without stating his own view, and without actually expressing support of his colleagues' policy, he sets forth the best defence of that policy which he can make. He probably deceives his constituents; but there are circumstances imaginable in which it would be far from clear that his course was morally wrong. Another man might tell the whole truth, and win perhaps a more whole-hearted approbation of his character; but that would be quite compatible with holding that his course of action was mistaken, even morally mistaken. It is a quite consistent moral judgement that expresses itself in such terms as these: "I think it was a mistake, but it was a mistake that only a man of fine character would make".

If the contention of this argument is sustained, it is at once apparent that about many moral judgements there is an irreducible element of uncertainty. Where the act in question springs from a well-defined relationship and there are no relevant complicating factors, we may pronounce unhesitatingly that one act is right and another wrong. But in many instances this is impossible. The problem may be too tangled for complete analysis by our limited understandings, and sometimes at least the personal quality of the agent is itself a relevant factor. In other words Ethics can never be an exact science, and absolute obligation therefore attaches not to the act, but to the will. It is my absolute duty to will the right; but there is no act which it is my absolute duty, independently of circumstances, to do or not to do. Murder is always wrong, because murder is such killing as is wrong; but it is often open to dispute whether or not a particular instance of killing is murder.

A useful distinction is drawn by Dr. Oman between Conscience and Conscientiousness.[1] Conscience is our judgement upon acts contemplated or accomplished. When the suggestion to act in some definite way arises, conscience approves or disapproves. That is always important, and no man who is in earnest about the business of right living will ignore that verdict of his moral nature. But he must not attribute to it infallibility. His moral sense requires training, and that training is never complete; the real nature of the act, conceived as the difference made, needs to be thought out, and often that process can never be complete. Especially is it dangerous to trust the approbation of an untrained conscience, or (still more) its acquiescence. When conscience condemns an act, there is likely to be something wrong with that act; but that conscience acquiesces or even approves is not convincing evidence that all is right with the act. Of course the "scrupulous conscience", which condemns when there is no occasion, is a familiar fact, but of less frequent occurrence than the conscience which acquiesces too readily. Conscience, which we here understand as the spontaneous verdict of a man's moral nature, is not by any means a completely reliable guide to life. It may be the best that we have got at any moment, and we must act by it, but always with readiness to revise its judgements. "What is absolute can never apply to any verdict of conscience, but only to conscientiousness in following the upward road, to always choosing what excels."[2]

Thus as we search for the proper subject of absolute obligation we are driven back from act to agent, from conduct to character, from the "Do righteousness" of

[1] *The Natural and the Supernatural*, pp. 312-329. [2] Oman, *op. cit.* p. 324.

the Law to the "Be righteous" of the Gospel. *The absolute obligation lies upon the will to choose the right.* In order so to choose, it must call for all thought that is available in the time allowed; but that is part of the activity of truly willing the right. The possibility of doubt concerning what is right presents insuperable difficulties to the attachment of obligation to acts as such; but it presents none to the attachment of obligation to the will to choose what is right according to the best estimate that can be formed. Dr. Ross repudiates the utilitarian's distinction between an act and its consequences, but limits his attention to that part of the train of circumstance initiated which is specified by the moral rule in question. It is my duty to restore what I borrow; and I am not to be content with taking steps reasonably calculated to this end; I must "ensure" actual restoration. But while my "act" is thus interpreted as more than my physical movement, it stops short apparently when the moral rule in question has been observed. But this is an unwarranted abstraction. Dr. Ross attaches the attributes right and wrong to the act so taken in abstraction, and is led by this process of thought to deny that there is any good or value in right acts. It is a duty to do them, and there is good in the doing of them (which is action); but there is no good in the act. But how can there be good in doing that in which there is no positive value when it is done? The distinction of the act from the action makes for clearness; but the distinction of the act from the totality of result is a false abstraction creating endless confusion.

So we come back to the common-sense view that the right thing to do is the thing that is best on the whole. This is the view most fully formulated in recent times by Professor Moore who interprets "right" as "productive of the best possible consequences" or "optimific."[1] Plato came near to the same position when he laid down the maxim, Τὸ ὠφέλιμον καλόν, τὸ δὲ βλαβερὸν

[1] *Ethics*, p. 181.

αἰσχρόν—the useful is noble and the harmful base.[1] A man's act is the whole difference that he makes; his obligation, which is absolute, is to see that this is the best possible. Dr. Ross seeks to annihilate this position, but his attack on it completely fails. He takes the case of a promise, and states the argument thus:

"Suppose, to simplify the case by abstraction, that the fulfilment of a promise to A would produce 1000 units of good for him, but that by doing some other act I could produce 1001 units of good for B, to whom I have made no promise, the other consequences of the two acts being of equal value; should we really think it self-evident that it was our duty to do the second act and not the first? I think not."[2]

With that verdict all must agree, if, as I presume, the satisfaction of A's reasonable expectation is excluded from the 1000 units of good. But Dr. Ross will not admit the reason which those whom he is here criticising would advance, and which he states as follows:

"By keeping my promise I am helping to strengthen the system of mutual confidence; by breaking it I am helping to weaken this; so that really the first act produces $1000 + x$ units of good, and the second $1001 - y$ units; and the difference between $+x$ and $-y$ is enough to outweigh the slight superiority in the *immediate* effects of the second act. In answer to this it may be pointed out that there must be *some* amount of good that exceeds the difference between $+x$ and $-y$ (*i.e.* $x+y$)—say $x+y+3$. Let us suppose the *immediate* good effects of the second act to be assessed not at 1001 but at $1000+x+y+3$. Then its *net* good effects are $1000+x+3$, *i.e.* greater than those of the fulfilment of the promise; and the utilitarian is bound to say forthwith that the promise should be broken. Now we may ask whether that is really the way we think about promises? Do we really think that the production of the slightest balance of good, no matter who will enjoy it, by the breach of a promise, frees us from the obligation to keep our promise? We need not doubt that a system by which promises are made and kept is one that has great advantages for the general well-being. But that is not the whole truth. To make a promise is not merely to adopt an

[1] Said to be a most excellent saying: *Republic*, 457 B.

[2] *The Right and the Good*, pp. 34, 35.

ingenious device for promoting the general well-being;[1] it is to put oneself in a new relation to one person in particular, a relation which creates a specifically new *prima facie* duty to him, not reducible to the duty of promoting the general well-being of society."[2]

All of this is well said; but it misses the point. If it be true that behind the special relationship created by a promise, and lending its sanction to the duty created, there is the very high general interest in maintaining mutual confidence, then what is required to release a man from the obligation of the special duty created by the promise is not an actual balance of good in the course which involves a breach of the promise, but a general recognition of the existence of such a balance, so that public opinion understands and approves the act as a true exception to the rule; in that case general mutual confidence is not impaired by the exceptional act. This may be otherwise expressed by saying that exceptions to moral rules may be made when, but only when, the exceptional character of the occasion is so clear that breach of the rule will in no way suggest neglect of it. And if we may anticipate the result of our further argument, it will be found that the balance of good in favour of breaking a promise, or of evading any other *prima facie* duty, is never found except when there is some other *prima facie* duty to be met and it is not possible to perform both. Dr. Ross's method gives us no means of determining our choice between two incompatible *prima facie* duties; to do each act is right; to neglect either is wrong; and it seems that we are driven to determine a moral question by reference to non-moral considerations. From such invasion of the sovereign rights of morality we are protected if we say that our duty is always to do the right thing, and that the right thing is the act or difference made which contains the greatest possible good, so that part of our duty is to ascertain what this is.

[1] Indeed one does not see why Dr. Ross thinks that it is this at all.

[2] *Op. cit.* p. 38.

portance, as a warning against any tendency to confuse convenience with obligation; but it does not help us positively to determine what is right, and of course it carries us very far from the principles or method of Kantian ethics.

Let us attempt a more concrete, a more organic,[1] method of treating the subject. We find ourselves living in a world that consists of inanimate nature, of animals, and of human beings. We know that experience has value for us as good and bad. At first we tend to interpret good and bad as consisting respectively of pleasure and pain; but from the first it is not only our own pleasure and pain. The child very early reckons as bad any suffering of pain by his mother; it saddens him that she should be sad. Later, but still early, he apprehends this as a principle; not only is his pain bad for him, but in his catalogue of bad things is pain suffered by any one whom he loves. It is not regarded as bad for him in any such sense as implies that his only reason for wishing it otherwise is that it causes him distress; that is a complete falsification of any unsophisticated experience. The child who is sorry to see his mother in pain does not wish that pain away in order to end his own sorrow; what he resents is not his sorrow but her pain. In other words, we are from the beginning, and by the very constitution of our nature, bound up with one another, so that the weal and woe of each is in itself the weal and woe of all others within the circle of intimate relationships.

As experience develops, self-consciousness develops also. The growing child, and still more the adolescent, becomes increasingly conscious of himself as distinct from his fellows. This may show itself in the form of doubt whether there is any need for him to rejoice in the joys of others or sorrow in their griefs; shall he not follow what has value for him, refusing to allow the

[1] *Ἔτι καὶ ὧδε φυσικῶς ἄν τις ἐπιβλέψειε τὴν αἰτίαν* (Aristotle, *Eth. Nic.* vii. 1147 a 24).

good and evil of others to present themselves to him as his own? As a matter of experience, very few really feel exactly this perplexity even if they seem to themselves to do so. They are not escaping from the bonds of human solidarity, but feeling the pressure of new bonds, which it is not easy to adjust to the old. The boy feels like a bold and bad self-seeker because he has become united in links of common feeling with a new group of friends, whose joys and sorrows are more vividly present to his consciousness than those of his family. If the claims of the two conflict, he may say that he intends only to please himself; but what he means is that he is more concerned to please his new friends than the old. He has not, as a subject of value-judgements, become an isolated unit.

In the very few instances where for a time some approach is made to such moral self-isolation, the person concerned very soon discovers that, even from the selfish standpoint, sheer self-seeking is unprofitable. The only life worth living is one which accepts the benefits of civilisation, and society takes care that it is not worth while for any one to receive all the benefits of membership in it without paying any regard to its demands. An attempt to organise life on a basis of selfishness would lead to a social order in which each individual would in fact conform to the requirements of the common good, even though only from selfish motives.[1] Selfishness thus contradicts itself. I can only serve myself by serving, at least a little, the common good; and this is so because I am in essence a member of society. Membership of family and nation is not an accidental appendage of my individuality, but a constitutive element in it. It is always vain to say "If I had been a son of Napoleon Bonaparte" or any such thing. I *am* the son of my own father, and if he had had no son, but Napoleon had had an additional one, that means that some one else would have been born instead

[1] Cf. Plato, *Republic*, 358-362.

of me. Membership, such as carries with it a share in a common weal and woe, is an essential element in our nature; and an effort to repudiate it is always found to be a reassertion of it by implication.

This actual membership of our own society, which is part of the constitution of our nature, is the root of the consciousness of obligation. As self-consciousness develops, there appears the contrast between that which seems to be for the interest of the self and that which seems to be for the interest of the community. It is through its contrast with the former that the latter acquires the characteristic of obligation. The fully moralised man, whose only pleasure is in doing good, is no longer conscious of obligation to do it; but if ever he lost his perfect equipoise and integration through the emergence of a strong impulse to do what was contrary to the general good, the claim of the general good would at once assume the form of obligation over against that unusual impulse.

In early stages the community of which membership is recognised is small and sharply limited. Moral progress consists largely in the widening of the area in which the obligations of membership are recognised. But this presents problems of its own. To call men to appreciate the limitations of their present objects of loyalty in the interest of a wider fellowship may have the effect of detaching them from the one without binding them to the other. The patriot often fears the internationalist, because he knows the real and great good that is in national loyalty, and is justly anxious lest this be lost and its place taken by a flaccid cosmopolitanism, calling forth no deep loyalty and no self-devotion. Yet the way of progress is from the smaller to the wider unit, till all human beings are recognised as possessing a claim upon us to treat them as our fellow-members in the human family.

Different codes of conduct are appropriate to the successive stages of this process. Whenever men have employed some degree of moral criticism in reading the Scriptures of the Old Testament, some have been perplexed to read (for example) that God commanded Jehu to entrap and slaughter "all the prophets of Baal, all his worshippers, and all his priests".[1] Our grandfathers dealt with this perplexity by explaining that God indeed is unchanging, but man's understanding of Him grows from stage to stage; the divine commands in the Old Testament which shock our consciences were all that men could understand of His will for them. To us it seems more adequate to say that God is indeed unchanging, and always wills the truest welfare of all His children; but at a certain stage of their development it is good for them to do and to suffer what at a later stage would no longer be good for them. Therefore, being then as always Holy Love, He may have chosen for the worshippers of Baal that they should be slain and for Jehu that he should slay them, even by treachery, because only by such means would Israel be turned from a religion that for them, at any rate, was worse than none, and only so could Jehu express and fortify such faith in the God of Righteousness as his gross nature was capable of holding. Such reflections are very dangerous, no doubt. We tend to use them in order to blunt our consciences. But the repudiation of them is, in the long run, still worse, for it tends to destroy the sense of obligation by attempting to force it artificially into activity. That sense of obligation is the spontaneous reaction of a person who is a member of society towards acts or suggestions which conform to or contradict the standards of conduct which under the influence of experience have come to be accepted in his community. That those standards are what they are is due to history—partly to biological, partly to social, history; the various moral codes that are to be found in different regions and different epochs are a deposit from the past and reflect present conditions as

[1] 2 Kings x. 18-28.

the outcome of former conditions. But not only is that so; it ought to be so. Our actual obligations depend on our membership of society and on the character of the society of which we are members. As a great philosopher of the last generation would have had us learn, the clue to most of life's problems is to be found in the phrase "My Station and Its Duties".[1]

But that does not affect the nature of obligation itself, or the inherent logic which makes it a principle of progress. For no stage or level of civilisation is satisfactory in itself; certainly no one proposes to leave all things just as they are in this present year of grace! The sense of obligation to serve the common good as apprehended at any time is inevitably a sense of obligation also to apprehend it better. The limitations set to the community in which membership, with its obligation of loyalty, is recognised are more and more evidently accidental or artificial. At one point after another it becomes manifest that the accepted convention is in fact contradictory of the principle of fellow-membership which is the root and moral sanction of all conventions, until the one universal law is known in the form "Thou shalt love thy neighbour as thyself", where "neighbour" is interpreted, as in the Parable of the Good Samaritan,[2] to mean any human being with whom even accidental contact occurs, and even though according to current convention he would be an object of hatred and contempt.

Membership is a fact of our nature, and the sense of obligation is its expression. But we are not creatures who live only by impulse or instinct. We are capable of reason, though we use it so little; and that is another way of saying that we are capable of apprehension of, obedience to, and fellowship with, what is absolute and universal. This gives to man as a subject of value-judgements a status far removed from that of a calculator of transient pleasures and pains. In the claims

[1] F. H. Bradley, *Ethical Studies.*

[2] St. Luke x. 30-37.

of Truth and of Beauty man is aware of something to which the sense of obligation responds. As he responds his mind finds what is akin to itself in the object, and he is on the way to learning that it is not only of a human community that he is a member, but also of a society which includes the myriad tribes of nature, animate and inanimate, because through all there lives and moves that Mind, or Other akin to mind, with which in his Science and his Art man enters into fellowship. It is because a man's relation to Truth and Beauty is thus a social relation—a relation to another Mind or Somewhat akin to Mind—that the claim of Truth and Beauty constitute an obligation, and not only the offer of an august satisfaction. In virtue of all this super-animal life, whereby he aspires and partly attains to fellowship with the universal and absolute, man is known as not only a subject of value-judgements, but a focus of actualised value. That is most plainly seen in the fact of obligation itself; when a man for duty's sake sacrifices his own interest or his life, he affirms himself in his capacity of membership to be more and better than his isolated self with all its pleasures and pains. To have a sense of absolute obligation is implicitly to claim inherent and ultimate value. Moreover that discovery by mind of what is akin to itself, which we found to be the essential condition of Value and to be characteristic of the attainment of Truth and Beauty, reaches its completest earthly expression in that very sense of membership which is the root principle of moral obligation. Here Person recognises Person, and the common principle of Personality in both.[1] But to find oneself in another, so that both are apprehended as one, is love. Therefore "love is the fulfilling of the Law".

It is this recognition of the ultimate value of Persons

[1] For the transition from Mind to Personality see my Lectures on *The Nature of Personality* and *Christus Veritas*, chap. iv. The main point is that Mind may be chiefly, or indeed wholly, concerned with the finding of means to fixed ends, whereas Spirit (the distinctive element in Personality) appears in the choice between ends, which is made possible by the capacity of Mind for "free ideas".

which clothes with so austere a sanctity those duties that arise out of special personal relationships. Dr. Ross is right to hold that the good to be gained by breaking a promise must be very great before it is right to break the promise, but he does not probe deep enough for the ground of his conviction. It is not because "a promise is a promise" that a man must keep it at great inconvenience to himself and even to others. It is because a promise creates a personal claim, and to break it for any reason which the man to whom it was made cannot be expected to regard as compelling, is to ignore his claim and so to flout the sanctity of his personality. Here we are close to the second form of Kant's Categorical Imperative: "So act as to treat humanity, whether in thine own person or in that of any other, in every case as an end withal, never as a means only".[1] Kant rightly advances from this to the declaration that "Morality consists in the reference of all action to the legislation which alone can render a kingdom of ends possible". We hold, as has been seen, that in the complex and varying circumstances of life, this may sometimes be action which the first form of the Categorical Imperative would condemn; but that, we now see, is because Kant interpreted his formula abstractly. The essential principle of his argument is that which in a more concrete form we have now been following.

The principle of morality is that we should behave as Persons who are members of a Society of Persons—a Society into which Personality is itself a valid claim of entrance. We are to treat all Persons as Persons, and all as fellow-members with us in the Society of Persons. Actual duties will depend upon actual personal relationship; there is a special duty of parent to child and child to parent; there is a special relationship between citizens of any one nation; the duty of an Englishman to a Frenchman is not to treat him as if he were an Englishman, or as if no national distinctions existed,

[1] *Op. cit.* p. 56.

but to recognise that devotion to France is as excellent in him as love of England is in an Englishman. In practice, no doubt, the main task of each man's moral life is to secure that his own self counts for no more with him than any one else's self. Here lies the danger of all particular loyalties. The Englishman should be loyal to England, not because it is his country, but because he is its citizen—not because in some sense it belongs to him, but because in a far deeper sense he belongs to it. And this stage is the more easily reached as we follow the sound principle of checking each narrower loyalty by what is wider. A man cannot do much to serve humanity as a whole directly; he must give his service to his own unit; but he can check the narrower loyalty by the wider, so that he will serve his family, but not at cost to his country, and will serve his country, but not at cost to mankind.

The perception that duty is concerned with all the varieties of persons, so that we may serve them best being what they are, leads to an apprehension of it as requiring infinitely delicate adjustments such as are not to be reached by deliberate ratiocination. Consequently those are right who insist that the voice of conscience as it is heard in relation to actual conduct does not utter the verdict of reflective reason. Moreover our reflective reason is sometimes quite unable to afford justification for what none the less remains an unassailably assured moral judgement. But for this unreasoned confidence we can assign two rational grounds.

(1) Reflective reason must accept from intuition the ultimate judgements of value, and the diversity of judgements pronounced by different people on different characters and different acts springs from a divergence at this point. We have commended, with reference to the estimate of acts, what is indistinguishable from "ideal utilitarianism". We have repudiated the intuitionism which holds that right and wrong are inherent qualities of acts, which can be perceived by

the mature and sensitive moral consciousness, and have said that a man's act is the whole difference he makes, and that this is right when it is the best possible. But here we part company with the historic school of Utilitarians. We hold that what chiefly matters is the judgement of what is "good" and of the various grades of good. The great Utilitarians held that the good is pleasure, and their error was not in being utilitarian as regards conduct but in being hedonist as regards the true ends of life. Plato also is utilitarian, as we have seen, as regards conduct; but if we say that "the useful is noble, and the harmful base", we must at once ask—Useful for what? harmful for what? And then Plato's answer is unmistakeable; the end is Righteousness. Moral value resides not in acts or actions, but in a certain type of character—the righteous character. This is the character which subordinates all other considerations to the claims of the community of persons. But because it is of persons, the highest interest of the community and of its members is a personal interest, the fulfilment of their being as Persons; and this is Righteousness. Plato speaks with the authentic voice of morality when he complains that those who had great repute as statesmen had "filled the city full of harbours and docks and walls and revenues and such trifles to the exclusion of temperance and righteousness".[1] For whatever is a truly personal good—a good which resides in a person—takes priority over all non-personal goods, because morality is the discovery or recognition by persons of personality in others, to whom by the common attribute of personality they are bound in the ties of community membership. What most concerns this is therefore the highest good. That is why moral considerations must take precedence of aesthetic, if the two conflict. The essential condition of Value is the discovery by mind of itself in its other; this is only perfectly accomplished when the other is itself a living

[1] *Gorgias*, 518 E.

mind or person. Therefore ethical good is itself the fulfilment of intellectual and aesthetic good, and Goodness supplies to Truth and Beauty their proper norm by which, if need arise, they are rightly regulated. The same consideration shows why it is better that thousands should die in tumults rather than that order should be preserved at the cost of injustice voluntarily done to one innocent man. For the suffering and death of the body does not involve deterioration of character; but that injustice should be inflicted on innocence is an outrage on the sanctity of personality, while voluntarily to inflict it is to repudiate that sanctity and the obligations which it imposes. The maxim of Caiaphas[1] had a meaning far profounder than he knew, and in that meaning it is true; but in the meaning of his own intention it is the quintessence of cynicism and detestably false.

Now personal relationships can seldom be precisely formulated; and as our actual obligations are such as arise out of our actual moral relationships they can seldom be represented by any formula. For this reason, as well as because in these relationships intuition so far outstrips reflection, it is best in action to rely chiefly on the spontaneous reaction of our moral nature to the situation confronting us. Because we are imperfect that reaction will be imperfect. But the cleansing of our characters is mainly a matter of constant discipline, not of sudden choice at the moment of action. A man is only fully moral who does the right because it is right; but he usually has not time to scrutinise his motives when the occasion for action comes. In his leisure he should criticise his conscience by reflection, and discipline his character by meditation; but at the moment for action he must act, being what he is, and knowing that his spontaneous judgements, however much they still need correction, have the authority of the garnered experience of the race.

(2) Yet that does not appear an adequate account of

[1] St. John xi. 50.

the majesty of moral law. It is not only that we may see ourselves as others see us or count ourselves for no more than others, that we must discipline our characters.

"For the judgement of oneself in action, which is of the essence of morality, is not a judgement of praise and blame, in which a man sees his own acts with the same eyes as those of his friends, and rejoices or despairs accordingly, making all allowances for defective equipment and restricting circumstance; it is something far more persistent and exacting than that, and much less respectful of existing fact. It is the tormenting consciousness of a stricter logic, a higher level of execution, always within reach if the spirit is willing, which leaves no room for rest or contentment; but yet justifies the act so far as it succeeds in pressing its claim. It is not egoism or altruism; it is no thought of self or others, or of the relation between them. But it may take Spinoza's name, the *conatus in suo esse perseverandi*, 'the effort to persevere in one's being'; for he who is committed to living is committed to living as well as he can."[1]

But how can it be that the inner logic of a man's nature should prompt him to ignore his own interest for that of his friend or his country? Does this not mean that man is by his nature shown to be created for love? And does not this again imply that in the ground of his being, and therefore in the ground of that natural order of which he is the most elaborately developed product within our knowledge, there must be the spring of that love which thus wells up in him? That question we must defer. But if an affirmative answer is given it will help us to solve the other open problem which our investigation has left on our hands. For the one satisfactory form of the moral law we have found to be—"Thou shalt love thy neighbour as thyself". But love is not at our command. We may force ourselves to act as if we loved, but it can only be with partial success; for where real love is absent there is failure also of the insight of sympathy by which the true welfare of the neighbour is discerned. Conscientiousness without love is clumsy. Moreover, we cannot force ourselves very

[1] J. L. Stocks. *The Limits of Purpose*, pp. 78, 79.

far in this direction; for the direction must come from the will; and, if there is no love, the will cannot force us or our lower nature, for it has no such desire in itself; and if it has that desire, that is love. We are enclosed in a net of helplessness. Only by love can we fulfil the law, and love is not at our command.

But if the ground of all the universe and of our own being is Personal Love, to which we owe our origin and our maintenance in being, then it may be that as we penetrate to that which is ever more than ourselves and yet is also the very life of our life, we may find the ability which we now lack.

If we anticipate the results of future discussion we can offer this summary of moral obligation: Your being is personal; live as a person in fellow-membership with all others who, being personal, are your fellow-members in the community of persons. Strive to grow in fullness of personality, in width and depth of fellowship; and seek to draw the energy for this from that to which you and all things owe their origin, the Personal Love which is Creator and Sustainer of the world.

APPENDIX B

THE MORAL PROBLEM PRESENTED BY A CONFLICT OF OBLIGATIONS

THERE is an excellent illustration of this problem in Mr. Sinclair Lewis's novel, *Martin Arrowsmith*. The hero is a medical student trained under the inspiration of a professor wholly dedicated to the pursuit of truth. When the student enters on his medical career, he is confronted by a series of temptations arising from the social life in which he finds himself from time to time as this affects both himself and his wife. In these the ethical problem is fairly simple, and the interest is chiefly the psychological interest of watching the hero's reaction to it.

The last temptation is different. The hero is sent to a plague-stricken island. A serum has been discovered which is believed to provide a certain cure, but it has not been fully tested. The professor urges his pupil to divide the island into two halves of approximately equal population, and then to treat with the serum all sufferers in one half and none in the other. Thus it would be possible to apply the Joint-Method of Agreement and Difference (the most reliable of inductive methods) and reach genuine knowledge concerning the efficacy of the supposed remedy. The professor points out that by taking this course his pupil will vastly benefit all future generations at the cost of leaving a few hundreds of people to die in agony, or to see their children die in agony, who would have been bound so to die before the remedy was found; service to humanity made, he argued, the same claim as loyalty to truth.

But the hero himself, confronted with the despairing anguish of those whom he attempted to repel, and who had a pathetic faith in the potency of the untried remedy, could not refuse their plea. He treated all inhabitants alike, and the professor died heart-broken that his favourite pupil should have failed in loyalty to truth. Which was right?—the pupil or the professor? We may admire the professor's devotion to truth, and perhaps to the highest interest of humanity in the long run. But we must say that he was ethically wrong and the pupil ethically right, because the course recommended by the professor involved treating one half of the sufferers as means only and not as ends in themselves. It could only be right to use those sufferers as material for experiment if they volunteered to be so used.

I have not read Mr. Sinclair's book for several years. If I have misrepresented it, I hereby apologise. It is the impression remaining in my mind and here set forth which supplies the illustration of my argument.

LECTURE VIII

PROCESS, MIND AND VALUE

It is necessary that we should pause at this point to review once more the relation of Mind to the Process in which and out of which it arises, to consider the significance of the Values which Mind discovers in its experience, and to determine the implications of our results for our view of Reality as a whole. We have completely repudiated the Cartesian separation of Mind and Extension, and have accordingly rejected by implication both Idealism (which starts with Mind and makes the extended world adjectival to it) and Materialism (which starts with the Extended World and makes Mind adjectival to, or epiphenomenal to, this)—though our starting-point is closer to Materialism than to Idealism. For we start with the picture which Science gives us of a world undergoing modification through the interaction of its constituent parts while as yet there is, apparently, no mind within it to observe its process. At a certain stage in the development of certain organisms, consciousness appears; and it first appears as an aid towards making effective the reactions of the organism.

But here at once a problem confronts us. For the consciousness which then makes its appearance must be either due to a combination of circumstances which are in their own nature not consciousness, or must be there inserted by a fresh creative act of whatever gives rise to existence in all its forms, or else must have been present throughout, though in a form so rudimentary as to be imperceptible and negligible. Of these alternatives the first may be immediately ruled out. To suppose that a combination of non-conscious physiological functions can be the cause of consciousness in the organism concerned is to assert so great disparity between cause and effect as to rob the notion of causation of all meaning. To suppose that a physiological organism becomes conscious only because its own evolution has brought it to a certain stage of complexity would be like supposing that the mechanical robot at a street corner will automatically turn into a policeman if the traffic is sufficiently congested.[1] If it be urged that upholders of this view only mean that on the occasion of a certain stage of complexity being reached consciousness always makes its appearance, we must reply that such occasionalism is an evasion of the issue. A philosophy which leaves the appearance of consciousness or mind as a brute fact incapable of explanation or of intelligible relation to the general scheme of things is self-condemned as bankrupt.

Are we then to posit a new creative act wherever consciousness is found, or to hold that it is present throughout and begins, at this stage of development, not to exist but to function perceptibly? When we have finished our discussion of the relation of Mind to Process, it will be evident that no ultimate issue hangs on the answer to this question; but there is the convenience of more obvious continuity if it be assumed that the novel factor at this stage is the appearance rather than the creation of consciousness. This view is implied in Dr. Whitehead's use of the word "feeling" to denote the interaction of non-conscious entities. Thus his interpreter says that "feeling of an external world as causally affecting us is prior to conscious awareness of it as an object of perception".[2] But while we may for convenience adopt this view, we do so provisionally only, regarding the question as one to be settled, if ever, by experiments which may test the presence of more than physical processes in the observed reactions of the entities examined.

When once consciousness has appeared, it introduces certain novelties. It delivers the organism from a mere

[1] Cf. Oman, *Natural and Supernatural*, p. 45.
[2] Emmet, *Whitehead's Philosophy of Organism*, p. 94.

repetition of routine. Even at a rudimentary stage it presents future events as grounds for present action, a thing impossible within the purely physical series of causation. At a later stage it takes a more complete control, and in the human being we find consciousness deliberately using reflection upon past experience in order to secure that future experience shall not be a repetition of it. In this familiar reflection upon the past to modify the future a great deal is implicit which we must shortly attempt to elucidate. What matters for our present purpose is that this entirely non-physical activity determines the behaviour of the organism. But the most minute introspection will disclose no transition from consciousness to movement; when I will to move my hand, as St. Augustine observed,[1] forthwith it moves. There is no trace of a causal transition, as though will moved the limbs as the cue moves the billiard-ball —by impact. In a healthy organism the movement is the bodily expression of the volition. The two, though distinguishable, are inseparable; they are organically one. If some lesion or other cause prevents the hand from moving, the volition is, no doubt, still present. But it is a thwarted volition. And when it has its proper expression in the movement of the hand, this is not an external result of the volition but is the volition organically active. The true nature of that one thing is mind, not mechanism. Whether or not there is rudimentary consciousness in all organic and even in inorganic entities, it is certainly true that in so far as mind takes control of any organism it becomes its real principle of unity. That is why bodily ills may sometimes be cured by suggestion, and Dr. Oman is fully entitled to say that "the plain presupposition of this power of mind over body is that the organic functions, however many mechanical operations they may use, are, in so far as life is essential to them, subconscious mental functions".[2]

[1] Cf. *Confessions*, Bk. VIII. chap. ix.
[2] *The Natural and the Supernatural*, p. 269.

Thus, starting without any of the presuppositions of Idealism, and from an initial view far nearer to Materialism, we are none the less led to an account of the living organism, and specially the human organism, as essentially and fundamentally spiritual, or at the least mental. Where Mind is found, it is found as potentially, and always in some degree actually, the principle of unity of that through which it is active. It is not another thing, so that we have to choose between the absurdities of psycho-physical parallelism and the semi-mechanical treatment of Mind involved in a theory of Interaction between Mind and Body. But where Mind is actively present with Body at all Mind and Body are one thing, of which the dominant character is Mind so far as Mind is active.

Mind first appears as an organ for the satisfaction of needs, and even of physical needs. The organism which is capable of self-motion must determine the direction of its motion, and so soon as there is a comparison of different possibilities of action with a view to selection between them, Mind is at work. But so soon also as such a comparison is instituted, it becomes apparent that it is the general quality of the various objects in the environment, and not their particularity, which is of importance to the organism.[1] Thus attention is fixed on general qualities, and science is become possible. For attention, in fixing itself on the general qualities of objects, detaches these in thought from the objects themselves, and so forms concepts, which the mind can handle in complete independence of particular objects, though they have application and meaning only in reference to particular objects. The mind may make a combination of concepts which is exhibited by no actual object, such as the Chimaera; but such combinations are justly called chimerical. Real thinking, though it makes use of concepts throughout its course, is directed to the actual world of objects, which are particular

[1] See Lecture VI. pp. 142-144.

instances of general qualities, and seldom, if ever, exhibit any general quality in precise correspondence to the concept, because the presence of other general qualities involves some modification of that which is the special object of attention. Consequently conceptual thought is more precise and clean-cut than the experience from which it abstracts its general qualities for detached consideration, and in theory as truly as in practice we should expect to find that some margin of variation must be allowed for in the transition from the conceptual to the empirical world.

But the mind, having the power to form concepts, is thus set free from bondage to particular occasions. The concept is a "free idea". "Only because man can take his ideas out of their context and apply them freely in any other context, could he either have created or applied his science."[1] In the next lecture we shall consider the importance of this freedom of the mind in connexion with man's moral responsibility and the control of his conduct. But we must first examine the nature of the free activity of mind, and what it implies with regard to the process within which it occurs.

The first and most conspicuous feature of the free activity of mind is its detachment from successiveness. This is the source of all theories which represent Reality as timeless, and treat Time (with Kant) as a form of perception imposed by the mind upon its experience in the act of apprehending it. But our view here is closer to Whitehead than to Kant.

> "The abiding value of the Kantian philosophy lies in the discovery that an act of experience is a process of construction. But according to Kant, the objective world is constructed by the subject experiencing; while in Whitehead's Philosophy of Organism the experiencing subject arises out of the world which it feels, and constructs its own nature from the way in which it feels it."[2]

[1] Oman, *The Natural and the Supernatural*, p. 244.

[2] Emmet, *op. cit.* p. 48.

That, so far, is precisely the view which we are here adopting. But one of the ways in which the human experiencing subject feels the world is to gather up in the span of a single comprehension an entire period of the process out of which it arises. A man is born at a particular point in history. At first his mind moves only in the service of his bodily needs; but even so it very soon uses memory of the past to guide action in the present. Gradually, as language is acquired, the general qualities offered by perceived objects are more and more detached from the empirical instances by the help of the names for these which language supplies; sequences are traced out; and at last something that may be called a historical grasp of personal life, of family, of nation, is found to exist.

What is implied in this? First, that "present" experience is apprehended as continuous with the "past" out of which it arises. The "present" is never the mathematical point at which past and future meet; that concept is a fruit of abstraction. The present is so much of the empirical process as is immediately apprehended. This is far more than the passing sense-impression of the moment. It is all which is apprehended as continuous with that impression. And this may be an indefinitely long stretch of duration. A great work of art is always a unity, adequately appreciated only when grasped as a unity. *Hamlet*, if presented without omissions, occupies several hours. But it is properly appreciated only when apprehended as an experienced unity. It is in such products of human art that the principles which we seek are best illustrated, because these are creations of the human mind, fashioned with reference to its capacities and limitations. If we try to build up the dramatic experience called *Hamlet* out of a series of successive "present" moments, we shall soon be baffled. *Hamlet* is a unit, divisible into shorter stretches of duration called Acts and Scenes, and even into lines and words. Every one of these occupies time which passes during the utterance even of a word. But if we begin at the other end, with the mathematical point of present time, we can never arrive at duration at all, still less at an empirical unit which is itself a process. Whitehead is admittedly involved in difficulties by his start from atomic actual entities, and indeed there is no solution of the difficulties inherent in that method of approach.[1] The primary datum of experience is a *continuum*; we may analyse it in any ways that are found useful for theory or for practice, and the result of every analysis is a group of actual entities. But they are not atomic. Nor is there any last point of all conceivable analysis which can be regarded as the ultimate constituent of reality. The world as given in experience is an articulated unit. We understand it by tracing out its articulations; but if we allow this process to obscure the continuity of the whole, we have let our thought lose touch with the given fact.

The mind is distressed by the apparent transitoriness of all things. *Arising out of flux, and itself in origin an episode of the flux out of which it arises, mind declares its own nature by demanding permanence.* It achieves this in two ways. One is by formulating changeless principles of the constant change of experience—laws which, themselves unchanging, describe the course of change which the various objects of attention follow; this is the method of science. The other is by holding a durational period in a single apprehension so that process becomes a constituent of the non-successive experience achieved. This is the method of Art. It is essential to the drama of *Hamlet* that the scenes should succeed each other as they do; if all were played at once, the drama would be destroyed; if their order were altered, it would be another drama. Process, and precisely this process, is indispensable; but the process is a unit, and ideally

[1] It is doubtful whether "atomic" is the right word to use, but it is Whitehead's own: cf. "Continuity concerns what is potential; whereas actuality is incurably atomic" (*Process and Reality*, p. 84).

should be complete in the apprehension of the spectator as a "present" fact.

No doubt it would seem curious to regard as present at 11.15 P.M., when the play closes, the rising of the curtain upon the opening scene at 8 P.M. But it is all a question of degree. We all regard as "present" what happened $\frac{1}{1000}$ of a second ago; why not what happened $\frac{1}{10}$ of a second ago, or a second ago, or an hour, or a day, or the thousand years which are said to be for omniscience as one day? Of course the drama is only part of the spectator's total experience; other, and artistically irrelevant parts of that experience are also in process. If to his aesthetic soul 8 P.M. is still "now" at 11.15 P.M., to the physical appetite the meal taken at 7 P.M. may be a long while ago. Art gives us, in a selected and deliberately ordered portion of experience, an illustration of what might be extended over the whole of it if our faculties were sufficiently developed. In every act of sensation there is already memory of its first instant, and when memory alone retains the sense-perception, it may still be "present" if its continuity with sensation is not only conceptually thought but organically felt. It is where the whole organic or personal being is involved, as the great dramatist goes far to involve it, that the "present" is extended to cover a great stretch of what to indifferent observation is "past". In other words, only Love is qualified to view the world *sub specie aeternitatis*.

The "past" is that which can be inferred from "present" sense-perception. We infer the death of Julius Caesar from documents and other extant forms of evidence. That is truly past. And in ordinary activities, when the mind is not specially stimulated to extend its span, continuity is felt as extending over very short stretches of duration, so that if I am to know what happened five minutes ago it must be by deliberate recollection or by inference; and then what happened five minutes ago is past. It is not become unreal. It is still "present" to omniscience, if that exists. It has its place in the real process; but that place is not "now", *i.e.* within my immediate apprehension.

The conception of an "Eternal Now"—the "moment eternal"—is thus seen to be by no means contradictory. Even in our own limited experience we find illustrations of the principle, not indeed in application to all Time, such as is required before the Now can properly be called "eternal", but with reference to periods of duration sufficient to put the principle itself beyond dispute. The question may, indeed, be asked whether Mind is not here taking flights beyond the warrant of experienced reality. Can we draw conclusions concerning the nature of the real process of the world from these characteristic activities of mind? If our whole scheme of thought is well founded, we can do so, and we shall confidently expect that whatever is a true characteristic of Mind throws light on the process out of which Mind arises. But there is a more pertinent consideration than that to be brought into the argument.

We have spoken of what is past in one view being also present (though as an earlier episode in the process) for a view based on the greater achievements of Mind. We have not brought into review the future. But when we consider Mind in action, and not only in contemplation, we find that it brings the future also into present action. Of course it is only the future as conceived or imagined in the present that affects conduct. But it is of capital importance to notice that man's deliberate conduct is far more determined by expectation of the future than by any kind of impulsion from the past. This does not necessarily imply that the future exists as part of a sufficiently extended "Now", as the past may do; but something of that sort is not only implied but actually experienced by the spectator of a drama that he knows well. And while it is his knowledge now of what he found in previous reading or watching of the play which enables him to hear the earlier words or see the earlier actions in the light of their results, yet it seems inconceivable that what is so essential a feature of the greatest dramatic art should be without some counterpart in the real world.

It is most significant that the Greeks, with their sure artistic touch, chose for their comedies unknown plots, with the possibility of surprise, while they chose for their tragedies plots familiar to the audience; the audience at tragedy appreciated the words and actions of the characters in the light of the coming events of which they were aware. This is the principle of the famous tragic irony. Certainly it makes a difference to our hearing of Lady Macbeth's cynical realism—"What's done is done"—when one knows that it will be replaced by the despairing agony—"What's done cannot be undone".

This method of dealing with the world vindicates itself in practice. The more completely a man acts on the supposition of real continuity in events, the more he is confirmed in his belief by experience. The most significant characteristic of Mind, after all, is not such knowledge as is possible to us while we are subject to the conditions of our present life, but purpose—not the apprehension of the world as it now is, but the constant effort to make it something else. And to the prophet or seer it never appears that he is being led by notions of his own; he feels that the future itself is luring him on. It presents itself as something which can never become actual or present without man's effort, but also as something which being extant, though not present, itself supplies the motive for its realisation. Those who have given their lives for the Kingdom of God have never felt that they were making their sacrifice for a dream of their own, but in order to bring into present actuality what is after its own manner already profoundly real. It may be that this experience is as yet so little developed that we cannot hope to give a clear account of it; but it seems certain that it is a real experience which bears witness to the true reality of the future, even though that future awaits man's effort to determine its mode of actualisation. We shall find that other considerations help to elucidate this notion, though it must remain to a great extent obscure.

When we come to Purpose we also come to Value. We have found that the general condition of the actualisation of Value is the Mind's discovery of itself, or at least of what is akin to it, in its Object. Value as actual belongs neither to the Subjective nor to the Objective side of the Subject-Object relation, but precisely to that relation itself. The picture may be beautiful, but the Value or Good of that only occurs when a mind appreciates it, though the appreciating mind finds the beauty in the picture, and does not put it there. And the Value once found is in some measure independent of the occurrence in which it is found. A mind that has once appreciated *Hamlet* has an apprehension of that aesthetic value, though no doubt in a lower degree, even when not reading or watching the drama. It enters the mind and becomes part of its life. The man who has let the great Shakespearean Tragedies make their own proper impact upon him does not afterwards have to say, in face of life's troubles, "I have seen the tragic side of life so revealed as to declare itself sublime, and I will face my troubles with the courage born of that vision"; but he looks on life with eyes which that vision has illumined, and in some degree himself sees tragic facts as in themselves sublime. The Value once possessed is in great measure retained; the mind which has found itself at home in one situation of terror, as in a tragedy, can afterwards face other situations of terror without—or at any rate with less—dismay. And when the Mind's discovery of itself in its Other reaches its climax in the love of friends, it is still true that the love, which is the excellence, continues even when companionship, which is its delight, is impossible. To love and be separated may be more pain than pleasure; yet no one who loves could wish to cease to love, because though love in such circumstances brings pain, it is yet known to be in itself supremely good. But while our minds attain to some power of retaining the Good or Value when its occasion is past, this power in us is narrowly limited; and for full fruition the occasion must be renewed.

But there is something much more important than this to be said about the relation of Value to Process. The successive events that constitute Process are, as events, unalterable. Whatever may be a true description of them at the time of their occurrence remains a true description throughout the whole course of time. Hamlet killed Polonius; no length of years can make it true to say that Polonius killed Hamlet. Conversely, if it is now true that the earth revolves, and from the formation of the solar system has revolved, about the sun, then it was never true to say that the sun revolves about the earth. In this sense the event is always unalterable, and not even God can change the past. But it is not true that the value of the past event is unalterable; when it is seen in the context and perspective of a longer vista of time, what was, as an isolated event, evil may be appreciated as an element in a total good—not only as a price paid for a consequent good, but as an indispensable element in what as a whole is good. And this again is not to be interpreted merely as a preponderance of good in a whole which also contains evil; the thing that was evil becomes a positive ingredient in a total good.

No doubt it is only by rhetoric that this can be called an alteration of the past; for the past event, as past, is what it always was. But the present appreciation of the past discloses a character which in the past was imperceptible. It would be inconceivable that any one should misunderstand the rhetoric which declares that the past is not unalterable, unless some persons had in fact misunderstood it. For it is the whole point of this way of thinking that the past *qua* past was what it was; if it was bad, it is now true to say that it was bad; but though it was merely bad, it is now an integral element in good. To turn at once to a supreme instance, the crucifixion of Jesus of Nazareth, interpreted as Christians have interpreted it, was for a moment the worst of all manifestations of evil; but throughout the ages it is the best of all manifestations of good; and the Christian scheme of redemption affirms, not only a preponderance of good over evil, so that the temporary victory of evil is wiped out by a more decisive victory of good, but the conversion of defeat itself into triumph. We are not now concerned with the actual truth of this conception in the particular instance adduced, but with the principle implied in it. That principle is that *the future does not merely disclose in the past something which was always there, but causes the past, while retaining its own nature, actually to be, in its organic union with its consequence, something which in isolation it neither is nor was.*[1]

Moreover, it is not only in the subjective experience of the estimating mind that this transition is effected. It is not only that we feel differently towards the event in question. Like all estimates of value, this is a genuine judgement, wherein we assert objective truth. Neither the aesthetic nor the moral judgement can be accounted for as a subjective reaction to facts which are in themselves indifferent. We must reiterate this point. No one who is sensitive to music (for example) can be content with the suggestion that the only objective fact is certain atmospheric vibrations which strike upon the drum of his ear and stimulate the aural nerves and portions of the brain. That is the physical fact—or rather it is the

[1] See Appendix C, pp. 221-222. Canon Quick has urged (*The Christian Sacraments*, pp. 47-49) that it is only the "instrumental value", not the "expressive value", of the past which can be thus altered. I should agree, if I accepted the distinction as ultimate. But both the past, and the present which effects an alteration in the value of the past, have their being within the whole which is the only reality. Consequently the value which the past has, or had, in isolation from the present and future is not its real value at all, whether expressive or instrumental. The evil thing remains in itself evil, but whereas it *was* a bad thing that it should happen it *is* a good thing that it did happen.

portion of the entire fact which is studied by the physical sciences. But behind this is the thought of the composer, who used those atmospheric vibrations as the medium and vehicle of the beauty which possessed his soul, and which, on occasion of those vibrations reaching their ears, possesses also the souls of listeners to that music. The beauty is quite as objective as the vibrations, and is truly prior to them (though, of course, not previous to them), as being the cause for which they were ever set agoing. The same holds good, even more evidently, of moral value. To a man who is thrilled with admiration at an act of moral heroism it would appear merely ridiculous to maintain that there is no excellence in the act, but only in his own, or the doer's, reaction to it. The value is in the action. And this objectivity attaches equally to the change of value which new conditions may effect in that action. An act of treachery is morally vile and purely deplorable; but if it reveals to the guilty person his own baseness, and he by repentance wins forgiveness from the person whom he betrayed, so that a new and deeper friendship springs up between them, he can no longer merely deplore that act. He must still deplore the baseness which found expression in the act,[1] but he can no longer deplore the act which led to the purging of his character and the closer relationship with his friend. And this change in his judgement of value is apprehension of an objective change in the objective value of the act; whereas it was, at the moment of its commission, a thing wholly deplorable, it now is, in the context of its consequences, an occasion for truly humble gratitude. No doubt it is because of its significance for appreciating minds that it formerly had the one value and now has the other; but it is always true that Value depends for its actuality on the appreciating mind. That does not mean that the Value resides in the subjective experience of that mind; it means that appreciation brings to actuality a quality of the object

[1] But even this needs qualification. See pp. 471-472.

which previously belonged to it really, but potentially and not actually—ὄντως but δυνάμει not ἐνεργείᾳ, for value is "objectively real, but subjectively conditioned".[1]

We have now reached these six results: (1) Process is real, and whatever has no relevance for the actual world-process is fictitious; (2) Mind arises in the course of the world-process, and is one of its episodes; (3) but it is an episode of which the distinguishing feature is its capacity, by means of "free ideas", to survey the process of which, initially, it is a part; (4) in that survey it apprehends process as an organic unity, such that not only does the past condition the present, but the future qualifies and even sometimes occasions both past and present alike; (5) it thus achieves a certain superiority to, and independence of, the process—not indeed such as to endow it with a life wholly detached from the process, but such that the process falls within its grasp, not it within that of the process; (6) in respect of value past events, as apprehended in the present, are not unalterable, but may still be so affected by the results won or wrought out of them as to become even the opposite of what at the time of their occurrence they were, and, when viewed in their isolation, still are.

If all these propositions are true, they involve consequences of the highest importance for the world process itself. We have already recalled how utterly impossible it is that Mind should owe its origin to what is not Mind. Either the Process from the beginning has the nature of mentality, which becomes apparent in the reaction of some living objects to their environments; or else Mind is superadded to the natural objects of which the Process has hitherto consisted, by a Mind which, if it could act thus, must be presumed to have been at work in or upon the Process throughout its course. The choice between these two, we said, was indifferent, and the reason for that view will appear later.[2]

[1] I owe this phrase to Professor Bowman.

[2] See Lecture X.

But if Mind is thus active within or upon the Process, we must interpret this Mind, and consequently also the Process itself, in the light of the most developed type of Mind known to us—the Mind of man as it displays itself in relation to Truth, Beauty and Goodness. Mind, which arises out of the world-process as something so alien from it that what has been observed of that process cannot account for its occurrence, none the less is found to be, or to afford, the clue to the interpretation of the process. Mind is only explicable in itself, if it is the explanation of all else besides itself. This is the truth which makes possible such heresies as subjective idealism, or the Kantian doctrine that in the act of experience Mind constructs, or at least imposes Form upon, its object.

If Mind, of which the vital principle is the aspiration towards totality, is the explanation of the world-process, that process must be itself a unity, a totality. If this involves the doctrine of a universe finite in time, as it is now said to be finite in space, so be it. But there seems no reason to regard this conclusion as inevitable. For the essence of an intelligible unity, or totality, is not that it has limits, but that it is informed by one principle. Now if there be a principle such that it is capable of indefinitely wide application and sets no limit, as a result of its own nature, to its application, there seems no reason why an infinite progress should not be both intelligible and satisfactory.

The choice which the philosopher has to make when he reviews the world-process is between the two apparently possible answers to the questions whether its interpretation is to start from the less or from the more developed stages known to us. Physical Science, and the philosophy which it inspires, with its maxim that any event must be accounted for by the lowest category found to be adequate, inevitably starts with the less developed phase. It begins with atoms, or with electrons, protons and neutrons, or with whatever is taken to be the ultimate term of scientific analysis. From this starting-point may be constructed an intellectual scheme of the physical universe, in Newtonian terms, or those of Einstein, or those of any man who shall devise a theory still more closely adjusted to meet the subtle intricacies of observed facts. But into such a scheme Mind and Value can only be inserted from without. The appearance of Mind is a breach of continuity, and must be accounted for either by treating Mind as an epiphenomenon which produces no modification in the process out of which it arises, or by postulating an external Creator, who has not been required for the account of the process hitherto, and is devised as a means of explaining the otherwise inexplicable. Of these alternatives, the former flouts the common experience of mankind, while the latter is a tacit abandonment of the theory it is devised to protect; for if there is a Creator capable of intervening in the world-process so as to intrude Mind into it at the appropriate moment, it is inconceivable that He should have no connexion with the process except at that point, so that the physical account of it was never complete after all.

Starting from the physical end we can never account for Mind; and Value shares its precarious lot. If primary Reality is purely physical, it is impossible to attribute Value to it in itself. Value, on that hypothesis, can only be found in states of Mind, when Mind has appeared on the scene. No doubt, certain physical occurrences could still for convenience be called good or bad according to the states of Mind which they induce. In that case, when a man calls a view beautiful, he only means that it evokes his admiration—or would do so if he were sufficiently sensitive; when he calls an act good, he only means that he approves it—or knows that it is such as is commonly approved. This conception of Value and of Value-judgements is not utterly without resemblance to what we believe to be the truth about them; but it is more false than true. In the first place, as has already been urged more than once, the Value-judgement certainly claims in its own nature to be as objective as any other. The man who says of a landscape or a work of art that it is beautiful does not suppose himself to be in reality pronouncing upon his own feelings; he does not think that the beauty of the view is grounded in his admiration for it, but that his admiration for it is grounded in its actual beauty. The Value only fulfils its essential nature, only achieves its essential excellence, in the moment when it is appreciated. It exists as value for Mind; Mind finds it and appreciates it; but Mind does not invent or create it in the act of appreciation. If man's mental activity in relation to the world is so totally at fault in this department that he mistakes for a judgement on the object what is really an expression of his own feelings, there can be little hope for any philosophic enterprise, and science itself could be trusted only so far as its results could be experimentally tested. To doubt the objectivity of Value is to adopt what has been called Scepticism of the Instrument in so extreme a form as to make all intellectual effort futile.

Even to this we might be driven, if by adopting the physical starting point we could produce an account of experience more comprehensive and more coherent than is otherwise attainable. But this is not so, for Mind itself is not thus to be accounted for at all. The recent tendency towards a physical account of reality is due solely to the recent successes of physical science in its own sphere; and inasmuch as its results can in large measure be experimentally tested, it affords a type of certainty that is out of reach where experiment is impossible. But its method ignores altogether the fact of knowledge itself; it concentrates all attention upon the object under investigation, and gives none to the attention so concentrated. It is natural enough that immense success in dealing with the objective world by a method which ignores the subject-object relationship altogether, should lead to a general habit of thought and intellectual outlook for which the fact of the subject-object relationship, and the problems arising from it, have little importance and no determining influence. But the simple and plain fact is that the scientific method wins its success by ignoring parts of reality as given in experience; it is perfectly right to do this for its own purposes; but it must not be permitted by a kind of bluff to create the impression that what it ignores is non-existent. Broadly speaking it is true that scientists themselves have long ceased to make any such attempt; the bluff now is not a consciously exerted influence, but a subconsciously accepted inference from the imposing success of the scientific method in its own field.

If we begin with mindless and valueless fact we cannot give any place in our scheme to Mind or Value without breaking up the unity of the scheme itself. The very activity which makes science possible remains unaccounted for in the theory of the world which men have constructed in the activity of science. It cannot be unscientific to prefer an alternative approach by which we may at least hope to find a place for science itself in its own world.

So much at any rate is secured by the method which takes the fullest development of any process to afford the surest clue to the interpretation of that process as a whole. Adopting that principle, we shall accept Mind as what we find it in experience to be, after study and analysis have done their utmost. That study will be hampered by no presuppositions drawn from the material world. If it appears that Mind is influenced by final causes as truly as by efficient causes, there will be no tendency to argue against this from the fact that physical science has for its own purpose dispensed with teleology.

It will not be claimed by reasonable disputants that we should be able, here and now, to produce a complete and tidy system of universal knowledge on pain of admitting that a philosophy which starts by accepting Mind as an active energy in the real world distinguishable from all physical forces is doomed to failure. But it may reasonably be claimed that this philosophy shall not break down at the same point at which its rival breaks down. The rival was discredited by its inability to effect the transition from the mindless physical system with which it starts to the reality of Mind as a fact observable within the total range of experience. Can our alternative do better?

It is here of primary importance to note that we are not attempting a mere inversion of the discarded view. We are not attempting to start with Mind and find the way to Matter. That was part of the Cartesian blunder. But we start with the totality of experience in which Mind is one given element; and we refuse to reduce Matter to any state of Mind or consciousness just as much as we refuse to reduce Mind to any combination of Matter. What is presented to us is a given articulated continuum in the form of a process, wherein, at a certain stage of development, Mind is found to be active. We take this Mind as what it appears to be, in its initial dependence on the data of experience, in its subsequent independence of particular circumstances, in its comprehension of succession and extension, in its purposiveness, in its freedom. Many of these marks of Mind will engage our attention in the next lecture. But we do not have to ask how Mind effects a transition from its own ideas to an objective world, because we see Mind first appearing as the consciousness of processes which had been going on in the physical world before that appearance. In Whitehead's words, "consciousness presupposes experience, and not experience consciousness"; "the feeler is the unity emergent from its own feelings".[1] The physical, chemical, biological,

[1] *Process and Reality*, pp. 72, 123. In the second quotation I take Whitehead to mean "emergent from a complex of feelings not hitherto united in a feeling subject"—*i.e.* feelings which become "its own" so soon as it is there to own them.

physiological process were there before Mind appeared as in less or greater degree superintending the life of any particular organism. When it appears, it appears precisely as that organism become, or becoming, conscious. There is no transition to be effected from Mind to Matter, because Mind, as we know it, *is* consciousness of an environment which is in one aspect material. How far or how truly Mind rises above the conditions of its origin is a question which must occupy us later.

But here we must note that Mind appears from the outset as apprehension of, or aspiration towards, value. From its first dawning, it is characterised by affection and desire.[1] So far as it is passive, it is the awareness of things as welcome or unwelcome, friendly or hostile; so far as it is active, it is a calculation of means to the attainment of ends apprehended as good. Later comes the choice between ends as between greater and lesser goods. But at no point is it other than awareness of Value—positive or negative—in its environment, that is, in the process from which it sprang. And Value we found to be grounded in the discovery by Mind of itself—or its own kin—in its object. If the object is apprehended as good—whether noble, beautiful or true, according to its own nature—that means that Mind finds there an expression, such as the nature of the object permits, of itself as it is or as it would wish to be. If the object is apprehended as bad, that means that Mind finds there either no expression of Mind at all, or else an expression of antagonistic Mind—the base, the ugly, the false.

So far, we have not tried to argue from Value to Fact any more than from Fact to Value; the latter indeed we found to be impossible. We have only claimed that in actual experience Fact and Value are given together, and that our conception of the world must make room for both and disclose a relation between them in a coherent scheme. In order to frame such a

[1] Cf. *supra* Lecture VI., pp. 141-143.

conception, we must at least enquire whether, if Fact is not of itself able to give rise in principle to Value, Value can in any sense give rise to fact. In other words, accepting Value as equally real with Existence, can we find in Value the clue to the interpretation of the totality which includes both.

We begin by considering again the Process, which is the first presentation of Reality which we apprehended. Arising out of it, and an episode within it, we find Mind, including our own minds, and the apprehension of the Process which Mind achieves. To put it otherwise, this Process, in certain of its constituent parts, becomes conscious of itself. And when it does so, that consciousness is at once an apprehension of value. The Process, in certain of its parts, apprehends itself as exhibiting that same character of Mind by which this apprehension is possible; for Value arises through Mind's discovery of itself in its object. *Mind, then, though it appears within the Process at a late stage, discovers throughout that Process the activity of Mind—universally in the form of Truth, commonly in the form of Beauty, sometimes in the form of Goodness. That Mind is pervasive of Reality is a necessary inference from this method of apprehending the world. If that method is justified, as we have tried to show that it is, the conclusion is inevitable. Mind is the principle of unity in Reality, or at least the fullest expression of that principle known to us.*

But Reality is first presented as Process. We have found that the Process is subject to Mind, and when Mind expresses itself through process, its activity is called Purpose. We are therefore led to enquire whether Purpose can be the governing principle of the world-process. It has, at least, this advantage as a candidate for that function; it is a principle of explanation which itself requires no further explanation. All other types of explanation set new problems; of every other answer to the question Why? we ask Why? again. But Intelligent Purpose is self-explanatory. When we have traced an occurrence to the Purpose of an intelligent being, we are satisfied. And this is natural enough, for in such a case Mind has referred the occurrence to itself as cause.

Now it cannot be said that we are under the same necessity to refer the course of the World-Process to Mind as its cause as we are to regard Mind as its governing principle; for there might be other causes unknown to us to which it could be referred. Yet if there is one and only one principle known which fulfils the requirement of supplying an explanation without demanding one, it is reasonable, at the least, to experiment with the theory that this does indeed supply explanation of the universe. But that theory is Theism in one or another of its forms.[1]

When we begin to follow up the theory that Mind Purposive, or Intelligent Purpose, supplies the explanation of the world, we are at once confronted with the fact that Purpose is directed primarily to Value or the Good, so that the theory involves the logical priority of Value to Existence. Objects come into existence, if this theory is sound, because they are good or because some good can be brought into existence by means of them. This does not mean that we can infer from the goodness of any state of things as conceived that such a state of things actually exists. For we ourselves exist, and conduct our thinking, in the midst of the World-Process and as part of it; and Values, as we have seen, are alterable, so that there may be goods which do not now exist and evils which now do exist, though the Process viewed as a whole is "very good".[2] Consequently *the reasonable attitude is not that which says "This is good, therefore it must be real", or "This is evil; how can it be*

[1] This argument is obviously modelled on Aristotle's argument to a First Cause, which must be an Unmoved Mover, in book Λ of the *Metaphysics*. But he developed it along lines of efficient causation; this is the same argument transferred to the category of final causation. Aristotle himself gave the hint in the famous phrase κινεῖ ὡς ἐρώμενον. But it is hard to be sure how much he meant by this. See below, pp. 256-257.

[2] Genesis i. 31.

explained?" but that which asks concerning every situation that arises how good may be won out of it, and how even what is now evil in it be made subservient to good.

For our minds, which are part of the Process, are not primarily occupied in knowing what the facts before us are, but in planning how to deal with them. Mind is first conative, and cognitive only in the second place as a means to acting wisely in the formation and pursuit of purpose. Our minds both exhibit and co-operate with the essential activity of the Mind which pervades and explains the Process. But before we begin to consider further the character of that activity we must determine more closely the relation of Mind as we know it in ourselves to the sequence of the Process in which it arises; in other words, we must form some conception of that freedom which is the most distinctive characteristic of Mind.

APPENDIX C

AN ILLUSTRATION FROM DANTE

MY friend, Mr. Geoffrey Bickersteth, whose translation of the *Paradiso* lately won so widespread a tribute of admiration, allows me to print here a letter in which he pointed out to me how Dante illustrates the point made on pp. 209-210 of the foregoing lecture:

"I should like to mention something to which I had meant to draw your attention in Dante's *Paradiso* xvii. 37-99, and especially verses 43-45, where a great, perhaps the greatest of all specifically Christian poets, is expressing *in terms of poetry* the truth which you were expounding *as a philosopher* in your eighth lecture on Process, Mind and Value, when you were employing the drama (*sc. Hamlet*) to illustrate how an experience *really* bad, and truly felt as such at the time it occurs, may acquire a wholly different value when judged (as in drama is possible) in the light of the whole in which it forms an element only.

"In this passage Dante, actually writing *after* the event—his exile, and *still suffering* the untold misery it brought him—it is important to notice that he is *still suffering*, for only so does one realise the magnificence of his faith—places (by a well-known device) the future (which he knows, since in fact it is now present and partly past) in the shape of a prophecy on the lips of Cacciaguida, who *within* the poem speaks of course in the present. [It is as if the audience in a theatre, knowing already the *whole* course of the action, were at the same time itself taking part in the action of which the outcome is unknown.] I pass over the six verses (37-42) on the relationship of contingency to necessity, with their strikingly apposite simile, and draw your special attention to verses 43-45. In these Cacciaguida, who (since in heaven) is, up to his capacity, one in his vision with God, *i.e.* seeing Dante's life past, present and future, *sub specie aeternitatis*, makes what must have seemed to the 'Dante in the poem' the perfectly astounding remark, in the context of the remarks following, that he beholds the poet's life on earth, a life of appalling suffering and of practically unrelieved misery, as a '*dolce armonia* da organo', with the implication that if only Dante himself could see as God sees, such would it appear to him also. And as Dante is writing the poem, that as a matter of fact is the way in which, *qua* poet, he *is* seeing it. Here, then, we have the actual sufferer at the moment of suffering (and *ex hypothesi*, therefore, incapable of being mistaken as to the *real* existence of his suffering) simultaneously with the poet seeing, in the timeless, spaceless experience of poetry, that suffering as an element in a 'sweet harmony'. The two values, the partial present, momentary, and the complete permanent, eternal, are here both fully realised in a single experience of the man to whose life they both refer. I know no other passage in poetry which goes so deeply to the root of the real meaning of suffering, or if meditated upon contains so much potential consolation to the sufferer—and all in three verses! And it is to be noted that they are the words of '*amor paterno*' (verse 35)."

LECTURE IX

FREEDOM AND DETERMINISM

THE great problem of spiritual freedom has usually been debated as if it concerned only the will, regarded in this connexion as the immediate determinant of moral action; and the subject has usually been discussed in specially close connexion with the notion of responsibility. Because this has been so prevalent a custom in philosophy, it will be convenient to take that starting-point. But we shall find reason to hold that, when so limited, the problem is insoluble. Just as our discussion of obligation pressed us back from action to character, and even from morality as commonly understood to something more fundamental, so our discussion of freedom will take us behind acts of choice to the whole life of mind or spirit.

The relation of freedom to responsibility is intricate. The superficial observer is liable to say that a man is not responsible for what he could not avoid, and that it we hold him responsible for an action we must attribute to him freedom to do it or not to do it. Freedom is thus conceived as freedom of choice at the moment of action. But if this freedom is complete, it seems to be as fatal to responsibility as its total absence would be. The culprit when charged with his offence might say that he did choose that course at that time, but he is not choosing it now; for all moral purposes he is now a different person. Responsibility, in short, involves continuity not only of physical organism, but of moral character; and this, in turn, imposes some limitation upon freedom of choice. The question is, indeed, whether the continuity requisite for responsibility does not preclude the freedom also thought to be requisite, so that responsibility seems to require both of two incompatible conditions. Some moralists have been led by this and kindred problems to regard "responsibility" as a legal rather than a moral term, connoting only accountability before the law but not fitness for moral praise or blame.

It is noticeable that for legal or civic purposes, it is easier to associate responsibility with Determinism[1] than with an extreme doctrine of Free Will. The difficulties created by the latter have been mentioned. So far as character is conceived as the source of conduct, an extreme doctrine of Free Will makes it uncertain whether the prisoner, though convicted of a crime, can justly be punished; for in what sense is he the same person who committed the crime? Determinism gives rise to no such difficulty. The judge may say to the convicted prisoner: "The Law, which I am charged to administer, takes no interest in the process by which you came to be what you are; but you are the perpetrator of a crime; and as such you must submit to the penalty prescribed by the Law, both that you may be thereby determined to a different course of conduct, and that others may be determined to avoid the conduct which is seen to incur such penalties". It is true that the administration of law on such a basis is likely to be callous and even cruel. The notion that Determinism tends towards sympathy and gentleness is due to mere confusion.[2] Determinism indeed condemns moral indignation as foolish; but it is ready to punish brutally though dispassionately, because fundamentally it treats Persons as Things, and will throw away the useless citizen as a man throws away a rotten apple, not thinking whether pain is involved or not, and quite sure that there is no such thing as free personality to be outraged.

This points the way to a change of approach to the question. For what is morally amiss in thorough-going

[1] Provided it be not mechanistic Determinism. See p. 238.

[2] Cf. R. L. Stevenson's fable, *The Devil and the Innkeeper*.

Determinism is not its impracticability in a civilised world, but its implied insult to personality. It is thus a theory destructive of all morality, which we found to consist fundamentally of respect for personality. The popular judgement is therefore right when it condemns Determinism as destructive of morality. But because it conceives morality as chiefly concerned with actions, it seeks to assert freedom (as the opposite of determinism) primarily in connexion with actions. And so it entangles itself in a complicated toil of difficulty from which there is no escape.

For even when it is admitted that freedom of choice is not absolute, but limited by continuity of character, and even when it is assumed that this limits freedom without destroying it, baffling questions still remain. Just how much freedom of choice is there on each occasion? Why does the "free will" choose as it does? and how does it effect its choice? If we say that it follows the strongest motive, we are returning to determinism; if we say that it chooses the motive by which it will be determined,[1] we are involved in a circle or an endless regress; for on what grounds does it make this choice? If this choice is motived it is not free; and if it is unmotived it is casual, not moral. Are we to say that it is a little motived, as the freedom is a little limited? The argument is leading us to nonsense.

The difficulty is nowhere so starkly exhibited as in Kant's treatment of it. He accepted the complete subjection of all experience to the category of causation; thus his doctrine of phenomena was determinist; but acts of choice are phenomena, so that concerning these also his doctrine was determinist. But besides phenomena, and in some sense the ground of them, he held that there are Things-in-Themselves, which are not subject to the Forms of Perception (Time and Space) or to the Categories of the Understanding (of which

[1] Cf. *e.g.* F. Temple, *The Relations between Religion and Science*, p. 80, and Gore, *The Philosophy of the Good Life*, p. 265.

Causation is one). The Thing-in-Itself which is the ground of acts of choice is the Will. This is not subject to Causation. It is free. Only of course it never acts. Kant's apprehension of the matter is presented in the mythical form of a free prenatal volition, of which all empirical choices are necessary and "determined" representations in the series of phenomena.[1] Kant was so near the truth that one is almost irritated at the completeness of his blindness to it. We saw in a previous Lecture that in his second version of the Categorical Imperative—"Treat humanity always as an end withal and never only as a means"—he found the true moral principle; but because he treated it, not as his starting-point, but as a corollary or restatement of his abstract formula—"Act at all times from a maxim fit for universal law"—he never perceived or elaborated its full significance. So here, in seeking the locus of freedom, he knows that it cannot be the momentary acts of choice which constitute the activity of the moral life, but looks for it in an abstract Will or Practical Reason instead of in the concrete Person, and so leaves it where for all practical purposes it has to be ignored.

By concentrating attention upon acts of choice, which are particular events or occurrences in the time-process, the traditional mode of discussion has presented the problem as though it were a question whether causality is present at all in relation to those acts; and inasmuch as the only alternative to causality is chance (if indeed that be a name for anything but blind causality), the defenders of freedom have often seemed in their own despite to be defending the principle of chance, and to attribute to chance just that which they desired especially to claim as the sphere of reason in action. Indeed nothing is further removed from chance than strength of will, which shows itself in constancy of character, not in unaccountable variations. Kant avoided a surrender

[1] Cf. Plato's more frankly mythical statement of a similar position in the Myth of Er—*Republic*, x. 617 D-620 D.

to chance, as we have seen, by delivering the phenomenal acts over to causation while he asserted the freedom of the noumenal will. But he shared with most others who have taken part in the debate the disastrous limitation of the notion of "cause" to efficient causation. Indeed this is a main source of the whole difficulty. The Kantian list of categories is framed under the influence of mathematical-physics and chemistry as typical sciences of the world of perception. It is no longer possible for us to be content with those categories. They are not easily applied to biology; if such students of that subject as Dr. J. S. Haldane are following a right course in their handling of it, these categories are entirely inadequate to it. In Psychology they lead to the absurdities of Behaviourism. In Ethics they prove their insufficiency by necessitating Kant's acceptance of a comprehensible incomprehensibility as the last word on the subject.

We must begin again at the beginning. Stark Determinism is stark nonsense, not only in Ethics but in every other field of study; for it declares that all objects are constituted by their external relations; and, if so, the process of mutual determination can never start. It may very well be true that every particular existent is what it now is because of the influence exerted upon it by other existents, perhaps even by all other existents. But it must have been something in its own being, so to speak, in order to be influenced by those others. And each of them must have been something in order to exert or submit to influence. Neither nothing-at-all, nor a perfectly undifferentiated homogeneous substance, could be the origin of a world of mutually determining constituent parts. Stark Determinism presents us with the spectacle of nothing-at-all differentiating itself into this richly varied universe through the mutual interaction of its non-existent parts. At whatever point we stop in our analysis of the cosmic continuum presented to us in experience, whether at the division of the classical four "elements"—earth, air, fire and water—or at the atoms of more modern science, or at protons, electrons and neutrons, at every stage we are confronted with aboriginal existents determining and determined by each other. How the term "aboriginal" is here to be understood is a further question. Theistic philosophy will interpret it in terms of creation, naturalistic philosophy in terms of self-subsistence. But whatever the interpretation, it remains true that every part of the universe confronts us with the mystery of Being![1]

There is a school of physicists which finds in the Quantum Theory not only a gap in the continuity of causation not yet filled by our knowledge, but a positive indeterminacy. There are other students no less eminent who scornfully repudiate this suggestion,[2] and are convinced that increasing knowledge will re-establish the reign of causation over electrons as over all other physical phenomena. For the Theistic philosopher the question has little interest, for the two views merely present him with two pictures of the constant activity of God. The one is a picture of perpetual directive acts, the other a picture of continuous directive activity; for the behaviour of Nature according to "Law" is no less a manifestation of the Mind of God, and thus an utterance of His Word, than its unpredictable behaviour from moment to moment would be. The indeterminist form of the Quantum Theory is hard to reconcile with Deism, no doubt; but Deism is not a living theory at the present time, and needs no killing. That any one should be turned from Atheism to Theism by a belief that electrons act unaccountably seems in-

[1] Cf. Coleridge, *The Friend*, Section II. Essay XI.: "Hast thou ever raised thy mind to the consideration of existence, in and by itself, as the mere act of existing? Hast thou ever said to thyself thoughtfully, It is! heedless in that moment whether it were a man before thee, or a flower, or a grain of sand,—without reference, in short, to this or that particular mode of existence? If thou hast indeed attained to this, thou wilt have felt the presence of a mystery, which must have fixed thy spirit in awe and wonder."

[2] So Einstein: "That nonsense is not merely nonsense. It is objectionable nonsense." See *Where is Science Going?* by Max Planck. p. 201.

conceivable. We may therefore leave the matter to the specialists, content to accept their decision whatever it may be.

There has indeed been some eager interest on the part of theologians and Christian apologists in the supposed discovery of indeterminacy at the basis of the physical world. This seems to be misplaced; for it is no more difficult and no less necessary to read the wholly determined course of nature as an expression of the will of God than it would be so to read the course of nature if indeterminacy were an inherent principle of it. And to welcome indeterminacy in nature as a supposed ally of such freedom of volition as is necessary to, or compatible with, obligation and duty, is a disastrous error. Concentration on acts of choice as the proper *locus* of freedom has led to the conception of freedom as indeterminism; but that, as we have partly seen and shall see more clearly, is a blunder. *Freedom is not absence of determination; it is spiritual determination, as distinct from mechanical or even organic, determination. It is determination by what seems good as contrasted with determination by irresistible compulsion.* The question is not whether certain events are determined or not, but what is the mode of the determination of any particular event; and we shall expect to find that this is appropriate to the distinctive nature of the agent.

We return then to our picture of the universe as consisting of mutually determining parts, where each none the less contributes something of its own to the totality. At the level of the simplest physical particles this contribution is such that (apparently) one could be substituted for another without perceptible difference in the result; each must indeed be somewhat on its own account, but its individuality counts for very little—so little as to be strictly negligible for all purposes except the metaphysical interest in the principle of individuality itself. But this principle is important, because if this has no application at the physical basis of the scale of being, it would be very hard to account for its appearance at other stages. We have seen, however, that unimportant as it may be for the purposes of physical science, the reactions and relationships studied in that branch of science presuppose individuality as a necessity of their own existence.

As we move from the simpler to the more complex structures, individuality counts ever more potently in the reactions and relationships observed. Where the rudimentary sentience, implied by the plant's turning to the sun, makes itself apparent; where the organism in search of nourishment detaches itself from its position and exercises powers of self-motion; where the animal develops interests and affections beyond what are relevant to the biological concern for survival; where the mind frames ideas drawn from, but also separable from, its particular experiences; where the moral person selects his ends independently of biological or even (in the narrow sense) personal, interests, aspiring, it may be, towards an ideal of which neither his own experience nor all recorded history supplies the origin—at every stage the individual is playing a greater part in determining his own reactions to the environment which is the field of his activity.

It is with this latest stage that we are now concerned. In the last Lecture we arrived at a conception of Mind as framing ideas based upon, but free from, actual experiences; thus it is able to seek in the future a goal by which to determine in the present the modification which it shall impose upon the inheritance bequeathed by the past; thus also it is able to find its own fulfilment in apprehension of, and correspondence to, a Being akin to itself though so transcending its scope as to seem almost wholly other and inaccessible. It is with the reaction of such an entity to the environment that we are concerned in the problem of Freedom.

There has been a tendency to maintain in connexion with volition and acts of choice what is really a survival of the old faculty-psychology, even though that form of psychology as a whole has long been discarded. Thus Bishop Gore held that the existence of a "central core of personality" was something which "philosophy must take over from common sense"[1]; and in like manner the existence of a distinguishable entity called a Will is often regarded as something which everyone recognises and can only be denied at the risk of absurdity. Bishop Gore himself, though without referring to a specific faculty of volition, attempted to solve the controversy about Free Will by simple introspection.[2]

But the difficulties attendant upon this conception of freedom, and the conception of Will commonly associated with it, are insuperable. They are the result of abstraction. When we consider the concrete person in action, they largely disappear. For the concrete person is a self-organising system of impulses, instincts, sentiments, emotions, ideas, and all the rest which psychological analysis may set out. The initial unity of all this phantasmagoria is the physiological organism. Any of the psychological elements can be stimulated into activity by the appropriate impact of the environment upon the organism. Thus at first the psychological life is disjointed and chaotic, but there are limits set to its chaos by the physiological organism which is its basis; for two incompatible impulses cannot simultaneously actuate the same organism. But consciousness is itself psychological, or, in other words, cannot be accounted for without remainder in the terms of pure physiology, because this does not allow for causation operating on the present from the anticipated future; and, because consciousness is psychological, the sense of value falls upon the psychological side of the line and begins very early to give to the psychological factor in the psychophysical system a preponderance which steadily in-

[1] Gore. *Can we then Believe?* pp. 151-156. The phrase in the text is quoted from a letter written by Bishop Gore to myself.

[2] *Belief in God*, pp. 139-144; *The Philosophy of the Good Life*, pp. 262-266.

creases. For while the organism makes demands for its own sustenance, its physical appetition is translated by consciousness into the appetites of hunger and thirst. Need becomes desire, and it is as desire that it influences movement and action. The "soul", to use a conveniently short term, cannot at this stage dispense with the "body", for indeed it is nothing as yet but the "body's" psychological counterpart; and its various activities arise out of "bodily" stimulations. But they are from the outset more and other than "bodily".

Desire, which is in its basis need-apprehended-in-consciousness, fastens, as we have seen, on the element of generality in those objects towards which it is directed, and thus out of the most "biological" element in the field of psychology there arises that apprehension of universals which makes possible the free and rational movement of thought. So science, which justly boasts its detachment from all desire except desire for truth, has its origin at the point where consciousness and organic process are most nearly allied. What is noteworthy for our purpose is the fact that freedom of thought has its source in the appetitive and conative part of nature. But Desire, though directed to the general character rather than to the particularity of its object, and thus supplying the starting-point of science, is in itself disorderly. Each desire is directed to its own satisfaction, and though each has reference at first to the needs of the organism and its survival, yet each also becomes active without regard to the economy of organic life. As consciousness develops, this trouble develops; for the power of imagination, whereby attention can be given to the general idea of what is not present to the senses, vastly increases the stimulation of desire, so that it may operate without reference to the proportion required by the life-process of the organism. Thus the same element in nature supplies the starting-point of the reasoning process which seeks order, and of the riot of appetite which destroys order.

Experience itself does something to restore harmony. The growing mind becomes aware that certain indulgences bring disagreeable consequences, and there arises an incipient purpose to hold the several desires in check. Under the discipline supplied by family and society this purpose is strengthened and defined, until, so far as education is complete, there is a wholly unified or integrated nature, controlling all its own elements to the fulfilment of its purpose. Of course education never is complete, and the process of integration extends throughout life; but that is its fundamental purpose—that out of the chaos which we are at birth order may be fashioned, and from being many we may become one: *ἕνα γενέσθαι ἐκ πολλῶν*.[1] When this process is still near its beginning, great difficulties often confront the educator. For integration is often commenced, yet is in such fashion incomplete that two or more alternative characters are active through the same body at different times, each in response to its appropriate environment. The schoolboy is often a different person in his home and at school, in the headmaster's drawing-room and among rowdy companions. For this he is sometimes accused of hypocrisy; but that is unjust; both groups of reaction are perfectly spontaneous and sincere; and to treat such a boy as if he deliberately adapted himself to his surroundings would be profoundly mistaken. He is not to be treated as having a perverted will, but as having a will incompletely formed.

For where in the initial welter of impulses is anything like a will to be found? And where in the schoolboy, whose impulses are organised in two or more groups but not yet in one, is anything like a will to be found? Will, if it means more than mere appetition, which is certainly not "free", first appears as an activity of a man's nature as a whole, or in chief part, exercising control over particular desires or impulses.

[1] Plato, *Republic*, 443 E.

Those impulses become active in presence of their appropriate stimulus; no motion of will is needed to set them in motion; will therefore appears at first chiefly as imposing inhibition on impulses and desires.

Will, then, as the agent in truly moral action is the whole organised nature of the person concerned; it is his personality as a whole; and so far is it from being an initial endowment of our nature, that the main function of education is to fashion it—a process which is only complete when the entire personality is fully integrated in a harmony of all its constituent elements. St. Augustine was, so far as I know, the first to perceive this truth, and the most fruitful parts of his immense influence on Europe have their origin in that perception. In a well-known passage[1] to which I have already alluded he asks why it is that when I will to move my hand, the hand immediately moves, whereas when I will to will the good, my will remains in the same state as before; and his answer is that in the second instance I do not completely will; for if I already willed the good, I need not will to will it; and if I will to will it, that proves that I do not completely will this. In other words, though the will can largely control my body, it cannot at any given moment control itself. It is what it is. If it is set on selfish ambitions or carnal pleasures, the fact that it is so set precludes it from changing its direction; it cannot change, because it does not will to change; if it did will to change, that would itself be the change. Of course there may be a most sincere wish to change; but that is different; it is something that may become a constituent part of a will to good; but so long as there are also present any forms of wish to enjoy what is evil, with motive power at all approximating to the wish for good, there are only two incompatible wishes, and no real or effective will.

The ideal is complete integration of personality, with all its elements included within its harmony. Wherever we meet that we admire it. It may be won at various

[1] *Confessions*, Bk. VIII. chapter ix.

levels of development and complexity. The "noble savage" has won it in a life of few relationships. The civilised man, with his vastly greater range of relationships, with all the varied interests and outlets for energy which they offer, has a harder task, but the attainment is so much the more excellent. There is a certain admiration extorted from us even by the man unified in sheer self-seeking, so that all scruples which might hinder his effectiveness in pursuing his own interests are removed—a Cesare Borgia, for example. But in fact that is always a mutilated unity. The scruples suppressed represent elements in nature for which no place has been found, and there is here no more true attainment of the ideal integration than in the life which, having failed to control certain elements in its nature, has gained unity by eliminating them. We must all offer our homage to the heroic souls who have plucked out the right eye or cut off the right hand to ensure their entry into life, for we are always doubtful if our will to life is sufficiently formed and stable to take the drastic and painful step. Yet we must also recognise that while to enter into life maimed is better than to perish with two hands, it is better still to enter into life with two hands. The once-born soul, if only it can acquire the same depth and earnestness, has the advantage over the twice-born soul, as we see at once when we pass from the study of Jesus of Nazareth to the study of St. Paul. But for the once-born soul to acquire that depth is very rare; perhaps indeed there is only the one recorded instance.

The will, then, is not an aboriginal endowment of our nature, but is something in process of formation throughout life under the influence of our environment, natural and social—and of any other sort that environment may be. It is the name for our personality so far as that is integrated. That process is never quite complete, but in the majority of men and women there is a dominant nucleus established by the time that the law recognises them to be of age. There is usually still very much that is not yet gathered into the positive service of the principle or goal which supplies unity to the dominant nucleus; but this has acquired an authority which can restrain those other elements from defying that principle or frustrating the attainment of that goal. This is called self-control. And strength of will first shows itself in certain splendid incapacities, as when it is said of a man accused of some base action, "He could never have done that". Where this control fails, and the as yet unco-ordinated impulses still act in defiance of the main purpose or dominant nucleus, there is moral weakness, and there is also a grave threat to mental stability, and even to sanity: sometimes this division of the soul amounts to complete dissociation of personality.

In considering this process of will-formation the most vital point to keep in mind is that the personality is largely a self-organising system. The importance of external influence is very great; scarcely any natural endowments are proof against certain combinations of circumstances; and in any case it is true that only such opportunities as present themselves can be utilised. But while influence plays a great part, it is never decisive by itself, as is shown by the differences in character often apparent in children of the same parents brought up under the same conditions. Each personality is largely a self-organising system, wherein the selection of elements to form the dominant nucleus is partly determined by the proportion which they bear to one another at the outset.

At first the process of integration is almost unconscious, but increasingly consciousness and its apprehension of values exerts an influence which at last becomes decisive. Its chief instrument is found in those "free ideas" which the mind forms for the tracing of connexions in the world of its experience. As these increase the scope of their embrace, they bring more and more of experience into some sort of unity. Among them are ideas which correspond to the purely scientific activity of mind, and other ideas which correspond to its aesthetic and moral activities. The trio of terms already discussed—Truth, Beauty, Goodness—supplies a rough classification of them; and in so far as a "free idea" manifests the quality denoted by one of those three terms it is apprehended as laying a claim or obligation upon the mind entertaining it. *Thus the mind finds itself equipped with leading principles for the co-ordination of that living entity of which it is itself the reflective awareness; by the direction which it gives to attention it determines the form of co-ordination or integration which takes place. It is here—in this constant direction of attention—rather than in the moment of action that freedom is found to be effectively present.*

At the moment of action it is still true that the person acting is a self-determining system, and even in that moment he can do something to mould the character that acts, especially if he is equipped with a truly adequate imaginative symbol of the right and good to which he may turn his attention at the critical moment. The element of self-determination in the act of moral choice is usually greatest when there is time for reflection and least when any action taken must be taken immediately. But in most cases the main decision is not made then; it is made by the discipline or non-discipline of the life of thought and imagination, which determines the general quality of character and consequently also the actions which will be done in the various combinations of circumstance that arise. The *locus* of freedom is the personality as a whole, but rather the life of thought than of will, so far as will is conceived as active in particular choices of alternative modes of conduct. Hence comes the profound significance of St. Paul's counsel: "Whatsoever things are true, whatsoever things are noble, whatsoever things are righteous, whatsoever things are pure, whatsoever things are lovely, whatsoever things are of good report, if there be any virtue, and if there be any praise, occupy your minds with these things."[1]

In what sense is the freedom of the self-integrating system of personal life sufficient to support legal and moral responsibility? For legal responsibility it is amply sufficient. All that is needed for that is a repudiation of mechanistic Determinism. If my bodily actions are a necessary outcome of the age-long play of material forces, so that my consciousness has nothing to do with them, then there is no place for responsibility at all. The State might still be wise in imprisoning or executing human organisms which preyed upon their neighbours, but it would be as one destroys vermin, not as one punishes crime. In fact the State itself, or rather the human organisms called State officials, would, on this theory, do whatever the disposition of gases in the nebula, from which the solar system has emerged, necessitated that they should do. But our view has nothing in common with that. It recognises that a human personality is a self-determining self-integrating system, and that ideas are the chief instrument of its self-determination. Moreover it is not wholly governed by the past, but by an imagined if not an actual future. What we have called the dominant nucleus may control and check some wayward passion under the influence of hope that one day the whole character will be something other than it is, or that through its self-discipline it may be able to help in bringing to birth a new social order. This is a form of determination; it is not indeterminism, but it is determination by other than efficient causation, though this, as always, plays its part. No knowledge of the person acting, or of his circumstances, at the moment previous to action will enable an observer to predict that action with precision, unless this knowledge includes apprehension of his unrealised ideals and the strength of their appeal to him; nor can he by self-observation predict his own future conduct or character. He is

[1] Philippians iv. 8

growing under the impulse of his own aspiration and the ground of his action is only revealed in the action itself. The acorn is potentially an oak, but so far as a man can predict the oak it is from observation of the growth of other acorns, not from analysis of this acorn. In the case of the child the same principle obtains, but here the prediction is still less informative, because here individuality counts for much, whereas with the acorn it counted for little. Therefore each moment as it passes reveals more completely the character that is moulding itself, and of every action the mature character must say "I did it, and what made me do it was myself". That is the freedom that supports both legal and moral responsibility, as commonly understood. It is nonsense in such a case for a man to plead compulsion; as Aristotle observed, no man is under necessity to murder his mother.[1] If he does it, whatever the motives, it must be because he has chosen or consented so to act, and the act is a manifestation of character. In relation to every moral choice, it is true to say that nothing compels the choice except the character of the agent, and that is something built up through the self-determining process of the whole personal life, limited by environment but not wholly directed by it. The self, which (like all other existing things) brings some original contribution of its own to the sum-total of existence, shapes itself according to its own initial nature and the influence of its environment and the reactions set up between these two. In some cases the self exercises a preponderating share of initiative; in others it submits to be almost passively moulded; but which of these it does depends upon what it is. Therefore the responsibility still lies with the self, even if it has contributed little beyond inertia to the process of its development. Consequently there is always credit due to the good character, however favourable the circumstances, and blame to the bad character, however unfavourable the

[1] *Eth. Nic.* 1110 a 26-29.

circumstances. In respect of the mutual relations of the moral agent and his environment the famous Kantian declaration is justified, "I ought, therefore I can",[1] for no environment can compel me to fail in duty or to do what duty forbids.

"I ought, therefore I can." Yet "The good which I would I do not, but the evil that I would not, that I practise. But if what I would not, that I do, it is no more I that do it, but sin which dwelleth in me. O wretched man that I am, who shall deliver me out of the body of this death?"[2] There is no logical incompatibility between the assertion of the philosopher and the ejaculation of the Apostle. Yet the difference between the two is fundamental. For of what use, after all, is it that I can, if I will, do what I ought if, in fact, I cannot so will? And though Kant argues truly that if I ought, I can, St. Paul meets that with equal truth by saying that, sometimes at least, it is even because I ought that I will not.[3] It is something to find that the cause of wrongdoing is in the self; but to diagnose the disease is not to discover the remedy. It is here that the popular doctrine of Free Will so hopelessly breaks down; for the will which is evil, or so far as it is evil, is not free to reform itself. If I am evil, then because it is due to myself that I am evil, I am justly held responsible for my evil state. But that does not help me to cure the evil. Every man lives at different levels of purpose and aspiration, and he may in his better moments take steps, by the direction of his attention, to extend these and their influence over an even greater portion of his life. But so far as his

[1] It was with great surprise that I failed to find this celebrated saying in any of Kant's works. The nearest parallel that I can find is this: "He judges, therefore, that he can do a certain thing because he is conscious that he ought" (*Critique of Practical Reason* (Abbott's translation) in Kant's *Theory of Ethics*, p. 119). (The original is: "*Er urteilt also, dass er etwas kann, darum weil er sich bewusst ist, das er es soll*".) Mr. Edwyn Bevan has sent me two other references, both in *Religion innerhalb etc.*, of which the closer to the familiar phrase is as follows: "*Wir sollen ihr gemäss sein, und wir müssen es daher auch können*" (*2 Stück, 1 Abschnitt* 8 *b*).

[2] St. Paul, Epistle to the Romans, vii. 19, 20, 24.

[3] *Ibid.* vii. 9.

will is genuinely set on evil, it cannot cure itself; for if it truly wished to be cured it would be cured already. To the man's better nature this evil direction of the will may seem something utterly alien—"sin that dwelleth in him". But, alien or akin, it is there; and its seat is the very focus of directive energy; so self-cure is impossible. The man is free, for the origin of his actions is himself; yet he is bound hand and foot, for from himself there is no escape.[1] Of what avail is it for Kant to say "You can" if this only elicits the reply "I will not"?

It may be answered that this is no concern of the moral philosopher, whose business is to give an accurate description of the facts presented by the moral consciousness, not to offer advice for their modification. But though the moral philosopher may thus escape, the metaphysician cannot. For if the moral consciousness of man has appeared only to taunt him with the realisation that his plight is miserable, and that he cannot cure his misery precisely because he is the source of it, then the fact that he is endowed with such moral consciousness is no evidence that the ultimate principle of reality shares his moral purposes or that as he pursues them he is in harmony with it. For the freedom that we have found in man so far is the bitterest form of bondage. Just so far as he is lifted above the brutes by the fact that his self-determination is self-conscious and guided by deliberately chosen ideals, he is also sensitive to his failures and harrassed by inability to attain to the ideals which he has chosen. The almost animal man is near to contentment; the man of moral aspiration is filled with self-contempt and despair. If his only freedom is that which assures him that because he ought he can, he will be conscious of bondage in proportion as his aspiration is noble. The freedom established by a non-religious ethical philosophy is a reality indeed, but is rather a

[1] Part of the supreme art of Shakespeare's tragedies consists in the power with which they illustrate this paradox. Cf. my *Mens Creatrix*, chap. xi.

curse than a blessing. It is fundamentally a freedom to sin; and while this, in contrast with an external compulsion to goodness, is the inevitable presupposition alike of vice and of virtue, yet no man can congratulate himself that he is free to sin. When regarded from within, the freedom not to sin is formal only; the self-centred will must choose selfishly. *Posse non peccare* is in fact an attribute of *peccaturus*; mere ability not to sin can only be predicated of one who does and will sin. Freedom of choice is a necessary pre-condition of morality; but it falls far short of true spiritual freedom.

True spiritual freedom would be the state of a man who, knowing an ideal which completely satisfied all aspects of his nature, always in fact conformed to it and could perfectly trust himself so to do; it is, in short, *non posse peccare*, inability to sin. We have already remarked that strength of will chiefly shows itself in splendid incapacities.[1] Here will is conceived as perfect. It is like freedom of choice, in that there is no external compulsion and action flows solely from the autonomous will. Yet it differs from freedom of choice because there is no selection between alternative courses of action regarded as equally possible. There may be real temptation, for pleasure and pain do not lose their qualities, and the mind still apprehends, with perfect clearness, the delights of comfort or indulgence, the anguish of suffering or renunciation. Yet there is now no doubt which course will be taken if it is clear on which side duty lies; there will still be consciousness of struggle, but no sense of a traitor within the fortress of the soul ready to open the gates to the insidious and plausible ambassadors of evil. There is a real conflict; but there is no doubt about its issue. Such a soul chooses indeed, but not between any "real alternatives", for by its very constitution it renders one of the alternatives impossible. That "inner logic of its nature" which we found to be the source of obligation now in a fuller

[1] Cf. *supra*, p. 236.

sense "obliges" the man to act in accordance with its dictates.

Such would be true freedom; and it is not ours. We see that it would bring with it the peace which passeth understanding, but that does not help us to reach it. For the trouble is that we are self-centred, and no effort of the self can remove the self from the centre of its own endeavour; the very effort will plant it there the more fixedly than ever. The man of science is drawn out of himself as regards one whole range of his activity by the concentration of his attention on the object of his study in his search for truth; the artist, by a similar concentration in his search for beauty; the good man, or public-spirited man, by a similar concentration in the service of his cause. But none of these cover the whole of life. Always there remains a self-centred area of life, and sometimes by a natural process of compensation those who are most selfless in the search for truth or beauty, or in public service, are most selfish, fretful and querulous at home. No ideal which a man purposes to himself will deliver him from the tyranny of self.[1]

But there is another environment besides that of nature and human beings; it is that Mind in which the Cosmic Process is grounded, that Spirit of the Whole, which is most adequately conceived on the analogy of Personality such as our own, but freed from our limitations and fulfilling all that in us is potential only. If it be possible to establish fellowship between the human soul and that Spirit, such fellowship would be the source of the true freedom of man. For just because it is the Spirit of the Whole, it is not alien from, however much it may transcend, any existing thing. The human spirit will find here something which has for it the appeal as well as the claim of kinship, and will be drawn to make a response, which is at the same time a submission, to the Spirit of the Whole, and therein attain to the fulfilment of itself in the freedom which is also peace.

[1] For a further development of this theme see Lecture XV.

Thus the soul which grows not only amid, but out of, the organic interactions of the physical world, by means of the free ideas that arise in it to guide its own reactions, becomes self-determining, using its environment as material for its own artistic enterprise of fashioning itself after its ideal; then, discovering its inability to satisfy itself because of the limitations inherent in its self-hood, it finds in fellowship with the Spirit of the Whole the power it needs to escape from self-determination to determination by that Spirit. Coleridge was right when he bade us think of "freedom as the power of the human being to maintain the obedience, which God through the conscience has commanded, against all the might of nature".[1] But that power belongs to man only so far as he is in fellowship with God.

Self-determination is the characteristic of man as a moral being, and without it he could never be called into fellowship with God. But it is not the last word of human development; on the contrary it contains the sentence of endless frustration as truly as it affords the opportunity of entry upon the spiritual enterprise. For the self which determines cannot carry the self which is determined above its own level. Self-determination must fulfil itself in the recognition of an Other which may lift it to heights for ever out of its own reach; self-determination fulfils itself in self-surrender to that which is entitled to receive the submission of the self.

But how can the self find the Other which is entitled to its homage? If it were possible for a man to comprehend the whole system of reality in its entire extent of time and space, he would have there an expression of the Spirit of the Whole, from which he might infer the character of that Spirit. But this is impossible. If he follows the guidance of his own experience of life, that is for this purpose accidental, and might lead to a multitude of divers conclusions, each of which would inevitably be inadequate. If he sets up his own ideals,

[1] S. T. Coleridge. *The Friend*, vol. i. p. 143.

and elevates to the throne of the Universe that which commands his personal admiration, he is back at the self-centred level from which his homage to this Other is to deliver him. There is in fact only one condition on which man can reach that true freedom for which his nature yearns; it is that the Spirit of the Whole should have offered to man a veritable self-disclosure, not only in the whole range of existence but in some act or series of acts such that man can apprehend them and direct upon them his concentrated attention. In other words, if God be such as to reveal Himself, and has revealed Himself, in a fashion apprehensible by man, then man by his homage to God so revealed may find the fulfilment of the destiny which his consciousness proclaims to be his.

That any particular event or series of events is truly the self-disclosure of God can never be proved; but it can be put to the test by whole-hearted experiment. If, as the experiment continues, the claim that in this event or that God is revealed finds vindication, then, though proof is out of the question, assurance becomes more intense and grounded in a wider range of experience. If it appears to be the fact that the mind which dwells on the alleged revelation finds that it is confronted with something akin yet transcendent, and discovers a new power of self-forgetfulness increasingly to pervade both thought and conduct, that will be strong evidence that this event is not a mere occurrence, which happened once and is now past, but is indeed a self-disclosure of that Spirit of the Whole, who sustains all things in being, but here offers Himself to be received into the minds of men. Man fulfils his natural destiny when the supernatural comes upon him, wins his loyalty, and transforms him into its own likeness, through his self-surrender to its determining appeal. But how this may be, is a topic for further enquiry.[1]

[1] See Lectures XII. and XV.

LECTURE X

THE TRANSCENDENCE OF THE IMMANENT

HITHERTO we have confined our attention to such forms of experience as are almost universal among civilised men and are commonly allowed to be in some measure veridical. Many who have no belief in God as Personal Spirit admit, and indeed insist upon, the august claims of Truth, Beauty and Goodness. In our own consideration of this famous trio we have noticed intimations, given through each, of a significance that carries us far beyond the meaning commonly attached to that name. But we did no more than notice these. We made no attempt to follow them up to their ultimate implications, or to correlate them under any principle that might account for them all, though it was plain that their indication, so to speak, was all in one direction. In other words, we considered only what was found to be, in the useful though tiresome current jargon, immanent in them, without enquiring how far this must also be transcendent. But we have now before us the material which enables us to take that further step. We must proceed to enquire how far, apart from any experience regarded as a direct self-disclosure of a Transcendent God, our general experience affords ground for holding that its deepest principle is not only immanent within the world as we know it but also transcendent over it. For this purpose some recapitulation may be useful.

We began our survey by considering the function of Natural Theology and the relation between Religion and Philosophy. That relation we found to be inevitably and properly one of tension. We then left Religion aside for the time and considered the structure of experience as it presents itself when no special prominence is given to Religion. Having noted the nature and consequences of what I must regard as the Cartesian aberration—a necessary and (now that we have escaped from it) even a wholesome aberration—we made an attempt to apprehend the World-Process within which human minds have their place. We remarked that the occurrence of minds within the process and as part of it tells us something of great importance concerning the process itself; it must at least be such as to give ground for the occurrence of minds. Proceeding to consider the most characteristic activities of human minds, and the objects to which those activities are directed, we found that alike in the apprehension of Truth and the appreciation of Beauty Mind is discovering itself in its object, and that the fundamental principle of Goodness is the recognition by personal Mind of its own character in all other persons, and action conforming to that recognition. And lastly we have seen that in the three activities corresponding to Truth, Beauty and Right, Mind achieves a freedom of movement by which alone those three objects are attained, and which is itself the potentiality of an extension of these characteristic activities such as seems to have no prescribed limit.

If this were all that is to be said, the result would be to encourage a certain religiousness of disposition and outlook, but nothing more. It would indicate that there exists, expressing itself in the universe, and most fully (within our knowledge) in man, a reality characterised by mind and, in some sense, by personality. The Truth of the world, that is to say its character as intellectually apprehensible, would reasonably be taken as illustrating the mental structure of that reality. To assume that the Beauty of the world expressed its nature would also be natural, though there would be no convincing answer to the sceptic who asked why its Beauty rather than its ugliness (which at first sight seems to be equally real) should be so regarded. We should wish to say, perhaps, that everything is beautiful if it is sympathetically apprehended, so that only Beauty is objectively real, while Ugliness is due to our defective apprehension. Yet this will involve difficulties, for in order to apprehend the supposed beauty of (say) cruelty, we must sympathise with cruelty, and that would at once create an opposition between our aesthetic and our moral activities.

If, again, after the example of Kant, we take the principle of these moral activities themselves as the basis of our religious outlook, there is great difficulty in relating it to the general character of experience. We do not find in nature or in history any clear indication that their sustaining principle is righteous. Kant himself, having invoked God to vindicate morality, has to postulate Immortality to supply Him with an adequate arena. We may believe as firmly as Kant in Duty, God and Eternal Life, but this adding of postulate to postulate in order to save from apparent unreality what is offered as an initial axiom is somewhat unimpressive, except, indeed, as a demonstration that the method is imperfectly adapted to the subject-matter of enquiry. And it is Kant himself who, in his intuitions, best points the way of escape from the entanglements of his argumentative method. For in his sheer reverence for Beauty and the Moral Law there is promise of a better way.

Our argument hitherto may thus be said to encourage a vague religiousness of outlook, which is likely to be more aesthetic than moral, and more intellectualist than aesthetic. In such a description we recognise the features of much contemporary culture. With such a view the thought of a specific divine revelation is not incompatible, but neither is it congenial. It would, on that view, be possible to hold that the mental reality, apprehended as finding self-expression in the structure of the world and its process, is also capable of definite and specific acts of revelation, and has in fact expressed itself also in such acts. Then these acts, accepted as being the vehicle of such self-revelation, would be taken as the clue to a fuller understanding of the process, and a whole scheme of theological philosophy could be constructed. But in that case the divine self-revelation would seem to be an abrupt intrusion of what, apart from these acts, was not known to be capable of effecting them. That is not of itself incredible; but it presents to the scientific and artistic mind difficulties so great that it is fully worth while to see whether closer inspection may not disclose a nearer affinity in men's deepest non-religious experience to that Being Who, according to the great positive religions, has declared His nature and will by authoritative revelation. For while all living religion is a response to what is recognised as authoritative, that response is possible with full justification and self-surrender only if the voice of authority completes, rather than contradicts, the deepest intimations of such experience as is unaccompanied by any note of special and peculiar authority.

We have indeed already seen that all experience has an authoritative quality. It commands our judgement rather than submits to it; for the judgement that we make upon it claims to be true concerning it, and thus is itself exposed to correction by the experience on which it is pronounced. The growing mind, in proportion as it is emancipated from the authority of other minds, comes under the authority of Truth itself. But we have also seen that in the apprehension of Truth, the mind is meeting with what is akin to itself. Moreover *the mind recognises in Truth, or in the Mind expressed in Truth, a proper object of reverence quite other than is appropriate as a part of the mind's apprehension of bare fact.* While a fact is apprehended as an almost bare particular occurrence, which is what it is but might as well have been something else, it evokes no reverence. The mind takes note, and passes on to other observations. But when it is apprehended as a constituent element in the system of Truth, it begins to acquire the qualities which compel reverence. Failure to observe this distinction leads to much confusion and bewilderment. The exalted language used about Truth and its sanctity perplexes those who think of it as a quality attaching to isolated bits of information. If I say "The sun shone all day in Glasgow on February 24, 1933", that statement, though admittedly improbable, is either true or false. But in neither case has it any sanctity. If I am mistaken about it, that does not greatly matter. To say it while knowing it to be false would be wrong, because to deceive people is to outrage their personality; but we are here concerned, not with saying what is thought, but with thinking what is true; and there is no sanctity in correct information about particulars, nor any calamity in being misinformed, unless this leads to calamitous action. Yet there is a sense in which Truth is august and compelling. *Willingly to believe what is suspected to be false is felt to be not only a degradation of the credulous believer's personality, but an offence against the order of reality. This feeling is quite unreasonable if the order of reality is a brute fact and nothing else; it is only justifiable if the order of reality is the expression of a personal mind, for the sense of moral obligation towards Truth is of that quality which is only appropriate in connexion with personal claims.*

I must confess that I know no way of arguing this last point, to which, none the less, I attach great importance. It is an intuitional judgement. It is only possible to recall the fact that the obligations arising from personal relationships have a special quality distinguishing them from, and giving them priority to, such obligations as are created by an appreciation of values conceived as impersonal. It is indeed one of the main contentions of these Lectures that the essential condition of Value is the meeting of mind with mind—or at least with what is akin to mind. But not all values are so appreciated by every one, or perhaps at all times by any one; and scientific Truth is perhaps that which it is least easy to appreciate as a directly personal relationship. My contention is that the quality of feeling entertained towards it by even materialistic scientists is often such as can only be justified if, in fact, the world-order thus apprehended is the expression of personal mind. It is no answer to that contention to say that this feeling is due to a surviving Theism which ought to be discarded, for such a reply admits the implications of the feeling, and these constitute the point of the contention. If on all grounds the conclusion is accepted that there is no personal mind expressing itself in and through the order of the universe, the existence of our feeling towards Truth may be explained by reference to the fact that during most of the ages of history men have believed that there was such a mind: the influence of that belief appeared in the form of reverence felt for Truth, and this feeling may be held to exist now as an anachronistic survival. I am not at present arguing against that as a possible hypothesis. I am urging only that most of us feel that reverence, and must either accept its implications or regard it as due to a mistake, and therefore deserving to be discarded. And it is very relevant to observe that this quality of reverence for Truth is specially evident among those who have felt bound, out of loyalty to Truth itself as they had been able to receive it, to abandon the belief which alone could justify it. It would seem as if there were some potent force compelling in them an attitude of mind which their own convictions have rendered obsolete. All this is intelligible on a basis of avowed Theism, but highly paradoxical on any other.

We have here then an intimation, though it is no more, that what the mind confronts in its search for Truth, and in the claim of Truth upon it, is something more than an intelligible system of uniformities; it is a Mind akin to itself, though so vastly greater as to be the controlling principle of that vast realm of being which our minds laboriously and very gradually apprehend. This intimation will be of great or little importance according as it receives or lacks support from other ranges of experience.

It finds support in an intimation similar to itself that comes from the pursuit of Beauty. But here the intimation itself is far clearer and more decisive. It is not only that the reverence which men feel in the presence of great Beauty, as before the claim of Truth, is such as to be reasonable only if in the appreciation of Beauty we are in communion with a master-mind, but because the apprehension of Beauty is in its own essence such communion. Lord Balfour made this point very forcibly, in a passage from which I have already quoted, in his most important Gifford Lectures on *Theism and Humanism*:

"If by some unimaginable process works of beauty could be produced by machinery, as a symmetrical colour pattern is produced by a Kaleidoscope, we might think them beautiful till we knew their origin, after which we should be rather disposed to regard them as ingenious. And this is not, I think, because we are unable to estimate works of art as they are *in themselves*, not because we must needs buttress up our opinions by extraneous and irrelevant considerations; but rather because a work of art requires an artist, not merely in the order of natural causation, but as a matter of aesthetic necessity. It conveys a message which is valueless to the recipient unless it be understood by the sender. It must be expressive."[1]

Lord Balfour was well aware that some would admit this of the relation of the work of art to the artist, but would refuse to go further:

"They would grant that a work of art must be due to genius, and not, in the first instance, to mechanism or to chance. But whether, in the last resort, mechanism or chance has produced the genius, they would regard as, from the aesthetic point of view, quite immaterial. Music and poetry must have a personal source. But the musician and the poet may come whence they will.

"And perhaps, in very many cases, this is so; but not, I think,

[1] Lord Balfour, *Theism and Humanism*, pp. 66, 67. The closing sentences are repeated on p. 78.

in all, nor in the highest. If any man will test this for himself, let him recall the too rare moments when beauty gave him a delight which strained to its extremest limit his power of feeling; when not only the small things of life, but the small things of Art—its technical dexterities, its historical associations—vanished in the splendour of an unforgettable vision; and let him ask whether the attribution of an effect like this to unthinking causes, or to an artist created and wholly controlled by unthinking causes, would not go far to impair its value."[1]

With these passages I must quote again the paragraph in which Lord Balfour proceeds to argue the same point with reference to the beauties of nature:

"The feeling for natural beauty cannot, any more than scientific curiosity, rest satisfied with the world of sensuous appearance. But the reasons for its discontent are different. Scientific curiosity hungers for a knowledge of causes; causes which are physical, and, if possible, measurable. Our admiration for natural beauty has no such needs. It cares not to understand either the physical theories which explain what it admires, or the psychological theories which explain its admiration. It does not deny the truth of the first, nor (within due limits) the sufficiency of the second. But it requires more. It feels itself belittled unless conscious purpose can be found somewhere in its pedigree. Physics, and psycho-physics, by themselves, suffice not. It longs to regard beauty as a revelation—a revelation from spirit to spirit, not from one kind of atomic agitation to the 'psychic' accompaniment of another. On this condition only can its highest values be maintained."[2]

Lord Balfour's appeal is to the judgement of those who have at any time entered into a deep appreciation of beauty. For what my own experience may be worth, it entirely confirms his interpretation. Further, as was remarked at an earlier stage, the mental attitude of deep appreciation is of its own nature akin to worship. The whole aesthetic experience is unintelligible unless there comes through it a revelation from spirit to spirit. *There is more in Beauty than Beauty alone. There is communication from, and communion with, personal Spirit.*

[1] *Op. cit.* p. 68. [2] *Ibid.* p. 81.

The same conclusion is involved even more inevitably in Moral Goodness as we were led to understand it. For here we found two relevant considerations. First, we found that the essence of morality is personal fellowship, or respect for persons as persons, so that the one true form of the Categorical Imperative is "Thou shalt love thy neighbour as thyself"—right acts being those which are prompted by such love fully and rightly understood. The second relevant consideration was that in the performance of duty, especially of difficult duty where the performance is heroic, there is a clear sense of corresponding to, and entering into, a reality which was always there, and which in itself has upon us that kind of claim which can only be exercised by persons. If it is reasonable, as it surely is, to be guided here by the standards of those who are ethically most sensitive, as in the sphere of beauty by those who are aesthetically most sensitive, there can be no doubt about the intimation of their experience. To fail in duty is felt by them not only as an injury to a neighbour, not only as a degradation of self, not only as a breach of that Moral Law on conformity to which all the welfare of man depends, but as the flouting of what justly claims our reverence. This feeling is most constant, no doubt, in those who believe that the Moral Law is the content of the Mind of God; and it is one of the chief practical advantages of a theistic belief in the moral sphere, that it enables people not specially sensitive in ethical matters by natural endowment, to feel towards the claims of duty as the most sensitive feel towards them without that added stimulus. But the feeling exists apart from theistic belief in many honourable souls, and it manifestly points to Theism as its only justification. *For no Law, apart from a Lawgiver, is a proper object of reverence. It is mere brute fact; and every living thing, still more every person exercising intelligent choice, is its superior. The reverence of persons can be appropriately given only to that which itself is at least personal.*

Throughout this recapitulation of the discussion of Truth, Beauty and Goodness, great emphasis has been laid on an element of experience designated by the word "feeling". But it is clear that it is "feeling" of a special kind. It answers not to *Gefühl*, but to *Ahnung*—to which so profound an influence was ascribed by Hegel's contemporary Jacob Friedrich Fries, whose importance as a philosopher Professor Rudolf Otto has lately emphasised.[1] To myself it is evident that to doubt fundamentally the intimations of these "feelings"—

> High instincts, before which our mortal nature
> Did tremble like a guilty thing surprised[2]—

involves so pervasive a "scepticism of the instrument" as to render all conviction impossible, and all opinion temerarious. If I may not trust what seems to me more sure than sight, more convincing than touch, I find no reason to accept any data of experience whatsoever. But I am aware that not every one finds these feelings or intuitions so self-evidently veridical, and while ready for myself to stand on them as a sufficient platform for the support of a theistic interpretation of experience, I yet gladly supplement them by a converging line of argument which leads to the same result.

We have directed our attention to the Process which constitutes the world of Nature. We have seen that, in the course of that Process, Mind appears—first in a rudimentary form, later in fuller development. In this fuller development we see Mind, though occurring within the Process and conditioned by it, yet capable in steadily increasing measure of selecting the direction of its own attention, and thereby determining the action which it initiates, even in the physical sphere. We cannot avoid asking for some explanation of this Process itself; and when we do so, three points immediately challenge our attention.

[1] See his lectures on *The Philosophy of Religion.*
[2] Wordsworth's *Ode on the Intimations of Immortality.*

(1) If it is indeed true, as we have found compelling reason to believe, that Mind thus initiates activity—which includes physical movements—in the physical sphere, then the physical universe is not a closed system governed only by its own laws. If the tides of the sea retard the rotation of the earth, then so does every motion on the earth's surface that is caused by the minds of men, whether that of their own bodies or that of other bodies set in motion by these.[1] The amount of difference that pygmies like us can make to astronomical movement is, no doubt, so small as to be negligible by astronomical science. But the principle stands. The dogma of the closed system of the physical world must be abandoned if the freedom of Mind is admitted.

(2) Any account of the Process as a whole—of Nature as known to us—must account also for the occurrence of Mind as an element within it. Its explanatory principle must contain the ground of freedom as against naturalistic determinism. It must be of such a character that the occurrence of free minds within the process is recognisably congruous with that character.

(3) The ground of the universe, by reference to which the universe is explicable or intelligible, must be such that it requires no further explanation of itself. But all ways of accounting for facts or occurrences in terms of physical laws call for further explanation—and that in two ways: they explain what is by reference to what was; but this in turn calls for explanation by reference to what was before that; and the physical law itself is not self-explanatory. Why is it so, and not otherwise?

Now Mind, determined by Good as apprehended, is such a principle of explanation as is required. When Aristotle in Book Λ of the *Metaphysics* desiderated a first principle of motion, an initiation of process, he found it in the analogy of an object of desire. The

[1] "Each time the child throws its toy out of its baby-carriage, it disturbs the motion of every star."—Jeans, *The Universe Around Us*, p. 198.

First Mover κινεῖ ὡς ἐρώμενον.[1] sets other things in motion, as an object of desire does; without motion on its own part, it sets in motion the bodies of those who desire it. Perhaps Aristotle had in his mind no thought beyond the observation that objects of desire do thus initiate motion while unmoved themselves, so that the notion of an unmoved mover is nothing wholly extravagant. But in fact he indicated a possible explanation of the world-process. When Mind, determined by Good as apprehended, initiates activity, no further explanation is needed. The enquiring mind, confronted with an example of what it perfectly understands as the essential characteristic of its own being, is completely satisfied. Whenever the subject of enquiry is traced to the action of intelligently purposive mind, the enquiry is closed; Mind has recognised itself and is satisfied.

To adopt the hypothesis that the process of nature in all its range is to be accounted for by the intelligent purpose of Mind is Theism. This hypothesis, and this alone of any ever suggested, accounts for all the three considerations that were said to arise on a review of the Process as a whole. If the Process is grounded in Mind it is in no way surprising that minds should appear as episodes in the Process, and there is no reason to suppose that the physical universe is a closed system. *Mens agitat molem*[2] —that is the brief, but sufficient, explanation of the entire series of facts.

Yet there are still ambiguities. Is this Mind, which pervades, sustains, and directs the Whole, so entirely expressed in it, as to have its whole being in it or is it something over and above all that the Process contains or ever could contain? Plainly it is immanent; is it also transcendent? It will be useful here to refer to Professor Whitehead, to whom the contention of these Lectures hitherto owes much, but from whom at this point sharp difference must be expressed. Professor Whitehead

[1] *Metaphysics*, Λ, 1072 *a* 3.

[2] Vergil, *Aeneid*, vi. 727.

recognises that the Process regarded as such stands in need of explanation, and is unable to supply this from itself. He says:

"The evolution of history can be rationalised by the consideration of the determination of successors by antecedents. But, on the other hand, the evolution of history is incapable of rationalisation because it exhibits a selected flux of participating forms. No reason, internal to history, can be assigned why that flux of forms, rather than another flux, should have been illustrated."[1]

The answer to this problem is found in the "primordial nature of God"—or rather that is the concatenation of vocables offered to any one who asks the question. An answer it is not. It is a mere name for a *desideratum*. For this "primordial nature of God" is nothing at all except the occasion for the initiation of the flux with which we are familiar. God is, indeed,

"the actual entity in virtue of which the entire multiplicity of eternal objects obtains its graded relevance to each stage of concrescence. Apart from God, there could be no relevant novelty."[2]

But this still does not tell us *how*, with God, there *can* be relevant novelty. Truly there *is* relevant novelty. To say that God is the ground of the possibility of this is to say nothing unless God is something other than such ground of possibility. To say God, or to say X, or to say *abracadabra*, is all one, if at the end we have only declared that the ground of possibility is the ground of possibility.

So again we are told that "God is the principle of concretion";[3] but how does that help us if He is no more than this? Moreover there is a force beyond God, called "creativity", and God in His primordial nature, is the first form of this. "The primordial nature of God is the acquirement by creativity of a primordial character".[4]

[1] *Process and Reality*, p. 64.
[2] *Ibid.* p. 229.
[3] *Ibid.* p. 345.
[4] *Ibid.* p. 487.

No doubt all this is supplemented by what is urged later concerning the "consequent nature of God". About this Professor Whitehead has much to say that is edifying,[1] but it is hard to see by what right he says it. One is glad to know that he has the consolation of believing that "the love in the world passes into the love in heaven, and floods back again into the world", so that "in this sense God is the great companion—the fellow-sufferer who understands".[2] This is very near the Christian Gospel, and if only Professor Whitehead would for creativity say Father, for "primordial nature of God" say Eternal Word, and for "consequent nature of God" say Holy Spirit, he would perhaps be able to show ground for his gratifying conclusions. But he cannot use those terms, precisely because each of them imports the notion of Personality as distinct from Organism. The very reason which gives to the Christian scheme its philosophic superiority is that which precludes Professor Whitehead from adopting it.[3]

The only reason to be found for his confidence in "the perfection of God's subjective aim" and the resultant "character of His consequent nature"[4] is the consideration that if this were true it would round off the philosophy of organism. Now it is certainly true that a union of comprehensiveness with coherence is a mark of truth. But it is rash to affirm propositions on the ground that, if true, they would, in combination with

[1] See Appendix D. [2] *Process and Reality*, p. 497.

[3] Miss Emmet complains of L. S. Thornton's book *The Incarnate Lord* on the ground that when it comes to consider the status of Jesus Christ in the World-Order "it sacrifices the conception of an organic connexion between the eternal order and the temporal series in order to preserve a finality of revelation" (Whitehead's *Philosophy of Organism*, pp. 254, 5, footnote). I am not concerned to defend Father Thornton, who is fully competent to defend himself. But it never occurred to me that he was using Whitehead's philosophy to *preserve* anything whatever; he seemed to me to be using that philosophy, for what it was worth and as far as it would take him, as a medium of exposition. In any case I should regard it as one of the great merits of Father Thornton's book that he does "sacrifice" (I would rather say "transcend") the organic connexion between the eternal and the temporal. This is necessary, not to preserve the finality of a revelation, but to secure the intelligibility of anything at all.

[4] *Ibid.* p. 489.

those already affirmed, achieve that union, especially if the data of ordinary experience are hostile. Professor Whitehead's optimistic conclusion is not a necessary, or in the judgement of many people even a probable, inference from the facts of ordinary experience. These point to a divorce of power from goodness at least as impressively as to their union in the perfection of a universe which is for ever being saved. The Professor finds the ground of his confidence in the "completeness" of God's primordial nature. But how does he know that it is complete in any relevant sense? Of course it is, by definition, the ground of all actual events. But to infer from this the kind of completion posited is to assume the Leibnizian theory of "the best of all possible worlds" which has previously been described as "an audacious fudge".[1] If on the other hand we are to estimate the character of the primordial nature of God from that of the events which it has occasioned, we have inadequate ground for concluding that, as He objectifies the world in Himself, "God is the poet of the world, with tender patience leading it by his vision of truth, beauty and goodness".[2] And how many questions are begged by the use of the word "patience"?

The fact is that in his beautiful closing pages Professor Whitehead surreptitiously introduces thoughts which properly belong to Personality, though ostensibly he stops short at the category of organism. Because he ostensibly stops there, he has to present God and the world as completely correlated to each other.[3] But because they are thus correlated, and each is explained by the other, the complex totality of God + World is not explained at all. It is what it is. If it is as described, we may be glad that it is what it is; but that is not the same as saying that we see why it is what it is. That could only be seen if qualities are ascribed to it which would carry us beyond Organism to Personality—beyond the

[1] *Process and Reality* p. 64. [2] *Ibid.* p. 490.
[3] See the series of antitheses on page 492 quoted in the Appendix to this Lecture.

notion of inner unification by co-ordination of function to the notion of self-determination by reference to apprehended good.

But Personality is always transcendent in relation to Process. Purposive action or reaction, which is a chief characteristic of Personality, differs from organic action or reaction precisely in the fact that not only is it determined by the whole being of the agent, but that the agent is determining himself both at other times and in the very moment and act of choosing his course of conduct. Here there is manifestly a reference to something over and above the observable activity. Organic differs from mechanical reaction in that the reaction is determined by the whole organism as a unity; if for example a condition arises which would increase the proportion of acid in the blood, the appropriate organs increase *pari passu* the supply of alkali and the balance is maintained. This results from the need of the organism as a whole for the maintenance of that balance. It cannot be accounted for on mechanical grounds; it is an instance of organic reaction. But while the organism as a whole and its vital needs thus determine the reaction of its several parts, it is the organism as it is at that moment which exerts this determining influence. There is nothing transcendent there. But in the self-determination of a personality something, which as yet is not, is envisaged as determining that which is. To say that the Self, being such as it is, acts in a certain way is to ignore the characteristic feature of this situation. The Self, being such as it is, but including in its present condition an aspiration to become what it is not, determines itself as reacting to the given circumstances, whatever they may be. Of course it is true that the future self does not exercise efficient causation upon the present self; such a contention would be manifestly ludicrous. It is the apprehension of what shall be, or at the least what may be, which exercises efficient causation over the self in its choice of conduct. But this is a form of causation that can only operate in or upon those to whom the future is a real factor in decision, as it is not for the organism. In the case of personal choice, there is more at work upon or in the "present" than is contained within that "present" as understood in the consideration of physical movements or of organisms. No doubt a personal self is a single organism, for its totality determines the behaviour of its "parts". But it is also more than an organism, because it is also determining itself by reference to its own ideal of itself, as an organism does not. To take at once a crucial instance; self-sacrifice, such as is seen in the surrender of life for a person or a cause by one who has no belief in a future life, is not what is ordinarily meant by an organic reaction. But this self, which frames ideals of itself, is certainly something more than appears in its actions. It may be that some very small selves, or some very full lives, have attained on earth a complete correlation of personality and activity, so that taking the life of each as a whole it could be said that the personality was immanent in the conduct and in no sense transcendent of it; but even then it would be transcendent of each particular action. What we have called the freedom of mind, with the kind of self-determination that results from it, implies also self-transcendence, and therefore a self that transcends.

Such self-determination we have found reason to regard as an established fact. The principle that is to account for the World-Process must account for this fact as (amongst other things) an episode in that Process. The principle of Organism will not do this unless it be so expanded as to deserve the name of Personality. But the principle of Personality is adequate. For it supplies, as has been already said, a ground of explanation which calls for no further explanation, thus delivering us from the infinite regress. Further, it is adequate in the sense that it is equal in richness of content to those episodes in the process which are richest, so that we are not under the necessity of explaining any existent by reference to a principle lower in the scale of being than itself. Thirdly, it is a principle of which the characteristic is action in the present with a view to a future fruition, so that it combines, as nothing else does, efficient causation with rational coherence; for when a person acts purposively his several actions cohere in one intelligible scheme, while in each action the present choice, which is at that stage expressive of the constant purpose, is an efficient cause of the changes effected in the environment.

But there is a further consideration deeper than all of these. Personality exhibits itself supremely in purposes of fellowship or love—supremely, because here is it furthest removed from the mechanical or organic. Therefore it needs, for its full self-expression, the existence of other persons. If we take as our ultimate principle Personality, not only as purposive mind, but as mind of which the actual purpose is love, then the occurrence of persons within the World-Process is truly explained by the principle to which that process is referred; and there is no other principle known to us whereby human fellowship, which is the culmination of the Process hitherto, is truly explained at all.

To make that hypothesis is to go beyond the evidence so far adduced as surely as Professor Whitehead's assumption of the "completeness" of the "primordial nature of God" from which he deduces the perfection of the "consequent nature of God". But it is a more justifiable adventure for several reasons. (1) It employs for the explanation of all things the "highest" category in our experience, whereas Professor Whitehead employs one less than the highest whereby to account for that highest with the rest. (2) It offers a real explanation alike of itself and of the World, whereas Professor Whitehead leaves us with a totality of God + World, wherein each explains the other but the totality itself is unexplained. (3) Most significant of all, it points to the reality of a Being of such nature as to disclose His character in specific acts, which revealing acts might supply evidence to set against the apparent evidence of ordinary experience. Professor Whitehead conducts to an optimistic conclusion those who follow him. And reason clamours for an optimistic World-view, for how can a world be reasonable if it were better that it had never come into being? But the evidence of ordinary experience, taken alone, allows no more, at best, than an open verdict. And it seems clear that Professor Whitehead's God, whether in His primordial or in His consequent nature, could not offer such disclosure of Himself in revealing acts as could be taken, if sufficiently authenticated, to outweigh the evidence of our admittedly restricted range of experience. And this is true of all ultimate theories of the world except the Theistic. But if on other grounds the Theistic hypothesis appears the most acceptable, as we have seen reason to hold, then it is capable of receiving confirmation, such as other theories altogether preclude, from events regarded as being revelatory acts of the Personal God whose existence is posited by the hypothesis. If I regard the Ultimate Principle as non-personal, I cannot afterwards regard any occurrence as a purposive self-revelation of that Principle; so I can only estimate its character, or its relation to my valuations, by observing the average tendency of the world as experienced. But if I regard the Ultimate Principle as Personal, then I am at least at liberty to interpret as acts of specific self-revelation on the part of that Principle any which can make good their claim to be so regarded; and I am then also at liberty—rather am bound in reason—to take these as indications of the character of the Ultimate Principle, even though the whole evidence of ordinary experience told the other way. In doing so I shall act by faith and not by knowledge, but by a reasonable faith.

So intimately bound up in one another are the Personality of the Ultimate and specific acts of revelation that an *a priori* argument for the former would be highly precarious if not supported by the latter. The general question of the actual possibility of such acts, the conditions of their occurrences and the criterion of their authenticity will occupy us in the next series of Lectures. Until these questions are handled our present argument lacks completion. *But our argument has led us, provisionally at least, to the conclusion that the explanation of the world is to be sought in a Personal Reality, or to use the historic phrase, in a Living God.*

But something remains to be said about the nature of His relation to the World and its Process. He is its explanation in such wise that it is dependent upon Him as He is not dependent upon it. Is it necessary, in order to be this, that He should be something more? We may readily agree that God's relation to the universe is not that of a carpenter to a box which he is making. He is not, in that sense, outside it and acting on it from without. He is Himself its life, its informing and vitalising principle. But in order to be that we have found that He must be Personal, and Personality always transcends its own self-expression. This does not necessarily mean that if we could apprehend the entire universe, spiritual and material, in all its extent of space and time, there would still quite certainly be something in God unexpressed in that panorama. It seems more natural to suppose that the Divine Artist has in His entire creation given complete expression to His mind and nature. But the contention that God is the explanation of the world because He is Person or Spirit does mean that if all else but God were abolished, God would still be Himself, whole and entire, capable of creating another world to take the place of the world which had gone out of existence. If God is Personal, He must express Himself; the Word was in the beginning with God; but His self-expression is not the self expressed; that remains always cause, never effect.

Are we then to think of God as expressed in, or immanent in, His creation as a poet in his poems? That is an improvement on the analogy of the carpenter and his box. But it leaves God too external to the world. When I read Shakespeare's plays, I find there the thoughts of Shakespeare, not Shakespeare the "thinking living, acting man". When I hear my friend speak, or watch his action, I find there his living self. The principle that explains the process of the world must be no less intimately related to that process than a man to his conduct. In nature we find God; we do not only infer from Nature what God must be like, but when we see Nature truly, we see God self-manifested in and through it.[1] Yet the self-revelation so given is incomplete and inadequate. Personality can only reveal itself in persons. Consequently it is specially in Human Nature—in men and women—that we see God. But Human Nature is a thing self-confessedly defective; whether still struggling to its true self-realisation, or fallen from an "original righteousness", it can give but a fitful and distorted representation of the Personal Reality from whom it springs. If in the midst of the World-Process there should occur an instance of Human Nature free from all blemish or defect, there might be found there the perfect self-expression of God to those who share that Human Nature. So it might come, but not otherwise; and only if it so comes can the great hypothesis itself be secure.

Yet once more, if the Personal God thus indwells the world, and the world is thus rooted in Him, this involves that the process of the world is itself the medium of His personal action.[2] It is commonly assumed by those who use freely the terms Immanence and Transcendence that God as immanent is unchangeably constant, while

[1] The parables of Christ strongly suggest such a view of the relation of Nature to God.

[2] "The world of nature cannot be understood by an intelligent theist otherwise than as the ever present working of a divine power."—A. S. Pringle-Pattison, *The Balfour Lectures on Realism*, 1933, p. 257.

God as transcendent possesses a reserve of resource whereby He can from time to time modify the constant course sustained by His immanent action. This seems to be a mere reflection of the wholly un-philosophic dichotomy of events into normal and miraculous. The naïve religious view is that God made the world and imposed laws upon it, which it invariably observes unless He intervenes to modify the operation of His own laws. From this naïve view springs the suggestion that it would better comport with the infinite Majesty of God that He should from the outset impose such laws as would never stand in need of modification. But if, as we have seen ground for holding, the World-Process is itself the medium of God's personal action, the whole situation is altered. There is nothing majestic about invariable constancy of personal action, which remains unaltered whether the circumstances are the same or not; rather should it be called mulish. Constancy of purpose is a noble characteristic, but it shows itself, not in unalterable uniformity of conduct, but in perpetual self-adaptation, with an infinite delicacy of graduation, to different circumstances, so that, however these may vary, the one unchanging purpose is always served.

If we adopt this view, we shall have also to hold that no Law of Nature as discovered by physical science is ultimate. It is a general statement of that course of conduct in Nature which is sustained by the purposive action of God so long and so far as it will serve His purpose. No doubt it is true that the same cause will always produce the same effect in the same circumstances. Our contention is that an element in every actual cause, and indeed the determinant element, is the active purpose of God fulfilling itself with that perfect constancy which calls for an infinite graduation of adjustments in the process. Where any adjustment is so considerable as to attract notice it is called a miracle; but it is not a specimen of a special class, it is an illustration of the general character of the World-Process.

At the present time, as was remarked in the last lecture,[1] leading students of physical science are disputing about the question whether there is, for the purposes of their science, indeterminacy in the conduct of atoms; is the movement of *Quanta* physically indeterminate? Sir Arthur Eddington and Sir James Jeans say, Yes; Einstein, Planck, and Lord Rutherford say, No. But the theistic philosopher is not greatly interested, for in either case he will maintain that in the last resort there is no indeterminacy; in either case the universal determinant is the purpose of God.

Because He is the all-comprehending Mind, the course which He sustains in Nature is orderly; that it should be in any way capricious would imply such characteristics in God as are manifest defects or limitations when they appear in men. When there is no sufficient reason for variation, none will appear. And for the vastly greater part of Nature's course there is, so far as we can tell, no reason at all for variation, and much reason for uniformity. All purpose in finite creatures—and therefore all moral purpose—depends on the reliability of nature. We could make no plans if the rising of the sun to-morrow were not reasonably certain, or if there were serious risk of failure in the custom of gravitation. Moreover, it is good for us to be subject to the discipline of accident, so that even those occasions when we are tempted to think that Almighty Love must vary the course of nature to avert suffering from ourselves or our friends, are still illustrations of our ruling principle that the uniformity of nature is grounded in the purpose of God. But when that purpose would be itself defeated by some anticipated occurrence, that occurrence is in fact impossible—as Christ suggested when he met the alarm of His disciples with the implication that the boat which carried the hope of the world could not sink.[2]

[1] See pp. 228-229.

[2] This is not, I think, an unfair paraphrase of Mark iv. 37. The astonishment of the disciples is that the storm ceased at His bidding—a minor matter. His astonishment was that they had any anxiety.

This is not popular doctrine in an age for which the metaphysics of every question is overshadowed by the physics, as in an earlier period the physics was by the metaphysics. Yet I am very sure that the conception of the Divine Personality is only tenable if it is taken in bitter earnest. And then it leads us to the conviction that the immanent principle of the World Process is a purposive Mind, guiding the movement of electrons and of galaxies by the requirements of its unchanging purpose, so that for the most part their course is constant, but the cause of their constancy is itself the cause of their variation when that serves the one purpose best.

Yet that which is found in the constancy and the adjustments alike—the immanent and self-adapting Spirit—is always the expression of the truly Personal Being whose self is thus manifested in successive partial disclosures. The immanent activity varies; but the transcendent Being is eternally self-subsistent and self-identical. God in the world acts now this way and now that as He carries to accomplishment His unchanging purpose. But God Himself, the root and ground of that unchanging purpose, eternally is. He is no more unchanging than He is changeable; for both of these express persistence through time. But God does not persist through time, for time itself is grounded in Him. He creates the world and guides it from phase to phase by His sustaining spirit active in and through it. But if He be no more than that sustaining spirit, we are back at the process which as a whole explains its parts but also as a whole is incapable of explanation. There is no need to fall back into that abyss if we are true to the principle of Personality. For a person is always somebody, so to speak, on his own account, over and above his activities. So too God is active in the world, and its process is His activity. Yet He is more than this; He is creator and therefore transcendent. Because He is, and is creative, He must create; therefore the universe is necessary to Him in the sense that He can only be

Himself by creating it. But He is necessary to it, because it only exists by His fiat. God and the world are not correlative terms. God as immanent is correlative with the world; but that is not the whole nature of God. The more we study the activity of God immanent, the more we become aware of God transcendent. The Truth that strikes awe in the scientist is awful because it is His thought; the Beauty that holds spell-bound the artist is potent because it is His glory; the Goodness that pilots us to the assured apprehension of Reality can do this because it is His character; and the freedom whereby man is lifted above all other nature, even to the possibility of defying it, is fellowship with Him. "Heaven and earth are full of His glory"; but He is more and other than all that is in earth and heaven.

APPENDIX D

I HAVE so freely alluded to the closing sections of Professor Whitehead's great work *Process and Reality* that it will probably be a convenience to the reader if I quote here in full the most important paragraphs; they are taken from the last pages of the book, pp. 488-497.

§ iii

"But God, as well as being primordial, is also consequent. He is the beginning and the end. He is not the beginning in the sense of being in the past of all members. He is the presupposed actuality of conceptual operation, in unison of becoming with every other creative act. Thus by reason of the relativity of all things, there is a reaction of the world on God. The completion of God's nature into a fulness of physical feeling is derived from the objectification of the world in God. He shares with every new creation its actual world; and the concrescent creature is objectified in God as a novel element in God's objectification of that actual world. This prehension into God of each creature is directed with the subjective aim, and clothed with the subjective form, wholly derivative from his all-inclusive primordial valuation. God's conceptual nature is unchanged, by reason of its final completeness. But his derivative nature is consequent upon the creative advance of the world.

"Thus, analogously to all actual entities, the nature of God is dipolar. He has a primordial nature and a consequent nature. The consequent nature of God is conscious; and it is the realisation of the actual world in the unity of his nature, and through the transformation of his wisdom. The primordial nature is conceptual, and the consequent nature is the weaving of God's physical feelings upon his primordial concepts.

"One side of God's nature is constituted by his conceptual experience. This experience is the primordial fact in the world, limited by no actuality which it presupposes. It is therefore infinite, devoid of all negative prehensions. This side of his nature is free, and unconscious. The other side originates and then acquires integration with the primordial side. It is determined, incomplete, consequent, 'everlasting', fully actual, and conscious. His necessary goodness expresses the determination of his consequent nature.

"Conceptual experience can be infinite, but it belongs to the nature of physical experience that it is finite. An actual entity in the temporal world is to be conceived as originated by physical experience, with its process of completion motivated by consequent, conceptual experience initially derived from God. God is to be conceived as originated by conceptual experience with his process of completion motivated by consequent, physical experience, initially derived from the temporal world.

§ iv

"The perfection of God's subjective aim, derived from the completeness of his primordial nature, issues into the character of his consequent nature. In it there is no loss, no obstruction. The world is felt in a unison of immediacy. The property of combining creative advance with the retention of mutual immediacy is what in the previous section is meant by the term 'everlasting'.

"The wisdom of subjective aim prehends every actuality for what it can be in such a perfected system—its sufferings, its sorrows, its failures, its triumphs, its immediacies of joy—woven by rightness of feeling into the harmony of the universal feeling, which is always immediate, always many, always one, always with novel advance, moving onward and never perishing. The revolts of destructive evil, purely self-regarding, are dismissed into their triviality of merely individual facts; and yet the good they did achieve in individual joy, in individual sorrow, in the introduction of needed contrast, is yet saved by its relation to the completed whole. The image—and it is but an image—the image under which this operative growth of God's nature is best conceived, is that of a tender care that nothing be lost.

"The consequent nature of God is his judgement on the world. He saves the world as it passes into the immediacy of his own life. It is the judgement of a tenderness which loses nothing that can be saved. It is also the judgement of a wisdom which uses what in the temporal world is mere wreckage.

* * * * *

"God's rôle is not the combat of productive force with productive force, of destructive force with destructive force, it lies in the patient operation of the overpowering rationality of his conceptual harmonisation. He does not create the world, He saves it: or, more accurately, He is the poet of the world, with tender patience leading it by his vision of truth, beauty and goodness.

§ V

* * * * *

"The consequent nature of God is the fluent world become 'everlasting' by its objective immortality in God. Also the objective immortality of actual occasions requires the primordial permanence of God, whereby the creative advance ever re-establishes itself endowed with initial subjective aim derived from the relevance of God to the evolving world.

"But objective immortality within the temporal world does not solve the problem set by the penetration of the finer religious intuition. 'Everlastingness' has been lost; and 'everlastingness' is the content of that vision upon which the finer religions are built—the 'many' absorbed everlastingly in the final unity. The problems of the fluency of God and of the everlastingness of passing experience are solved by the same factor in the universe. This factor is the temporal world perfected by its reception and its reformation, as a fulfilment of the primordial appetition which is the basis of all order. In this way God is completed by the individual fluent satisfactions of finite fact, and the temporal occasions are completed by their everlasting union with their transformed selves, purged into conformation with the eternal order which is the final absolute 'wisdom'. The final summary can only be expressed in terms of a group of antitheses, whose apparent self-contradiction depends on neglect of the diverse categories of existence. In each antithesis there is a shift of meaning which converts the opposition into a contrast.

"It is as true to say that God is permanent and the World fluent, as that the World is permanent and God is fluent.

"It is as true to say that God is one and the World many, as that the World is one and God many.

"It is as true to say that, in comparison with the World, God is actual eminently, as that, in comparison with God, the World is actual eminently.

"It is as true to say that the World is immanent in God, as that God is immanent in the World.

"It is as true to say that God transcends the World, as that the World transcends God.

"It is as true to say that God creates the World, as that the World creates God.

"God and the World are the contrasted opposites in terms of which Creativity achieves its supreme task of transforming disjoined multiplicity, with its diversities in opposition, into concrescent unity, with its diversities in contrast. In each actuality there are two concrescent poles of realisation—'enjoyment' and 'appetition,' that is, the 'physical' and the 'conceptual'. For God the conceptual is prior to the physical, for the World the physical poles are prior to the conceptual poles."

* * * * *

"In God's nature, permanence is primordial and flux is derivative from the World: in the World's nature, flux is primordial and permanence is derivative from God; also the World's nature is a primordial datum for God; and God's nature is a primordial datum for the World. Creation achieves the reconciliation of permanence and flux when it has reached its final term which is everlastingness—the Apotheosis of the World."

* * * * *

"The theme of Cosmology, which is the basis of all religions, is the story of the dynamic effort of the World passing into everlasting unity, and of the static majesty of God's vision, accomplishing its purpose of completion by absorption of the World's multiplicity of effort."

* * * * *

§ vii

* * * * *

"There are thus four creative phases in which the universe accomplishes its actuality. There is first the phase of conceptual origination, deficient in actuality, but infinite in its adjustment of valuation. Secondly, there is the temporal phase of physical origination, with its multiplicity of actualities. In this phase full actuality is attained; but there is deficiency in the solidarity of individuals with each other. This phase derives its determinate conditions from the first phase. Thirdly, there is the phase of perfected actuality, in which the many are one everlastingly, without the qualification of any loss either of individual identity or of completeness of unity. In everlastingness, immediacy is reconciled with objective immortality. This phase derives the conditions of its being from the two antecedent phases. In the fourth phase, the creative action completes itself. For the perfected actuality passes back into the temporal world, and qualifies this world so that each temporal actuality includes it as an immediate fact of relevant experience. For the kingdom of heaven is with us to-day. The action of the fourth phase is the love of God for the world. It is the particular providence for particular occasions. What is done in the world is transformed into a reality in heaven, and the reality in heaven passes back into the world. By reason of this reciprocal relation, the love in the world passes into the love in heaven, and floods back again into the world. In this sense, God is the great companion—the fellow-sufferer who understands."

PART II

THE IMMANENCE OF THE TRANSCENDENT

LECTURE XI

THE IMMANENCE OF THE TRANSCENDENT

Our review of the cosmic process, of our own place in it, and of our apprehension alike of the process itself and of our relation to it, led us to the conviction that there is at work within and throughout it a Mind which also transcends it. When Mind, by means of its free ideas, becomes active not only in choosing means to ends, but in choosing between ends, it is rightly called Spirit. This activity manifestly belongs to that Mind in which the cosmic process is grounded, so that this Mind is fitly called the Supreme Spirit. For the process, of course, is process; as such, its successive moments come into being and pass away. But among the successive occurrences—or, more accurately, occurrents—are entities of such sort as to be the subject of value-judgements—to wit, ourselves; these entities find their circumstances, and indeed also themselves, to be good and evil. They find in their experience not only events but significance. As they seek to understand this quality in things, and how it can be possible, they are led to postulate a general significance of the process itself; they leap to the assumption or the demand that taken in its entirety it is good; and they make experiment, both theoretical and practical, with this hypothesis, thus becoming philosophers or pioneers. Those who have made the initial demand or assumption with the most vigorous apprehension of its nature usually find that experience fortifies them in that basic conviction. Those who begin more tentatively are seldom led by their own experience to any very confident affirmation, though they may be infected with the enthusiasm of others and so led confidently and energetically to make of life and experience the demand which hitherto they had put forward with hesitation. Those who make no initial demand that experience shall show itself to be good will seldom be converted by its course to a belief that it has that character. Moreover, it is energy of action rather than range or subtlety of thought which is as a rule found most potent in confirming the optimist hypothesis.

These considerations do not provide a basis for any hope of creating universal agreement in favour of belief in the goodness of the world or against it. Whatever a man starts by believing, it appears that experience is likely to confirm him in that belief. The process, which throws up human intelligences as episodes of its unending transitoriness, endows some of them with an optimistic temper and some with the reverse; and whatever outlook it supplies, it offers a corresponding view to be looked-out upon. So it appears. And it may at once be said that this is so far true that hardly any one was ever turned from pessimism to optimism by any activity of intellectual reflection, though some have been turned the other way by brooding over "the slings and arrows of outrageous fortune". The conviction that there is a meaning in life and that this meaning is good belongs not to science but to faith; and while a faith which is shown to be irrational must perish, faith is never a product of scientific observation and induction alone.

Yet this does not mean that from the standpoint of reason there is nothing to choose between optimistic faith and pessimistic agnosticism or despair. The whole endeavour of the former series of these lectures was to show that there is a vast abundance of evidence in our experience which calls for the optimistic interpretation. There is also, no doubt, very much that tends to deny it. So far the balance may hang evenly. But if it appears that the optimistic hypothesis supplies an explanation of what tends to pessimism without distorting this, while the pessimistic can only handle the portion of experience which tends to optimism by explaining it away, then the former must be pronounced to have the wider range of comprehension, and therefore, on a scientific view, the higher probability.

Now the first of the elements in experience challenging this choice of methods is the occurrence in the world-process of intelligences which even purport to estimate value and to find things good or evil. At the risk of tediousness we must once more, and for the last time, claim for this fact a place in the field of attention which men of science are often unwilling to accord it. Quite as impressive as the vastness of the universe or the infinite delicacy of its articulation is the apprehension of these qualities by beings who, from one point of view, are mere episodes of its continually changing process.[1] This apprehension of the whole—or at least of stupendous ranges of it—by very small parts of itself cannot be taken for granted and passed over as without significance. If all theories which seek to relate this fact to the nature of the Whole itself are found to present insuperable difficulties, we may be driven to fall back upon a materialism which regards this fact as an interesting but uninstructive episode, or upon an agnosticism which avowedly refuses to attempt any explanation of that fact which, in all our experience, most loudly demands one. It is clear that to adopt either of these latter courses is to proclaim the bankruptcy of philosophy. And this verdict on such a theory would not be in the smallest degree affected by a complete demonstration, were such a thing possible, that consciousness and thought are a secretion of the brain. No mystery could well be greater than that the brains of certain organisms should produce secretions which correspond with the structure of the universe in such a way that to act upon the impulsion supplied by them

[1] Sir James Jeans writes a book to describe the Mysterious Universe. But he is himself quite as mysterious as all that he describes: and nothing is so mysterious as the fact that he can describe it.

is found to result in further correspondence with a modified structure of the universe at a later date, as appears to happen, on this theory, when we calculate the hour of to-morrow's sunrise, lay plans accordingly, and put them in practice when to-morrow comes.

Repelled by such Bedlamite ravings, we adopt instead the hypothesis to which all scientific activity points, and assume that mind as we know it in ourselves is akin to what guides and orders the universe in all its parts. It seems, as has been said, not to affect our argument whether it be held that all existence and all existing things are in some degree mental, though in stocks and stones this element is so rudimentary as to be negligible, or that the whole is the self-expression of a Mind which is able to use what is truly non-mental and even inorganic, as well as what is organic and mental, as the vehicle of its utterance. That may be in itself an interesting enquiry, and, before any philosophy can be final, it must rest on or supply a correct answer to that question. For us at this stage it is enough to establish the kinship of the human mind with the Principle which rules all things, and of that Principle with the human mind.

This human mind is not merely an energy active in tracing out logical correlations or observing uniform sequences. It is also, as we reminded ourselves at the outset of this lecture, a centre of value or subject of value-judgements. Indeed this characteristic is empirically prior to its purely logical qualities. It only begins to seek truth because it is already appreciative and appetitive of good; at first the good it aims at may be the comfort of its own organism; to secure this it must correctly apprehend the nature and reactions of a considerable part of its environment. Later, in the activity of seeking truth as a means to quite non-intellectual ends, it becomes aware of good in the very search for truth itself and in the grasp of it. Thus science is born. And it would seem strangely paradoxical to say that though science is a product of the mind as appreciative of value, yet value and appreciation have no ultimate significance or importance in that real world which science apprehends. We must repeat at this level the arguments of the former section. When we remember the place which belongs to mind as a subject of value-judgements in the initiation of scientific enterprise, it becomes absurd to say that value itself has no place in the world which science seeks to comprehend. For, once more, the thinking and valuing mind is part of that world; it is indeed the part which makes possible the existence of science. The man of science is part of the world which he studies, and for our purposes the most important part. Let him by all means be self-forgetful when he studies stars or electrons; but let him not generalise about the moral character of the universe or the mind expressed in it on a basis which omits the only evidence relevant to that subject.

Mind in pursuit of good is purposive and is known as Will. Will, we have seen, is the only principle known to man which supplies a finally satisfactory explanation of anything whatever. The effective action of will is, almost certainly, the prototype of all concepts of causation, and it is noticeable that all attempts to account for efficient causation otherwise than by reference to Will have broken down. Some scientists urge us to abandon the category of causation as being hopelessly obscure and confused. But in fact we cannot do without it.[1] And this will cause no dismay to any one who is ready to find the explanation of the world in a Cosmic Mind which is akin to the mind of man, and which is therefore appreciative and purposive as well as accurate and coherent.

So far we have been engaged in recapitulation of

[1] I cannot claim to have seriously studied the recent discussions of Causation, but an effort to follow their general course leaves me persuaded that nothing important has been added to Lotze's treatment of the subject in his *Microcosm*, vol. i. pp. 259-261, 276-283.

points urged in the former series of lectures. It is unnecessary here to refer to special occasions which seem to require a transcendent rather than a purely immanent Mind to account for them. They are found in connexion with all the three traditional forms of ultimate value—Knowledge, Beauty, and Goodness.[1] But the notions of Immanence and Transcendence themselves call for further consideration.

It is not difficult to see what is meant by an immanent principle; indeed the difficulty is to see how a principle can ever be other than immanent. On the other hand it is very difficult to see what is meant by an immanent person, or how a person can be other than (relatively) transcendent. This contrast states the most relevant points in the meaning of all the four terms; and it may be well to affirm dogmatically, before we go any further, that the *main interest alike of philosophy and of religion is with the question whether the Cosmic Mind is truly conceived as personal.* Yet there is a provisional convenience in the familiar terms, and an examination of their appropriate use will help us to avoid ambiguities; in the course of this examination we must repeat, from a different angle of approach, certain considerations urged in the last lecture; for we are in this series beginning where the last series left off and in some sense covering the same ground in the reverse direction.

The classical case of Immanence is of course the relationship of mind to body in any rational organism. Mind is immanent in the body which is organic to it.[2] A conception of the relation of God to the World, based on this analogy, is expressed in Pope's famous couplet:

> All are but parts of one stupendous Whole
> Whose body Nature is, and God the soul.[3]

[1] See pp. 249-255.
[2] We should maintain that mind transcends it; that is to say, the mind never receives full and exhaustive expression through the body: it is always more and other than the ground of the body's movements. But this is a further consideration.
[3] Pope, *Essay on Man.*

But to represent the cosmic system in this crude way as the body organic to the Divine Mind involves, not only the difficulties noted in our last series as besetting Whitehead's presentation, but also quite special and ruinous difficulties when we consider the relation of the Divine Mind to our own; for our minds, and the bodies which they govern, are not organic to the Divine Mind in the sense of always moving in immediate conformity with it. We may return to this analogy of mind and body. At present the terms with which we began will serve us better.

A principle is properly spoken of as immanent in the occasions or processes which conform to it. These illustrate it, and it is other than they; but it has no being apart from them. Gravitation does not first exist on its own account, and compel material particles to conform to itself. It exists in the mutual attraction of the material particles. So Nationalism is a principle to which certain policies and politicians conform; it explains their particular methods and actions. It is other than these, but it has no existence apart from these. In other words it is distinguishable, but not separable, from them. And because it is not separable from them, it has no element of transcendence.

A person is properly described as transcendent of his acts. He is expressed in these, but he has an existence apart from them. His circumstances on any occasion may be strictly accidental; that is to say, the causes conditioning them may be wholly other than his own will or any causes conditioning this,[1] so that it is possible to conceive him, while himself unaltered, being at that time in other circumstances instead. His acts in the two sets of circumstances would be quite different. Indeed he would express that special identity which he is by the difference in his acts in different circumstances. His self is not only distinguishable but separable from

[1] An "accident" is an event due to the convergence of two independent chains of causation. See *infra*, p. 291.

the acts in which it is revealed. What is important in the assertion of transcendence is the affirmation, not of unexhausted resources, though this may be true, but of capacity for that infinite delicacy of adjustment to varying conditions in which purposive as distinct from mechanical or chemical action consists. An unusual or unexpected act may appear to exhibit a special volume of energy, but that is because our minds are obsessed by the mechanical categories, and we suppose that additional energy is needed to counteract a supposed natural tendency to do always the same thing—a moral inertia. But what is required for heroic sacrifice as compared with selfish acquisitiveness is not more volitional force; it is a different volitional direction. *What a true doctrine of divine transcendence will assert is not a reservoir of normally unutilised energy, but a volitional as contrasted with a mechanical direction of the energy utilised.*

In what sense, then, if any, can a person be described as immanent? We may mark certain distinct grades. It is sometimes said, though probably only by those who wish to illustrate something else, that the thought of an inventor is immanent in the machine constructed in accordance with his idea, or that the mind of a poet is immanent in his works. Certainly in the case of a machine it is only the inventor's thought that can be so described, not his mind as possessed of subjective functions. There may be thought in the machine in the sense that it expresses and corresponds to thought; but this does not mean that the machine thinks. When men speak of divine immanence they always mean more than this. We come nearer to what is intended in the other illustration. For when a man says that the mind of Shakespeare is immanent in his plays, he does not only mean that Shakespeare's mind determined the arrangement of the words which we read (as the inventor's mind determined the arrangement of wheels and rods), but that when we read the plays we are entering into a certain commerce with the mind which conceived them, analogous to that intercourse of mind with mind which takes place in conversation but conducted through the medium of written instead of spoken words. So far as the change is in the medium of communication, the substitution of marks on paper for vibrations in the air, no important or relevant difference is discernible. The difference, which is obviously great, lies in the fact that the play is written and remains unaltered by any comment of ours, whereas when we hold conversation with a living person we receive not only an expression of his mind, but an expression of it adjusted to correspond to the expression of our own; we watch not merely the expression of that mind as fixed once for all, but the living play of that mind in sympathetic reaction to the play of our own. The text of *Hamlet* will not be affected by anything that I may say as the play proceeds; but my friend's next remark may be very greatly affected by my reply to what he said last. It is for this reason that there is still a sense of uneasiness in any doctrine of immanence which tries at once to assert the personality of the being held to be immanent, and yet to illustrate his immanence by reference to the relation of a poet to his poem.

The only true immanence of a person is in his conduct as it occurs. A person is not immanent in his past conduct, or in the record of it. You may infer his personality from these, but you cannot meet it in these. There is, however, a real sense in which a personality is immanent in his present conduct; it gives to that conduct its direction, its quality, its energy. And the conduct itself consists of that perpetual and delicate adjustment to varying and never wholly foreseen contingencies wherein the life of personality or purposive intelligence resides. Shakespeare himself was immanent in the composition of his plays; he is not himself immanent in the plays composed. You may interrupt *Othello* or insult it in its actual process, and provoke no personal reactions; if you interrupted the actual composition of *Othello* you might provoke a personal reaction which would illustrate that treasury of language from which so many dramatic characters drew the vehicle of their self-expression.

The more the matter is considered, the plainer does it become that we can only speak of the immanence of what is personal in processes which are not irrevocably fixed but are open to determination by the activity of mind, which, as we saw, is in varying degrees free from the pressure of that process in and out of which it emerges, and directs its activity according to its own principles and interests. To assert the immanence of a personal being in a process is to assert the indeterminacy of that process when considered in abstraction from the mind supposedly immanent in it.

The point we have reached may be put in another way, and it will then be seen that our contention is diametrically opposed to the interest with which the notion of divine immanence has commonly been invoked. It has commonly been suggested that immanent Deity may be conceived not only as a constant principle of action, but as a principle of constant action, while transcendent Deity, or Deity *qua* transcendent, possesses reserves of power which may be exercised by way of miracle and in a manner unpredictable by us. It is easy to see how this conception arose. Natural science was tracing uniformities of procedure in one department of existence after another, and asserted the uniformity of nature as the one indisputable axiom. Science triumphantly vindicated its methods by its resounding success. It was not easy at first for philosophy and theology to keep their balance. There was an obvious duty to welcome the new revelation. In some sense at least, science was grasping truth. If as we look back we judge the philosophers and especially the theologians of the latter nineteenth century and first decade of the twentieth to have been rather pusillanimous we must, in fairness to them, remember the immense impact of a scientific movement which seemed to be united in itself, and especially united in its proclamation of the dogma of uniformity. In our day the scientific phalanx has dissolved into unco-ordinated units; men of science repudiate one another's conclusions; the same scientist works at different times with contradictory theories; and many students of science are become sceptical about the capacity of science to lead to any apprehension of the real world. It is easy now for the theologian to be bold in claiming for the branch of experience and study which is his special concern its full weight in any philosophy which purports to be a survey of reality.

Yielding to the pressure of their times, the theologians of the last two generations submissively accepted the dogma of the scientists, and then set themselves to relate this to that belief in divine personality to which every western or Biblical religion is committed, by means of the thought of divine immanence. The laws of nature were taken to be a mode of that immanence; God as immanent was thought to be constant in His action, in the mechanical sense of constancy. There was also posited a divine transcendence, whereby God was conceived as able to modify His normal constancy of action by the occasional exercise of reserved powers in acts called miracles. Then of necessity came the struggle to eliminate or to establish this transcendence. For if it were established, it introduced an uncertainty into our expectation that laws of nature will continue to operate; who knows when they may be set side? But if the belief in divine transcendence be abolished, religion is in a parlous state, for a mechanically constant order (which is all that is then left, however much it be called divine immanence) is no object of worship or fount of love.

The mistake was to admit the assertion of natural uniformity at the physical level, or to suppose that variations in it must be due to the introduction of some power not normally utilised or the action of some "higher law" not normally operative. Obviously it has a provisional truth, which has been enough to carry science to its victories. The theologian who quarrels with science on its own ground is but a presumptuous fool. But the scientist who quarrels with theology on its own ground is no better. If there is mutual respect and common reverence for truth in all its forms there may still be divergence and even what we have called tension; but there will be no quarrel.

The impressiveness of the scientific advance in the nineteenth century was mainly due to the fact that science was then preponderantly occupied with physics and chemistry, and what is most intimately allied to these. It is true that the chief public controversy of the century was concerned with biology. But it was very early apparent that in this field there was less unanimity among students than in the others. The general hypothesis of Evolution was accepted, but its precise mode was debated, and for philosophic purposes the precise mode is as significant as the general hypothesis. It is obvious that for some students at least the impulsion towards acceptance of "natural selection" as the one and only mode of evolution came from a mechanistic habit of mind and a desire at all costs to dispense with providential "design". That is sheer prejudice of a grossly unscientific character. The fact is that "uniformity" takes a new meaning when applied to organisms, and when applied to persons is so transformed that it is misleading to use the word without careful explanation. Its true sphere, in the sense in which it was for a time dogmatic among scientists, is the sphere of what can be precisely weighed and measured—the sphere of mass and motion; beyond that it expands until in the spiritual sphere it becomes the "principle of sufficient reason".

The day is past, then, when the theologian can with self-respect accept from a department other than his own a dogma which reduces his own to insignificance, and then, by what is little more than verbal jugglery, try to save from the wreck what is vital to his special interest. He finds that the religious interest demands the assertion of personality in the Ultimate Reality itself. Further he finds that on a survey of existence in all its grades as a single whole he has abundant reason for this same conviction. We have attempted in the former series of lectures to show the grounds for that conclusion and have already recapitulated some of these. From that conviction, therefore, we now make our start in the endeavour to trace some of the ways in which the Personal Reality thus affirmed is related to our life and experience. In that enterprise we inevitably follow the analogy of personal conduct and action, though fully aware that this is in human beings subject to many limitations which can have no application to the ultimate Being.

Now so far as a person is made known in his conduct it is by a perpetual variation of reaction to varied conditions, which has its explanation in the identity of his personality and character. In so far as this is still in process of development under the discipline of experience, there may be actions which are really inconsistent with each other. Because of such growth, we do not call a man a liar on the ground that he is known to have told lies as a schoolboy. There may also be inconsistency, because even in mature life character has not been fully formed. But personality in a grown man shows its special quality neither in mechanical constancy of reaction, such as that of those who always, or never, fall in with suggestions made to them, nor in caprice, so that they are unreliable, but in a discriminating control of actions in the light of accepted principles of established sentiments. Thus the good father may be indulgent to one son and stern to another, if at different times they commit some outwardly identical offence, because from his knowledge of their characters as thus far formed he can be sure that he is in each case supplying what will most help moral progress. But no one could forecast his action who did not intimately know him and the sons and his love for and knowledge of them. It is thus that a person is immanent in his conduct. And if a personal God is to be described as immanent in the world, this must mean that the action and reaction of all parts of the world are determined at every moment by the wisdom of God, and if they are observed to be constant, that is because the wisdom of God so orders. Socrates was quite right in principle when he demanded of Anaxagoras, who had said all things were in chaos till reason ordered them, that he should say whether the earth is round or flat by showing which it is better that it should be.[1]

But though the principle was right, it was inapplicable by any finite mind. For no finite mind can say with certainty what is that good of the whole universe which dictates the detailed arrangements of its parts. In the sphere of morality we can without question or hesitation condemn some types of character and principles of action as bad, and commend others as good. But to determine the truth about the levels of being lower than the ethical and aesthetic by means of value-judgements passes the wit of man. We have here to call in aid the distinction, dear to Aristotle, between the order of being and the order of experience or discovery. It may be perfectly true that all things are as they are only because the Will of God, which is the Good as efficient cause, has so decided: good determines fact. But we can only find out what is in accordance with the Will of God in other than the ethical and aesthetic spheres by observing the facts and remembering that they are as they are because God so willed. In this activity of observation and in co-ordination of the facts observed, science has its being. It must not itself call in the hypothesis of Divine Volition in relation to any particular event, for that is to leave observation and co-ordination

[1] Plato, *Phaedo*, 97 D, E.

for the value-judgements which, admittedly, have here no scientific application. Yet if it be true that the Divine Will, though we can never fathom it, is none the less the real cause of all things being as they are, then science must admit that its own method affords only provisional assurance with regard to its results.

What follows from such a view? There is a point at which the behaviour of the natural world directly affects the moral interests of men; it is the point where natural conditions are integral to men's fulfilment of their intentions. What men call an "accident" is an event in which some causal sequence in nature comes into intimate relationship with the purposive action of a mind that had not taken that sequence into account. All purposive action of men rests upon and presupposes the constant operation of natural forces. I plan for to-morrow and for next year on the supposition that the revolution of the earth upon its own axis and about the sun will continue. If in following up my plan I walk along a street at the precise moment when a chimney is blown down so that it nearly or quite kills me, that is an "accident"; the fall of rocks from a mountain into an empty valley is not called an accident unless there is a person, or a building representing the purpose of a person, near where the rocks fall. It appears then that while the constancy of natural processes is the necessary prerequisite for intelligent, purposive and moral action, that same constancy may sometimes cut across the sequence of purposive actions and hinder the fulfilment of purpose. It is at such times that religious people are driven to ask why God permits the occurrence of events that involve apparently useless waste and sorrow. It would hardly be appropriate in this series of Lectures to discuss the principles on which it may be possible to "justify the ways of God to men" in the detail of personal experience.[1] But some of them may be indicated.

[1] I have attempted the outline of such a theology of accident in *Christus Veritas*, pp. 192-199.

First, the whole possibility of that moral life, from the implications of which the difficulty arises, depends upon the general constancy of natural processes, which leads to the particular regretted accident. If that constancy is to be modified every time it would lead to what is in itself regrettable for somebody, it would become a totally insecure foundation for the purposiveness of the moral life. Secondly, it is good for a man to know that the course of nature is not devised for his convenience; for his benefit indeed it is devised—for it is to his benefit that his individual convenience should not be considered. Consequently there is an immense *a priori* probability that it is good for the normal process to take its course, even though it make havoc of many human purposes and even of human affections. But the religious man's difficulty is not imaginary; it springs from a principle more fundamental than that of nature's constancy; it springs from recognition of what is implied by belief in Divine Personality.

For Personality, as was said, manifests its identity through an infinite variety of adaptation. The man who always acts in the same way, whatever the circumstances, is reliable indeed, but is not strong or loving or wise; he is only obstinate and stupid. If we believe in a personal God, we may believe that having created the world He leaves it to move by the laws implanted in it by the act of creation, or we may believe that He guides and governs it at every stage. If we accept the former view, we exclude present divine action from the greater part of the world of our experience. If we thus make a total severance between God and the world, as between a carpenter and a box that he has made, or, to take Paley's famous illustration, between a watchmaker and a watch, we are on the way to that separation between sacred and secular which ends by making religion a special and peculiar interest of persons constituted in a particular way. Moreover, it is of little help to attribute capacity for intervention to the Creator who normally leaves the mechanism of the universe to grind remorselessly on, for it appears that the instances of His intervention are, at any rate, very few, and indeed we see good reason why that should be so. God, who is in this fashion transcendent only, is too remote to be object and occasion of the religious experience of mankind as that has actually occurred. We are left with this result: a purely transcendent God, who intervenes often to give special direction to the course of events, is incompatible with a scientific apprehension of the world; while a purely transcendent God who never intervenes at all, or has done so only once or twice in recorded history, is incompatible with vital religion. The only way to hold together a vital religion and a scientific apprehension of the world is to assert some form of Divine Immanence.

We do a great disservice alike to philosophy and to religion if we minimise the divergence of the tendencies proper to science and to religion at this point. Because science works with uniformities it is unable to allow in its own processes for any variability in nature; and it is not easy for the man of science to admit that such variability may be real, even though science can take no account of it. Similarly because religion is concerned with Divine Personality it must assert the variability of a natural order which is the expression of that Personality, though for such variation, as for constancy, there must be "sufficient reason".

The scientist is free to pursue his own method and justified in pursuing it; but he must not dogmatise about what can or cannot happen; he must not allow the habit of mind which is appropriate and congenial to his special studies to become exalted as the only habit of mind appropriate to and worthy of the Creator of the cosmic system and of the purposive intelligences which inhabit it, apprehend it, and, in their degree, modify it. The religious man is free to insist that in every detail of experience the mind and hand of

God are traceable, but he must not suppose that he sufficiently apprehends the nature and scope of the divine purpose to say independently of evidence what has happened or is about to happen. Above all, he must not postulate reserves of energy or power which may break in upon the ordinary course of events from without but must recognise that the normal constancy of nature expresses the will of God no less truly than occasional variation, and that the explanation of what he calls a miracle is exactly the same as the ultimate explanation of the most commonplace event.

There is here a genuine difference between the outlook natural to religion and that natural to science. "Modern Science", says Dr. Streeter, in a lecture which (he assures us) was submitted for criticism and amendment to a scientific friend,

> "is founded on two closely related conceptions, mechanism and law; and it works mainly with two implements, experiment and measurement. To a scientist the verbs 'to explain' or 'to understand' mean to see the individual fact as an instance of a general law, or to see a departmental law as an instance of a more general law, and then to see all the phenomena concerned as connected in a relation of cause and effect *mechanically* conceived."[1]

To the religious man the verbs "to explain" or "to understand" mean to see the phenomenon in relation to the Divine Purpose. These are not necessarily incompatible; but they are very different. And the religious outlook has this advantage, that it is able when taken as ultimate, to allow free play to the scientific interest, provided only that this be regarded as provisional and not exclusive or ultimate ; while the scientific interest, if treated as ultimate, cannot find room for the religious interest or interpretation at all.

If the insistence on this point is becoming tedious, I must urge that it is of crucial importance and is commonly ignored. If uniformity in nature is not only

[1] B. H. Streeter, *The Buddha and the Christ*, p. 11.

usual but universal—still more if it is necessary—the personality of God is denied, unless God is conceived as purely transcendent in the way repudiated above. If the personality of God is affirmed, this affirmation carries with it that of the essential variability of nature. There is a sharp choice to be made here; the tension between the habit of mind congenial to religion and the habit of mind congenial to science is acute. But the way to deal with it is not to deny it, nor to let one habit extrude the other, nor to mitigate the tension itself, but to recognise its necessity and its origin, so that neither religion nor science may in practice encroach upon the other.

This position should not involve difficulty for any except believers in mechanical Determinism. If in any sense man has freedom to choose and to act on his choice, this of itself involves a breach in the rigid uniformity of nature. I am free to choose whether I shall stand still or walk across the room. If I choose the latter, I effect a redistribution of the mass of the world and shift its centre of gravity. That I only do so to an extent negligible in the most precise astronomical calculation possible to man, does not affect the principle. And if I can do this to any extent at all, then God, if He exists, can do it to any extent that He pleases.

Personality, whether human or divine, is, in so far as it is immanent, a principle of variation. There is in the world an immanent Reason—a Logos. If this is impersonal, it may be only a principle of logical coherence. If it is personal, it must be a principle of perpetual adjustment according to "sufficient reason". But behind, or above, the successive moments of conduct in which personality is immanent, there is the personality itself, transcendent, and, in proportion to its completeness of integration, unchangeable. *Miracles, if they occur, are as much the manifestation of God immanent as are the regular processes of Nature. God immanent is a principle or energy of adjustment and therefore of variation; God transcendent is the eternally self-identical—the I AM.*

But while personality is immanent in all its conduct, it is not equally expressed in all. The hero and the coward perform most actions of their lives quite indistinguishably; nothing reveals the heroism of the one or the cowardice of the other until some crisis arises—truly called a crisis, because it is the judgement on their two characters. The hero does not at that moment become brave or the coward timid; but the event displays what each had been in the time when no difference appeared between them. The heroic act is not done by some strange power which the agent had not previously called into play; his will, which had caused all his previous and undistinguished actions, now, because circumstances require it, causes the act of courage. No doubt the human hero becomes braver through doing the brave action, but that is an accident of finitude. If he were a perfected character in all respects it is still true that his constant will would express itself in undistinguished action when this is appropriate and in awe-inspiring self-sacrifice when that is appropriate. But it is the latter and not the former which exhibits his character truly.

So the Personal Deity universally immanent—the Logos—may for centuries act in ways that very imperfectly disclose His Character; yet when time is appropriate may Himself submit to conditions which reveal that Character as it had always been. There is no novelty of causal energy. If He use some way of becoming Himself an historical episode other than that by which other similar episodes are initiated, such for example as birth from a Virgin, this is no manifestation of new and usually dormant power, but is due to the same cause as other and normal births, namely, the Will of this same Logos, now aiming at a special and unique result. In other words, if the immanent principle is personal, we must not only see the whole universe as the expression and utterance of His activity, but must expect to find in its course special characteristic and revealing acts, which are no more truly His than the rest, but do more fully express Him than the rest.

There is ground for believing that there are infinite gradations of such adjustment and adaptation as find their climax in these alleged revelatory acts. The actual practice of religion in any of its forms admits men to experience of the personal action of God in many degrees of self-disclosure. This field has not been worked over by scientific students of the subject with the diligence which it deserves. That is natural enough, because precise and critical observation is very difficult and experiment is from the nature of the case impossible. What is very startling to the philosopher whose mental habit is controlled by scientific interests is the abundance of testimony given by those who have had intimate experience of men's spiritual life to the conviction that in the early stages prayer receives literal fulfilment with great frequency; that later on this becomes less frequent, until it seems almost to cease, as though God at first gives encouragement of the most obvious kind and later withdraws this in order to evoke a deeper trust. Such theories call for scientific investigation; the evidence should be weighed and tested. But if this very common assertion of the persons best qualified to know is well founded, it indicates not only a power, but a readiness, to practise with much freedom that adaptation to circumstances which we have asserted as a necessary inference from the Personality of God.

To assert the adaptability and variability of nature is not to introduce chaos or caprice as a characteristic of the universe, because the assertion is made concerning the immanent activity of a Personal Deity, who, because Personal, is also transcendent, and as transcendent is eternally Himself, self-identical, "with whom is no variableness neither shadow of turning". His Will, that is to say His Character in action, is the explanation of all that is. If Nature is uniform, it is because, for His own purposes, He so wills; if it is variable, it is because He so wills. That it is sufficiently uniform for us safely to assume its uniformity for action and for study of its own processes, is evident. To assert that it is absolutely uniform is not open to any man unless he either denies the existence of Divine Personality or else can show, as Socrates demanded of Anaxagoras, that this is best. The believer in Divine Personality will not be ready to accept with credulity stories of capricious behaviour in nature, but if he is given evidence of some apparent variation where there is also moral or spiritual occasion, he will receive it with respect and investigate it without prejudice.

Immanence and Transcendence are not sharply contrasted terms. It is the Transcendent who is immanent, and it is the Immanent who transcends. If the norm of immanence is taken to be the relation of mind to body, then a doctrine of divine immanence may easily lead to an assertion of that parallelism of God and Nature which Dr. Whitehead outlines in the closing section of *Process and Reality*, and to which reference has already been made. But such a view supplies no "explanation" of the world; the sum total of God-plus-World remains a brute fact—it is what it is, and there is no more to be said. It does not explain itself—and it is marked by this fatal defect because it seeks to reduce all relations to those of the organism to its own parts or to its environment. Only Personality is a true principle of explanation, for only of its intelligent purpose has reason no desire to reiterate its perpetual question "Why?"[1] If, however, with the classical instance of Mind and Body we couple that of Person and Conduct—or indeed if we only remember that impersonal mind is always undeveloped mind, so that mind in its true nature is always personal—then our doctrine of divine immanence must be that which has been outlined in this

[1] See Lecture VI., p. 145.

Lecture. The living God is indeed at work—fully at work—in Nature, in human experience, and in the course of history. But He is at work as a Person, exhibiting the identity of His character in the infinitely delicate variations of adjustment to varying circumstance. He is not at work there as a static principle, always acting in the same way, though reserving in His transcendence a capacity to intrude with variation into the uniformity of His own immanent action; He is at work there as a living Person, expressing His constancy through appropriate variations, which are guaranteed against caprice or incoherence by that transcendent self-identity in which they are grounded. Such a view gives to science all it needs or can rightly claim in assurance of the actual constancy of Nature, while it also secures for religion its vital need for a God who is in all things supreme and unfettered.

For some it may make clearer the point that is being urged if it is put in the traditional terms of Christian theology. God as immanent is the Eternal Logos, the personal expression of the divine character, thought and purpose; this Logos is the explanation of all things that occur,[1] whether it be the regular and customary growth of the seed into the plant, or the birth of His own fleshly tabernacle from a Virgin-Mother;[2] neither of these is more or less divine than the other; neither represents a divine intrusion from without; each is a manifestation of divine activity appropriate to the occasion. But in the variety of activity there is no instability or incoherence, if only because the personal Logos does nothing of Himself, but in all things expresses the transcendent God.[3] Yet once more, that transcendent God is unknown to finite minds except through His self-expression in the immanent activity of His Word or Son.[4]

For this, too, is involved in our position. God—the

[1] St. John i. 31.
[2] St. John i. 14 (cf. 13).
[3] St. John v. 19, 30.
[4] St. John i. 18.

Absolute, Eternal, Self-identical God, whose only Name is I AM THAT I AM—is for ever unknown and unknowable except so far as He reveals Himself. And every revelation is an utterance of His Word. His Eternity becomes known in the variety of its temporal manifestations. The God whom we learn to know in Nature or in spiritual experience is no other than the eternal God. There is no "Veiled Being" behind that "Invisible King" who governs the series of temporal occurrences.[1] We know that God is more than His actions in time, as a man is more than his conduct. But He is known by His actions as a man is known—not by a doubtful and precarious inference, but by the certainty of sympathetic apprehension. God is known only as He reveals Himself; but He truly is what He reveals Himself to be. As our consideration of the world in which He is self-expressed led us to the assertion that His immanent presence and energy therein pointed to that transcendence which is proper to personality, and before which alone, when it is personality at the full, our personalities may fitly bow in the total self-surrender of adoration, so now we are led to the conviction that in that evidence of divine transcendence which our experience affords we have the true explanation of the immanent activity of God and therefore of the universe and all that it contains. To use the Johannine term once more, the "Word" is not adventitious to God but integral. There is at the heart of things such a balance or parallelism as Dr. Whitehead sets forth; but it is not directly between God and the World; it is between God transcendent and God immanent—not between God and the World, but between the eternal God and that Word, wherein He is self-expressed and the World is implicit.

[1] The terms are taken from Mr. H. G. Wells' book, *God the Invisible King*.

LECTURE XII

REVELATION AND ITS MODE

We have found reason to assert without mitigation the full Personality of that ultimate Reality in which the whole universe is grounded. That is another way of asserting the doctrine of Creation. If we begin with the conviction of a Personal God, the relation between Him and the world must be that of Creator to creature; if we begin with the world and find that it points us to a personal ground of its existence, the relation of the world to such ground of its being must be that of creature to Creator. For the essence of the doctrine of Creation is not that God inaugurated the existence of the world at a particular moment of time, but that it owes its existence—not only its beginning—to His volitional activity. The doctrine of Creation denies that the world proceeds from the Divine Being by any process of inevitable emanation; it denies that God and the World are correlates, so that each depends upon the other for existence in the same way; it asserts that the world exists because God chose to call it into being and chooses to sustain it in being. If He is personal, and if He is the ground of the world's existence, this follows as an inevitable consequence. The word "choose" may have associations that are out of place, and the same may be true of all other human language. But the word "choose" expresses what chiefly needs to be expressed—that God is under no external compulsion to make and sustain a world; He does it because it seems good to Him so to do. "Thou hast created all things, and because of thy will they were, and were created."[1]

But our enquiry did not lead us to the bare assertion

[1] Revelation iv. 11.

that the world owes its origin and continuous existence to the Divine Will, but also to the consequent conviction that all things are in their measure an expression of that Will which sustains but also moulds and guides all things, so that the unity of the world, its principle of rational coherence, is the Divine Personality in self-expression.[1] Further we were brought to the view that because the world's principle of unity is personal its manifestation will not be through invariable uniformity but in such variability of adaptation as expresses the constancy of the divine character in face of the various moments of universal history. For the most part we shall expect to find, as we find in fact, a widespread uniformity; because where there is no special and sufficient occasion for variation, its occurrence would argue caprice rather than constancy. Moreover, we have seen that, so far as the moral quality of human life is matter of concern to the Creator, it supplies a reason, not so much for variation to meet special contingencies as for a uniformity sufficiently general to be the basis of purposive action. But where there is sufficient occasion, the creative will may vary its more usual activity; when this occurs, it is not through the intrusion of some normally inoperative cause, but through the action of what alone accounts for all existences and occurrences, the volition of personal Deity. It is thus characteristic of God that He should usually act by what to us is uniformity (though the appearance even of this may conceal variations too delicate for our perception and too small to affect our confidence in action), just as it is characteristic of Him to vary His action when the occasion is sufficient. Yet there is inevitably a peculiarly revealing quality in the occasional variations, both because they show what occasions are in the divine judgement sufficient, and because they are the issue of a specially directed activity in face of the sufficient occasion,

[1] This is the conviction which finds expression in St. John i. 1-3 and Colossians i. 17.

whereas the general uniformity obviously does not issue from such specially directed activity. That God did not intervene in answer to my prayer to save the life of some friend during the Great War by deflection of a bullet may perhaps be indirectly a manifestation of His love both for my friend and for me; but if He raised Jesus of Nazareth from death, that is a much more direct manifestation of His relationship to the Life and Death of Jesus.

Now many religions have in their traditions the record of events which from the standpoint of a believer in absolute uniformity must appear abnormal. To the historical critic this is an occasion for vigilance, if not for suspicion. He is aware of the tendency towards belief in miracle as a characteristic of religion, and is bound accordingly to discount the evidence for such events to some extent. On the other hand, the student of religions is bound to notice the fact that this tendency is present in religion. It is possible, of course, to set it on one side as one of the superstitions which continually beset religion; but before this is done, care must be taken to ascertain how much of what is regarded as essential to religion is bound up with this tendency. For it may be that even though our intention be only to distinguish between superstition and genuine religion, yet the repudiation of what has been condemned as the former may carry with it the evisceration of what has been commended as the latter.

Professor Otto lately called attention to the characteristic element in religion to which he gave the name of "the numinous". It is possible to be grateful for his general insistence upon the presence of this element in all vital religion without accepting the whole of his account of it. In primitive forms of religion there is no distinction drawn between the veritably awe-inspiring and the occasion of shuddering fears. But on the whole these last go with conceptions of Deity as uncanny and capricious, a cavernous darkness out of which unknown terrors may leap upon us. And with that conception of Deity religion parts company as it develops to the height of its own stature. The Infinite must for ever remain incomprehensible to the finite; but this is not because it is in itself the unintelligible; it is because of the limitation of our power to understand. "God is light, and in Him is no darkness at all";[1] towards such a declaration all progress in religion is, and ever has been, pressing. God is the utterly reliable. There is nothing of the morbid or the occult in our awe before Him; but in that awe is the very heart of worship and of religion itself.

The whole course of our argument forbids us to draw any sharp distinction between the works of God so as to regard some of these as constituting His self-revelation and the others as offering no such revelation. We can make no truce with any suggestion that the world for the most part goes by itself on its own way while God intervenes now and again with an act of His own. The course of thought, which enables us to hold together religious faith in the living God and the picture of the world with which science provides us, renders the whole notion of such divine intrusion from without intolerable and incredible; for this course of thought has perpetually recurred to the insistence that all occurrences find their ultimate ground in the Divine Volition. But if we stopped here we should only have affirmed that in the entire course of cosmic history there is to be found the self-revelation of God; and that, no doubt, is true; but as no man can ever hope to contemplate that history in its entirety, it cannot be said to afford a revelation to us or for us. Moreover, this affirmation by itself concerns cosmic history as a whole, as though it proceeded on its course uninfluenced by any agents within it who are completely or partially free to influence that course. If there is ground for holding that such agents exist, then we

[1] 1 John i. 5.

must expect to find instances of divine action relevant to the situations which their free acts create, and while such action will be no more divine than the constant purpose which sustains all things in being, it will have a specially revelatory quality, because it is an expression of the divine character in face of critical situations, and not only an episode in the age-long energy of God. It is always in dealing with persons as persons that personality most truly expresses itself. It tells us something about a man's character if we know that he rises from bed every day at the same hour; it tells us much more about him if we know that he even once rose a great deal earlier to do some act of kindness. The main field of Revelation must be in the history of men, rather than in the ample spaces of nature, though it is also true that if nature were so severed from God as to offer no revelation of Him at all, it would mean that there was no Being fitly to be called God, and therefore no revelation of Him either in human history or elsewhere.

We saw at an earlier stage that man's relationship to Truth, to Beauty and to Goodness is such as to imply that in each of these a Personal Spirit is calling to him and claiming him.[1] This prepares us for a more intimate expression of what thus receives august but not unfamiliar intimation. The revelation to which Religion in many of its historical forms appeals is therefore nothing alien from such a view of the world as we have been led to form, but is something very much more than is discoverable except in such supposed revelation. Here the Divine Mind in which all Nature is grounded speaks direct to that Human Nature which, of all Nature known to us, is nearest to itself because, like itself, it is personal and spiritual. The personal God can only be adequately revealed in and through persons; but then such revelation must be distorted by any defects in the persons through whom it comes. The revelation given in the majesty of the starry heavens may be perfect

[1] See Lectures VI. and VII.

in its kind, though its kind is markedly inadequate; the revelation given through the reason and conscience of men is more adequate in kind, but in that kind is usually imperfect.

We have not yet spoken of the problem of evil except to refer to it as the distinctively religious problem among all those which call for intellectual solution, and the discussion of it must be postponed until we can give undivided attention to it. But the existence of evil in its worst form, that of sin, introduces a defect, and it may be a distortion, into all revelation given through the medium of human personality, unless there be found an instance of this which is free from sin. This defect or distortion is something more than limitation in fullness or completeness; it affects the quality of the revelation in ways that are not capable of ascertainment in advance; and this fact must be borne in mind in any attempt to set forth the general conditions of the possibility of revelation.

We affirm, then, that unless all existence is a medium of Revelation, no particular Revelation is possible; for the possibility of Revelation depends on the personal quality of that supreme and ultimate Reality which is God. If there is no ultimate Reality, which is the ground of all else, then there is no God to be revealed; if that Reality is not personal, there can be no special revelation, but only uniform procedure; if there be an ultimate Reality, and this is personal, then all existence is revelation. Either all occurrences are in some degree revelation of God, or else there is no such revelation at all; for the conditions of the possibility of any revelation require that there should be nothing which is not revelation. Only if God is revealed in the rising of the sun in the sky can He be revealed in the rising of a son of man from the dead; only if He is revealed in the history of Syrians and Philistines can He be revealed in the history of Israel;[1] *only if he chooses all men for His own can He choose any at all; only if nothing is profane can anything be sacred. It is*

[1] Amos ix. 7.

necessary to stress with all possible emphasis this universal quality of revelation in general before going on to discuss the various modes of particular revelation; for the latter, if detached from the former, loses its root in the rational coherence of the world and consequently becomes itself a superstition and a fruitful source of superstitions. But if all existence is a revelation of God, as it must be if He is the ground of its existence, and if the God thus revealed is personal, then there is more ground in reason for expecting particular revelations than for denying them.

The massive impressiveness of nature's apparent uniformity leads some religious students of natural science to suppose that it is more consonant with Divine Majesty to impose upon nature one order never to be varied than to meet successive situations with appropriately varied activity. We have already commented on this view, which seems to make the Divine Will more external to the natural order than the course of our argument would suggest, and also ignores the fact that personal wisdom is not shown in rigid uniformity of behaviour, but in constancy of purpose expressed through infinitely various response to different conditions. Our task now is rather to consider what forms religious people have supposed that special revelation to have taken, in which their trust is reposed, what is implied in such forms of revelation, how far they are philosophically justifiable, and what are the conditions of a fully satisfactory revelation. For our purposes it will be sufficient, and will prevent confusion, if we confine ourselves, except for occasional illustration, by way of similarity or contrast, to the religious tradition with which we are familiar.

Most people who share our cultural tradition, if asked where Christians supposed that a particular revelation of God is to be found, would probably answer that it is in the Bible. At once the question arises whether the Bible is supposed to be itself the revelation, or to be the record of the revelation. Is the revelation in the book or in the events which the book records? Plainly it could not be in the book unless it is first in the events. And this is the witness of the book itself; for the prophets, who claimed that the word of the Lord came to them, were largely occupied in reading the lessons of history to the people whose history it was. Living by faith in the personal and living God, they saw His hand in all that affected the people with whom they were concerned. This is a conception in full harmony with the general position that we have outlined. But it is to be frankly recognised that it is by no means the traditional doctrine of Christendom. The traditional doctrine has rather been that the Book itself is the revelation than that it contains the record of it. The position stated with emphasis in the Vatican Decrees and still more pointedly reaffirmed by Leo XIII. in his Encyclical *Providentissimus Deus* of 1893[1] is that which has been traditional in Christendom throughout the greater part of Christian history. For our present purpose the importance of this fact resides in the testimony which it affords of the natural craving of religion for a final and unquestionable authority.

The Natural Theologian is not concerned with the question whether there has in fact been given an authoritative revelation of this kind. But he is very much concerned with the question what would be involved in its occurrence, and also with the question whether there is not another view of revelation more consonant with such a conception of the universe in relation to God as we are led by general considerations to frame. Now this traditional doctrine of revelation implies, first, that God has so far overridden and superseded the normal human faculties of those through whom the revelation was given as to save their utterance by voice or pen from all error in its communication. That God is able to do this we need not be concerned to deny; the question is whether it is consonant

[1] See below, p. 309.

with what we otherwise know of His dealings with men that He should wish to do so, and also whether this view of the general nature of revelation is consistent with the actual content of the revelation supposed to be so given. In order to deal with the first of these questions we must anticipate some results of future arguments, and especially that concerning human freedom before God. For it seems that while it cannot without spiritual disaster be contended that man apart from God is free to do the will of God, it is also indispensable to faith and to morality to hold that God empowers men to do His will through the enlightenment of their natural faculties and the kindling of their natural affections, and not by any supersession of these. But to provide, by some process of suggestion, oracles directly expressive of divine truth—that is, of the divine apprehension of the reality which includes Creator and created universe—would be to repudiate this principle alike as regards the prophet and as regards the hearers. If Amos and Isaiah and the unknown author or authors of the Books of the Kings wrote (as Leo XIII. phrased it) "at the dictation of the Holy Ghost,"[1] in any sense of those words which could at all justify the use of them—for what "dictation" means in this context is by no means obvious—then no doubt their content must be regarded as truth, but it is truth conveyed in a manner wholly without either parallel or analogy in the normal relationship between God and man, and even contradictory of that relationship.

That would not be a fatal obstacle to belief in this theory if it could be shown that there is sufficient occasion for a departure from the norm, and also that the particular departure in question is consonant with the

[1] *Dictante Spiritu Sancto.* The full passage in the official translation runs as follows: "All the books, which the Church receives as sacred and canonical, are written wholly and entirely, with all their parts, at the dictation of the Holy Ghost; and so far is it from being possible that any error can co-exist with inspiration, that inspiration not only is essentially incompatible with error, but excludes and rejects it as absolutely and necessarily as it is impossible that God Himself, the supreme Truth, can utter that which is not true."

revelation given by means of it, and appropriate for the purpose for which it is given. That there is sufficient occasion is beyond dispute. Whether we take the view that apart from any "Fall" man's nature is such that he can have no true knowledge of God through normal processes, or the view that only by the "Fall" has he come under that disability,[1] or even the view that he is in principle capable of reaching the saving knowledge of God but has not in fact by his own powers attained to it—in any case the conveyance to man of this knowledge is a matter of import so transcendent, and an activity of love so characteristic, that it must be regarded as offering as adequate occasion as any could ever be for a departure from normal procedure.

But there are far greater difficulties when we turn to the relation of this method of revelation to the content of the revelation so conveyed. The Fathers of the Church saved the situation by means of allegorical interpretation. Thus St. Thomas quotes with approval the teaching of St. Augustine that there are two rules to be observed:

> "The first is to hold the truth of Scripture without wavering; the second is that since Holy Scripture can be explained in a multiplicity of senses, one should adhere to a particular explanation only in such measure as to be ready to abandon it, if it be proved with certainty to be false; lest Holy Scripture be exposed to the ridicule of unbelievers, and obstacles be placed to their believing."[2]

The necessity of recourse to the second of these principles as a means of adhering to the first is sufficiently obvious. But it destroys the whole value of this form of revelation. I am to believe whatever is the true meaning of Scripture; but I have no way of knowing what that

[1] The Thomist and Augustinian views, respectively.

[2] *Summa Theologiae*, Part I. Q. lxviii. A. i. (E.T. by the English Dominicans) "Sicut Augustinus docet, in hujusmodi quaestionibus duo sunt observanda. *Primo* quidem, ut veritas Scripturae inconcusse teneatur. *Secundo*, cum Scriptura divina multipliciter exponi possit, quod nulli expositioni aliquis ita praecise inhaereat, ut si certa ratione constiterit, hoc esse falsum, quod aliquis sensum Scripturae esse credebat, id nihilominus asserere praesumat ne Scriptura ex hoc ab infidelibus derideatur, et ne eis via credendi praecludatur."

is; what I take to be the true meaning may be proved to be in part false, whereupon I am to say that the mistake was mine and that this was not what Scripture meant. Unless the revelation is not only indubitably true but also unmistakeable, it fails to fulfil the function which this theory of revelation assigns to it. We need not wonder that where once men had set their hearts on having some infallible authority in the realm of spiritual truth, they were driven by the logic of their own desire from the infallible Book to the infallible Church and to the infallible spokesman of the infallible Church. Only by those expedients can the desire for infallible guidance be satisfied, or the theory of oracular revelation perform its function.

When we turn to the consonance of this theory with the content of the revelation to which it is applied a similar result follows. For the Historical Figure in whose career the story finds its culmination, and who is acclaimed as its crown and illumination by those whose theory is under review, is in nothing more remarkable than in His unfailing respect for the spiritual liberty of those with whom He had dealings. Though the record presents Him as capable of miraculous action, and as having recourse to it for purposes of mercy, it also presents Him as steadily refusing to allow such acts to become the basis of men's adherence to Him or to His cause. He appears as desiring none but willing disciples; and to them He gave teaching designed rather to stimulate and direct their thought than to provide formulated doctrines claiming acceptance on His authority. The revelation, if given at all, is given more in Himself than in His teaching, and the faith in which His early followers believed that they had found salvation did not consist in the acceptance of propositions concerning Him nor even in acceptance of what He taught in words concerning God and man, though this was certainly included, but in personal trust in His personal presence, love and power. Doctrinal or credal formulae had their importance as pointing to Him, by trust in whom His followers had found peace; they were not themselves the revelation, but sign-posts indicating where the revelation was to be found.

All this was in line with the earlier and supposedly preparatory revelation. For this, as has been already suggested, consisted primarily in historical events, and secondarily in the illumination of the minds of prophets to read those events as disclosing the judgement or the purpose of God. What we find in the Old Testament Scriptures is not mainly, if at all, authoritative declarations of theological doctrine, but living apprehension of a living process wherein those whose minds are enlightened by divine communion can discern in part the purposive activity of God.

Revelation so conceived is the full actuality of that relationship between Nature, Man and God which throughout these Lectures we are seeking to articulate. First there is the world-process, which, in its more complex components, if not throughout, is organic in principle; secondly, we have the fact that certain organisms, to wit ourselves, occurring as episodes of the world-process, are able to apprehend and in part to comprehend that process; thirdly, we infer from this that the process, in order to give rise to such episodes in its course, must be regarded as itself grounded in a mental principle; fourthly, enquiry into that interaction of the intelligent organism with its environment, which we call thought, compels the assertion that the principle in which the world-process is grounded, is not only mental but spiritual and personal; fifthly, this leads us to the conviction that the process itself and all occurrences within it—including the intelligences of men—are due to the purposive action of that Person whose reality has been established as the governing fact of existence. *He guides the process; He guides the minds of men; the interaction of the process and the minds which are alike guided by Him is the essence of revelation.*

But His action in guiding the world is not constant in a mechanical sense; rather its constancy, as that of all personal action, is found in its infinite adjustability to present conditions. It is true that the conditions are themselves due to the divine action, but that does not affect the argument if we recognise two facts: first, that the divine action in or upon the world is not the essentially dead action of an immanent principle, but the essentially living action of a transcendent Person; and secondly, that among the conditions are the attitudes adopted by, and the situations created by, the relatively free acts of finite intelligences like ourselves.

Much of the divine action which sustains the world is such as to produce apparent uniformity in the world-process. We have already seen why this should be so, even from the standpoint of human interests. But of course this apparent uniformity may itself be due to an elaborately designed balance of multiform adjustments. If those scientists are right who regard recent developments as having introduced indeterminacy into the basis of Physics, so that laws of causation are to be understood, not as real uniformities but as statistical averages,[1] the theistic philosopher will be prepared with the account of the (physically) indeterminate behaviour of electrons and of the resultant constancy of natural processes, which has just been offered. If on the other hand the older scientific view of uniform causal processes ultimately prevails, for this also the theist has his explanation, both in the constancy of the Divine Nature which will vary its activity only for sufficient reason, and in the need for substantial uniformity as a basis for moral action. The more modern view supplies a greater measure of that continuity between different stages of evolutionary complexity, and this may recommend it to theists who share the common scientific interest in such continuity. The Natural Theologian is not

[1] A sociologist may know how many people will commit suicide in Great Britain next year, but he cannot know which individuals will do so.

concerned in the dispute; either alternative is equally agreeable to him.

Whatever be the final view of that matter, it will remain true that, while the apparently uniform process of the world is in its measure a revelation of God for those whose minds are alert to its significance, it is less fully revelatory than specially adapted activities for the meeting of such contingencies as give sufficient ground for such activities. It is therefore not unnatural or inappropriate that the term Revelation should be commonly used with a specialised reference to these occasions. But these must be understood as particular and conspicuous illustrations of the principle of revelation already stated—the interaction of the world-process and the minds, both being alike guided by God. In these events too—be it a deliverance of a nation from bondage in despite of all calculable probabilities, be it the Incarnation in a human life of that Self-Utterance of God which is the ground of the created universe—there is no imparting of truth as the intellect apprehends truth, but there is event and appreciation; and in the coincidence of these the revelation consists.

There is obviously neither need nor possibility to draw any dividing line between the revelation which is continuously given in the whole course of the world-process as men's minds are enlightened to appreciate this, and the revelation which is given in special and signal occasions. Among the events which are conspicuous in the record accepted by Christendom as in a special sense Revelation, those which accompanied or facilitated the Exodus or the retreat of Sennacherib may be more easily referred to normal processes, while those which preceded the birth or followed the death of Jesus Christ are more difficult to classify under that head. Yet even here, for those who start, not from efficient causation but from divine intention and efficacy, it may be that we have the most strictly natural way of bringing about a divine self-incarnation, and a strictly natural issue of the bodily death of humanity when rendered sinless by divine indwelling.[1] If we make the mistake of beginning with the thought of God as normally acting by way of immanence, while holding His transcendent resources in reserve against emergencies, we may fairly be challenged to say under which heading any particular occasion should be classified; and scientifically trained minds then appear to have some justification for the protest, to which they often are inclined, that it would be more consonant with divine Majesty so to order the world that no interventions disturbing to its order should be required. But if the contention of the last Lecture is sound, and divine immanence is always and only the activity of a transcendent Personality, and operates, after the manner of personal action, by infinitely various adjustments which exhibit constancy of character in face of varied situations, then there is no need for any dividing line, nor any possibility of drawing one. All things are grounded in the divine volition, which acts on each occasion as is appropriate for the fulfilment of the divine purpose. All therefore is alike revelation; but not all is equally revelatory of the divine character. We find revelation at its highest where God finds occasion for unusual action, and we find it then both in the choice of occasion for such unusual action (for the divine character is revealed in its estimate of such and such an occasion as sufficient) and in the mode of action taken.

But whether we think of the unceasing revelation afforded in the whole world-process or of the occurrences which constitute revelation in the specialised sense of the word, *the principle of revelation is the same—the coincidence of event and appreciation.*[2] Here we have

[1] The phrase attributed to St. Peter with reference to this event in Acts ii. 24—"because it was not possible that he should be holden of it (*sc.* death)"—suggests such a view.

[2] The appreciation need not be contemporaneous with the event. But till it comes, the event, though revelatory in its own character, is not yet fully revelation. If no one had recognised Christ, the Incarnation would have occurred, but it would have failed to effect a revelation of God.

at its fullest development that living intercourse of mind and world-process which we found to be the true life of thought. For here the mind, which arises within, and out of, the process, apprehends the process for what it truly is—the self-expression of that Creator-mind in the kinship of which created minds are fashioned. From the occurrence of our finite minds within the process we were led to believe that the process which contains them must be grounded in mind; the finite mind in developing its intercourse with its environment finds itself the subject of intellectual judgements, aesthetic appreciations, moral obligations, thus becoming aware of the reality of Truth, Beauty and Goodness in that environment; considering these experiences it finds in all of them evident marks of personal relationship, and learns to recognise the environment as the self-communication to itself of a personal Creator. In the characteristic moments of revelation this apprehension and appreciation is at its highest point of development.

Its essence is intercourse of mind and event, not the communication of doctrine distilled from that intercourse. The contrary opinion, which has so long held the field, is due to the false estimate of conceptual thinking held by Greek and Scholastic and Cartesian philosophers. Through the greater portion of Christian history it has been held by Christians that

> "the kind of knowledge which Revelation gave consisted in exact, clear-cut truth-statements. It was an immediate communication of truths as they existed in the Divine mind, even though their communication might involve some measure of accommodation to the human mind's power of reception."[1]

So writes Canon Lilley in his recent Paddock Lectures, and comments as follows:

> "The fact that the actual revelations of Scripture had very seldom anything approaching this character was for tradition

[1] Lilley, *Religion and Revelation*, pp. 144, 145.

something of a scandal, a difficulty to be explained away. For us the difficulty does not exist. The scandal becomes the clearest witness to what we should expect in man's attempt to translate the knowledge he had received through God's immediate action upon his rapt and expectant soul. The effect of that action upon man is to exalt him into a mood of perception in which the mind is as it were dazed by the wonder revealed. Through figure and image and symbol it translates the awed impression of a truth whose vastness and sublimity must ever evade its clear grasp. The typical medium of revelation is not the thinker but the seer."[1]

That is finely said. But it seems to me to be only a part of the truth, and it can only be true at all if conceptual thinking is, as it was described earlier,[2] an *interim* procedure. If such thinking as finds expression in the propositions of traditional Logic were the actual apprehension of reality, revelation must offer itself in such propositions or forfeit the right to its name. But if that mode of thinking properly corresponds to the analytical study of the score between two occasions of hearing great music, we shall not expect the divine self-disclosure to be made at that stage or in that form. Rather we shall expect to find it in the tumultuous surge and the serene calm of the world's music itself. Theologians will play the part of musical critics, analysing and summarising; but they too will return from theology to worship, as St. Thomas passed from the *Summa Theologiae* to the *Lauda, Sion, Salvatorem*. *From all this it follows that there is no such thing as revealed truth. There are truths of revelation, that is to say, propositions which express the results of correct thinking concerning revelation; but they are not themselves directly revealed. On the other hand, this does not involve the result that there need be anything vague or indefinite about revelation itself*. Canon Lilley does not wholly avoid the suggestion of such indefiniteness, because, while denying revealed truth, he does not altogether escape the influence of the view that revelation is primarily something which

[1] Lilley, *Religion and Revelation*, pp. 144, 145. [2] See pp. 116-118.

happens within the mind. It is true that "the typical medium of revelation is not the thinker but the seer". But it is also true that the typical *locus* of revelation is not the mind of the seer but the historical event. And if the revelation is essentially an event or fact, then it can be perfectly definite, although it neither is nor can be exhaustively represented in propositions. Moreover, it can be a focus of unity for people whose interpretation of it is various.

But we have to add that though the revelation is chiefly given in objective fact, yet it becomes effectively revelatory only when that fact is apprehended by a mind qualified to appreciate it. Like Beauty,[1] Revelation exists or occurs objectively but is subjectively conditioned. Revelation is given chiefly through events to minds enlightened to receive it. Some direct self-communication no doubt there also is from God to the soul. It would be strange if He acted only in the inorganic and non-spiritual, and dealt with spirits akin to Himself only by the indirect testimony of the rest of His creation.

This intercourse of the human mind with God will be more fully considered in the next Lecture under the heading of religious experience. It is conditioned by religious tradition, but may carry its recipient beyond that tradition. The signal instance of a conviction that must be credited to a divine self-communication given by means of such intercourse is the prophetic faith in the righteousness and holiness of God of which the intellectual formula is Ethical Monotheism. This was certainly not an inference from experience; it was an illumination arising from communion with God in the activity of conscience and in adoration, in the light of which the prophets read the history of their times. Even so, it was not a communicated "faith", but a crystallisation of thought and feeling under pressure of facts experienced or anticipated, as when Abraham

[1] Cf. pp. 154-155, 210-212.

exclaimed, "Shall not the Judge of all the earth do right?"[1]

The spiritual impulse within us is as yet rudimentary, and is called into action chiefly by way of response to the acts of God objectively presented to us. In the language of Christian theology, God utters Himself in His Word as Creator and Providential Ruler; that same Word, according to Christian belief, becomes incarnate in the world created by its agency; to all this activity of God in His Word or (to us) objective self-utterance, a response arises from within us who are parts of that world, and this response is the movement in us of the divine Spirit. It is powerful in proportion as the objective self-disclosure is complete in itself and also completely apprehended,[2] so that it is only as response to the fullness of revelation that the Spirit is known in plenitude of power.

For two reasons the event in which the fullness of revelation is given must be the life of a Person: the first is that the revelation is to persons who can fully understand only what is personal; the second is that the revelation is of a personal Being, who accordingly cannot be adequately revealed in anything other than personality. Moreover, if the Person who is Himself the revelation is to be truly adequate to that function, He must be one in essence with the Being whom He reveals. Professor Pringle-Pattison, in his Gifford Lectures on *The Philosophy of Religion*, comments on the traditional Christian doctrine as follows:

> "In every religion the question at issue is the character of its God or Gods; for on that depends its whole conception of human duty and its views of human destiny. The lesson of Christianity is that we have to think of God in terms of Christ —*sub specie Christi*, if we may adapt a great phrase—in terms, that is to say, of his recorded teaching and of the spirit of his

[1] Genesis xviii. 25.

[2] By "Holy Spirit" St. Paul and St. John, at least for the most part, understand the fullness of response called out from men by the fullness of divine self-manifestation in Christ; cf. Romans viii. 9-27, specially 14-17 and 23; St. John vii. 39; xvi. 7.

dedicated life and death. And in order to give us authentic tidings of the character of God, Jesus did not require actually to *be* God."[1]

Professor Pringle-Pattison betrays the weakness of his position by the use of the phrase "give us authentic tidings of the character of God". It is a phrase that belongs to conceptual thinking. Tidings about God are such accounts of Him as can be expressed in propositions and communicated by speech. It is true that the Professor had spoken of "the spirit of his dedicated life and death", but he evidently regards the life and death as rather the symbol of ideas than as themselves the unveiled life of God. He is still under the influence of the intellectualist conception of truth, and not free from the attitude of condescension towards all symbolic presentations which is characteristic of intellectualism. Tennyson's expression of this attitude is familiar:

Tho' truths in manhood darkly join,
  Deep seated in our mystic frame,
  We yield all blessing to the name
Of Him that made them current coin.

For wisdom dealt with mortal powers
  Where truth in closest words shall fail,
  When truth embodied in a tale
Shall enter in at lowly doors.

And so the Word had breath, and wrought
  With human hands the creed of creeds,
  In loveliness of perfect deeds
More strong than all poetic thought;

Which he may read that binds the sheaf,
  Or builds the house, or digs the grave,
  And those wild eyes that watch the wave
In roarings round the coral reef.

Still clearer is the suggestion of an earlier and less poetic stanza:

---

[1] Pringle-Pattison, *The Philosophy of Religion*, p. 252. What the believer needs to know is not only that "God was in Christ reconciling the world unto Himself", or that Christ is the truest representation of God up to date, but that he may worship and trust in the eternal God as actually known in Jesus Christ. See Appendix E.

O thou that after toil and storm
  Mayst seem to have reached a purer air,
  Whose faith has centre everywhere,
Nor cares to fix itself to form,

Leave thou thy sister when she prays
  Her early Heaven, her happy views;
  Nor thou with shadowed hint confuse
A life that leads melodious days.[1]

The suggestion clearly is that the highest truth is something purely conceptual. The embodiment of it in a tale may make it acceptable to simple folk like farm labourers, and bricklayers, and grave-diggers, and South Sea Islanders; and the cultivated young man who is exhorted not to unsettle his sister—(the poem is of the Victorian era)—may find that even he needs the help of the tale or else in this naughty world may "fail for want of such a type".[2]

Now if the whole contention of these Lectures is sound, knowledge of God can be fully given to man only in a person, never in a doctrine, still less in a formless faith, whatever that might be. There is a use for vague aspiration, though it is a very limited use until the vagueness gives place to some measure of determination; and there is great use in formulated doctrine, because it points us to that in which many have believed themselves to find the revelation of God. But the life of faith is not the acceptance of doctrine any more than the life of the natural man is the acceptance of mathematical equations, or the life of the artist is the acceptance of aesthetic canons. The canons and the equations assist the effective adjustment and intercourse of organism and environment, but the life of art, or of mere organic continuance, has its being in that adjustment and intercourse. So too sound doctrine assists the psycho-physical organism, which is a man, an organism now recognised to be spiritual as well as aesthetic and animate, to achieve satisfactory adjustment to and intercourse with its environment, now known to be divine

[1] Tennyson, *In Memoriam*, xxxvi. and xxxiii.

[2] *Ibid.* xxxiii.

as well as beautiful and nutritive. But it is in that adjustment and intercourse that living faith consists. In more familiar language, faith is not the holding of correct doctrines, but personal fellowship with the living God. Correct doctrine will both express this, assist it and issue from it; incorrect doctrine will misrepresent this and hinder or prevent it. Doctrine is of an importance too great to be exaggerated, but its place is secondary, not primary. I do not believe in any creed, but I use certain creeds to express, to conserve, and to deepen my belief in God. *What is offered to man's apprehension in any specific Revelation is not truth concerning God but the living God Himself.*

The enquiry whether such and such a creed is well founded, or whether any particular type of revelation has in fact been given, lies beyond the province of Natural Theology; but it is very much the business of Natural Theology to describe the mode of Revelation which is consonant with the conclusions which on other grounds are found to be most probable concerning the nature of God and of His relation to men. It is still open to question whether any such Revelation exists, and it is still possible to accept on grounds of its supposed inherent authority a revelation that derives no support from those conclusions. Natural Theology has fulfilled its function in this regard when it has shown what mode of Revelation is consonant with the conception of God, man and the world, which its own course of argument has led it to adopt. Our argument has led to a conception which suggests as the essential principle of Revelation the appreciation by divinely enlightened minds of divinely directed occurrences, and further requires that for fullness of Revelation the occurrence should take the form of personal life of such sort as to be intelligible to, and elicit sympathy from, those persons to whom the revelation is given; it must be no mere theophany, but an Incarnation.[1]

[1] See Appendix E.

The question still remains—By what means does the revelation authenticate itself? From the nature of the case it must offer its own credentials; that revelation should have to appeal to anything beside itself to establish its character as revelation, would be patent absurdity. The older tradition found the authentication in miracle and fulfilled prediction. God, being the supreme power in the universe, was held to give evidence of His special activity in it by setting aside its normal process and accomplishing some transformation by His creative fiat. So Moses was to convince his people of the authenticity of his mission by the conversion of his staff into a snake.[1] Whether God ever does such things in accommodation to primitive minds is not a question for Natural Theology; if He could want to do it, He could also do it; but the probable explanation of this and similar episodes is to be sought in hypnotism. At a more developed stage there arises a demand for fitness in the sign offered, and some coherence with the spiritual content of the revelation. I could not expect my hearers to be any the more ready to accept my philosophy if I were able before their eyes to turn my pen into a stick of sealing-wax.[2] So it is also with fulfilled prediction. Great attention has been given, for example, to the close resemblance between the details of Psalm xxii. and those of the story of Our Lord's Passion, but this is a false line of argument; not by any irrelevant thaumaturgy in either the physical or the psychological realm does the Lord God Almighty make His presence known. Yet when we turn from essentially trifling details to broad principles, the old attention to miracle and prophecy is seen to be justified. The evidence of God's special activity is indeed not to be found in what baffles the intelligence, but rather in power active for such purposes as may reasonably be supposed divine. Where power and mercy are combined, there is God manifest; where we see right-

[1] Exodus iv. 1-3.

[2] Cf. Matthew Arnold, *Literature and Dogma*, p. 95.

eousness or love, we see the character of God; where we see these triumphing, there we see God in action; where we see them achieve their purpose despite all calculable probabilities, there we acknowledge God signally self-revealed. We do not know that it costs Him more (to speak humanly) to work the most startling so-called miracle than to maintain the habitual motion of the planets; but where that happens which former experience leads us to expect, we are less impelled to ponder on the divine nature as therein disclosed than when our expectation is negatived by an exhibition of that character in ways unpredictable by us. All is of God, but not all things equally display His character, and not all things equally call our attention to His character as displayed.

So too with prophecy: if God makes Himself known we shall expect to find progress in man's apprehension of Him, and even in that which He discloses. But if He is active in the progress, the progress must bear the marks of His continuing guidance; its earlier stages must be incomplete, and one condition of advance is that men become aware of the incompleteness of what they have. So the earlier look forward to the later, groping after it, adumbrating it. Some parts of the adumbration will be mistaken, arising from the human limitations of the prophet or seer; but some parts will be filled in and completed, being gleams of the light that lighteth every man, which, if it ever shines in full brilliance, must be recognisably their completion. This continuity of development along constant and converging lines is evidence of a continuing illumination; and if in some event the converging lines of development meet and all find their fulfilment, that is corroborative evidence of authentic revelation alike in the preparatory and in the culminating stages.

These, then, are the marks of a true revelation, of which we have already described the necessary mode: a union of holiness and power, before which our spirits bow in awe, and which authenticates itself by continuous development to some focal point in which all preparatory revelation finds fulfilment, and from which illumination radiates into every department of life and being. Whatever claims to be revelation makes good that claim in the degree in which it approximates to the ideal thus described.

APPENDIX E

A REPLY TO PROFESSOR PRINGLE-PATTISON

PROFESSOR PRINGLE-PATTISON, in his volume on *The Philosophy of Religion*, pays me the high compliment of associating me with Professor H. R. Mackintosh as typical representatives of the traditional Christology which he is concerned to discredit. He quotes with approval some sentences from my essay on "The Divinity of Christ" in *Foundations*, and contrasts these with some sentences in *Christus Veritas*. But the contrast is fallacious. It is indeed most true that "the wise question is not 'Is Christ Divine?' but 'What is God like?'" The whole point of my essay in *Foundations* was to insist that the religious importance of the belief in the Deity of Christ is that it alone supplies an effective answer to that question. Professor Pringle-Pattison thought the answer could be detached from that belief; my contention is that he could only think this because his concern was with intellectual belief about God, not with personal communion with Him. For this latter purpose it makes an entirely vital difference whether Jesus of Nazareth is an inspired man who "gives us authentic tidings of the character of God" or is Himself personally God.

The Professor held that I had fallen back upon those categories of substance which I had declared to be in essence materialistic (p. 246). I can only refer to the relevant chapters in *Christus Veritas* and say that I made, at least, an elaborate attempt to substitute other, and personal, categories. He represents me as differing from the Kenotic theory of Professor Mackintosh by adopting a "view that the Kenosis did not go so far" (p. 249). In fact my view, set out at length in *Christus Veritas*, is that there was no Kenosis at all. The Second Person of the Trinity laid aside nothing, but added to His divine attributes the experience of a strictly human life.

That this view leads to difficulties insoluble for minds which are human only, I readily admit. But I deny that these constitute "a sufficient *reductio ad impossibile* of the dogma which gives rise to them, the deity, namely, of Jesus in a metaphysical (or shall we not rather say, in a physical ?) sense". If God became Man, the psychology of the God-Man must necessarily be beyond our grasp; a theory which professed to comprehend it would be thereby condemned. What we may require is that the difficulty should arise at the point where, from the nature of the subject-matter and of our own minds, it ought to arise, and not elsewhere. In that case the difficulty is no proof that the alleged event from which it arises did not occur. If the Professor were still among us, I should urge him to read again in Browning's *Ferishtah's Fancies* the poem entitled "The Sun".

I will deal with one more point. The Professor writes as follows:

> "Dr. Temple says at one point in his book that 'if standing before them in the flesh, Jesus had said to those devout Jews, "I am God", he would have reduced them to mere bewilderment.' He fails to realise that his own language in presenting the same claim often produces in his readers a similar sense of stupefaction."

It is needless to observe that I have never failed to realise this. But I regard the stupefaction now as unreasonable, whereas then it would have been not only reasonable but inevitable. The difference is made—for

Christians—by the Cross, the Resurrection, and experience of communion with the Risen Christ.

Having thus entered for a moment into controversy with the Professor, I would add the expression of my personal admiration and gratitude for his work, and my sense of the loss to British philosophy involved in his death. At least I am sure that his scrupulous fairness would support me in the contention that, if he could rightly use a Gifford Lecture to discredit the traditional doctrine of Christianity, I am guilty of no breach of trust when, in an appendix to a Gifford Lecture, I offer some rejoinder to his argument.

LECTURE XIII

SPIRITUAL AUTHORITY AND RELIGIOUS EXPERIENCE

Our account of Revelation has presented it as a special form of religious experience, in which both the objective and the subjective elements afford a special manifestation of that divine control which directs all things. Just as the complete course of history would disclose the divine character and intention to a mind qualified to appreciate its meaning, so the particular events in history which are specially described as revelations disclose the divine character and intention to those who have eyes to see. The divine self-disclosure in the objective event claims authority because it is such a disclosure; the apprehension and appreciation of it as such a disclosure is a specific religious experience. Thus the two terms Authority and Experience are both involved in the very occurrence of revelation; and as the relation between them has been the subject of far-ranging controversy, it may be well to see in what way our general view enables us to formulate this relation. How far is all religious experience dependent on the authority of given revelation? How far does objectively given revelation hamper the free development of religious experience? What is the relation of that spiritual Authority, which is an indispensable element in all vital religion, to the particular vehicles—Scriptures, Institutions, Ceremonies—through which it is mediated? Some answer to these questions may be attempted by any one who seeks to understand the actual religion of men or to use it as part of the data for an interpretation of the universe.

In the primitive stage of development it is impossible to distinguish between the objective and subjective aspects of the experience in which the presence of the divine is apprehended. As with other forms of primitive experience, perception and interpretation are indistinguishably fused into one another. In the same act of experience is found also what will later be distinguished as social obligation. Progress begins with a rudimentary sense of these distinctions, so that it becomes possible to have awareness of the divine apart from any particular external occasion, while the object or event which has been or even which still is, an occasion of such awareness, may be apprehended by certain minds without any stimulation of religious feeling. That stage has long been reached in certain departments of experience by any of our species who stand near enough to ourselves to make possible a secure estimate of their beliefs or feelings. And when that stage has been reached, we find authority and experience acting upon one another in every gradation of mutual interdependence. The supposed conflict between Authority and Experience in religion is really a tension between two indispensable elements. For the individual, Authority, whether as tribal custom or as alleged Revelation, is prior to Experience; in the race as a whole Experience is prior to Authority. Both have their origin in the stage of indistinguishable fusion, but they have become distinct —so distinct as sometimes to appear as hostile opposites—and yet they remain essentially interdependent.

There are two broad divisions of tradition to be observed in this connexion, according as primacy is given to intellectual or to moral interests. The purely intellectual treatment of experience, with the yearning for wholeness or totality which is the mainspring of logic, leads to the conception of God or Ultimate Reality as the Absolute One, or, in Lord Balfour's less exalted phraseology, as "the logical glue which holds multiplicity together and makes it intelligible".[1] Such a conception of God imposed by the authority of tribal

[1] Lord Balfour, *Theism and Humanism*, p. 20.

or national custom leads religious experience, where it occurs, to approximate to the type of mystic union in which the distinction of worshipper and deity disappears. But we have seen that though philosophy has often tended to such a conception, yet it is philosophically unsatisfactory, for the Absolute One is not self-explanatory, and as nothing from without can explain it (for nothing is outside it), it remains a mere brute fact, however august. Philosophy can only find its own satisfaction by going beyond the purely intellectual process in which its life consists, and consenting to receive illumination from the complete personal and spiritual life of which it is a part. Truth for truth's sake is falsehood; for truth's own sake we must say—Truth for good's sake. In our discussion of Truth and Beauty (Lecture VI.) it became clear that the principle of Truth is one which finds its full expression in Good as the meeting of Mind with itself. What is said above is, therefore, no pragmatist subordination of Truth to some thing alien or extraneous: Truth is one form of Good, but a secondary form; the primary form is Love, and this requires Truth for its own completeness. The one self-explanatory fact is the full energy of spiritual life active in the achievement of the good. This brings us at once to the other conception of God, which we may also describe in Lord Balfour's words:

"When I speak of God, I mean something other than an Identity wherein all differences vanish, or a Unity which includes but does not transcend the differences which it somehow holds in solution. I mean a God whom men can love, a God to whom men can pray, who takes sides, who has purposes and preferences, whose attributes, however conceived, leave unimpaired the possibility of a personal relation between Himself and those whom He has created."[1]

We may later on be able to see how this conception satisfies the needs which lead to the formation of the other; indeed we have already seen that it alone is in

[1] Lord Balfour, *Theism and Humanism*, p. 21.

principle adequate to the function which any conception of God is philosophically required to discharge. The thought of a personal Creator would really explain the world and all things in it, if only as we look upon the world we could see that it is good, sharing the estimate of it attributed by the Biblical myth to the Creator Himself.[1] This at any rate is the predominant conception of God in the Bible and in those religions which owe their character to its influence. Where these religions are prevalent, religious experience tends to take the form of a communion of persons in which the distinctness is never lost; one is Creator, the other creature; and if the special quality of the Christian religion is also potent, one is Redeemer, the other redeemed: and of course it is only with such a conception of God that the idea of revelation as grounded in a special divine activity is compatible at all. The Absolute appears in its appearances; only the living God can reveal Himself in action. Hinduism here as elsewhere attempts a combination of mutually destructive elements; its *bhakti* is incompatible with its metaphysics.

The form taken by religious experience in the individual is always dependent on the influence of religious tradition, or in other words of authority. But the authoritative quality of tradition is at its maximum where the tradition is taken to be or to contain a specific revelation. This special quality of authority may both stimulate a personal experience responsive to itself, and also give to experience a deeper tone, a greater intensity. But inasmuch as the tradition is not the only influence moulding character and thought, it may be that any particular mind responds more readily to other influences; and then the tradition with its authority is felt to be a barrier erected against the free movement of the spirit. Thus we trace the difference between the attitude to tradition and its authority which is characteristic of the Middle Ages, and that which is typical

[1] Genesis i. 12, 18, 21, 25, 31.

of the Reformation; or again the difference between both of these on the one hand, and, on the other, the attitude of some modern types of religion to the tradition of the Church and to the variety of new influences which have become powerful alongside that tradition, such as, at one time, the new classical scholarship of the Renaissance, or, at another time, the new scientific achievements of the last hundred years. The extent to which any individual revolts against the authority of the religious tradition of his civilisation, without stimulus from some other great influence in his environment, is probably very small. There may have been some brought up under the static unity of the Absolute as presented by Brahminism and the other Eastern traditions, to whom God has directly revealed Himself as righteous Will, apart from any external influence of which the Bible was the ultimate source; but we do not hear of them, or find their influence in history, unless it be claimed that Zoroaster was such an one; and if he is, then he is truly an exception that proves the rule, because the strongly ethical character of his teaching was quickly "obscured or submerged in superstition".[1] When once a religious tradition has established itself, the unaided individual consciousness cannot escape from it. But, of course, there is escape provided by other forms of experience or thought. When the sole supremacy of the mediaeval tradition had been undermined by the Renaissance, the path was open for Luther to find his way back to the Scriptures of the Old and New Testaments relatively unencumbered by traditional interpretation, and thus to receive the stimulation of his religious experience from the almost forgotten doctrine of St. Paul concerning Grace and Faith. So experience initiated a new tradition which was capable of becoming as tyrannical as its predecessor. But Luther did not begin from an immediate experience of the divine; he began with St. Paul and the effect which

[1] Gore, *The Philosophy of the Good Life*, p. 54.

St. Paul produced in his religious history. *As usual, external and internal, objective and subjective, are found together; but priority, also as usual, is with the external and objective.*

Where several influences of diverse proximate origins are at work, the current orthodoxy or distinctively religious tradition is commonly felt as a restraining rather than as a stimulating factor. Some men reach experience of God in other modes than those supplied by the religious tradition of their age and country, and as these owe less to that tradition they easily appear to be more spontaneous. Thus a supposed contrast is drawn between religions of authority and religions of the spirit. But this is a false division. The less orthodox form is not independent of authority; it only finds its authority in a new place—in natural science, or in art, or in the momentary phase of literary fashion. And there is no reason to suppose that the religious tradition which was till a slightly earlier date authoritative was any less than these representative of the divine spirit. Yet the tension will continue until the various influences have been re-synthesised by the natural activity of thought, and there is again an accepted tradition possessed of an authority now seen to be that of the divine Spirit Himself. Thus orthodoxy is constantly refashioned so that its permanent essence may be synthesised with an ever-growing range of experience.

Perhaps the world has passed beyond the stage when such a complete adjustment and synthesis is to be expected; even if it is achieved, it is sure to be shortly broken up again. The question, therefore, how Revelation, Authority, and spontaneity of religious experience may best be related to one another is not only of great interest to the student, but of great importance to the practical life of religion. In handling it the Natural Theologian does not rely on any revelation, though he must allow for the fact that all religions assert its reality, and does not submit himself to authority, though he must notice that the essence of his subject-matter—Religion itself—is such submission; he will therefore most easily begin with religious experience.

It is impossible to use that phrase without recollection of William James and his Gifford Lectures on *Varieties of Religious Experience* delivered at Edinburgh thirty years ago. The immediate value of that book was very great. Its freshness, its candour, its openness of mind gave it a very strong and wholesome influence in encouragement of the tendency of thought to recognise the reality and authenticity of religious experience, and to claim attention for it from those who construct systems of thought purporting to unify all fields of experience. But if the immediate value was great, there is doubt about the balance of value in the long run, for William James had a great share in associating the thought of religious experience with moments of specially intense awareness. He used the word experience in that sense which enables us to prefix to it the indefinite article or to employ it in the plural. When a man speaks of "*an* experience" or of "experiences" he is thinking of special and isolated moments in his experience as a whole. Now there can be no doubt about the occurrence of such religious experiences. But if they stood alone, they would be of comparatively small importance. They derive their importance from the fact that each is a focus of a quality that pervades the whole life of some persons, including as a rule those to whom the special moments of experience occur. It is not religious experiences, but religious experience as a whole, that is of chief concern —that is to say, the whole experience of religious persons. For the religious man is not only religious when he prays; his work is religiously done, his recreation religiously enjoyed, his food and drink religiously received; the last he often emphasises by the custom of "grace before meat". He does his duty religiously; above all, his failures in duty affect him religiously. For duty is to him the "stern daughter of the voice of God", and while he may be conscious of God in the doing of it, he is perhaps most vividly conscious of God in his failure to do it. Other men find in such failure a breach of moral law, an offence against society, a disgrace to self; the religious man finds there disloyalty to a king, betrayal of a friend. This judgement on the self and its conduct may or may not be accompanied by a specially vivid awareness of God, but it proceeds from belief in God and an acknowledged relationship to him. It is the whole reaction to circumstance resulting from that belief and from that acknowledged relationship that should be uppermost in our minds when we speak of religious experience and its significance—the apprehension by the psycho-physical organism of its environment as (amongst other things) divine. Like other forms of awareness, this has its moments of special intensity; but these moments derive their chief importance from the fact that they bring specially vivid awareness of what is matter of constant apprehension. In those moments the religious man does not enter on a novel and otherwise unknown type of experience; rather in those moments he is vividly conscious of what he then knows perfectly well to be a permanent element in his experience as a whole.

In any individual the type of religious experience will depend upon the religious tradition prevalent in his social environment. That remains true even when it takes the form of conscious and deliberate rebellion against the authority of that tradition, just as a political rebellion must needs take its form from that of the government which it seeks to overthrow. From this follows the immense importance of securing that the traditional and prevalent belief of any community is in the closest attainable correspondence with truth, alike by the exclusion of falsehood, which, in this field, is idolatry or superstition, and by the inclusion of all truth which is relevant. Correctness of belief is of high importance to the individual, for reasons which will engage our attention shortly.[1] But it is very much more important to the community, because whatever is the prevalent belief of the community will be accepted uncritically by great numbers of individuals and will predispose them towards forms of religious experience, and of its issue in religious and moral practice, corresponding to that belief. Heresy may be compatible in the individual with deep religion which as a whole is sound; but the Church is bound to regard heresy as for its purposes a more serious evil than some aberrations which in the individual would be more pernicious.

But while, in the individual, experience very largely depends on belief, and this again on tradition, it is none the less true that in the totality of religious history tradition and belief depend on experience. No doubt it is true that in the primitive phase of human existence in which both have their origin they are not yet distinct from one another; but it was because men actually found the divine element as one among others in the field of their experience that they formed a conception of the divine. It is the task of anthropologists to trace out the long process by which man's vague awareness of Something—call it "the numinous" or what you will—developed into the positive religions of mankind in the historical era. This is a subject of profound interest, and is full of warning against hasty judgements. But it is not directly relevant to the study of religion as it exists among civilised men; for whatever may be the process of development which has led to this result, the massive fact of human religion is there before us to be evaluated.

Within the historic period development has come in two ways—by religious experience itself and by philosophical reflection. Each is chiefly a contribution of individuals. The religious experience of a multitude—whether Church or nation or group—is almost certain to conform closely to an already prevalent tradition, which, in the case of Church or group, is actually con-

[1] See pp. 352-353.

stitutive of the common life. This may be of supreme value in strengthening faith or in evolving zeal to live conformably with faith; but it will contribute little to the purgation or the expansion of faith. This must come through individuals, whose activity will at first render them suspect to all who are content with the tradition. They may proceed by philosophical reflection, which must be taken to include the comparison of religious tradition with the ethical consciousness of the community. Thus the canon of Xenophanes—If Gods act basely they are not Gods—provided a principle of ethical purgation for application to the Greek mythology, but its method was that of philosophy, not of direct religious experience. It is the philosophic counterpart of the plea of Abraham: "Shall not the Judge of all the earth do right?"[1] But Abraham is applying an apprehension of the divine character to a particular suggested action; Xenophanes is offering a general principle for application to a tradition. By the efforts of philosophers man's thought of God has been purified and enlarged; but philosophy can contribute little of that definiteness wherein lies most of the driving power of any actual faith. The labours of philosophers from Plato to Hegel might have sufficed to provide a criterion of superstition, and perhaps, in the long run, its elimination; they might have saved religion from shallow ridicule by showing its inherent dignity and its place in the thoughts of those whose thought is most worthy of attention. But it is hard to suppose that the thought of God resultant from those labours would have stopped infanticide, and homicidal public spectacles and slavery,[2] or studded Christendom with hospitals, or inspired crusades against prostitution. Something more than truth and loftiness of thought is necessary to endow religion with converting power.

[1] Genesis xviii. 25.

[2] These are, according to Lecky, the three signal achievements of Christianity in the sphere of social ethics; cf. *History of European Morals*, vol. ii. pp. 20-84.

The growth of religion as a dynamic force comes rather from the side of religious experience, though this is less potent than the other in the elimination of superstition or in the expansion of the thought of God so that it may be adequate to the range of secular knowledge. This religious experience is conditioned by the prevalent tradition, as we have seen; but it may carry men far beyond it. Individuals, who are specially responsive to those elements in the tradition which are qualified for permanence, receive through their religious experience so vivid an apprehension of the aspects of truth which these express, that these elements assume an altogether new proportion; the perspective and emphasis of the tradition is thereby changed, and sometimes, under the influence of that change, elements, which had at one time been accepted with a reverence equal to that paid to any part of the tradition, sink into recognised unimportance and finally drop out altogether. Such a process is probably, though not necessarily, assisted by philosophical reflection and criticism; but its first impetus comes from an empirical apprehension with new clarity of the element which is destined to remain. This is clearest when this apprehension comes in a definite moment of time to an individual; and usually there is such a prophetic apprehension at the outset; but it retains its essential character when it occupies several generations and advances by the slow change in the point of view of a whole people.

It is easy to suggest illustrations of this point. There are comparatively few Christians who remember where is to be found the first proclamation of the familiar words "Thou shalt love thy neighbour as thyself". It is in a passage which clearly shows that its writer had no notion that in that phrase he was enunciating the fundamental principle of all morality.[1] It was just one incidental precept, and moreover "neighbour" meant "fellow-Israelite"—one of "the children of thy people".

[1] Leviticus xix. 18. High Jewish authorities, including Dr. J. H. Hertz, the Chief Rabbi (see his work *The Pentateuch and Haftorahs; Leviticus*, pp. 201, 2; 220–222), claim that the scope of this command is already universal. I find it hard to accept this in view of the combination of phrases in the text. But it is unfair for Christians to refer to the passage without mentioning the claim made by Jewish scholars

Before this maxim could be recognised as the true categorical imperative, two creative transformations were required. The first was accomplished when Rabbis of the school of Hillel drew it out from its obscurity and set it side by side with what was already recognised as the supreme requirement of the Law.[1] The second was accomplished when Jesus of Nazareth, accepting this combination of precepts as a summary of the Law, declared by the Parable of the Good Samaritan that the word "neighbour" must be understood as meaning any human being that a man happens to meet, even a member of a hated nation.[2]

The supreme example of religious progress, occasioned by direct religious experience is that of the Hebrew Prophets. There is no means of accounting for their fresh apprehensions of truth by reference to current movements of thought either in Israel or among the surrounding nations. At least for any believer in Theism, the simplest and most natural explanation of the impressive fact of Hebrew prophecy is offered by the Prophets' own interpretation of it as issuing from a real communion between God and the Prophets, in which the initiative lay wholly on the divine side.[3] Devout men, loyal to the religious faith of Israel as hitherto developed, they were receptive of divine intimations consonant with it but going beyond it, or else so magnifying as to transform certain elements within it. The supreme prophetic intuitions—that God is Righteous, that God is One, that the One God is the ruler of all nations, so that not only Israel but also the enemies of Israel are His peoples[4]—were all present as elements in a faith which originally gave prominence only to the first. But that primary conviction of the

[1] Deuteronomy vi. 4, 5. [2] St. Luke x. 25-27.

[3] I could not go so far as Bishop Gore appears to do in *Belief in God* (the first section of "Reconstruction of Belief"), where he seems to make the fact of Hebrew Prophecy a main ground for Theism itself. If I did not accept Theism on other grounds, I should have to accept even an improbable psychological account of prophecy rather than resort to so immense a hypothesis to account for it.

[4] Cf. especially Amos ix. 7; Isaiah xix. 24, 25.

Righteousness of God, of which the emergence into clear consciousness is typified by the story of Abraham, and of which the distinctive form of a covenant-relation between Jehovah and Israel came to clear expression in Moses, made those who accepted it receptive of the other two. The essence of polytheism is the attribution of diverse characters to Deity; it was the conviction of the absolute righteousness of God which prepared the way for Monotheism, and that in its turn for belief in universal providence. But the prophets did not make this great advance by any form of argumentation. They did not plead that what man already believed involved certain other beliefs which they did not yet accept; they presented themselves as the spokesmen of divinely imparted oracles: "The word of the Lord came unto me saying, Thus saith the Lord".

But it would be a false account of the prophetic writings which would suggest that these divine oracles came to the prophets' consciousness unmediated by either tradition or external event. They are not simply divine utterances in which the prophet is used as a mouthpiece. They are stimulated by events in the contemporary world—the religious and moral decay in the court of Samaria, the enmity of Syria, the advancing thunder-cloud of the Assyrian Empire, the fall of Nineveh and rise of Babylon, the triumphant career of Cyrus. These and other historical events supply the external occasion of the prophetic intuition, and the divine communication is, for the most part, an illumination of the prophet's mind, in congruity with his inherited faith, enabling him to apprehend with new freshness and vividness that truth concerning God which at once explains the external event and indicates the right way of acting in face of it. The prophetic oracles are not formulated theological doctrines, presented in detachment from the practical needs of the moment. The prophets were not Gifford Lecturers with the advantage of some special "guidance". They were men faced with practical problems of political, moral and spiritual life: how is this invasion to be met? how is that act of oppression to be punished? with what manner of hope may endurance be braced or the disappointment of high aspiration be checked from turning into despair and faithlessness? As the prophet faces some actual human need, that truth of God which bears upon it irradiates his mind and he proclaims it in words that thrill our hearts to-day.

In all this there is communion of the divine and human spirit; but it is not unmediated; it is mediated by the tradition which has prepared the human spirit to receive it, and it is occasioned by the external circumstances of the moment. The prophet is enabled to interpret the circumstance as it falls within the divine purpose; in other words, we have here the perfect example of revelation—divinely guided external event interpreted by a mind divinely illuminated to that end. Such revelation escapes from the perils of pure subjectivism, which always accompany special moments of religious experience, for the reference of the illumination is not to a feeling but to a historical fact. And to historical facts the prophets habitually appeal in recalling men to faith in Jehovah—above all to the deliverance of Israel from Egypt. The principle reaches its fullest expression in that event which Christians regard as the culminating point of revelation interpreted as Christians interpret it; for here it is claimed that the external fact is not merely a divinely guided event but a life that was lived by God Himself, which those, whom He "chose that they might be with Him", were enabled by His Spirit to understand for what it truly was.

Now it is evident that such Revelation carries with it a great, indeed an overwhelming, authority for those who so accept it. But what is the nature of this authority? If our account of the revelation itself is true, two allowances have to be made, which entirely prevent the authority from being decisive for any other person than the prophet. The first is that though it consist in an experience where both objective and subjective factors are subject to divine control, yet this control is not unmediated. The prophet's personality and religious history—including the tradition under which he grew to maturity—are the vehicle, the medium, of the divine communication; and it is quite impossible to determine with precision the extent to which this may have affected the divine communication itself. Indeed that mode of expression allows too much for the thought of a divine oracle which, if only it could be disentangled, would be a direct utterance of God, entitled as such to unquestioning acceptance. But that is very rarely presented as occurring. What we have in the prophetical writings of the Old Testament—in which the Jews quite rightly include the historical Books—is the record of, or judgment upon, providentially guided history, proceeding from divinely illumined minds. There is not a divine message, other than the prophetic utterance itself, which has been distorted into this by the medium through which it has passed. That utterance is the only message, but it comes out of an experience of communion with the divine which endows it with more than human authority, though not with the inerrancy of a divinely dictated oracle.

Secondly, with the exception of the Shema to which reference has already been made,[1] and what may be regarded as comment upon this, almost every divine message has direct application to a particular occasion, and it is impossible to declare with certainty how far it applies to any other occasion. Each is characterised, no doubt, by universal truth; but it is only a part—for its occasion the relevant part—of universal truth, and does not contain guidance for its own application elsewhere nor for the supplementing of it that may be called for at other times. Even the moral code of the Decalogue calls for supplement or for completely

[1] Deuteronomy vi. 4, 5; see p. 339.

transforming interpretation before it will correspond to what we know of the will of God for ourselves.

Pharisaism, therefore, was, and is, a perversion. It was a very noble perversion. It had its roots in reverence and in loyal desire to obey God's will. But by converting occasional legislation and direction into a code for all times and places it corrupted the true character of the revelation in which it was grounded; and the same condemnation awaits all who follow the Pharisaic principle of seeking to order life by immutable rules. The revelation itself came in a living experience; that in it which is of permanent authority is not capable of being stated in formulae; it is the living apprehension of the divine will in living intercourse of the human spirit with the divine. It is one mark of the supremacy of the New Testament scriptures that in them this, which was actually true also of Old Testament revelation, came clearly into consciousness.

But all this does not mean that revelation has no authority, or that in religion authority is altogether out of place. On the contrary, consciousness of authority and submission to it is the very heart of true religion. It is because of this that religious history is so full of tragic submission to authority of the wrong kind, and of consequent reactions in which men try to practise religion apart from authority and fall into every variety of phantasy. The heart of religion, as has repeatedly been emphasised, is acknowledgement by the finite of insignificance before the Infinite, by the sinner of pollution before the Holy, by the creature of total dependence before the Creator. It is in its essence a submission to authority.

This authority actually presents itself to the individual in two ways: in the well-proved and attested religious tradition of his community; and in personal experience of the divine as calling, sustaining, judging. If there is any divergence between these two authorities, there is always an initial presumption in favour of the tradition, for it represents the deposit of innumerable individual apprehensions; none the less, it must be remembered that it is by fresh individual apprehensions that the tradition has been developed, and to reject the new intimation may be, not the suppression of a human aberration, but a quenching of the divine spirit; and where the individual apprehension is sufficiently vivid, it may be found in practice irresistible.

Religious tradition has taken many forms. In Hinduism it is chiefly embodied in custom; in Buddhism it is partly represented by custom, partly by the supposed precepts of the Buddha and his chief disciples; in Confucianism, chiefly by the ethical maxims of the sage. But in none of these could it have the special form that belongs to it in Christendom and Islam as the vehicle of a divine revelation. In Islam the sacred writings are regarded as divine oracles to be accepted and obeyed without question. In Christendom a similar view has struggled to maintain itself alongside the complicating factors of a living and very active Church, and of a personal loyalty to a personal Lord which is recognised as more fundamental and more vital than any other element. It is therefore in Christendom that the various forms and repositories of spiritual authority are most in evidence, and for this reason, as well as because the data are here the most familiar to ourselves, we do well to examine and evaluate the modes of spiritual authority by reference to Christian history and experience. We have then to ask what kind of authority belongs of right, according to our general view, to Scripture, to Creeds, to ecclesiastical decrees and customs? And what is the relation of each and all of these to the spiritual experience of individuals or groups, and what is the individual to do when recognised authorities diverge? Plainly we are not concerned with what may be called the disciplinary aspects of these questions. Societies must have rules by which members of those societies are bound so long as they continue to enjoy the privileges of membership. A society may even hold that its own rules are of divine appointment, so that modification of them by any human authority is in itself an act of profanity. With such matters we are not now concerned. Our concern is with genuinely philosophic questions concerning the general nature of spiritual authority and its general relation to its own agencies.

The essence of spirituality is freedom. The quality of that freedom has already been discussed in its relation to the order of physical nature;[1] its relation to the supremacy of God who is Himself spirit will concern us later.[2] But spirit manifests itself by its activity in the initiation of processes not initiated or governed by the causal processes of the physical world. The spirit is controlled, not by force or physical causation, but by the Good in one or other of its forms, among which beauty, truth and moral goodness are the chief. This control only becomes operative through appreciation on the part of the spirit subject to it. Consequently *the essential principle of spiritual authority is the evocation by Good of appreciation of itself; for only when this occurs is authority exercised over the spirit.* Where conformity of conduct, or even of opinion, is secured by any other means than that of persuading the person affected that such conduct is good, or such opinion is right, the authority exercised is less than fully spiritual. Of course a man may act in a certain way out of loyalty to his Church or his country or his party, without being persuaded that the act is in itself right, and such deference to the collective wisdom may be fully spiritual in quality, because it is grounded in a recognition that obedience or conformity in itself is good even though the justification of the particular requirement is not perceived. This is a very frequent experience, and while it is always an advance when the particular requirement also is recognised as good, yet there is plenty of room for sheer obedience within the freedom of spiritual life. The

[1] See Lecture IX. [2] See Lecture XV.

important distinction is not between individual judgement and authority, but between action determined by appreciation of good either in the act itself or in obedience to the authority requiring it, and action undertaken for the avoidance of pain and inconvenience or for the enjoyment of pleasure other than that of doing what is seen to be good.

Confusion of thought at this point is very common, and it may be worth while to elaborate the distinction thus drawn. If a man seizes me and throws me over a cliff, my fall (so far as my part in it is concerned) is due to physical causation only; there is nothing spiritual about it. If he seizes my wife and says he will throw her over unless I jump over, I may choose to jump over rather than accept the alternative; and I am free in that choice of alternatives; for I choose that which I see to be good, in the sense of being the better of the two possibilities before me. But it would be misleading to say in such a case that I jumped over the cliff by an act of my own will; that action cannot be taken in detachment from its immediate context; it was adopted under moral, though not physical compulsion. If now instead of threats the man offers me a great reward, say some large sum of money, if I jump and survive, I may decide that the risk is worth taking, even though the chance of survival is small; and then my action is more clearly voluntary, but can hardly be described as due to spiritual authority. But if, once more, I can be persuaded that by jumping to certain death I may be the means of rendering some great service to my country, as when Curtius leapt into the pit in the Roman story, then my action becomes a free choice of good, and is taken under the spiritual authority of the law of service. In other words, there are various degrees of distance from pure spiritual freedom, according to the degree in which any action is truly voluntary. But we leave the truly spiritual realm as soon as other determinants of choice than the good, in itself and for itself, are introduced.

The spiritual authority of revelation depends wholly upon the spiritual quality of what is revealed. If what comes to the human soul in its religious experience is a sense of impending doom upon itself unless it conforms to the supposedly divine command, that is not an exercise of true spiritual authority. A genuine revelation may take that form, because it may be that the soul is incapable of free response to the appeal of the Good, so that, in order to give opportunity to its better instincts, a purely disciplinary use of fear may be in place. But if so, this means that God Himself makes use of authority other than purely spiritual in dealing with His creatures. Authority does not become spiritual in its own nature because it is exercised by a spiritual being; and a truly spiritual being will have recourse to other methods only as preparatory to the exercise of truly spiritual authority. But there is a point to notice which is for our immediate purposes more important. This supposed revelation of impending doom would only have any effect at all in so far as the recipient supposed it to be true. To that extent the free play of his own judgement is involved. If on calm reflection he dismissed what seemed like revelation as after all no more than the phantasy of a moment, his conduct would be unaffected. But that is the limit of spirituality in the determination of his conduct. He does not really choose the divine will; what he chooses is avoidance of threatened doom, and conformity to the divine command as a means thereto. This may be better than nothing; it may be the best of which he is capable; but it is all on the level of coercion and inducement, which is mental certainly as distinct from physical, but is not yet spiritual.

On the other hand submission to authority, even to human authority, may be purely spiritual. To take the most familiar instance, if a man accepts some doctrine of the Church, some article it may be, of the Creed, or if he conforms to some ecclesiastical regulation, though he himself has no perception of the truth of that doctrine or the rightness of that regulation and conforms solely on the ground that he thinks the Church likely to be right, that submission to its authority is fully spiritual; it is a free exercise of judgement concerning the good. But if a man decides to accept the direction of the Church, not because in one way or another he has come freely to believe that it is likely or even certain to be right, but because he thinks it may just possibly be right and that there is risk of very great pain or inconvenience to himself, here or hereafter, if it is, then his judgement is no longer of the good as such but is merely a prudential calculation concerning his own pleasure or pain; his choice then is a mental, but not a spiritual act. And it must be plainly admitted that though mere obedience to the Church may be spiritual in principle, and may even be the best and wisest course for many individuals, yet it is a limitation of the area of full spiritual response, and if all questions were regarded as settled by the Church, the exercise of spiritual faculty would be very disastrously curtailed for its members.

Now it may be held that God exercises authority over finite spirits as their Creator who is capable also of being their destroyer.[1] Yes; He does exercise such authority; and the believer will be confident that He will exercise it in wisdom and love. But it is not a truly spiritual authority. The spiritual authority of God is that which He exercises by displaying not His power, but His character. Holiness, not omnipotence, is the spring of His spiritual authority. In such a vision as that of Isaiah there is awe-inspiring majesty; but what leaps to the prophet's consciousness is not the sense of his powerlessness before the Almighty, but the sense of his uncleanness before the All-Holy.

The true contrast, then, is not between religions of the spirit and religions of authority, for authority may be fully spiritual, and cannot be truly authority at all if it be not partly spiritual; there is no proper authority

[1] St. Luke xii. 4, 5.

in physical compulsion, or coercion by fear, or inducement by bribery. The true contrast is between the authority which exacts deference through its own inherent quality, and that which exacts deference through any non-spiritual form of sanction. The use of sanctions may be perfectly justified, provided its aim is to develop a character that will no longer require them; but it must be clearly recognised that sanctions do not become spiritual in virtue of the fact that they are imposed by a spiritual Being or Society; they approximate to the spiritual when they are such as to make a spiritual appeal; thus excommunication is more spiritual than flogging, because a completely unspiritual person would be indifferent to it, and to him therefore it would be no sanction at all. This may therefore be described as a spiritual sanction; it is an appeal to the free recognition of good in one department of life, designed to correct the consequences of failure to recognise it in another. The point is that spiritual authority always operates within that sphere of the discovery by mind and spirit of itself or of what is akin to itself in its object, which we have already found to be the essential condition of actual value.[1] Where the soul freely chooses or seeks an object for that object's value alone, there is, in principle, determination by the good—there is spiritual activity; and the spiritual authority of God Himself consists, not in His having the power to create and to destroy, but in His being the appropriate object of worship and love.

The disclosure of the divine character is made through creation;[2] through the principle of reason found to be active in the human mind and discovered to be exemplified in the physical universe; through the history of mankind; through religious experience, especially as providing the interpretation of history; and also (according to Christian belief) in the historical occurrence of a personal Life as interpreted by those

[1] Lectures VI. and VII.

[2] Romans i. 20.

who were qualified by sympathetic companionship with that Life to become its interpreters. We have spoken already of the revelation through creation and the principle of reason.[1] We are concerned now with the authority of the revelation that reaches us through the record of certain historical events and through certain persons supposed to be qualified by their intercourse with the divine Being to read His purpose and character therein. Concerning all of these, except that personal Life in which this supposed process of revelation culminates, we must say two things: first, that millions of spiritually sensitive souls have found here what they are bound to acknowledge as the very Word of God; secondly, that the message is none the less so inextricably human and divine in one, that no single sentence can be quoted as having the authority of an authentic utterance of the All-Holy God. The message comes through the broad impact of the revelation as a whole upon the human spirit; this may be gathered up in summary phrases, but these are only indicators pointing to elements in the living experience of the living God of which the Scriptures give the record. Such summary phrases belong to conceptual thinking, which is in its own nature of an interim character, enabling us to enter more fully into the fruition of living experience. For this very reason such summary phrases are not the proper subject-matter of revelation. Specific Revelation, if it exists at all, is revelation of God, not of propositions about God; and God is not a concept.

It follows that everyone who makes any use at all of the alleged revelation of the Old Testament must make what he can for himself out of it, gaining, if he is wise, all the help that he can from those who by spiritual insight and careful study are qualified to assist him. How far is this still true of a revelation given in a Person believed to be both God and Man? If Christ had written a code of precepts or a manual of theology, those

[1] Lectures V.-XI

who accepted Him as the Incarnate Self-Utterance of the Eternal God might have found it impossible to deviate from what was so laid down. But in doing this He would have confined the fully spiritual response of His followers to their general acceptance of Him as Lord; Mohammed did, by the kind of authority which he claimed for the Koran, confine in that way the spiritual response of Moslems. If Christ designed to evoke a response spiritual in every part, He must write no book, but leave the general impact of His Person and Work to reach mankind in general through the account of Him which His disciples would give. Here once more the human element intervenes with all its limitations, not only those inseparable from the perfect humanity attributed to the Incarnate Lord Himself, but also those of His faithful but not infallible disciples. And the purely spiritual authority of the revelation is secured by this removal of what would otherwise have been the almost coercive quality of its divine origin. For Christians must exercise their own insight and their own intelligence, not only in judging whether or not to submit themselves to Him as Lord, but also in estimating the claim on their allegiance of any particular recorded direction. Any individual Christian may accept a recorded utterance as final for himself, as some "pacifists" take certain sayings in the Matthaean compilation known as the Sermon on the Mount and let these decide their personal attitude to war. But the decision to accept those recorded sayings as decisive is a personal decision. The mode of the revelation as it reaches us renders inevitable a large exercise of private judgement, which is the essentially spiritual principle; and the spiritual authority of the Gospel for those who accept it is secured by the fact that it is transmitted in a form which perpetually calls for private judgement.

In the case of Christ as fully as in that of the prophets we have to allow for the occasional character of the recorded utterances. It is true that He refers every occasion to its appropriate principle; but it does not follow that this is the only principle appropriate to some other occasion. The duty of thinking out what duty requires still remains. But it is precisely in virtue of this occasional quality of His words and acts that His truly spiritual authority can be regarded as universal. If He had committed Himself to the formulae of conceptual thought, He would have laid a fetter upon human spirits, nor could any formula of action be applicable to all circumstances or stages of social progress. But occasional words and acts display the spirit in its living relation to the facts confronting it; and it is the spirit that is universal in its scope, it is the spirit that is entitled to authority; and its authority can only be recognised by an act of private judgement, or rather, a private act of judgement.

But private judgement need not be individualistic; indeed to exercise it in a spirit of independence or self-assertiveness is the distinctively diabolic as contrasted with the merely animal way to alienation from God. That an individual, who is called to the august responsibility of determining his own response to what he accepts as in some sense at least the self-revelation of God, should fail to make use of the best help that he can find, would be wanton arrogance. He will find wisdom in submitting his judgement very largely to the guidance of that accumulated understanding of the revelation to which devout souls and profound thinkers in many generations have contributed. He will think it most unlikely that he should be right and the common testimony of the saints be wrong. But that testimony is enshrined of necessity in the propositional form of conceptual thinking; no creed or doctrine can, because it belongs to that stage of apprehension, have full spiritual authority in itself. It can only be an indicator, pointing to the place where true spiritual authority may be found. Among Christian theologians it has been common to point out that most articles of the Creeds were adopted in their familiar form as a warning against a line of thought proved to be disastrous to some element in that full revelation and corresponding experience which Christians believed themselves to possess. So far as that is true, it would follow that the authority of the Creeds resides in their warning to avoid denial of any article rather than in a claim that any article should be accepted and believed exactly as it stands. In any case, the function of the Creed is not to be itself an object of faith, but to point men to what is worthy to be accepted as an object of faith, and it is in that proper object of faith, and not in the Creed, that true spiritual authority is to be found.

It has been a traditional Christian doctrine that a Creed becomes authoritative only by the *consensus fidelium*; and this is a clear recognition that the source of its authority is the mind of the living Church—not, indeed, that of the contemporary Church alone, but also not that of the Church of past ages alone. Here we come back to the truly spiritual realm of personal intercourse, but in doing so we leave behind the possibility of infallible guidance. The Christian will believe that he has an infallible authority in the Mind of Christ; but he should also know that he has no infallible means of ascertaining this in application to given circumstances. There always remains necessity for private judgement either upon the matter under consideration, or else by reference of the decision to an authority known to be fallible. Infallible direction for practical action is not to be had either from Bible or Church or Pope or individual communing with God; and this is not through any failure of a wise and loving God to supply it, but because in whatever degree reliance upon such infallible direction comes in, spirituality goes out. Intelligent and responsible judgement is the privilege and burden of spirit or personality. A man may have full and (in psychological fact) unshakeable assurance concerning the will of God, or the rightness of his Church, or the character of his friend; but though his assurance cannot be shaken, it does not rest on certain knowledge or deem itself infallible; its root is personal trust.

The revelation to the prophets was a personal revelation to persons, even when the medium of revelation was a historical event or course of events; the words of the prophet are the expression of the prophet's personal apprehension of the Divine Character and activity as disclosed. The words are not the revelation but the vehicle of it. The precise oracles of Isaiah or Jeremiah, for example, are not in themselves revelation for others. But countless persons have been convinced that through those oracles the Word of God has come home to their own souls. And when it comes it always comes with authority claiming obedience. What is revealed is not truth concerning God, but God Himself. It may be that this revelation is sometimes given to a community of persons rather than to individuals in isolation; it may be that an individual believer recognises an obligation to defer his judgement to that of his religious community. But all such questions are secondary. The primary fact concerning revelation in its essence is that it is a personal self-disclosure to persons, and has authority as such. In the Hebrew-Christian tradition, God is revealed as holy love and righteousness, demanding righteousness of life. *The real acceptance of such revelation is not only intellectual assent; it is submission of will. And this must be submission to the revelation as personally received, not only to the record of it as received by some one else. Every revelation of God is a demand, and the way to knowledge of God is by obedience. It is impossible to have knowledge of God as we have knowledge of things, because God is not a thing. We can only know a person by the direct communion of sympathetic intercourse· and God is personal. But besides this He is Creator, so that the communion of man with God is communion of creature with Creator; it is worship and obedience, or else it does not exist.*

God is personal; revelation therefore is the self-disclosure of personality to persons; its authority is its capacity to satisfy those aspirations which God Himself has implanted in persons. Other forms of persuasion may be used to lead men away from interests that have no promise of satisfaction; but the authority of God over the soul does not arise from anything external which He may bring to bear upon the soul; it arises from the intrinsic nature of God and of the soul—of God as creative, holy Love, and of the soul as creature, yet free to respond to love and holiness with willing obedience and with worship.

LECTURE XIV

FINITUDE AND EVIL

All theistic schemes of thought are confronted with one great and apparently insoluble difficulty—the fact of evil. The difficulty presented by this fact is felt with acuteness varying directly with the completeness of conviction that God is good. If reality consists only of happenings, void of all purpose and tending to no goal, it may then be impossible to understand it at all, but at least there is then no special difficulty about the occurrences described as evil. Whatever causal processes are recognised to exist are sufficient to account for these events, as for others. The very fact that evil is felt to be a problem even by many of those who avow no theistic faith, is evidence of the natural tendency of the mind to seek some explanation of the world in other terms than those of purely efficient causation. But as soon as that principle is pronounced insufficient, there is no alternative recourse save to the principle of purpose; and if that be adopted the difficulty presented by evil at once appears.

It must always be with anxiety that a philosopher approaches this part of his subject. So many promising schemes have failed at this point. Either the evil element in experience is so directly referred to the divine initiative as to preclude the attribution of perfect goodness to God, or it is so marked off from His activity as to involve the intolerable difficulties of ultimate dualism; or else it is itself so minimised that the resultant account of experience seems to be wholly detached from actuality. No extant solution of this triangular problem is altogether satisfactory. We have to recognise to the full the reality, and the radical badness and wrongness, of evil; the universal sovereignty of God; and His perfect goodness. It is not likely that our attempt will be successful where so many advanced by far more competent guides have failed. None the less it must be made, and its failure may contribute to the success of another.[1]

Evil is Negative Value. The essential condition of Positive Value has been found to be the recognition by mind of itself, or of what is akin to itself, in its object. We note in passing, and reserve for future discussion, the apparent subjectivism and relativism of this view, only remarking that the real good and evil are what appear such to the Divine Mind or to a finite mind that is fulfilling its divine vocation.

When Mind in its aesthetic activity of contemplation finds what is strange and alien, that is the experience of Ugliness. When Mind in its scientific activity of analysis and synthesis finds itself bewildered and baffled by its environment, or when it acquiesces in an apparent recognition of its own principle in that environment, to which other facts than those under observation are recalcitrant, that is the experience of Ignorance or Error. When Mind in its ethical activity of determining personal relationships either fails to find its counterpart, or finds it as something akin, indeed, but hostile, that is the experience of Moral Evil. For in the ethical sphere where the relevant relationship is that of person to person there are two kinds of Evil—the absence of the kinship sought, and the perversion of this so that the very condition of good is become a fount of evil.

Now as Moral Good—the Good of personal relationships—is alone absolutely good, so we find that it stands in a special relation to all forms of Evil including Moral Evil. For Truth and Beauty can both be subordinated to Moral Evil, and the Evil is all the worse because of the prostitution to its service of what

[1] Cf. Hume, *Dialogues on Natural Religion.* "A very small part of this great system, during a very short time, is very imperfectly discovered to us; and do we thence pronounce concerning the origin of the whole?"

intrinsically is good; thus the good of physical Beauty can be prostituted to the service of lust, and the good of extensive Knowledge to the service of selfish ambition. But Moral Good cannot be subordinated to any form of Evil. When it occurs in the midst of an evil context it shines like a jewel and makes the evil whole which includes it the less evil for its presence.

In each main sphere Evil can be subordinated to its corresponding Good. Error subserves Truth when the explanation of its occurrence illustrates, as a well-founded explanation must, the rational order of the whole within which the error occurred. The climax of Art is found when the great artist takes the repellent and hostile elements in experience and, welding them into the completeness of his harmony, makes them—while still in their isolation horrifying—constituent and contributory elements of the sublime.

But the inherent predominance of Good over Evil is nowhere so clear as in the moral and spiritual sphere. The presence of what is morally good in a process or occurrence which as a whole is evil cannot add to that evil, nor can the good become in any sense an evil thing. But the presence of evil can enhance the excellence of what on the whole is good, and the event or act which in isolation is evil can be itself an integral and contributing part of a whole which, as a whole, is good.[1] To cite once more the supreme instance; the crucifixion of Christ is (in the Christian scheme) supremely bad when taken in isolation, but when taken as part of the whole scheme of which it is the pivot, it is supremely good.

As we set ourselves to consider what may be the place of evil in a world regarded as divinely created and divinely governed, it is worth while to remind ourselves at the outset of this possible subordination of evil to good. Indeed, if that were all that could be said, it would be sufficient to save Theism in principle, sup-

[1] See *supra*, Lecture VIII.

posing that on other grounds it could establish itself. But that would leave us still without any real understanding of the place of evil in experience, and it is this which we must now try to reach.

We have two questions to consider, which may or may not turn out to be identical—the cause of evil, and the justification of its occurrence. First we must enquire how evil finds a place in the world-process as we have conceived it, and secondly, whether, when its origin is so understood, its occurrence is compatible with the belief that the world is created and ruled by a God who is both infinite Goodness and infinite Power.[1]

In the first stages of its existence the world exhibits neither life nor consciousness. At a certain point of its development life appears in rudimentary vegetable form. This life is void of consciousness. But again at a certain point in its development, life exhibits consciousness. Consciousness supervenes upon an organic existence which has already established a habitual routine. That routine includes the process in which one organism becomes food for another. If there is no consciousness, that cannot be called evil. If the organism that becomes the food of another is conscious, there is perhaps already evil in that combination of facts. But this seems less than certain; for the merely conscious organism lives in the present, and an extremely constricted present, so that consciousness perishes almost if not quite simultaneously with the occurrence of the event which in combination with continued consciousness would be evil. At this level then there is perhaps a very little evil, perhaps none at all. But once more at a certain stage in development consciousness becomes self-consciousness. The organism is now not only conscious of its environment as offering occasions for satisfying appetite, or for flight from danger. It is now conscious also of itself as distinct from its environment, and of possible states

[1] We are here concerned only with the former question. The latter is taken up at the conclusion of our enquiry, in Lecture XX.

of itself as distinct from its actual state. It is, in Green's phrase, a self-distinguishing and self-seeking consciousness. Its time-span is increased. The "present" is now for it a longer stretch of clock-time, and it has memory of a past and anticipation of a future. Events now have value for it, and it is become a centre of value-judgements.

As we look back we see that at any stage which we choose to isolate, prior to the human, there was a possible balance or harmony comprising the best possible good at that stage. It was in principle possible that each self-conscious organism should pursue its own interest in such ways that the good of life should on the whole at least outweigh the evil. There seems to be no doubt that life in the jungle is, on balance, good. The larger beasts must kill the smaller to maintain themselves; but though this involves for the smaller beasts moments of terror, it seems clear from the accounts of naturalists that even for them enjoyment of life is the prevailing tone or colour of experience. And though there is already some problem concerning the occurrence of any evil at all, yet at this level there is reason to be satisfied with a balance of good over evil. That is not all that we have to say about it. But it is all that arises at this stage; and at this stage it is enough. For the stage at which evil may be taken up into good and made part of its own excellence is the stage of definite moral values. If life at the animal stage is good on the whole, then as a whole it is good, and no question of its justification arises. If later developments appear to offer a justification of the subordinate element of evil which it contains, that is to be welcomed in the interest of a completely rational interpretation of the world; but even without it we can safely pronounce that the best understanding we can frame of the animal world offers no obstacle to a reasonable Theism.

It is with the advent of man that the problem assumes proportions so overwhelming. Mind, as known in man, early achieves a certain detachment from its basis in the physical organism by its use of "free ideas". But it actually holds these ideas by means of its capacity as imagination. The mind cannot think without either percept or image.[1] The use of the Figure in Geometry is more than a convenience; it is a necessity. But it need not be drawn on paper or on a blackboard. It can be constructed in imagination. The mind is not strictly thinking about the Figure—the triangle ABC, for example; it is thinking about the universal triangle; but it can only do this by means of a particular triangle, taking care to avoid reference to any peculiarity of the particular triangle. Now imagination, just because it exists to offer particular instances of general qualities, offers to desire the stimulus which the appropriate physical objects offer to appetite. Hence comes a great, and in principle unlimited, expansion of the life of desire, which initially functions only as expressive of the vital needs of the organism or as stimulated by appropriate objects in the physical environment. Desire as so expanded may take the form of aspiration or of lust. No doubt it always takes in fact both forms at first, and one way of expressing the purpose of educational discipline is to say that it aims at directing the whole force of desire away from lust towards aspiration. When this process is corrective rather than preventive it is commonly called "sublimation".

From these considerations it is clear that so far as Evil is a product of exaggerated or misdirected desire, the condition of its occurrence is identical with the condition that makes possible all the higher ranges of human life. The ancient Hebrews had ample justification for tracing sin to the "evil imagination". But to imagination also must be traced the possibility of all forms of distinctively human excellence. All depends on how it is used. To take up the thought of our earlier discussion of Freedom, all depends on the direction of

[1] οὐδέποτε νοεῖ ἄνευ φαντάσματος ἡ ψυχή, Aristotle, *De Anima*, 431 a 16, 17.

attention;[1] and this is largely within the mind's own control.

But this gives us rather the mechanism of evil as known in men than its mainspring. If the mind can control the direction of its attention, why does it so often give it a bad direction? It is easy to answer by attributing this to perversion or sin in the mind. But that hardly helps us. What is the source and nature of this perversion of mind? That any man ever chose evil, knowing it to be evil *for him*, is to me quite incredible. He may say, under an impulse of defiance, "Evil, be thou my good"; but his pursuit of it is then due to the fact that he has adopted it as his good and not because it is evil. To desire evil strictly for its own sake is impossible. To hate the human race so as to desire as good for one's self what is evil for all others, and even because it is evil for all others, is possible; but this evil for others is still desired as supposedly good for him who desires it.

In other words, a man is governed by what effectively appears good to him, which we shall henceforth term "the apparent good". And what appears good depends on the condition of his mind. It is not a reflective judgement with which we are now concerned. No one, probably, *thinks* cruelty good—certainly not as a general proposition, and hardly in a particular instance. Yet men do cruel things; they do them because at the moment those things appear good through gratification of some lust for self-assertion, or through their power to allay some panic fear. A man's character determines his apparent good at any moment; his apparent good determines his conduct.

If this process is working out to a bad result it is because the apparent good is not the real good. Sometimes it is possible to change the apparent good by setting beside it some presentation of the real good. There are many who habitually gain control of evil desires by turning their attention to the Figure of

[1] Cf. Lecture IX.

Christ, in contrast with which the object of the evil desire appears no longer good but abhorrent. Sometimes again it is possible to think out the full implication of what presents itself as good, and to see that taken in its real completeness it is bad. But as a rule the real good will be impotent against the apparent good unless it can be made equally apparent; and this means that it must be presented to the mind in some form apprehensible by the senses or in imagination. A man may know as a matter of general principle that stealing is not only wrong but bad—bad, that is, for him. But if he sufficiently desires an object that is within his grasp, he may none the less take it unless there is also before him the sorrow of the person robbed, or the penalty which he is likely to bring upon himself. Most of us have been able to master our covetousness of possessions sufficiently to be free from these temptations. The force of temptation is more felt in the region of bodily appetites, or of personal resentments, or of professional or commercial ambition, or of political sentiment. But the principle is the same. There may be a genuine apprehension of the true good in conceptual form; but this will not prevail against the vivid attraction of an apparent good unless it is presented in a form that is as effectively apparent. Imagination is usually the connecting link between thought and volition, and if the apparent good is to be changed otherwise than by conversion of the character, it must chiefly be through the occupation of the imagination with the things—and the relevant things—that are "pure, honourable and of good report."

But we have not yet come to the heart of the problem. Why is there a difference between the apparent and the real good? or, to put the question more usefully, why are we such that what appears to us good is other than the real good? For there is here an unquestionable bias or tendency to evil in human nature. Theologians have called this Original Sin; and if those words mean that every human being has in one respect or another such a bias or tendency to evil, they do not stand for a mysterious doctrine but for an evident and vitally important fact. Our task is to relate that fact to belief in the divine government of the world; but it will assist us if we first enquire further into the ground of the fact in human nature and its place in the world process as our argument has led us to envisage this.

The point which here concerns us is this. Mind arises within the world process as one of its episodes; but it is a peculiar episode in two ways. First, it is peculiar because it is able to take the process in which it occurs within the embrace of its awareness and its comprehension. Viewed from one standpoint, a man is a trifling occurrence—a midget breathing and moving for a brief span in one corner of a universe overwhelmingly vast. Viewed from another standpoint, he is himself the master of that universe, able to comprehend it as it can never comprehend him, and bending the mighty forces of nature to serve his purposes. He tames the force of lightning, turning it on and off with a switch. He regulates the waves of ether, bidding them carry accounts of his very games round the globe. To his lightest whim the august energy of Nature must be subservient. There may be rational minds domiciled in other planets, or in stars and nebulae. On the planet called Earth such minds have appeared, and their achievements make even the suns look small. That is one way in which Mind is peculiar as an episode in the world process.

The other, which more concerns us now, is this. Till Mind appeared as an episode in the world process, all other episodes had value in potentiality only, not in actuality—so far at least as the process itself supplied the condition of its actualisation. In the sight of God, and it may be also of spirits other than those born in the world process, that process and its episodes had value. But with the coming of minds there came also for the first time episodes within the process supplying to other episodes the condition for the actualisation of their value. Here, even more than in the impressive achievements lately enumerated, is the supreme peculiarity and distinction of mind. *The human mind is a focus of appreciation. It has knowledge of good and evil. The winning of that knowledge is called the Fall of Man, because acts, which before he won it were merely instinctive reactions to environment, become through that knowledge sins against the light. Again, because they are done against the light, they are done with a new degree of self-assertion. And, once more, because imagination is so potent to stimulate desire, there is an additional impulse to those acts. Man in so far as he is evil is worse than any animal; and in every man there is the bias or tendency to evil.* We are now in a position to track this to its source.

Mind, as it occurs as an episode in the world-process, takes the form of finite minds. It is indeed confined within extremely narrow limitations. It cannot attain to any grasp of the true proportions and perspective of the world in which it is set. Certain things have a value for it and are its apparent good. There is no inherent and absolute necessity for this to be other than the real good; yet the probability of divergence is so great as to amount to certainty for all practical purposes. The finite, and indeed very narrowly limited, mind appreciates the gigantic fact of good and evil. But its limitations hinder it from apprehending the full significance of these, or the true nature of the various objects which present themselves as apparent goods. *The mind by a necessary tendency of its own nature attaches more importance to values which find their actualisation in itself than to those which find it elsewhere; or to put it crudely, each man cares more about what seems to be good for him than about goods which he does not expect personally to enjoy. Even so far as he knows of these, they take a second place for him; and about many of them he knows nothing. So he becomes not only the subject of his own value judgements, which he can never cease to be, but also the centre and criterion of his own system of values, which he is quite unfit to be.*

Accordingly, as man rose above sub-human forms of life through the development of mind within his psycho-physical organism as an increasingly dominant factor, he found himself self-centred. The animal also is self-centred. But in the animal this is an innocent state, because it is merely a given fact of nature; the animal self does not compare its actual condition with a conceived or imagined ideal; it is a consciousness but not a "self-distinguishing and self-seeking consciousness". Consequently it is self-centred without being self-assertive. But as soon as consciousness advances to full self-consciousness, so that the self, distinguishing itself from its environment, not only chooses what appetites it shall satisfy but even what ends it shall pursue, self-centredness becomes self-assertion. The good-for-self is alone effectively apparent good, and good in a fuller sense, though recognised to be real, is relatively powerless as motive. It is not utterly necessary that this should be so; and therefore it is not true to say that God made man selfish, or predestined him to sin. But that it should be so was "too probable not to happen"; and it is true to say that God so made the world that man was likely to sin, and the dawn of moral self-consciousness was likely to be more of a "fall" than an ascent. Human sin was not a necessary episode in the divine plan; but was always so closely implicated in the divine plan that it must be held to fall within the divine purpose. To the problem thus presented we must return at a later stage.[1]

The individual members of human society are not mutually exclusive atoms of consciousness. Each is a partly self-determining, self-integrating system of experience; but the content of that experience is derived from environment. The part of that content with which we are now concerned is derived from social environment. We are, in part, reciprocally determining beings. We make each other what we are. Therefore the existence of one self-centred soul would spread an evil in-

[1] See Lecture XIX.

fection through all who come within its range of influence. This happens both positively by suggestion and negatively by repulsion. If A is self-centred, B tends to become so by imitation; but also B becomes so in self-defence. The instincts of gregariousness and of fear combine to produce the same result. And this process continues, so that A and B perpetually develop their own and one another's self-centredness. Actual human society is to a large extent, though never completely, that network of competing selfishnesses, all kept in check by each one's selfish fear of the others, which Glaucon describes in Plato's *Republic* and which Hobbes made the basis of his political philosophy in the *Leviathan*.

This may, perhaps, be called an evolutionary account of the origin of moral evil. But it must be sharply distinguished from any theory of moral evil which accounts for it by reference to a survival of animal impulses into the rational stage of development. The centre of trouble is not the turbulent appetites, though they are troublesome enough, and the human faculty for imagination increases their turbulence. But the centre of trouble is the personality as a whole, which is self-centred and can only be wholesome and healthy if it is God-centred. This whole personality in action is the will; and it is the will which is perverted. Our primary need is not to control our passions by our purpose, but to direct our purpose itself to the right end. It is the form taken by our knowledge of good and evil that perverts our nature. We know good and evil, but know them amiss. We take them into our lives, but we mis-take them. The corruption is at the centre of rational and purposive life.

The suggestion which we have repudiated belongs to the phase of "faculty-psychology". This presented the soul as a complex entity in which reason and passion exist side by side. Passion, according to this view, comes from our animal ancestors and is already strongly developed when reason appears; reason at first is feeble, and very slowly develops capacity to control passion; the devices of education aim at keeping passion in check while the development of reason is hastened. At last it may be hoped that reason will take complete control, and then all will be well.

Of course that picture is not wholly false. But it is more false than true, because it misses the most vital point. That point is that reason itself as it exists in us is vitiated. We wrongly estimate the ends of life, and give preference to those which should be subordinate, because they have a stronger appeal to our actual, empirical selves. That is why the very virtues of one generation lead to the miseries of the next; for they are contaminated with the evil principle, and it is truly said that "our righteousnesses are filthy rags". *We totally misconceive alike the philosophic and the practical problem of evil if we picture it as the winning of control over lawless and therefore evil passions by a righteous but insufficiently powerful reason or spirit. It is the spirit which is evil; it is reason which is perverted; it is aspiration itself which is corrupt.*

And yet it cannot be said that the principle of selfhood is evil. To say that would be to accuse the constitution of the universe itself and therefore also God its Creator. Moreover it would be, for us at least, self-contradictory. For we have found that the essential condition of Good is the discovery by mind of itself in its object, which reaches its culmination in the love that binds different souls into the unity of perfect fellowship. If the highest good is found in personal relationships, it must be ludicrous to contend that persons or selves are inherently evil in principle. But the persons or selves which occur in the World Process are finite; they are extremely limited in range of apprehension. Their own well-being is dependent on the principle of the Whole in which they are no more than episodes; but this is not within their apprehension; if they so ordered their scale of values as to conform to it, that would seem to be a lucky accident which had occurred against all the balance of probability. Some of them at least must be expected to order that scale wrongly because of the falsified perspective due to their limited range of apprehension; and that will be enough, as we saw, to infect the race. It is still more likely that all will thus err, and then mutually infect with error one another. Because it was not necessary that we should err, we cannot say that our sin is itself God's act; it is our fault, not His, in the first instance. But that we are finite selves is directly due to God's act, and we cannot doubt that God foresaw the issues of conferring selfhood upon finite beings, so that sin falls within His purpose, and is even part of it, though it can not be said that He directly willed or wills it. What He faced was a probability so great as to be distinguishable only in thought from certainty. "I speak after the manner of men"; of course there is, for God's *eternal* knowledge,[1] no such thing as "probability" but apprehension of all reality in its ordered completeness. Yet that distinction in thought is important. For it means that God did not directly cause any man to sin.

The sin of each man is a new element in the World Process. It is what, being himself, he contributes to it. And its essence is not that he is a self, but that being a self he is self-centred. What matters to him bulks larger in his estimate of value than what matters equally or even more to others. He does not love his neighbour as himself, but allows himself to count for more in the direction of his attention, and therewith his life, than his neighbour does. It is not wicked to be finite; but it is so improbable as to be beyond all reasonable estimate of practical possibility that finite selves, if left to themselves, should not be wicked.

When once the spiritual principle of evil had established itself through the adoption of themselves as

[1] *Sc.* as distinguished from His temporal knowledge. We find ourselves obliged to attribute both modes of experience and knowledge to God; see Lecture XVII, specially pp. 444-448.

centres of their systems of value by all, or by any, selves, its calamitous authority would spread apace. Each would infect, and be infected by, the others. The great system of mutual support in evil would be established, which Dr. Inge describes as "co-operative guilt with limited liability".[1] As was noted above, it spreads itself in two different ways, both by positive suggestion, and by putting on the defensive those who find that their neighbours, being self-centred, will attack them if interest so prompts. The young soul, still plastic and rather timidly making its adventure in the world, sees that others fend for themselves, and resolves to do the like; it also finds that in a world so conducted it is likely to be overwhelmed unless it does the like. However small its own perversion, resulting from its own finitude, may have been, it is firmly rooted in self as its centre by its intercourse with others who were perhaps at the outset in their own outlook and estimate of the goods of life no more perverted than itself. And in each this process is intensified by the activity of imagination, which not only stimulates desire beyond its proper province, so that it becomes lust, but also, being specially responsive to fear, exaggerates the peril proceeding from the rivalries and antagonisms of the competing individuals and groups, poisoning all thought and feeling with rancour and bitterness.

This is the account of that indubitable fact, called by theologians Original Sin, which coheres with our general account of the World Process and of man's place within it. Because mind when it appears in that process is finite, and even narrowly restricted in scope, it attaches undue importance to those goods and evils which it apprehends as affecting itself; its perspectives are falsified; what is near at hand looks larger than it is, and what is far off, smaller than it is. This initial aberration of (probably) every finite mind is magnified by the activity of imagination and by the reciprocity of

[1] Inge, *Speculum Animae*, p. 35.

social influence till the Apostolic catalogue is no exaggerated account of the state of man: "foolish, disobedient, deceived, serving divers lusts and pleasures, living in malice and envy, hateful, hating one another".[1]

It is not suggested that this is a complete account of human nature or of any actual phase of human society. But the evil aspect of human nature and society is all that has been said and more. It is no solution of the difficulty which such a view presents to Theism, to say that there is also much good in human nature. If the world is the creation of Almighty Righteousness, we should expect to find good in abundance; that causes no perplexity; but the occurrence of any, even minute, instance of evil causes great perplexity.

With that perplexity, however, we are not yet in a position to deal. Our present endeavour is to apprehend with substantial accuracy the actual moral situation of mankind. And for this purpose it is necessary to allow its fair place to the good that is in human nature despite its perversions, and (no less important) to those potentialities for good which are bound up with the very source and occasion of evil.

First, then, we notice that the earliest experience of the child is almost always predominantly good. The love for its mother which is part of the child's first conscious apprehension is almost purely good. It is not a perfect good, because it is a love wherein from the outset self-interest plays a part. It is in some respects truly disinterested, but is also in a certain sense self-centred.[2] It is *φιλία*—the love of friendship, where the well-being of the self is an element in the complex of motives determining the friendly relation, not *ἀγάπη*—the love of utter self-giving and self-forgetfulness. Therefore it can be stifled and quenched; for if no kindness meets it, its element of self-regard will turn acid within it and corrode it till it vanishes away. Ἀγάπη

[1] Epistle to Titus iii. 3. [2] See *infra*, p. 392.

cannot be so quenched; for as in it the self has been freely given from the outset, the absence of kindness only lets it prove its quality more perfectly. It is necessary to notice this contrast here, not in order to cast a blight upon the loveliness of a child's love, but to remind ourselves both of its possible decay and of the more splendid love which is alone divine and safe from evil infection.

That earliest experience, being good, creates in the soul a tendency which is not easily quite obliterated. And if the home be happy, and early years are spent in a society where love prevails, the good tendency may often be established so firmly that nothing can now prevent its becoming the controlling determinant of character throughout life. Yet the soul will still have its own element of perversion due to self-centredness, and is inevitably hardened in this by the play upon it of the selfishness in the world, from which even its early home is sure not to have been quite exempt. Nor can it be said that every soul trained in a loving home is less selfish than every soul trained under the pressure of grinding selfishness. There are some whose natural responsiveness to the goodness and beauty of the world gives them a centre outside themselves, which is only established the more firmly in resistance to the shocks administered by selfish surroundings.

"Centre" is a spatial, even a geometrical term. Its main suggestion in this context is clear enough, but we must not be misled by its limitations. A circle can only have one centre, but a soul can have two or more. If precision of geometrical metaphor is to be more nearly observed we may then speak of these as foci. Certainly it is the fact that very few, if any, lives are wholly self-centred; that could only happen through great spiritual mutilation, a mutilation which is perhaps impossible. For though our reason, as empirically active, is perverted, yet the essential principle of reason is incorruptible, and those mystics are probably right who hold that in every soul there is a divine spark which never consents to sin.[1] Life cannot be fully integrated about the self as centre; it can only be fully integrated when it becomes God-centred. For God is the real centre of the real world; His purpose is its controlling principle; only in Him therefore can all creatures find a centre which brings them all to harmony with one another and with themselves. But God is immanent in the world, making Himself apprehensible through the Truth, the Beauty, the Goodness which call forth from men the allegiance of discipleship. Consequently there is a constant lure to every soul to find itself at home with Him, and this influence works in the world side by side with that influence of inter-reticulated evil which was earlier described. The soul which all through life is fashioning itself by the exercise of its mental freedom under the pressure of all these forces, good and evil, pursues its difficult and commonly wayward course, with always some element of self-seeking, and almost always some element also of sheer self-giving.

In the process of history the pressure of self-seeking and the impulse of self-giving tend increasingly to converge, making outward conformity to standards of sound morality easier, but also for many souls making progress in inward and spiritual morality more difficult. Selfishness, for its own sake, puts a check upon its expression in acts. If each fights hard for his own hand, no man's hand will retain what it has grasped. Covetousness itself will prompt a prohibition of stealing; for the thief who ignores his neighbour's property rights desires to be protected in his own. As selfishness learns by experience it attains to prudence, and those who zealously follow the best policy will about as often as not be honest. Outward morality is thus encouraged even by the immoral principle itself. Some genuine progress is thus made; but to an almost equal extent conscience is confused and the edge of its witness blunted.

[1] This must be read in connexion with what is said on pp. 367 and 368.

Moral and social progress is, no doubt, mainly due to the activity of positive good influences. But it is of great importance, both practical and theoretical, to notice that lower motives, and even that principle of self-centredness which is the very fount of moral evil, play their part in the empirical development of good. Very often the wisdom of a trainer of character or a reformer of institutions is shown in the extent to which he can secure that the lower motives support the higher in promoting right conduct. Often the elimination of self-centredness is best assisted through the stage of enlisting it in support of what public spirit and even the highest claims of absolute morality require. Few actions are guided by one motive alone, and the vital question in practice is not whether the motive of an action was noble or mean, but whether the just order of priority among motives has been maintained, so that when divergence arises the higher check and control the lower, and the lower do not control or check the higher. The argument, frequent on the lips of a certain kind of moral idealist, that virtuous conduct sustained by fear of the consequences of vice is worthless, only proves that he who uses it is a bungler. Even if nothing sustained the virtuous conduct except fear, it would still be better than vicious conduct, both because it is beneficial instead of harmful to society and because its own excellence at least has the opportunity of making its appeal to the conscience of the person acting, so that imperceptibly another and better foundation for the virtuous conduct may be fashioned. Moreover, impulses which are refused any expression in conduct may atrophy, provided that the energy represented by them is utilised in other ways. It is quite possible for character to improve under the pressure of disciplinary sanctions, and for self-regard to be partly undermined by appeal to self-regarding motives.

Even more evident is the improvement in social relationships which may be assisted by the considerations of an enlightened selfishness. To a quite appreciable extent respect for law rests on the need of every citizen for the law's protection. So through the action of self-regarding motives men may be led to an appreciation of justice. So far as civilisation needs prisons and a police force, the general good is served through appeal to particular interest.

Yet when all this is admitted, it is still true that the self-regarding principle is a precarious support of moral progress, and that a point is reached in connexion with each successive phase of development in individual or society, at which it becomes a barrier to further advance. Where it exists—which is everywhere—the practical statesman and the practical pastor must alike recognise it as a fact and allow for it in the plans which they make to assist social or moral progress; they will try to enlist it as an ally in an advance that is really dictated by higher principles than itself. But man cannot be saved, nor either individual or society attain to perfection, except by the total elimination of self-centredness. Only by truly disinterested love does man enter into completeness of fellowship with God.

That goal, it is clear, will never be reached by the aid of self-regarding motives. Indeed the inevitable utilisation of those motives for the earlier stages of progress constitutes a special difficulty for the final stages—a fact which has led rigorists to make the attempt to crush the self-centred motives from the outset. The actual effects of rigorism in ministering to spiritual pride are evidence that this method is unsound. Consider the spiritual rancour that took a large part of the place belonging of right to charity in the soul of Jerome! The effort to crush self-concern by exaggerated austerities only leads to transference of concern from the self subjected to discipline to the self imposing it. There is a place for austerity in a wise self-discipline, and most of us would be the better for a fuller use of this aid to progress. But it is no more than an aid. It may be that all men need it, and even that the best are those who can and do use it most. But fullness of life is in itself good, and all austerity impoverishes this to some extent. In any case, austerity must be temperately adjusted to the soul's capacity to accept it, not forcibly imposed by one nucleus of desires or aspirations upon another.

Moreover, it is constantly to be remembered that, as has been already said, it is self-centredness that is evil, not selfhood. Selfhood is a pre-condition of all true good. There can be no discovery by mind of itself or its kin in its object unless mind be active as a self or conscious system of experience; and this, which is the essential condition of value, only reaches its completeness in the personal relationship of different selves. The self therefore is not to be destroyed; its need is to understand and feel its creatureliness, its dependence, and its own subordinate place in the entire scheme of things. But this it cannot do by its own effort. *So long as the self retains initiative it can only fix itself upon itself as centre. Its hope of deliverance is to be uprooted from that centre and drawn to find its centre in God, the Spirit of the Whole.* Towards this it is brought by all in which the Spirit of the Whole is manifest as such, by Truth and Beauty and Goodness. In its response to these it is in some measure drawn from its self-centredness and subjected to the Spirit of the Whole who is the one true centre for that self as for all else. Far gone as human nature is in corruption and perversion, it is not so far as to have become insensitive to all forms of goodness; otherwise redemption and recovery were impossible, and impossible also the heroism and self-forgetful love which every one of us has witnessed. But the response, though real, is not always pure, and its influence is seldom, if ever, all-pervasive. The scientist who labours devotedly in the service of truth is sometimes very jealous about the credit for his discoveries; the artist who is true to his own ideal of beauty is not always generous in appreciation of other artists; the philanthropist who sacrifices ease and comfort in a life of service is sometimes extremely self-willed as regards the kind of service which he or she shall render. And any one of these may be an exacting member of the home-circle.

If deliverance of the self from its self-centredness is to be complete it cannot be through response to any partial manifestations of the Spirit of the Whole "by divers portions and in divers manners".[1] That Spirit must personally appear before the self in a form truly apprehensible by that self. Only such a manifestation can effectively claim the submission of the self in all its being. Whether such a manifestation of the Spirit of the Whole has been given is not a question which Natural Theology can answer. But Natural Theology can, and as I think must, declare that if, and only if, such a revelation has been given, finite spirits may find there the cure for the ills of finitude; remaining and rejoicing in their finitude they will then accept their own place in the economy of the universe, bound to one another by a love which is indeed the fulfilment of all morality, but which has its source beyond those relations of the finite which are the sphere of morality, in that "Love which moves the sun and all the stars".

[1] Epistle to the Hebrews i. 1.

LECTURE XV

DIVINE GRACE AND HUMAN FREEDOM

It has been frequently observed that belief in Predestination does not have upon those who seriously entertain it the effect which detached observers tend to anticipate. Observers usually suppose that it must lead to moral and spiritual torpor; for if all is settled by divine decree, what place is there for human effort? Must not the Divine Will be left to fulfil its purpose, as assuredly it will? But history records a very different result. St. Augustine and John Calvin were not quiescent spectators of the drama of divine activity; John Knox was not content idly to observe what Providence might bring to pass in Scotland; or, to take a yet greater name than these, St. Paul, who had much to say about the passivity of clay in the Potter's hands, was not one who accepted from his master, Gamaliel, the doctrine that man's wisdom before what purports to be an act of God, is to wait and see whether history will vindicate that claim. He fought it while he believed it was not of God, and "laboured more abundantly than they all" when he found his error. Saul the persecutor and Paul the missionary are one in vivid consciousness of a duty laid upon man to decide and to act.

We have here an illustration—perhaps the most conspicuous illustration—of a principle common to many phases of religion. The content of religious faith can only be expressed in propositions; but because of the nature of faith, these are of necessity in part misleading. The propositional, or conceptual, or scientific, phase of thought is, as we saw, an *interim* process, helping us to appreciate more fully the reality empirically given in the actual life of the organism.[1] Religion, when it is more than conventional belief or a body of philosophical conclusions, is of all forms of experience the most vital and personal, so that it loses even more than art itself when an attempt is made to translate it into propositional form. The translation must be made; and the doctrinal formulations, which are the result, are of indispensable value for pointing to the source of vital religion those who have not yet experienced it or whose experience of it is as yet rudimentary. But intellectual acceptance even of correct doctrine is not by itself vital religion; orthodoxy is not identical with the fear or the love of God. This fact of the inadequacy of the truest doctrine is a warning that to argue syllogistically from doctrinal formulae is to court disaster. The formula may be the best possible; yet it is only a label used to designate a living thing. To draw conclusions from it by the methods of subsumptive logic may very likely involve us in results which are either quite irrelevant or even contrary to truth, because the inadequacy of the formula will be quite as potent in determining the course of the inference as its appropriateness to the personal relationships for which it stands.

It may assist apprehension of this point if we turn to an illustration other than that with which we are most immediately concerned, though not wholly detached from it. St. Paul undoubtedly argued that human sin was a special opportunity for divine Grace. Those who had no experience of that Grace drew the formally correct conclusion that we should "do evil that good may come" or "continue in sin that grace may abound".[2] With regard to the former slander, the Apostle is content to retort upon its utterers the gloriously question-begging observation "whose damnation is just". The second form of the inference supposedly drawn from his doctrine supplies an opportunity for fuller reply; and the reply is not a denial of the major or minor

[1] See Lecture V. pp. 116, 117.

[2] Epistle to the Romans iii. 8; vi. 1.

premise, nor a criticism of the logical form of the argument, but an appeal to experience showing that whole course of argument to be irrelevant to the spiritual facts. For the Grace of which he speaks abounds only to those who are "in Christ"; and for them there is no open question whether they should continue in sin. The inevitable form taken by the propositional expression of the experience of Grace is such that inferences drawn from it with absolute formal correctness may be, in their practical suggestion, not only irrelevant but the diametrical opposite of truth.[1] Theologians do well to check every step in their procedure by reference to the living experience of personal religion. This living experience is the initial fact which they are to articulate and, so far as may be, render intelligible, and to this they must come back for that richer appreciation which their study and reflexion has made possible.[2]

A man who from outside all religious experience reflects upon the probable effect of any vitally held faith is almost certain to reach wrong conclusions. In relation to the matter now under consideration, he tends to suppose that anyone, who is convinced that God controls all things absolutely and without reserve, will feel himself relieved of responsibility and will adopt the attitude of "wait and see". But the man to whom divine control is not the major premise of a dialectical process but a dominating fact of intimate experience does not in this way settle down inertly to watch the activity of that control; the consciousness of control is itself an overmastering impulse, urging him to incredible enter-

[1] This is not the fault of logic. It is true, as well as a correctly drawn inference, that I have nothing to do except respond to grace. It is the interpretation of this by minds which have no conscious experience of grace that leads to error. This interpretation is illicit, because it uses a term in the conclusion in a sense different from that which it bears in the premise: but though illicit, it is in practice inevitable.

[2] Perhaps yet another instance may be given in a footnote. I should hold that a common mediaeval conception of the Presence of Christ in the Eucharist is proved to be mistaken by the mere fact that it was possible for it to lead to such enquiries as what happened to the Presence if a mouse ate the species. Their formula may have been good, even the best possible. But those who debated such a question were misapprehending the reality. See below, Lecture XIX.

prises and impossible endeavours. So St. Paul found that a necessity was laid upon him; his abounding activity is no credit to him; rather, woe to him if he desists.[1] And of course it must be so. To feel God's hand upon one impelling and directing, and to find oneself actively pursuing some course or serving some cause, are not two experiences but one. The doctrine of the universal Sovereignty of the divine will is paralysing so long as it is doctrine only; but when it is matter of personal experience, it becomes impulse and energy and inspiration.

With this preliminary reflection we may turn to consider two closely allied questions: *how is the divine control of the human will effected? and what does man need which only divine control can offer? The answer to both questions will be found to involve at once the denial of all human freedom over against God and the affirmation of complete human freedom in submission to God.*

The divine control is exercised at various levels. Man is a product of Nature, and in his dealings with Nature is subject to its laws. A man may dive off a rock into the sea, and swim there in safety; but he cannot dive off a cliff into the air and swim in that. Man's range of free choice is limited by natural necessities. By study of nature's laws he is able to overcome this limitation to some extent. Thus by inventing a glider he has enabled himself to dive from cliffs or precipices with safety; and by inventing aeroplanes he has become able in a certain sense to swim in the air. How far he may be able to go in achieving such an indirect emancipation from the limits initially imposed by nature on his range of choice it is impossible to forecast. The emancipation is indirect, in the sense that it is only achieved by means of

[1] 1 Corinthians ix. 16. Of course the vast majority of Christians fall between the two extremes described. They neither vividly experience divine control nor argue about it, but simply believe in it. If that simple belief is more than intellectual assent and takes the form of a confidence which controls the will, that is a living and saving faith. But it is the vivid experience which most clearly refutes the false inferences in question.

appropriate instrument; it remains true that a man cannot swim in air as he can swim in water. But though indirect, the emancipation is effective. Man's range of action, and consequent liberty of choice, is vastly increased by his scientific knowledge; and this expansion of liberty continues.

The present phase of the world's history prompts the reflection that expansion of liberty on one side is balanced by an equal contraction on the other, and that the same cause is responsible for both. It is by machinery that man has gained the wider liberty, and now he is imprisoned by the machinery which sets him free. "Things are in the saddle and ride men." In the competition which machinery has intensified, men find that they must conform to the established process or starve; and even if they are ready to conform by offering their labour, there may be no room for them in an industrial organisation which is almost as completely mechanised as its own productive processes. But true as this may be, and in its own context supremely important, it is to be noticed that the compulsion exerted by competition or any other social force is not physical compulsion. It is only regarded as compulsion because the alternative to conformity is regarded as indubitably undesirable. But a man might choose to starve rather than labour in the only way open to him. In other words, this compulsion acts through the will and not apart from it. Even in a period when man is controlled by his own machinery as much as he controls it, the emancipation from physical restraint upon his freedom of choice remains.

That physical restraint is part of the divinely fashioned constitution of the universe; and from that, by use of his divinely given power of thought, man has in part emancipated himself. So far as it operates, that restraint is a control that makes no reference to man's will. It is merely a limitation of the possibilities before the will. Such a limitation itself supplies an element in the rudimentary discipline of moral character. It teaches us the futility of crying for the moon. That is not an advanced lesson, though some of us never quite learn it. But it is only concerned with wise or unwise ways of seeking a selfish satisfaction; it has nothing to do with the actual direction of our purpose. It is only when this level of concern is left behind that the real problem of divine control and human freedom is reached. A form of external compulsion exercised through divinely instituted laws of nature may minister to our discipline; it has nothing to do with divine control of the will. Indeed it is not control of the will at all; nothing can properly be called control of the will which does not determine the direction of the will itself, as distinct from the conduct to which the will assents.

This principle affords guidance when we come to the stage where we may rightly speak of control of the will. For if compulsion is not real control of the will, no more is bribery. Conduct may be controlled by a system of rewards and penalties; and such a system may have a disciplinary use in fashioning the will, by holding in check certain lawless impulses and thus allowing an opportunity for the dominant nucleus to establish itself and become a rudimentary will. And thereafter this will may itself direct conduct in accordance with right moral principles because it is itself concerned with the winning of rewards or the avoidance of penalties. But in such a case the will is not really directed to moral principle; it is directed to pleasure and pain; and if ever it has hope of gaining a greater preponderance of pleasure by deserting the moral principle it will do so without compunction. Rewards and penalties, in this life or another, may have some disciplinary and educative value; but they are not means by which the will itself can be controlled. Not by such means can God be Sovereign in this portion of His creation.

Are we then to say that He only becomes sovereign over the spiritual world by the self-initiated movement of the finite will towards submission to Him? That would make His sovereignty highly precarious. Moreover, such self-initiation of volition is very hard to understand. It has the appearance of a surd—an irrational entity in the midst of what should be reason's own domain. But if that is unwelcome, are we to say that all depends on the action of God in making to each self or will the appeal to which its nature will lead it to respond? If so, why does not God make that appeal at once, ending the misery and havoc due to the self-centredness of all existing selves? This question has been argued repeatedly in the history of religion. Doctrines of Irresistible Grace, of man's co-operation with divine grace, of man's deserving grace by congruity of conduct, and the like, litter the libraries of Christendom. Let us see whether our method of approach to all such problems enables us to set the various factors in any intelligible relationship to each other, only demanding in advance that the matter should be considered in the closest possible connexion with living religious experience.

We have seen mind establish itself as the dominant principle, or principle of unity, in organisms that are themselves episodes of the world-process. We have agreed that this fact is evidence that the world-process is grounded in mind. We have observed mind detaching itself from the needs and movements of the organisms in which it appears by means of its free ideas. Thus it acquires a freedom to be itself—a freedom "against all the might of nature". This freedom is chiefly exercised in control of the direction given to attention, whereby the mind selects its own nutriment and therefore also its own course of development. Being thus to a great extent a self-determining system of experience, though always less than perfectly integrated, it is free in conduct in the sense of being the true source of its own actions. External compulsion is now irrelevant to it, even when such compulsion still determines conduct, for, as we have just noticed, the will is then either not concerned at all, or else is directed not to the acts nor to their principles, but to the sanctions under which they are commended. *The will is therefore a real power of choice; nothing forces it to choose one way or the other; it follows its own "apparent good". It is not undetermined. It is determined by its apparent good, and itself determines—not by specific choice but by its actual constitution in each self—what shall be to it apparent good. Hence it has—or rather is—the freedom which is perfect bondage. It is free, for the origin of its actions is itself; it is bound, for from itself there is no escape.*[1]

So it seems. Yet there is at least partial escape along three roads—the roads that are followed in the pursuit of truth, of beauty, and of goodness. They are the roads marked by inherent value, of which we have found that the essential condition or formal cause is the recognition by mind of itself or of what is akin to it in its object. This recognition can lead to the escape of the self from its self-centredness because it involves a submission of all that is special or particular in the self to the impress of the object. The man of science must not so study nature as to find only that evidence which supports the theories to which he is already committed. If what he looks for is not the mind that meets his mind in its nature as *mind*, but a structure that corresponds to his mind in its nature as *his*, he is no seeker after truth but an advocate thinking to a brief. The mind which seeks truth is not pronouncing judgement on reality but submitting itself to be judged by reality. Thus the impulse towards truth is an impulse away from self-centred particularity to the whole, and humility is at once a condition and a result of success in any genuine search for truth.

The same thing is equally, if less obviously, observable as regards the search for beauty. At first we find beautiful whatever gives us aesthetic pleasure; but those who are content to remain at that self-centred

[1] See Lecture IX. p. 241.

level never reach the deepest apprehensions of beauty. For this there is needed the docility which is willing to be guided by a richer experience.[1] And when the deepest forms of aesthetic apprehension are reached, the mood of the apprehending mind is more of reverence than enjoyment; a man may enjoy himself, in the proper sense of the words, as he witnesses a comedy; but if he is to appreciate high tragedy he must forget himself and be absorbed into the drama presented to him.

Supremely is this principle illustrated in the aspiration towards goodness. We have already seen[2] that so far as this is a self-centred effort, it is doomed to perpetual frustration. As the mind which seeks truth submits itself to the impact of reality; as the mind which seeks beauty finds itself, in proportion to its success, drawn out of itself in a reverence that borders on worship; so the mind that seeks goodness finds that the very essence of what it seeks is that it so give itself to the personal beings in whom it finds itself, that it ceases to be the centre of its own social relationships, and becomes one member with the rest in a totality or community of persons, wherein even for itself it counts for one and for no more than one. For this is to love one's neighbour as one's self, which is the true principle of moral goodness.[3]

Now to many people these three roads are open and the lure to travel them for at least a certain distance is sufficient. But the movement from within is a response to the truth or beauty or goodness apprehended as presented from without. The seeker for truth repudiates the notion that his real desire is to invent it; his desire is to reach what is truly there. The artist does, indeed, in some sense invent or create the beauty of which his artistic masterpiece is the medium or vehicle; yet his own attitude to it is much rather that he has given to it a form whereby it becomes communicable. He has not

[1] See *supra*, Lecture VI. [2] See Lectures IX. and XIV.
[3] See Lecture VII.

really been himself the source of it. Blake's disclaimer—"Not mine! Not mine!" represents the attitude of the greatest artists to their own productions. Alike in science and in art, the movement away from hampering self-centredness is a movement of response. It is an adaptation of the organism—an organism in which mind is the dominant principle—to its environment. The environment has the initiative.

But this environment is the medium of divine activity. The truth and the beauty in it are God's self-utterance, His Word or Logos. Already here we find at work that divine priority which theologians have called prevenient grace. All possibility of good is due to the grace of God in creation—His creation alike of the object-world and of the subject-minds which are part of the process of that object-world. And the movement of response within man's mind, which not only enables him to find in the object what is akin to the mind in him, but also proves him to be akin to the mind revealed to him in the object world, is for that reason known to be a divine movement recognised as due to the spirit of God.[1]

But these deliverances are never more than partial. The search for Truth may dominate a man's intellect and dictate the course of his life, as with Browning's Grammarian, who gave all his energy to the study of Greek grammar and syntax. But we do not hear of his courtesy or lack of it in dealing with those who brought him his meals. It is not always true that a man utterly selfless in pursuit of Knowledge is uniformly considerate to the people with whom he lives. Nor does a similarly complete devotion to Beauty always issue in the social graces. Beethoven was a passionately conscientious artist, but he was not specially easy to live with. Truth and Beauty draw the self from its self-centredness, but only in respect to certain functions. The deepest springs of life are not yet touched.

[1] See pp. 445-447.

It is otherwise with the appeal of Goodness, so far as it is effective. That is a call to desert self-centredness altogether. There may be real progress towards this goal, but the goal can never actually be reached by continuous progress. At first or at last there must be the sharp break which has been called, in the language of religion, conversion or the new birth; or else there may be a series of conversions affecting different areas of life; but there is need for real discontinuity. Often, indeed, a particular conversion takes a long time and is effected through a gradual process; yet even then its completion takes place at a moment, and though the transition effected in that moment may be very small, yet it is in its essential nature abrupt. Most of us have watched the sun setting behind a sharp horizon. Its disc slowly disappears; at last there is only a speck of light; then suddenly it is gone. Its going is a gradual process; but between the last moment when it is visible and the first when it is entirely hidden there is abrupt transition for the eyes that are watching it. The contrast between "nearly" and "quite" is, in the realm of Quality, entirely different from the contrast between any two degrees of approximation, however far apart. Regarded as matter of Quantity or measurable movement, the setting of the sun is a continuous process; and there is a greater difference between the moment when the lower rim of the sun touches the horizon and the moment when only a dazzling point remains, than there is between that latter moment and the moment when nothing remains to dazzle the eye at all. But in Quality it is not so. Throughout the longer period there is the dazzling brightness; then in a moment it is gone; and the difference is absolute, however small, while the other difference is relative, however great. So it is with the setting of the self as it passes over the horizon of its own contemplation. Whether it be in relation to Truth, or Beauty, or Holiness—or that entire dedication of life which alone deserves the Christian name of Love—the self may gradually forgo its grip upon its own activities or it may relax it suddenly; but the vital difference comes when the grip is gone and the object of contemplation or aspiration has free play with it. For that moment there may be long preparation, or it may come as a lightning-flash. Regarded from one standpoint it is, like the sunset, a continuous process; regarded from another, the process is crowned by a moment which is not itself process at all; that moment is decisive for the quality of life so far as the type of conversion involved affects it. In religion the quality thus induced is called saintliness. And it is most important to notice that this, like the parallel devotion to Truth or Beauty, may be departmental. A man may have been lifted clean out of himself in some functions or activities, and brought into fellowship with the Holy and Eternal, and yet remain in many respects unconverted and self-centred. Such are fanatics—men who are capable of combining with true spiritual exaltation the utterly self-centred passions of cruelty and malignity, or who are ready to speak falsely on behalf of truth. This may happen even when the conception of God intellectually accepted is true; for not all that is intellectually accepted is translated by imagination into that apparent good which sways the conative elements in the self and therefore also the will which these combine with intelligence to constitute. There have been cruel saints, and contemptuous saints, and unscrupulous saints; such saintliness is very incomplete, but may none the less be genuine in itself. And there have been saints who in the unconverted functions of their nature care so much for their own saintliness that for it they are ready to cause great pain to others. It is evidence how mortally deep is our self-centredness that even our deliverance from it in respect of many sides of life may become itself an occasion of self-esteem. This is that demon of spiritual pride, which most of us are not nearly good enough even to encounter, but which, the saints assure us, is waiting as it were on the top rung of the ladder of perfection to catch us even there and throw us down. It is not mere self-satisfaction at our own goodness like that of the Pharisee in the parable, though this is often confused with it. It belongs to a far more advanced stage of spiritual progress. It occurs where the self, being by nature self-conscious, which is indeed the condition of all spiritual progress whatever, contemplates its own state of deliverance from self-centredness and finds in that a self-centred satisfaction. It is not merely pride in being good; it is pride in being delivered from pride; it is pride in being humble. It turns even self-sacrifice into a form of self-assertion. In the language of our simile, it is a last effort of the sun of self to keep itself above the horizon. Of course it is only possible when the deliverance is not complete; but it is compatible with, indeed it is occasioned by, a deliverance which judged from the lower level looks complete. Though so complex in its formula and so insidious in its activity, it is quite simple in its principle. On an altogether lower plane, we easily see that wholesome desire is for the objects that will satisfy it, as hunger is desire for food. The satisfaction of the desire brings pleasure; if desire is now diverted from its appropriate object to the pleasure of attaining or enjoying it, desire is turning into lust. So the proper object of the self's surrender is the Spirit of the Whole which we call God; but if attention is diverted from God Himself to the self's satisfaction in being surrendered to Him, adoration itself is poisoned. The satisfaction is real, and there is no reason for refraining from attention to it so long as it is in the second place. Man's chief end is to glorify God and (incidentally) to enjoy Him for ever; but if a man were to say that his end was to enjoy God for ever and (with that aim) to glorify Him, he would be talking pernicious heresy. *The true aim of the soul is not its own salvation; to make that the chief aim is to ensure its perdition;*[1] *for it is to fix the soul on*

[1] "Whosoever would save his soul shall lose it."—St. Matthew xvi. 25.

itself as centre. The true aim of the soul is to glorify God; in pursuing that aim it will attain to salvation unawares. No one who is convinced of his own salvation is as yet even safe, let alone "saved". Salvation is the state of him who has ceased to be interested whether he is saved or not, provided that what takes the place of that supreme self-interest is not a lower form of self-interest but the glory of God.

It is time to return from this consideration of the ultimate goal and of the last perils that may hinder our attaining it, and to consider the ways of progress, so that we may ask how far they can bring us. Truth and Beauty, as we have seen, may effect a real emancipation with regard to certain activities of life—an emancipation partial in the range of interests affected though capable of being complete in type. On the other hand the claim of Goodness, so far as it wins response, effects an emancipation capable of being complete in range though apart from one condition it is always incomplete in type. For the claim of Goodness is upon the complete will. Certainly the response is not always given with completeness; an all-round development of all the virtues simultaneously is a rare occurrence. To some extent their psychological bases are different and even divergent, and this is true even of virtues apparently similar. Thus, for example, moral and physical courage are very differently conditioned; the power to face danger is increased by dullness of imagination, while this will make almost unattainable the power to face obloquy or mockery or the censure of a man's own circle. Still the claim of goodness is for the allegiance of the whole will, that it may be resolute to take the best possible course in relation to any and every combination of circumstances. This will include the right attitude to Truth and Beauty, but the distinctive sphere of this demand is that of personal relationships.

Now there are two main ways in which the self is delivered from self-centredness and its resultant antagonisms in those relationships. One is by the activity of genuine and disinterested love within the self; the other is by the widening of the area within which obligation and loyalty are recognised as holding sway. The natural self is capable of disinterested love; indeed it is probable that every child has for its mother a love which is in part disinterested so soon as it is capable of any true emotion as distinct from animal desire.[1] The vitiation of selfhood by self-centredness is never complete, though it is very pervasive and there are few children who come to years of so-called discretion in whom self-interest has not contaminated what elements they once had of disinterested love. Yet the capacity for such love is always there in some degree; it is part of selfhood as God designed and created it. By grace of creation man is made in the image of God, and however much that image may be blurred, it is seldom if ever effaced, and never until the corruption of self-concern has eaten deeply into the very constitution of the self.

Disinterested love and devotion are called out chiefly by persons who have some special affinity for the person concerned, or by the society or nation to which he belongs. This love and devotion may attain to very great heights, even beyond the sacrifice of life to that only true self-sacrifice which is the ignoring or forgetting of every self-centred interest. But admittedly this is rare; and even when it occurs two facts are to be noticed which give warning of grave limitations. The first is that this response, so far as it is given to persons, is given only to a few or to one, and so far as it is given to a community is always to a limited community; it is therefore compatible with antagonism and even hatred towards other persons or communities, and sometimes seems, at least, to be deepened and intensified by these. The other fact is closely connected with this, namely, that this devotion, with all its selflessness, is called forth by some affinity to the self, so that the lover not only

[1] Cf. Lecture V. p. 125.

belongs to the beloved but the beloved to him, the patriot not only belongs to the country but the country to him. The paradox of this devotion is not so great as that of the love of Launcelot for Guinevere, whose

> honour rooted in dishonour stood
> And faith unfaithful kept him falsely true.

Yet it has in it the same essential contradiction. It is a self-devotion resting on appeal to the self in its particularity; it is the devotion of the Englishman to England, of the Frenchman to France and so forth; it is the discovery of himself not only in his other but specifically in his own other. In such devotion the sun of self may be setting behind the horizon, but it never quite disappears; and if it did, it would destroy the occasion of the devotion. This natural love may be truly disinterested; it is its own reward and looks for no return; yet it is in itself a return, and depends for its very existence on being so. A loves B because B is the appropriate object of A's love. A does not love B for the sake of any result, nor even for the enjoyment of the sentiment of love; A loves B for being B. Yet this love is rooted in the special appeal which B has for A, and which neither does B exercise over others, nor does A find exercised over him by others. Consequently the complex unit AB may be exceedingly self-centred.

Similarly with devotion to group or country, the patriot's love for his country depends on its being his. Consequently patriotism may be a genuinely disinterested love, and yet co-exist with antagonism and hatred towards other countries. It does not appear that the way to true emancipation from self-centredness is to be found in this natural capacity for devotion. It is very noble; it is akin to God; but it is, as Nurse Cavell said of Patriotism, "not enough".

It was remarked that moral progress, which comes partly through an activity of disinterested love within the soul, also comes largely through widening of the area in which loyalty is recognised as an obligation. And that is real progress. So also is the growth of sympathy such as marks the humanitarian movement characteristic of the last hundred years. The diminution of that callous cruelty, in which men were content to inflict suffering on others, is true progress. The civilisation of the penal code is true progress. In each of these there is a movement away from that crude selfishness which sharply contrasts the self and others, which acquiesces in the infliction on others of what would be passionately resented if inflicted on self, which greedily grasps for self what is thereby made unattainable for others. Such greed continues, and is in our bad economic order made almost synonymous with efficiency. But conscious cruelty is really diminished. The world is effectively learning that all forms of malignity and antagonism of person against person are genuinely bad. Rivalry and emulation may have a rightful place, and such competition as is the expression of those principles. But enmity is always an evil, at least in its consequences. So much the world is visibly learning. Perhaps it will go on to learn that greed or acquisitiveness is no less an evil, though it has hardly begun to learn that yet. And in all this learning there is real progress, real approximation to conformity with the Divine.

And yet when all is said, *advance which comes as continuous progress is an expansion of the circle of which self is still the centre. It may theoretically be so expanded as to include all mankind, even all spiritual beings. But self is still the centre, and if God Himself be included in the circle, He is peripheral, not central; He is, for me, my God, not God whose I am.*

At first it may even seem that, in so far as moral growth is only the expansion of the circle of which self is the centre, the greater the growth the greater the evil; to make much centre on the self is worse than to make little, and to include God on the periphery is worse than to exclude Him altogether. But this is to press the spatial metaphor beyond its intention, and it is equally true to say that the self which is centre to a large circle counts for less relatively to that circle than it would relatively to a small circle; and where God comes in at all, He begins to count for what He is even where that is not as yet accepted.

It is, perhaps, idle to speculate whether the purely moral progress, which consists in lengthening the radius of the circle drawn round the self as centre, could bring satisfaction to man in respect of his temporal interests. Probably it could not do this. For the interests envisaged from the various self-centred points of view—the "apparent goods" of the multitude of self-centred souls—would almost certainly be not only different but incompatible. Quite certainly the course of progress to be travelled before that road can lead to satisfaction is very long. The clashing units which have expanded from tribe to nation, from nation to empire, would become larger. If the nations now civilised so strengthen their League as to become a Federal State, there looms behind that achievement the menace of the Race Problem. And the same threat of clashing systems hangs over our economic development. There is no quick way to peace and fellowship, if we start in that direction. But these are considerations for the practical moralist rather than for the student of Natural Religion. What is more to our purpose is that the colossal structures of enlightened egoism to which that way of progress leads will never effect the deliverance of the self from self-centredness, but can only seek to make self-centredness compatible with final well-being. And this it can never be, if God exists; for it fixes the self in a false relation to God; it makes self prior and God secondary; at best it makes self and God two entities equal in type and principle, however much one may exceed the other in scale. But this is to relapse, at the religious level, into that correlation of God and World which we found to be the capital error of Whitehead's Philosophy of Organism,[1] as of many another philosophical structure. Moreover this false relation, apart from the intrinsic evil of falsity, must needs set up tensions between God and the self which will make it impossible for the self, perhaps for God also, to experience the peace of attainment until they are overcome.

The error of the Barthian school of theology—for that it contains error when judged by the canons of either natural reason or Christian revelation I cannot doubt—is, like every other heresy, an exaggeration of truth. To deny the reality of moral progress, or that moral progress is an increasing conformity to the Divine, is wanton. To deny that revelation can, and in the long run must, on pain of becoming manifest as superstition, vindicate its claim by satisfying reason and conscience, is fanatical. But that revelation is altogether other than rational inference from previous experience is vitally important; that only by revelation and by his surrender to its spiritual power can man be "saved", is a profound and irrefragable truth; that even when man's salvation is complete there is still the impassable distinction between Creator and creature, Redeemer and redeemed, Sanctifier and sanctified, is the heart of metaphysical and religious sanity. In so far as God and man are spiritual they are of one kind; in so far as God and man are rational, they are of one kind. But in so far as God creates, redeems and sanctifies while man is created, redeemed and sanctified, they are of two kinds. God is not creature; man is not creator. God is not redeemed sinner; man is not redeemer from sin. At this point the Otherness is complete.

With this reflection we pass beyond the morality of areas of loyalty and obligation. The problem now is not the relation of finite selves to one another, in isolation or in groups. The problem now is the relation of the finite spirit to the infinite. It is easy to see that the only reasonable attitude of the finite is that of worship. But it

[1] See Lecture X.

is not so easy for the self-centred finite self to adopt that attitude. For it will follow in action, not what reason generally demands, but what presents itself in vivid form as apparent good; and this depends upon its own whole structure and orientation. *What is quite certain is that the self cannot by any effort of its own lift itself off its own self as centre and resystematise itself about God as its centre. Such radical conversion must be the act of God, and that too by some process other than the gradual self-purification of a self-centred soul assisted by the ever-present influence of God diffused through nature including human nature. It cannot be a process only of enlightenment. Nothing can suffice but a redemptive act. Something impinging upon the self from without must deliver it from the freedom which is perfect bondage to the bondage which is its only perfect freedom.*

Whether in fact there is such a redemptive act, or what is its mode, may be declared by positive religion; it is no question for the Natural Theologian. But Natural Theology may very well enquire what its conditions must be if it is to satisfy the requirements of the problem as that has defined itself.

Man, being an organism in which mind is the increasingly predominant element, is free from purely mechanical determination except so far as his body is actually propelled by physical force greater than his own. He is free from this, not because his action has in it any element of indeterminism (which is indistinguishable from chance or nonsense) but because he is determined by Good as it appears to him. His freedom from "the might of nature" consists in his necessity to follow the apparent good. But what this is depends upon what he is. If from the first he had realised his dependence upon God, and had ordered his whole experience in the light of that progressively comprehended dependence, what appeared to him good would at every stage have been the real good. But it has not been so; and while in abstract principle it was possible for it to be so, the probability against this was always so high that we must regard not only the risk, but also the expectation, of sin as part of the divine intention. Yet it is none the less sin for that; it is alienation from God, for it is the centring upon self of a life whose very nature requires that it should be centred upon God. And this sin has been, as it was bound to be, indefinitely infectious. So we have the self not only taking itself as centre and thus falsifying its whole scale of values, but confirmed and hardened in self-centredness by both the attraction and the repulsion of the other self-centred selves among which it must live. It is by no means wholly corrupt, if that means that there is no aspiration after good left in it; on the contrary, pursuit of good is its only motive of deliberate action—even of wrong action—though its vision of good is distorted, so that this leads it astray. But it is wholly corrupt if by that is meant that there is no part of it untainted by this corruption. There is much in it that is the very stuff of good, the ineffaceable image of God. But there is nothing that is unadulterated good, and the image of God is blurred.

How can God deliver such a soul? The soul is helpless, fixed in the vicious circle whereby it both determines and is determined by its apparent good. And the ways of escape which we have considered, while they offer a real liberation, never lead to a complete deliverance. The soul or self can contribute nothing except a certain passivity of response. If salvation comes it is the gift of God alone.

In what sense, then, is there spiritual freedom in man before God? As against mechanical determinism, to be spiritual is to be free; in that context the two words mean the same thing. But when we turn to the relationship of man to God, is there any freedom here? It is tempting at first to say that though God gives the call, and the strength of perseverance to him who responds, the response at least is the free act of the human soul. And this is not wholly or merely untrue. For whether or not the soul responds is determined by the moral character of the soul. The divine claim is presented; some refuse it, some respond to it; and so they are judged.[1] Which they do depends on what they are. And that is not wholly determined by past history or present environment, because every self is in part an original contribution to the scheme of reality and is moreover, in the very act of giving or refusing its response, a self-determining system of experience. The fact that the soul or self responds, or refuses to respond, is a result, in part at least, of what comes into being with that self. It is free, because nothing outside the self compels it.

And to that very freedom the divine appeal must be addressed. If God exercised compulsion by forcing obedience or by remaking the character of a self against its will, He would have abandoned omnipotence in the act which should assert it, for the will that was overridden would remain outside His control. The only obedience congruous with the nature of either God or man is an obedience willingly, and therefore freely, offered—a response which is given because the self finds it good to offer it. Our question therefore is this: How can the self find it good to submit willingly to removal from its self-centredness and welcome reconstitution about God as centre? There is in fact one power known to men, and only one, which can effect this, not only for one or another function of the self (as beauty and truth can do) but for the self as a whole in its entirety and integrity. When a man acts to please one whom he loves, doing or bearing what apart from that love he would not choose to do or bear, his action is wholly determined by the other's pleasure, yet in no action is he so utterly free—that is, so utterly determined by his apparent good. And when love is not yet present,

[1] "We preach a Messiah on a cross, to Jews a scandal and to Gentiles an absurdity, but to the very people who are called, both Jews and Greeks, a Messiah who is God's power and God's wisdom."—1 Cor. i. 23, 24.

"This is the judgement, that light is come into the world, and men loved the darkness rather than the light."— St. John iii. 19.

there is one power and only one that can evoke it; that is the power of love expressed in sacrifice, of love (that is to say) doing and bearing what apart from love would not be willingly borne or done. *The one hope, then, of bringing human selves into right relationship to God is that God should declare His love in an act, or acts, of sheer self-sacrifice, thereby winning the freely offered love of the finite selves which He has created.*

Here the last great problem confronts us. For one great religion at least consists in the conviction that God has so revealed Himself; but not all within whose experience that revelation has been proclaimed have offered their response. What is still lacking? Is the decisive step which is required a step to be taken by man or by God? If we say that God must first act, we seem to be involved in all the difficulties of Predestination: does God then arbitrarily choose to call some with the appeal that will stir their response, leaving others to await in vain the transforming touch? If so, how is He just or even loving? But on the other side, if we say that man's is the decisive step, we make him master of his fate even over against God; if God's grace is a universally bestowed assistance, the use of which depends upon ourselves alone, then we are again in the centre and not God.[1]

Against this all deep religious experience, and all the authority of reason, loudly protests.

"There is no faith without in the end ascribing everything to God. . . . If God will only act when we begin, or continue acting as we fulfil certain conditions, then in the last issue our reliance is on man and not God."[2]

"Once the principle that grace must come first has been

[1] I once heard the following conversation between two theologians, the one an Augustinian, the other a semi-(or semi-demi) Pelagian:

S.-P. "No doubt the call is from God, so the initiative is with Him; but whether or not I answer the call depends on myself."

Aug. "I see; so your address to the Almighty is: 'For that thou didst call me of thy grace I thank thee; but for that I answered the call I thank thee not, but rather tender my most respectful congratulations'."

[2] J. Oman, *Grace and Personality*, p. 24.

admitted, nothing is lost by adding that it must also come second, and last as well—that man can never at any point bestir himself in pure freedom to good actions—that he needs, in the language of the Schoolmen, *subsequent* as well as *prevenient* grace. The semi-Pelagian doctrine that, once the first grace has been given, man must co-operate with it of his own free-will, must always lie under the suspicion of inconsistency with its premises."[1]

If there is any reality at all in the experience called Religion, we must admit and affirm both the priority and the all-sufficiency of God. For the only idea of God that is possible to the scientific and philosophic reason is such as to claim for Him these qualities. Moreover, religious experience when it is most intense confirms this.[2] *All is of God; the only thing of my very own which I can contribute to my own redemption is the sin from which I need to be redeemed.* My capacity for fellowship with God is God's gift in creation; my partial deliverance from self-centredness by response to truth, beauty and goodness is God's gift through the natural world which He sustains in being and the history of man which He controls. One thing is my own—the self-centredness which leads me to find my apparent good in what is other and less than the true good. This true good is the divine love and what flows from it appreciated as its expression. In response to that good, man finds his only true freedom, for only then does the self act as what it truly is and thus achieve true self-expression.

It is hard to know which is the more important aspect of truth to emphasise. No one can be "saved" against his will or otherwise than through his willing co-operation; but this co-operation cannot be offered except by a purpose divinely implanted or elicited. St. Paul's celebrated dictum observes the true balance: "Work out your own salvation with fear and trembling: for it is God which worketh in you both to will and to

[1] K. E. Kirk, *The Vision of God*, p. 546.

[2] Nothing in my hand I bring,
Simply to Thy Cross I cling.

work".[1] No doubt it is wholesome to distribute the emphasis of attention differently at different stages of spiritual development. The man who is as yet without any experience of divine grace as an active power in his life had better reflect that it is his own state of mind and character which makes him insensitive to the divine appeal. But as he advances towards some beginnings of fellowship with God, it will be good for him to understand that it is only divine grace, or in other words the love of God at work upon him and within him, which has brought him to that fellowship. As the experience of grace becomes deeper, the conviction of its all-sufficiency becomes more inevitable and more wholesome, until at last a man knows, and is finally "saved" by knowing, that all good is of God alone. *We are clay in the hands of the Potter, and our welfare is to know it.*

But this knowledge must be the knowledge of experience, not merely of intellectual conviction or acquiescence. If it is of the latter type, it is very liable to suggest inertia as its practical inference, as the clay offers only inertia to the potter. But here the analogue to clay is the living will, and the only man who has experience of being shaped by divine grace is the man whose will is in fact surrendered and is become the energetic instrument of that grace; such a man can never suppose that his proper reaction to the doctrine that all good is from God alone is to be found in inertia. His experience of the fact formulated in the doctrine consists in conspicuous activity. "I laboured more abundantly than they all; yet not I, but the grace of God which was with me."[2] The inert soul is precisely the soul which has *not* understood its relation of utter dependence; it is inert, because it is self-enclosed. Evangelists, pastors and teachers, who are agencies of divine grace, try to bring it to an understanding of its true dependence. As soon as it admits that dependence, with any appreciation of what that is upon which it depends, its inertia will be ended.

[1] Philippians ii. 13. [2] 1 Corinthians xv. 10.

The real difficulty of the position concerns the relationship of God to those selves whom divine grace has not called, and apparently is not so far calling, out of their self-centredness. If grace can call the Buddha or St. Francis to the great renunciation which inaugurates their career of sacrifice and service, why does it leave so many unstirred? We cannot say that it is because these responded, while others do not respond, to the activity of grace everywhere equally active, for it is only by grace that they could respond. Is it that God elects some to salvation and others to perdition? We all know the history of that doctrine, and in our recoil from it have often failed to make due allowance for the strength of the argument leading to it. But it will not stand. Neither justice nor love could be intelligibly predicated of a God who could act so; and if these be denied, Deity is denied. Yet we cannot escape the doctrine of Election in some form; it is not so much an inference as the only possible reading of the facts when Theism is accepted. What its ultimate issue is to be lies beyond the bounds of terrestrial experience, and must be considered in connexion with Eternal Life.

LECTURE XVI

THE COMMONWEALTH OF VALUE

It has been already suggested in these Lectures that the period of European thought and history commonly called Modern is even now reaching its natural term. That fact is, indeed, a main occasion of the bewilderment characteristic in our era—a bewilderment to which there is no parallel since the time when the transition from the "mediaeval" to the "modern" epoch was effected. The ancient Mediterranean civilisation gave place to the chaos of the Dark Ages. Gradually a new order was fashioned under the twofold influence of the prestige of the Roman Empire and so much of the Christian revelation as had taken a hold upon the minds of men. The result was mediaeval Christendom, ordered under the authority of the Papacy, which Hobbes was not wholly incorrect in describing as "the Ghost of the deceased Romane Empire, sitting crowned upon the grave thereof".[1] This order was shaken by the Renaissance and shattered by the Reformation. The characteristic of the new period was departmentalism—politics, art and science all winning emancipation from theology, the queen of the sciences, who had once been a benefactress through the bestowal of universal order but was becoming a tyrant in that this order was too narrow for an expanding experience. The disappearance of the old order led to new forms of authority—in politics the divine right of the state as actually constituted, in art the acceptance of beauty as a value not only ultimate but absolute, in ethics the unquestioned supremacy of individual conscience.

There is no possibility of going back on this. Our

[1] Hobbes, *Leviathan*, Part IV. chap. xlvii.

new appreciation of the Middle Ages as a period when a theory of world-order was accepted, however little conduct conformed to the theory, must not lead us to suppose that recovery from the modern welter is possible by any retracing of our steps. The antithesis of Luther and Descartes has so shattered the thesis of Hildebrand and Aquinas that it cannot be re-established. But the antithesis also is moribund if not extinct.[1] We are driven, whether we will or not, towards a synthesis which resembles mediaevalism in possessing an order and which resembles the modern period (soon to be described as the last or late period) in accepting liberty for individuals and associations, so that the Empire and the Sovereign States give place to the League of Nations, while universal civilisation increasingly assumes a federal structure, and in the moral sphere dogmatic authority and unfettered individualism give place to the Commonwealth of Value.

Our discussion of Moral Goodness[2] left us with some problems on our hands which seem to provide the best starting-point for our next advance. The popular riddle concerning the reconciliation of an absolute moral obligation with the variety of actual moral codes or conventions did not of itself cause very much trouble, for we found that universal obligation attaches not to particular judgements of conscience but to conscientiousness. What acts are right may depend on circumstances, social history and context, personal relationships, and a host of other considerations. But there is an absolute obligation to will whatever may on each occasion be right; in practice we have even to say whatever may on each occasion *seem* to be right, but then it is necessary

[1] With this view Professor Whitehead agrees; see *Adventures of Ideas*, chap. x. But he advocates a reconstruction on lines of pure Immanence, which we have already seen reason to discard. It is most significant that he advocates (as an illustration) the substitution of Pericles' Funeral Oration for the Revelation of St. John the Divine. That Thucydidean composition is an exquisite expression of purely pagan ethics. The conduct it commends would befit a Christian; but the scale of motives which it would cultivate is the diametrical opposite of the Christian scale.

[2] In Lecture VII.

to remember that this includes an obligation to secure that what seems right and what is right are as nearly as possible identical. But though that riddle seems easy, it is after all the superficial reflection of a very serious difficulty. For when we turned to ask what acts are right, we found ourselves driven to the view sometimes known as Optimific—that is, the view that those acts are right which are productive of most good; and then we had to recognise that this criterion, however sound in principle, is inapplicable on any large scale in practice, partly because no one knows the whole train of consequences that will follow from his action, but partly also because it provides no criterion by which to frame a comparative estimate of different kinds of good. If, for example, I can either add to the world's store of beauty by painting a masterpiece or else remove some one instance of acute physical pain, which is the greater good? I am to do the greatest good that I can, but how am I to know what that is? And this perplexity we found to be crossed by another. For there are some acts which are right if done by the right agent, but wrong if done by any one else. And the Optimific theory gives little help in determining who are the proper agents of such acts. We found a provisional resting-place in the recognition that the one absolutely and universally binding form of the Moral Law is the command "Thou shalt love thy neighbour as thyself", and that the Good of personal relationships is the highest form of Good, and also in the perception of a certain logic of our true nature which requires of us conformity to its conclusions. So long as we remained on strictly ethical ground it was not possible to go further.

But we have seen sufficient ground for the conviction common to all great religious traditions, that the whole universe, the whole process of the world, is grounded in the Will of creative Deity, so that this divine Will is at once the source of world-order, and also the determinant for every finite mind of its special place within that order and of the appropriate contribution of each such mind to the life of the whole. If this be true, *the solution of the outstanding problems of Ethics is to be sought in terms neither of Utilitarianism however ideal, nor of Intuitionism, but of Vocation.* Admittedly this carries us beyond the sphere of scientific Ethics; but to claim that Ethics, or any other departmental enquiry, must be able to solve all its own problems is to accept the fissiparous tendencies of the late epoch and to renounce the hope of recovering some form of world order. The moralist, if he would retain that hope, must, therefore, like every other student of a department of reality, either claim that his own study supplies the norm for all departments besides its own, or else admit that his department like the rest is only rightly understood when it is seen in the context of the whole and is subjected to principles which inform the whole. Those principles are the various strands that are combined in the divine purpose. Therefore, as the chief practical problem of ethics is solved not by volition but by conversion, so the chief theoretical problems are solved not by reference to a Categorical Imperative but by reference to Vocation.

Inasmuch as vocation is of its very nature individual, and to each individual his own vocation is peculiar, the guiding of men towards the discovery of their vocations is a task for the evangelist and pastor rather than for the philosopher. But the discussion of the general conditions to be fulfilled may be undertaken by the philosophy of religion or natural theology, and the implications of the actual occurrence of vocation can hardly be ignored. It is evident that the whole doctrine of Providence is involved. For the divine will or purpose, which determines my vocation, also determines all events or occurrences whatsoever, at least in the sense of fixing the order within which they take place. It must therefore be possible in principle for a man to discover his vocation by considering with sufficient thoroughness his own nature and his circumstances. In practice, however, to achieve the necessary degree of thoroughness is often so difficult as fairly to be called impossible; where all possible effort has been made to ascertain by such means the direction of vocation, it is sometimes at least found by a conscious communion of the mind with God. Such guidance by an Inner Light is an experience common among those who make a serious practice of religion in any of its higher forms, and in some of these, as, for example, among Christians in the Society of Friends, it becomes the dominant element of a great tradition. But it is not only so that vocation is discovered; it may also be found by the ordinary exercise of a mind which has in prayer committed itself to the divine guidance. That vocation exists, and where experienced provides the practical solution of the main ethical problems, is the clear testimony of religious history.

This principle enables us to bring together the two apparently incompatible lines of thought concerning *acts* and *actions* which we found ourselves led to follow at the earlier stage. A man's *act*, we said, is the whole train of consequences which he initiates; and the right act is the best possible train of consequences. That, so far as it goes, is an objective account of rightness; the question of motive does not yet come in. His *action*, on the other hand, which includes his motive, and is not the train of consequence initiated, but precisely the initiation of it, must in practice be determined not by a full calculation of the best possible effect to be produced (for accurate knowledge of this is unattainable), but by the logic of a man's own true nature, which leads him, being the man he is, to act thus and thus in view of circumstances being what they are. It has lately been suggested that what is sound in these two can be combined by adopting as our watchword "the Rightness of Goodness".[1] The proposal is that we should invert the Optimific or Maximalist doctrine, and, instead of

[1] P. Leon, "The Rightness of Goodness" in *Mind*, N.S. 166, pp. 180-185.

saying that the right act is right because it is the best train of consequences, we should say that the act is the best because it is right. Our view would agree that "whatever is right is *eo ipso* best", but not by making either right or good subordinate to the other, except so far as right is a form of good and therefore a narrower term than good. Our contention rather is that when the act is apprehended in its completeness as the entire train of consequence initiated by the action, right and best, as predicates of that act, denote the same quality in the act, while right connotes obligation and good connotes fruition. Right is the Good as presented to mind practical; Good (as applied to an act) is Right as presented to mind contemplative. But this thoroughgoing identification of Right and Good is only possible on the hypothesis that history is itself an ordered process in which the order is expressive of divine purpose.[1]

Admittedly each individual's obligation must be discharged within some relatively confined area of relationships. Social obligation in principle extends to the limits of humanity, and is not even restricted to men and women alive at the moment of action. But we cannot offer direct service to mankind as a whole, partly because we cannot envisage the good of mankind in sufficient detail, partly because the structure of Humanity regarded as a unit is itself composed of other social structures within it; if there is any structure of mankind as a whole, it is, in Mr. Leon's phrase, a "structure of structures".[2] A man must in practice serve his family, his city, his firm, his trade union or what not; the over-riding obligation to the entire spiritual fellowship can in practice only be expressed through the prohibition of any service to the narrower unit or structure which involves injury to the wider.[3] And the man is himself a "structure", with its own immanent logic. There is no

[1] The identification of Right and Good, except in the form stated earlier, is impossible for Mr. Leon because of his view that history is a chaos: *op. cit.* p. 173.

[2] Cf. *Mind*, N.S. 166, pp. 183, 184.

[3] Cf. *supra*, Lecture VII. p. 192.

solution, even in principle, of the divergent claims thus indicated unless there is one creative Mind which orders both the structure which is a single moral agent, the social structure in and on which he acts, and the ultimate "Structure of structures" which is the universal spiritual fellowship. But if there be such a Mind, in whose creative activity all other existents are grounded, then the following by each individual of his own immanent logic—the fulfilment of his true being—must issue in the right act, conceived as the best possible train of consequences. It does not follow that the right act for him is also right for all agents and not only for this agent. It is the best train of consequences for him to initiate because it is his destined contribution to the all-inclusive divine purpose. So far we must agree that it is best because it is right; but on another view it is equally true to say that it is right because it is best, for the essential wrong in any deviation from it is the breach of the order of that fellowship wherein all social good consists.

In actual practice it is seldom possible to trace these various lines of enquiry. A man must follow his own conscience, which is more closely connected with the inner logic of his being than with estimates of the total effect of his activity. But the fact that the latter alone supplies the test of the rightness of his act should remind him that he is not morally at liberty to do harm with benevolent intention. His duty is both to intend and to accomplish good.

The principle of divine vocation wherein we have found the solution of our outstanding ethical problems not only relieves the moral philosopher from every claim that he should so articulate the conception of moral good as to provide clear guidance for individual action; it positively forbids him to attempt any such task except to the extent—always so small as to be negligible—to which he apprehends the divine purpose in detail; to apprehend it in principle is his function, and to fail here is to fail completely; but the detail must ever escape him. As the general ethical problem finds its solution in general religious principles, so the personal problem of each individual finds its solution in personal religious practice. In the life of personal devotion to God, known as Righteous love, the answer to problems of conduct otherwise unanswerable may be found. Thus the adventurous element, found to be always present in moral choice,[1] is discovered to be no leap in the dark but the hazard of confident faith, and the individualism admitted to be ineradicable from the practical problem of moral judgement is found to be the expression not of general chaos but of providential order. There are some acts of which we can say with confidence that they are wrong; and sometimes positive obligation is also plain. But the difficult choices, in which the individual is most conscious of the need for guidance, are not capable of determination by general principles alone. When the philosopher has stated what are the general principles bearing on the situation his task is finished. Each finite mind must find its own solution of its own problem, without definitive direction from any other finite mind. The sympathetic friend may help with suggestions and so come nearer to the concrete issue than the philosopher with his general principles. But even he cannot safely make the delicate choice. That each must do for himself, and none may rightly judge his act. "A man's soul is sometimes wont to bring him tidings more than seven watchmen that sit on high on a watch-tower."[2]

This point has been, perhaps, more laboured than enough so far as it concerns moral judgement. There is, however, another aspect of it which, if practically less important, is of the highest significance for any world-view. We have found that there are at least some Goods of which it is true to say that though Objective in essence they are subjectively conditioned. Of these the

[1] *Supra*, p. 183. [2] Ecclesiasticus xxxvii. 14.

most conspicuous is Beauty. The aesthetic experience repudiates with vehemence any suggestion that Beauty has its being in the mind which appreciates it; and though, if there is no appreciation, the good of Beauty is potential only, yet when appreciation occurs the good is in the Beauty as appreciated, not in the appreciation. The appreciation is the condition of its potential good becoming actual, but the good remains objective. There is a good also in the appreciation, but this is derivative and secondary; it consists in the joyous apprehension of the good that is objectively present as Beauty. Now if the good which resides in appreciation were the only good, or the chief good, in question, it would be a matter of comparative indifference how many minds had this experience. The more, the better—no doubt. But the non-existence of any would only involve loss on the part of so many enjoying minds. As *ex hypothesi* those minds would not exist at all, there would not be any unfulfilled promise in the actual scheme of things. There is, indeed, a bewildering abundance of such unfulfilled promise in the lives of multitudes whom circumstances have hindered from fulfilling their own true destiny; in that fact the social reformer finds a great part of the impetus which urges him to action. But our problem is a different one. If Beauty as a positive good is subjectively conditioned, then there is much Beauty which can be no more than potential good until the condition is supplied. As I write these words the Everest expedition is on the march. Those mountaineers are passing through scenes never before beheld by human eyes. We must suppose that there are sublimities now, by the fact of appreciation, passing from potential to actual good. For the form of appreciation made possible by the expedition is different from any which was possible to angels or other discarnate intelligences, or even to God Himself.

For as the Divine Mind cannot experience error or sin as among its own states, but only as states of other minds and as contrary to itself, so it cannot in its divine infinity directly experience the appreciation won by courage and toil, through which the finite mind gives actuality to some new aspect of Beauty. It may be that within the mystery of Godhead there are such distinctions as make possible for God a real experience of awe; perhaps (if Christian terminology be assumed to shadow forth reality) in the relation of the Son to the Father there is the divine counterpart of that wonder and joy which in men is reverence, awe and adoration. But if God Himself is conceived as sharing such emotions, both feeling subject and occasioning object must be within the divine being; it is not possible that God should feel awe towards anything other than Himself. That appreciation which certain mountaineers are feeling as I write towards the Himalayan splendours is not only new in itself but supplies the condition hitherto lacking for actualisation of part of the value of that Sublimity. There is a new good, as well as new appreciation of good, in the universe; a new element in that good, for the sake of which God is Creator, has been actualised; and therein a purpose of God is fulfilled.

This is a consideration of the very highest importance for any effort to understand the world in relation to God, and therefore for the enterprise of natural theology. The instances cited, indeed, are not of the highest importance; but the principle involved undoubtedly is. That principle is twofold: first it asserts that *there is potential spiritual worth which awaits appreciation as the condition of its actualisation; secondly it asserts that there is an appropriate appreciation for each individual to exercise, so that each contributes to the entire scheme of good not only his individual fruition but also the actualisation of potential worth or good which this occasions*. These assertions give a new emphasis to the place in the world-process not only of consciousness in general, but of the finite consciousness associated with particular organisms; for the special experience of each organism supplies the consciousness which arises as a function of it with the special opportunity for appreciation that is proper to it.

But if this conception heightens the cosmic significance of the individual consciousness, still more does it emphasise the central importance of what Plato called Justice. For the contribution to the scheme of things which is due from each finite consciousness will be forthcoming only if each finds and fulfils its own place in that scheme. This may be missed, as is evident, in a great variety of ways; the road to destruction is not only broad, but has many different tracks along it, whereas the way that leads to life is narrow and, for each pilgrim at least, has only one track. It may be true that all who start down the way to destruction are called back before they reach its end, and even that when so called back they are found to have contributed to the excellence of the whole scheme—the "joy in heaven"—more than those who never left the right way. But if that is true at all, it is most conspicuously one of those truths which are dangerous while held as general propositions and only become safe when apprehended in living experience. For the man who holds Universalism as a general proposition may easily draw the conclusion that what he does is of no consequence, because it will work out to good anyhow; but such moral indifferentism is quite impossible to the man who is conscious of the appeal of divine grace winning the response of his heart and will, especially if with this he is conscious of an infinite cost to the divine love willingly accepted, which saves that appeal itself from the charge of moral indifference and at the same time makes it effective.[1] There is much in the relations between God and man which we can only apprehend truly as we look back upon the event when it is past, not as we look forward to it while it is still in the future. It may be bad for the sinner to know that God is going to save him, unless he has at least some present experience of the process of that salvation; but

[1] See *Christus Veritas*, pp. 259-264.

it is supremely good for the sinner to know as a fact of his own experience that God has saved him—indeed that is, in the last resort, the only good for him that there is.

This salvation, however, if all our argument has any validity, is not a fixed state, identical for all, to which each mind individually and separately attains. It is in its own nature a fellowship primarily with God, and secondarily (and derivatively) of all souls with one another. At this point our argument demands some doctrine of Immortality. It does not appear to be possible that there should be eternal life for any isolated finite mind. For if eternity is a mere everlastingness, that for the isolated finite mind would be intolerable. The finite self is constituted in very large measure by its social relationships, and only attains to real unity or to self-consciousness through those relationships. To exist in isolation from them would be spiritual death. And if eternity, as will be argued later,[1] is something more than everlastingness, then the finite self needs its neighbours as the condition of reaching and maintaining its superiority to the flux of successiveness and the divisive force of mere extension. A mind to which "then" is merely "not now", or to which "there" is merely "not here," or to which "They" are merely "not I", is no candidate for eternal life. But so far as the finite mind is isolated from other minds, it is condemned to this relation to time and space. It may expand its "now"—its "specious present" which we have seen to be the real present—to cover the period of its own existence; it may expand its "here" to cover all of which it is directly conscious in space: but so long as space and time, with the events of which these are the forms, have meaning for it only as related to itself, that meaning is so chaotic that the world must appear mad and reduce to madness any mind condemned to feed upon it as its only object of contemplation. Everlasting life for the

[1] Lectures XVII. and XIX

isolated soul is neither possible nor (for any one who knows what he is talking about) desirable; so far as it could occur it would be hell.

But there is no reason to suppose that such an isolated finite mind either does or can exist. Finite minds are, indeed, marked from their origin with a self-centredness which is disastrous in whatever degree it persists. But that is never the whole, or the only, quality of the finite mind. From its origin it also has love and trust, or at least is marked by the germinal form of these. And the only question of ultimate importance for each finite mind is the question whether love or self-centredness is becoming predominant over the other. All distinctions between venial and mortal sins are provisional makeshifts to be applied with great caution and elasticity of rule. In the last resort there are God and Self; and the soul is at any one time, and in any one department of its life, increasingly finding its centre of reference in one of these or the other; that alone is of vital consequence, though all the elaborations of moral theology and of psychology are useful as means to assist diagnosis of each soul's disease and to suggest appropriate remedies.

Here something further must be said about the relation of natural generosity and pagan virtue to the religious doctrine of divine grace. The difficulty is rather to find expressive and unambiguous language than to see the principle involved. According to the position which we have adopted, and which is at least so far identical with the universal tradition of Christian theology, all movement of love within the soul is a movement of the divine spirit. Consequently we shall say without hesitation that the atheist who is moved by love is moved by the spirit of God;[1] an atheist who lives by love is saved by his faith in the God whose existence (under that name) he denies. Then what is to be said

[1] Cf. 1 John iv. 16. God is love; and he that abideth in love abideth in God, and God abideth in him.

of such a declaration as that made in the thirteenth of the Thirty-nine Articles of Religion:

"Works done before the grace of Christ and the Inspiration of his Spirit are not pleasant to God, for as much as they spring not of faith in Jesus Christ neither do they make men meet to receive grace, or (as the Schoolmen say) deserve grace of congruity: yea rather, for that they are not done as God hath willed and commanded them to be done, we doubt not but they have the nature of sin."

That the Article is unfortunately, even calamitously, expressed, is evident. In the stress of the Reformation men had little leisure to remember that the light which is declared to have shone forth in its fullness in Jesus Christ is by equal authority spoken of as "lighting every man".[1] If we limit "the grace of Christ" and "faith in Jesus Christ" to the activity of God in Jesus of Nazareth and the response of men to Jesus of Nazareth, it would indeed be rash to make the affirmation of the Article. But Christians believe that in Jesus Christ that Eternal Word was Incarnate, by agency of which all things were made, so that to every soul of man at all times and in all places that Word, which Christians know as Jesus Christ, has spoken and is speaking; and the answer that arises in their hearts is fashioned by the inspiration of His Spirit. So there may be many a heathen or Moslem whose works were "done as God hath willed and commanded". The question is not primarily concerned with our relation to a historic Figure, but with our relation to the divine wisdom and love incarnate in that Figure.[2]

But to say that only may be deceptive. In most human generosity there is much of self as well as of love. No Christian dare deny that there may be instances of genuine sainthood among the heathen; but knowing his own heart, and the source of any emancipation from self-centredness that has been given to him, he will sympathetically recognise how very hard it must be to

[1] St. John i. 9. [2] Cf. Spinoza, *Epistle* lxxiii.

reach fellowship with the Eternal Word of God for one who has not heard any clear and definitive utterance of that Word.

If the spiritual realm consisted only of finite spirits, it would be no more than reckless speculation to conceive them as so interacting upon one another that in the end the full self-realisation of each ministered to the perfect harmony of all. It is true that the calamity resulting from self-centredness is evidence that the order of life proper to finite selves is co-operative in fundamental principle rather than competitive. But though the self *qua* self may be "naturally" co-operative, the finite self *qua* finite is, as we have seen,[1] inevitably and, at least in that sense, "naturally" competitive. The spiritual republicanism of Dr. McTaggart's Absolute appears to be a postulate which explains nothing, facilitates nothing, and contradicts the plain testimony of experience. There is nothing about the society of finite spirits as now known to us to suggest that its inmost reality is a perfect harmony; the main practical problem of individuals and statesmen is to turn it into harmony from jangling discord and sheer cacophony. To be told that the discord belongs to appearance, but that the reality none the less is harmony in the Absolute, is small comfort; for to us (on that view) the appearance is more important than the reality. Such a proposition is, no doubt, a blasphemy, and argues a profane mind in him who makes it. Yet it is an inevitable blasphemy and a predestined profanity, unless it can be shown how this appearance springs from or helps to sustain that reality. Of Optimism Bradley has said that "the world is the best of all possible worlds, and everything in it is a necessary evil".[2] But he does not ask us to take this very seriously. Yet it is something like this that Absolutism leaves on our hands unless it can show how the evil is necessary to the good, so that the good is a permanent end to which the

[1] Lecture XIV. [2] *Appearance and Reality*, p. xiv.

evil is a transient means or in which it is a subordinate moment. This, of which the possibility is illustrated elsewhere,[1] is part of the meaning of History. But at this point it is appropriate to notice the difference that is made by our doctrine of divine transcendence and of the mode of divine immanence. For if the divine spirit is only something "deeply interfused" it is hard to see what security we can have, other than a baseless optimism, for supposing that the spirit immanent in the world we know is guiding that world to such a harmony as by resolving present discords shall make them contributory to an all-embracing perfection of harmony. We find indeed noble achievements and aspirations in man; and we infer some power in the source of man's being that is adequate to give rise to these. Yet, as has been already argued, this would seem a precarious basis on which to rest a refutation of the view that the universe, though embodying the principles of intelligence as known in ourselves, and especially mathematical principles, is altogether indifferent to human values, when so much of actual experience can be cited in support of that view. Admittedly the argument for the supremacy of goodness must be *a priori*; and the claim that the ground of all things must be such as to account for human goodness is, in that form, irresistible. But to insist that only the greater goodness of Ultimate Reality itself can suffice for this is temerarious if there is no more to be said.

Our whole argument, however, consisting of many interwoven strands has led us to claim that the ground of all things is not an immanent principle, of which the character must be inferred from the whole range of observed occurrences, but a living God, able to make Himself known by decisive and characteristic acts. If He has thus made Himself known, that manifestation becomes a possible focus for the universal harmony of the various subjects of value-judgements. As each finds

[1] See Lectures VIII. pp. 209-212, and XX. pp. 509-511.

there the centre of his own being he is also related to all others who do the same. The Commonwealth of Value is a real possibility if it is also a Monarchy; on republican principles there is no sufficient ground to hope for its actualisation. It is the main contention of these Lectures that the monarchic basis is assured, so that the hope can be reasonably entertained.

This hope posits, however, something besides Theism. In itself it is one form of the doctrine of Freedom, for it asserts that each mind is its own master in the sense at least that it is governed by its own conception of good and can—nay, must—stand by that "against all the might of nature", if the two conflict; and though in the end it can only attain to its own true freedom by surrender to the grace of God, yet this never overrides or coerces it, but controls it by causing the true good to appear as good to it, so that in its surrender the mind is still adhering to its own essential principle. Our conception of the Commonwealth of Value starts from this belief, adding a new insistence upon the distinct individuality of every finite mind, which is an element in the doctrine of Freedom. It is not surprising to any one acquainted with the history of thought to find any part of this doctrine leading first to a fresh emphasis upon Theism and next to a demand for Immortality.

We have already said that for the isolated self everlasting existence would be undesirable and even unendurable. We have now to see that for the self in fellowship everlasting existence is desirable, and for the ideal perfection of the fellowship is necessary. The life of the mind or soul depends on perception and assimilation of its environment, as the life of the body depends on the reception and assimilation of environment. But the relevant environment is different. The body, being physical, receives and absorbs elements of the physical environment, assimilating these by digestion, so that its food becomes part of its own texture. So the mind receives and assimilates its environment of truth, beauty and goodness, so that these become part of its own texture. To forward this is the task of "education"; that very word means "nourishment", for which the vitally important matter is not the mere absorption of food and drink, but its assimilation. The self-centred or self-concerned soul, making itself the object of its contemplation, and seeing all else as related to itself, is trying to feed upon itself. The food may be congenial, but the process is inevitably one of wastage. Such a soul must shrink and shrivel, suffering at last both the pain of unsatisfied hunger and the pain of contraction. On the other hand, the mind or soul that is set on an object capable of truly feeding it may still, and perhaps for ever, suffer the pain of expansion, as it seeks to absorb a proffered wealth to which its capacity is unequal, but that pain is accompanied and transmuted by the joy of perpetual attainment.[1]

Now finite souls are to a very great extent reciprocally constitutive of one another. We have our whole being in fellowship with each other, and are what we are because of the tradition that we inherit and the influences that play upon us. Something of our own we bring to this, but only the omniscience of God can discriminate between this original contribution and the work of social influences. It is partly because of this essentially social character of finite mind that self-centredness and self-concern are suicidal; they set up an absolute contradiction between the activity of mind and its own nature. But if the mind or soul is thus constituted, then it may at least reasonably be regarded as requiring for its own fulfilment the special social relationship that may exist between it and every other mind, while every other will be the poorer for the lack of social relationship with it. Moreover, what is in question here is not only the good enjoyed by each in proper

[1] Cf. F. Von Hugel, "What do we mean by Heaven and what do we mean by Hell?" in *Essays and Addresses on the Philosophy of Religion*, pp. 195-224.

appreciation of the other, but the special good of each waiting to be actualised by others' appreciation of it. It is possible, no doubt, to conceive the Commonwealth as a series of eccentric circles, each representing the sphere of social relationships proper to an individual soul. And some such notion would be natural if not inevitable if the Commonwealth itself were conceived on republican principles, that is to say, as a fellowship cohering by the attachment of members to one another. But we have seen reason for conceiving it as a Monarchy, so that the fellowship coheres by the allegiance of all members to the King or Head, and to one another in and through Him. The conception congruous with this is that each member should have, or be destined to have, through Him a fellowship with all others who owe to Him the same allegiance.

Such a commonwealth must bind into unity all spirits of all periods of time. In other words it involves everlasting life for all who are its members; but this life is something more than everlasting. It must, at least progressively even if never completely, partake of the nature of eternity, wherein all successiveness is united in a single apprehension. Only so could the whole value of all the social relationships comprised in it be actualised. That the human mind is capable of such apprehension on a limited scale we have already seen in our discussion of the relation of Process to Value.[1] We found not only that the mind can apprehend a stretch of successiveness as a unit, in the way in which an aviator sees below him a great stretch of extension as a unit, but that the unity of the successive is so intimate that the course of events may lead to an alteration in the value of a past event when it is seen in the light of its own consequences. This conquest of the mere successiveness of the temporal can be rendered more complete by practice in the appropriate exercise of concentration. It finds its most intimate and vivid illustration in the

[1] See Lecture VIII.

experience of forgiven sin, and its most penetrating and pervasive illustration in the constancy of a dedicated life. But it is only possible when the mind has been endowed with that objectivity of direction which is called humility, and which consists not in thinking little of self but in not thinking of self at all. The forgiven sinner who rejoices chiefly in his own forgiven state has not fully appropriated the forgiveness offered or fully escaped from the sin which called for it. The fully forgiven man does not rejoice in his own forgiven-ness but in the divine love to which he owes it; and his past sin persists in his experience no longer as a source of shame but as the occasion of a new wonder in his adoration of the love divine. It is such a going-forth of the mind to greet what is akin to it in its object that may fitly lead it to desire everlasting life that it may achieve a joy in God and His creation that is perpetually nearer to being in the full sense eternal.

But we are not primarily concerned to argue that the Commonwealth of Value requires for its perfection the eternal life of those who are its members, for in any case it is not itself the true ground either of eternal life or of belief in it. That ground is God Himself and God alone. What is now our primary concern is the truth that the condition of eternal life is such a Commonwealth of Value. *If every finite spirit had the same experience of Value, even in the apprehension of God, there would be no advantage, except for each such spirit separately considered, in the eternal life of finite spirits. But if each is different both in itself, and in what it apprehends, and therefore also in respect of the value which by its apprehension it makes actual, then eternal life must be the life of such a Commonwealth and of spirits that know themselves to be members of it.* This knowledge need not, of course, be theoretical or present to consciousness in the form of any proposition, nor will propositional knowledge of itself suffice; the knowledge required is that of living and active experience, wherein each spirit actually finds its joy in fellowship. On the other hand for the self-centred spirit there can be no eternal life. Even if it should exist for ever, its existence could only be an ever deepening chill of death. Because it seeks its satisfaction in itself, where none is to be found, it must suffer an always intenser pang of spiritual hunger, which cannot be allayed until that spirit turns to another source of satisfaction. In the self which it contemplates there can only be successive states. The self is not sufficient to inspire a dedication such as brings purposive unity into life. Self-seeking may express itself as aspiration after wealth, or power, or popularity, or any other occasion of self-gratification. And any one of these may occupy a man's energies in the few years of his life on earth,—may even give to them a concentrated unity to which among those whose devotion is to worthier objects only the saints attain. But there is in these no abiding value. Even the soul that lives to be loved by others, and has thus in a perverted fashion understood that love is the supreme good, yet fails of its object, because it is impossible to win and hold the love of others if no love goes forth to them; and as soon as it does, that soul already lives to love, not only to be loved, and its salvation is begun. Eternal life is the life of love—not primarily of being loved, but of loving, admiring, and (in love and admiration) forgetting self. Such a life is not only an entering into, but is the actual building of, that fellowship of mutually enriching selves which we have called the Commonwealth of Value.

This Commonwealth finds its centre and even the ground of its possibility in God. And God Himself, unless all our experience is illusory, claims for the fullness of His own delight in His creation the special excellence that resides in each finite spirit as it both achieves and appreciates the values that are proper to it alone.

> Morning, evening, noon and night
> "Praise God!" sang Theocrite.

But the unwise admiration of a sympathetic friend kindled an ambition in the boy to praise God "the Pope's great way". An archangel carried him to St. Peter's and took his place; but he could not give to God the joy of Theocrite's appropriate praise.

> God said, "A praise is in mine ear;
> There is no doubt in it, no fear;
>
> . . . . .
>
> "Clearer loves sound other ways;
> I miss my little human praise."

Then the Archangel took Pope Theocrite and set him again in the craftsman's cell, saying:

> "I bore thee from the craftsman's cell
> And set thee here; I did not well.
>
> "Vainly I left my angel-sphere,
> Vain was thy dream of many a year.
>
> "Thy voice's praise seemed weak; it dropped—
> Creation's music stopped!"[1]

The whole harmony of creation depends upon the offering by each humblest spirit of its own appropriate note of music which no other can sound without discord. It is impossible to stress too strongly the individualism of the spiritual world; each is himself alone, and each, because an object of divine love, has infinite value. But it is equally impossible to stress too strongly the communism of that world, if for once we may use the word "communism" with what ought to be its meaning; for each individual becomes his true self only so far as he fastens his attention not on his own fulfilment but on God and on God's work in creation. This is the road which leads to Peace, "that Harmony of Harmonies which calms destructive turbulence and completes civilisation", and to which, as an "intuition of permanence" in the midst of "the passing of so much beauty, so much heroism, so much daring", Professor Whitehead calls

[1] Browning, *The Boy and the Angel.*

our attention in his latest book.[1] It is indeed "the peace of God which passeth understanding". It is a Harmony of Harmonies, for it takes into itself all lesser loyalties and fellowships, using them as elements in its own abundant richness, preserving them from doing to each other injury through any self-centred temper still unpurged from them; it is the peace of eternity, wherein all successiveness is comprised and all discords are resolved. We have called it the Commonwealth of Value; its Christian name is the Communion of Saints; its perfection is in eternity, but to bring its divided and warring members into that Harmony and Peace wherein alone it is actual is the purpose which gives meaning to History.

[1] *Adventures of Ideas*, pp. 367, 369.

LECTURE XVII

THE MEANING OF HISTORY

AT an earlier stage of these Lectures we considered the accepted trio of ultimate values—Truth, Beauty and Goodness. We found that in every case the essential condition of the value in question was the discovery by mind of itself or of its own principle in its object. Further we found that though the value only becomes actual through appreciation, yet its existence is objective and not subjective; it is objectively real though subjectively conditioned. The three terms—Truth, Beauty and Goodness—we interpreted as signifying the objective counterpart of three modes of mental activity, the intellectual, the aesthetic and the ethical. These three seem to exhaust the distinguishable activities of mind, or at any rate may be so understood as to do so. Every such activity we found to arise through reaction to, or in correspondence with, some aspect of the objectively given environment, so that each is a mode of apprehending reality.

But there is an activity of mind which is found to combine all of these in one. The importance of History, whether subjectively or objectively considered, has not until recent times received from philosophers the attention which it deserves. Objectively regarded, History is the sum total of events. The relation of those events and of their totality to what is real but other than event, is one main theme of metaphysical enquiry. Subjectively regarded, History is the apprehension and interpretation of events; and so far as what occupies attention is the series of events initiated or modified by human volition, it is found to unite in itself all the three activities previously considered. The historian must be scientific in his treatment of evidence; he must exert himself to ascertain truth to the utmost. But a catalogue of events is not history. He must so present the events which he records as to exhibit their significance and not only their occurrence. This calls for the aesthetic or artistic activity of mind alike in apprehension and in expression. But, once more, it is not possible for the historian to record all the events of the period which he studies, partly because he cannot ascertain them all, and partly because, if he could, he has not space for the narration of them. He must select; and his selection must be governed by some principle, which, being a standard of judgement upon the values of human experience and action, falls within the sphere of ethics. Science, art and morals are all involved in the study of history. It is even probable that philosophy in its most specialised sense will be involved also; for the principle of selection among events, and the suggestion or articulation of the significance of those selected, can hardly be detached from ultimate questions concerning the nature of Reality.

The earlier philosophers paid little attention to History, and indeed History itself, as we understand it, is a recent achievement of the human mind. From early ages men have recorded the events of their own or immediately preceding times; and from Thucydides onwards many have applied to this activity all the powers of the mind—scientific, artistic and ethical. But the effort to recover the course and significance of a buried past, and to contemplate a whole stretch or reach of time as a single panorama in a synoptic apprehension, begins, on the great scale, with the great work of Gibbon. He was quickly followed by others; the acceptance of evolution as a biological, and then as a cosmological, hypothesis, reinforced the new tendency, until to-day historical successiveness is the aspect of reality with which our minds are most familiar. Our effort to understand any event or phenomenon usually begins with the attempt to place it in its historical context, and to see it in the light of what preceded and of what followed it. Contemporaneously and coherently with this tendency appeared the belief in progress, and the conviction that change is a necessary function of life. Our forefathers took for granted, not change, but stability; they assumed that social customs and political constitutions normally remain unaltered through incalculable periods, while change was admissible only as a rare adjustment of this essentially changeless structure. As late as 1832 Lord John Russell pleaded for what then seemed a drastic measure of Parliamentary Reform on the ground that if this were adopted it would prove a final settlement of that vexed question. In the second quarter of the twentieth century we do not expect final settlements of any terrestrial question. We take change for granted; stability we call stagnation, and associate it in our minds with death.

For this profound and pervasive change of outlook the historians and biologists prepared the way. But the main cause of it was the actual and perpetually renewed transformation of the social structure of many countries under the influence of steam-power and electricity. The idea has followed the fact. But the result is that whereas for the people of former generations it was almost self-evident that ultimate reality is eternal and unchanging, for our contemporaries the passing event is alone indubitably real, while the very existence of any eternal object is matter for debate.

Oriental philosophies have often so stressed the eternal as to represent the transient as illusory; this world with all its happenings, including our moral strivings, is *Maya*. Indeed it is inevitable that exclusive concern for the eternal should make the temporal appear meaningless. But exclusive concern for the temporal has the same result. It condemns not only the eternal but the temporal also to insignificance. Mysticism at least finds meaning in the eternal; materialism can find it nowhere. The successive as such cannot display meaning. If History is a mere succession of events, it must be quite meaningless. There is now this and then that; and there is no more to be said. But actual temporal experience is not mere succession; it is always a unitary apprehension of a successive manifold. Moreover, there is a non-successive unity in the life of any organism, still more in the life of a self-conscious, and especially of an ethical, organism. There is such a unity also in the life of a species or (in some degree at least) of a nation. This unity finds expression in the successive events; it is not fully expressed in any of them separately, but only (if at all) in the whole series; nor has it any objective existence apart from the events; the successive and non-successive are here bound to one another indissolubly. One may be the logical *prius* of the other, but not in such sense that it could exist without the other.

The nature of such unities of the successive is most easily studied in those instances which are due to the deliberate activity of human minds, though there are points at which the artificial character of these may render misleading the analogy which they supply. In some sense the thought which the poet expresses is real as a thought in his mind before he gives expression to it. But in some instances at least—and those precisely the instances which give the strongest impression of "creation" as distinct from "construction"—it appears that the thought is fully apprehended by the poet only in the very act of its articulation. The poet himself is prior to his poem temporally as well as logically; but the poetic thought is temporally prior to the poem only as an embryonic phase of consciousness, or even (it may be) as organic feeling. Further, as has already been observed, the thought or meaning, which is the ground of necessity for every part of the poem, is only given when the end of the poem is reached; for it is expressed in the whole and not in any part or series of parts less than the whole. That is always so for the reader of the poem; but if it be true that the poet only apprehends his own thought in the process of articulation, it is true for the poet also. In that case the meaning, which is the ground of the poem's existence, only comes to actuality in the process of the poem's composition. Here, then, is an instance of a rational unity of the successive where the unity and the successive series become actual together.

This is a type of unity perfectly familiar in experience, though we do not often pause to formulate its characteristics or to consider the relation of the non-successive unity to the successive elements in which alone this has actuality. When we do so, there is no difficulty unless our minds are obsessed with the abstractions of clock-time or with the notion that efficient causation is the only relation between ground and consequent. Every one who utters a significant sentence is actually employing efficient causation as a subordinate instrumentality for the actualisation of a meaning which determines the sounds or signs that express it and yet may only become actual in those signs and sounds.

In such a series there is real unity—the meaning; and this is a ground of necessity to all parts of the series; but regarded successively, it is only fully extant when the series is complete. This consideration carries with it a consequence of the highest importance. For it means that *there exist series of successive parts, so ordered that when regarded forwards no necessitating ground is discernible, but which are seen to be governed by an immanent necessity when regarded backwards, from the view-point of the completed series.* In no sense does the first line of the poem determine the second, except perhaps by striking a keynote with which certain developments would be unrelated. Sometimes this is very marked, as with such a line as

> It is an ancient marinere

where, incidentally, the archaic spelling is indispensable.

Sometimes the poet takes longer to announce, as it were, the poem's atmosphere. As the poem proceeds, its type becomes more defined, and the range of possible development is narrowed. But not till the last line, and the last word of the last line, is necessity present. Then, if the poem is a good poem, necessity is apparent. In order to be that poem, and express that meaning, it had to consist of exactly that series of words arranged in that order, with that rhythm.

In some men's lives the same principle is exhibited, though never (perhaps) in the same completeness. At each stage there is a variety of open possibilities. The boy may give more attention to letters or to science, having an aptitude for both; the young man may take up an academic or a political career. Every choice narrows the range of possibilities for the future; but there are still some open alternatives to the very end. Yet at the end, those who knew him may look back and see a unity in the completed life which makes it the perfect expression of his personality. In such a case each choice, which seemed at the time so open as to depend almost upon chance, is seen to proceed from a constant element in character which may then have had its first opportunity or occasion for expressing itself. It is not in any way denied that there are lives in which some decisive choice depends on external or even irrelevant considerations, and which then exhibit a real unity along the line so laid down for their development. But where the character is strongest it is felt afterwards as having been the real determinant of all its choices.

This self-expression of a constant and constantly developing character is what we have called Purpose.[1] Some objection has been raised to the use of the word with so wide a significance; it is urged that it properly means the pursuit of a definite end. But that seems arbitrary; for the end pursued may be the maintenance of a type of character or a certain relationship to neigh-

[1] Cf. Lectures XI., XII., XIII. and elsewhere.

bours. This will express itself in a vast variety of actions, no one of which is itself the end proposed as a guide to conduct; it would be misleading to speak of the man's purpose as directed to them; it is directed to something permanent which finds expression in them; it is directed to its own preservation; it is Spinoza's *conatus in suo esse perseverandi*.

Something akin to this is often traceable in the life of a nation. Its character is gradually formed by the coalescence of a diversity of ingredients; in the growth of experience and the alternating relationships of friendliness and hostility with other nations it acquires a body of tradition and sentiment the maintenance of which becomes a chief element in the national purpose. As the citizens of a country look back over its history, being themselves in very large measure products of that history, so that they appreciate it with true intimacy of sympathy, they see in its general course the expression of something which they know and value in themselves; there are probably episodes which they deplore and for which they feel shame; but they see in process of formation a character which they value because in it they find themselves or what is akin to themselves.

There is no nation which exhibits in its history so complete a unity of the successive as some men have shown in their lives; and no man (perhaps) has shown so complete a unity in his life as is to be found in an artistically successful poem. But the same principle is found to be operative in the indefinitely various complexities of personal and national life as are clearly observable in the work of art, which may be said to be deliberately constructed in order to embody or illustrate this principle. In other words, there is found as a feature of history an element which may properly be described as an immanent purpose. To exhibit this is one essential function of the historian. He is not called upon to formulate the immanent purpose of a nation's life, or of a civilisation or a culture. But he is rightly expected to set forth the facts which he narrates in such a way that they are felt to express a more or less constant tendency which gives unity to them. He must not be content to compile a chronological table; he must make a story of it, and a story must have, at least, coherence, which is a form of unity.

The points which have been under consideration are of importance when we return to the question what is the meaning of history for eternity. There are three main ways in which this has been regarded. (1) The first is expressed in the familiar Platonic *dictum* that Time is the moving image of Eternity.[1] On this view, the eternal is what it is independently of the temporal, which in some sense proceeds from it and expresses it, but makes no difference to it. (2) The second view is that eternity is just the sum-total of the temporal simultaneously apprehended. (3) The third is that the eternal is in itself constant; that it is somehow the initiating cause of the temporal, and that the temporal in some way returns to it. (4) A fourth view, however, is possible which seeks to combine the other three in such a way as to allow each to correct the deficiencies of the others. Our programme, therefore, from this point onwards is to consider the three views first described so as to note their strong and weak points, and then to construct our own more synthetic view.

(1) The view commonly, and with some reason, ascribed to Plato makes History in the last resort meaningless—not in the sense of having no unity, but in the sense of supplying no ground for its own existence.[2] If Time is the moving image of Eternity, we may hopefully seek in the eternal the explanation of the temporal. But then Eternity itself is conceived as so detached from Time that, though it supplies an explanation of the content of Time, it gives no ground whatever for the existence of a temporal world. The Eternal is unaffected. It, or He, eternally abides. I AM

[1] *Timaeus*, 37 d.

[2] Plato had also another view; see below, p. 443.

THAT I AM must be His only form of self-expression. History occurs because of Him; but it makes no difference to Him.

Now this is true and important for both philosophy and religion, provided it is understood in a certain sense. For only by a doctrine of thoroughgoing Transcendence is the universe explicable[1] or the religious impulse satiable. In the sense in which God is necessary to the world, the world simply is not necessary to God. Apart from Him it has no being; apart from it, He is Himself in plenitude of being. The World – God = 0; God – the World = God.

But if that is all that can be said, History is metaphysically unmeaning. In itself it has meaning, for in some degree it expresses the eternal realm or Being whence it flows. But it has no ultimate meaning—no meaning for God. Consequently our view, in its concern to exalt the Majesty of God, attributes to Him an activity—Creation—which is from His own point of view meaningless. Philosophically, therefore, this view is deeply unsatisfactory. Religiously regarded it is even worse. For we find that the higher any religion is in the scale of spiritual, ethical and intellectual value, so much the more is it rooted in History.[2] Certainly for Christianity it is impossible to accept a view which makes History of no ultimate importance. For Christianity affirms an act of God within History itself and rests on this affirmation. History is of importance to Buddhism so far as reverence for the Buddha is deepened, and obedience to his precepts stimulated, by the conviction that he actually existed on this earth and attained to Enlightenment. History matters to Islam so far as the authority of the Koran depends upon its having been actually given by divine inspiration to Mohammed. But beyond this, those religions are indifferent to History. For Christianity it is otherwise. It is not

[1] Cf. Lecture XI.

[2] Cf. C. C. J. Webb, *Problems in the Relations of God and Man*, pp. 62, 63.

primarily a system of ideas divinely communicated, nor a way of life divinely enjoined or guided, nor a method of worship divinely taught. It is, according to its own claim, primarily a self-revelation of God in a historical Person, and in that Person's life, death and resurrection. Because it is this, it is open to attack on the historical plane as no other religion is. Because it is this, it is involved in all the difficulties that attend the treatment of the temporal and contingent as possessing the value of the eternal and absolute. These are peculiar difficulties of the Christian religion, from which others are free. But they arise from the central essence of that religion. At any rate it is impossible for Christianity to acquiesce in the view that, however much the historical depends upon the eternal, the eternal is unaffected by the historical. Sin is for Christianity a temporal phenomenon; but it matters sufficiently to the Eternal God to lead Him to take self-sacrificing action for the world's redemption. And most Christians to whom the Gospel has been a living power would have been much startled by the suggestion that the Death of their Lord upon the Cross made no difference to the eternal life of God.

In this insistence upon the real and ultimate importance of History, Christianity is at one with the deepest ethical consciousness of mankind. Morality has its very being in the effort to maintain loyalty to certain principles in the changing circumstances of time; those principles are not generalisations concerning successive phenomena;

> *οὐ γάρ τι νῦν γε κἀχθές, ἀλλ' ἀεί ποτε*
> *ζῇ ταῦτα, κοὐδεὶς οἶδεν ἐξ ὅτου 'φάνη.*[1]

> Not of to-day or yesterday are these,
> But ever living; none knows whence they sprang.

They are phases or aspects of the Eternal; but their ethical importance is found in their application to passing and changing conditions. As has already been

[1] Sophocles, *Antigone*, 456 f.

observed, the man who persists in a moral purpose is conscious therein of special fellowship with the eternal; the man who sacrifices his immediate interest and even physical life in order to bring into being some good as yet not actualised, feels himself in that act to be not so much creating a new temporal good as conforming to an eternal good. For men, at least, it is true that fellowship with the eternal is most fully achieved by a certain mode of successive behaviour in relation to the temporal. And Christians have found the fullest entry of the divine into human nature, not in the moment of some mystic trance, but in the continued life of obedience to the divine Father; not in any episodic transfiguration, but in constant loyalty to love and its purpose through agony and crucifixion.

(2) Such reflections incline us to begin our enquiry afresh from the other side, and instead of regarding Time as the moving image of Eternity, to conceive Eternity as the integral totality of Time. Such a view at once endues History with an eternal significance. We are ourselves in Time, and cannot see the future which is to grow out of the present and the past. Consequently we cannot see the present and the past themselves in the proportions and perspectives which belong to them when seen as parts of the whole; and there may be rectifications of value which will be brought about in the future,[1] and which will profoundly modify the judgement on past and present which our present knowledge makes inevitable. We understand why the world as known to us is full of unsolved problems; their solution lies in the unknown future. We are delivered from the dilemma which bids us either deny our own moral judgement on the strength of a dogmatic conviction that the work of God is good, or else deny that the world is grounded in the divine creative act because it manifestly is not good. We are enabled to say that, seen from our standpoint, it is partly, even largely, bad,

[1] See Lecture IX.

and yet to cling to the hope that in the totality, which is beyond our grasp, all discords are resolved, all hatreds turned by love's own sacrifice to love, and every bitterness accepted as a price well worth the paying for the sake of the sweetness drawn from it. The integrity alike of moral judgement and of religious hope is thus preserved. And History itself, the scene of our moral striving, is invested with capital importance, for its course positively constructs the content of that eternal experience, which is History as an integrated whole.

But if the advantages of this view are great, the difficulties attendant upon it are formidable. For how are we to be sure that the future of History, which is unknown and also *ex hypothesi* contingent, will be such as to set our experience in the context and perspective that may justify it? Our view is strong just so far as it gives ultimate importance to our moral choices whereby the course of History is not so much determined as constituted. But if so, while the responsibility that rests on us is undoubtedly real, it is also insupportable. For it appears that upon our moral action depends the content of the eternal experience of God Himself. And if this apotheosis of Pelagianism is avoided by the hypothesis of such divine intervention as may be sufficient to overrule our choices to the fulfilment of the divine plan, then the question arises whether our supposed freedom and responsibility are not essentially fictitious and the whole course of History no more than a projection of the divine nature. And then we are back at the first view for which Time is the moving image of eternity. For if every thing after all is thrown back upon God, and God is conceived as Himself altogether outside the process, then the process is not in an ultimate sense constitutive of eternity at all but wholly episodic in relation to it.

(3) This conception of History as episodic to Eternity is frankly accepted in the third view which we have to consider. This may be called the naïve religious view.

It does not start with Eternity and seek to effect the transition to History; nor does it start with History and try to effect the transition to Eternity; but it starts with both as data, or at least as postulates, and seeks to effect a relationship between them. No doubt, being naïve, its conception of the Eternal is hardly more than that of somewhat, which persists unchangeably through Time. The Eternal God, so conceived, launched into being the world of successive events. As a rule this act is regarded as having some date, however remote; Time is conceived as having once begun; Time and the created world began together. And they will end together, except in so far as the temporal world contains spiritual beings, who will survive the wreck and dissolution of this world-order, and will then enter a condition determined by their moral response to the opportunities presented to them during their life as parts of this world-order.

This view, no doubt, is rather mythological than philosophic. It collects together the various points of certainty, and then relates them in a picture presented to the imagination rather than in a logical structure presented to the intellect. It is none the worse for that, if its true nature is recognised. The myth can often present reality more fully than any argument. The view which we are considering has these great advantages. Almost equally with the first it recognises the sole and complete supremacy of the Eternal—whence all springs and whither all qualified for such communion aspires to return. Almost equally with the second it recognises the ultimate significance of History and of the moral choices which (at the human level) constitute it, at least for those who are in their own nature historical entities and qualify for Eternity by their historical conduct. In addition to combining in high degree the advantages of the other views, it has this further point of strength, that it conceives the climax of History, for those who are centres of value-judgements, not as a mere prolongation, but as translation to a new and previously inconceivable world-order.[1]

This is a new point of so great importance that some further elucidation of it is required. It is sometimes said that an infinite progress is unmeaning. But that seems to be a mere mistake. Progress need not be the continuous approximation to a goal; judged as such an approximation it is, no doubt, true that infinite progress is only another name for perpetual failure. But Progress may take the form of an ever wider application of a principle which sets no limit to its application, and then there is nothing self-contradictory in the idea of infinite Progress. Yet if that is all that the future offers, it is hard to see how it can ever justify the historical experience of human and animal nature, in the sense of exhibiting these as appropriate products of an all-wise and all-good Creator. If we postulate Immortality, so that those who have ended their days upon this planet may still share the endless Progress, this alone does little to redeem the past. Religion has never been content with such a prospect. It has usually conceived the course of Progress to come to an end in a static condition of the fullest happiness which it can conceive, or else it has thought of the immortal state as one that we can only describe by negation of all earthly analogues. The naïvely religious view which we are now considering points forward to a state, whether static or progressive, which is quite other than a mere prolongation of earthly existence, though some foretaste of it here is possible, and the lot of each individual in that state is determined by his conduct here.

But this view, as ordinarily presented, still suffers from grave defects. The connexion which it sets up between History and Eternity is very external to both. There does not seem to be a sufficient reason why the Eternal should have launched into being the historical process. The supremacy of the Eternal over the his-

[1] *E.G.* 1 Corinthians ii. 9.

torical is not complete. The process of History has for its own denizens an ultimate importance, but not, apparently, for God. It is a view which, like many naïve and mythological presentations, puts together the best points of other views at the cost of compromising all. We must now attempt a synthesis of our own which may be free from that accusation.

(4) In entering on this task let us premise that we do not expect complete success. The essence of the enterprise is that we who are finite are seeking to comprehend the infinite, in order to define its relation to our finite selves. In such an attempt apparent success must be certain failure. Further, our method must be one of analogy and not of demonstration; for the Eternal ever eludes us, and we cannot without certain error form a definition of it which might be the starting-point of logically cogent argumentation. But by analogy we may make progress, and our hope will be that if we reach a stark antinomy, this may arise in regard to that which we know we cannot comprehend, and that at all other points our difficulties may be such as to give way before us even though we never reach their ultimate solution.

The three points of strength in the three views considered are: in the first, the complete and all-controlling supremacy of the Eternal; in the second, the ultimate importance of History and its moral choices; in the third, the expectation of a climax of History inaugurating a new world-order. With these in mind let us turn to our analogies. We naturally direct our attention to that human activity wherein the mind launches into being, as it were, a miniature history. Dramatists have declared that when once they have set their several characters in motion, they have no further control over the conduct of those characters. Indeed in so far as a dramatist creates after the fashion of those poets who apprehend their own thought in the act of expressing it, it must be so. Yet in another sense the dramatist retains an absolute control, even to the extent of cutting short the composition and destroying it. His thought, active in self-expression, is immanent in the play; the play is made by it, and apart from it no episode in the play takes place;[1] further, the vitality of every episode comes from the relation of that episode to this thought.[2] Yet the dramatist himself is absolutely transcendent in respect of the play. Upon him it depends whether there shall be a play at all. The play depends upon him for its existence; he does not in that sense depend upon the play at all. But because his vocation is to be a dramatist, he fulfils his nature by writing plays; if he did not write them he would be untrue to himself. The self-expressing thought through which the play comes into existence is part of the principle of his being. Consequently the play itself, and its content, is of vital consequence to him.

We now turn to another form of human creativity, which we have the highest religious sanction for regarding as an analogue of the divine. The father in a human family is to his children at once the source of their existence and a present Providence. Because they will represent before the world the results of his training of them, because they bear his name and may bring to it either honour or shame, but most of all because of his love for them, prompting him to give up what he values most if so he can serve their welfare, their doings are of vital concern to him. He gave them being; to a great extent he shapes their circumstances; perhaps his influence over them is so great that they will never knowingly act against his wishes; yet they are free to respect his wishes or not; if they do so, it is because it appears to them good to do so; when he controls them, he does not coerce them, because his control is effective through their wills and not either apart from or against their wills.

The analogy of the dramatist breaks down because his creations are not substantially alive; the analogy of

[1] Cf. St. John i. 3. [2] *Ibid.* 4.

the human father breaks down because the father himself is only another finite spirit, subject to successiveness in the same way as his children. But if we can think the two analogies together we find ourselves adumbrating a conception which seems to meet some at least of our requirements. Let us attempt the articulation of that conception, knowing that we can only speculate, and accepting a "likely tale"[1] concerning a theme too great for our scientific apparatus.

We start then with the conception of the Eternal God, perfect in the plenitude of Being. We know that He creates, for here is the world, and to attribute it to any other source than to Him is to attribute to Him finitude and limitation. In that case we should have to assume something greater than God, to wit, God *plus* the world, or whatever that may be in which both are grounded. The insuperable difficulties of this way of thinking have already been indicated.[2] We can only understand the world at all if it is grounded in the Will of the living God. He is therefore known to us as Creator. That He should create cannot be a mere accident of His being; it proves Him to be of such a nature as to create. Following our analogies of human creativity, we may connect this with the sheer satisfaction of creative activity—which is not by itself the highest even of human motives and therefore is not by itself an adequate spring of the divine action—and with the desire for self-communication. This latter, suggested by Plato as the motive of creation, is an expression of love, and coheres with the essential condition of good as the finding by mind of itself, or its kin, in its object.

In the inorganic world we may imagine that the divine mind takes delight, as that world in vast expanse and tiny detail expresses the perfection of quantitative relationships. It is a delight both scientific and aesthetic, and if here perhaps the scientific preponderates, we may

[1] εἰκότα μῦθον ἀποδεχομένους, Plato, *Timaeus*, 29 d.
[2] In Lecture X.

assume that there is preponderance of aesthetic satisfaction in the loveliness exhibited by every form of organic life from the "Tyger! Tyger! burning bright"[1] to the delicacy of a butterfly's wing, so that in every changing phase of nature "God renews his ancient rapture".[2] He looks upon His own creation and finds it "very good",[3] and therein also finds the fulfilment of the purpose with which He made it. It is His work, and in it He finds the counterpart of His own mind, so that the human student of creation is, in Kepler's words, "thinking God's thoughts after Him".

Upon one planet attached to a certain sun (whether also elsewhere or not we have no knowledge), His creativity expressed itself in beings able in some measure thus to enter into His mind and understand His work, so that in them He found a fuller counterpart than elsewhere of His own being. Rooted in nature they yet are not swayed only by natural forces, but by that which appears to them good, that is to say, by that in which they find themselves as God seeks to find Himself in them. They, like all else, exist only in dependence on His will. But since He has thought it good (that is, has found Himself in determining) to fashion them in so complete a resemblance to Himself, He must now control them according to the law of their being which He has imposed on them; He must control them through what appears to them good and their power to appreciate it—that is, through their unforced affection and will. Thus He Himself does not know *beforehand* exactly how they will respond to the various modes of His manifestation of Himself to them. So far as He is Himself at work within the process of Time, the precise mode of the future is unknown to Him, though its general issue in the fulfilment of His purpose is secure. Yet, all the same, because He is not in His own nature within the Time-process any more than the dramatist is personally within the play, and all that happens utterly depends on Him,

[1] William Blake. [2] Browning, *Paracelsus*. [3] Genesis i.

He knows it all with utter certainty. To Him the contingent is still contingent, as not being compelled by its own past; yet the whole is necessary, and therefore also all its parts; and the whole is the expression of His will. So He knows the contingent as contingent and yet knows it with certainty.

There is something here which we cannot fathom; but the difficulty arises where it ought to arise, in our attempt to understand the divine nature itself. The profoundest religious intuitions do not here lead to a scheme of thought perfectly comprehensible by men; they do, however, lead to apprehensions germane to the speculations which we have sought to follow out. In many religions they have led to some form of Trinitarian doctrine. In Christianity they have led to a form of Trinitarianism which may consonantly with our line of thought be presented as follows:

The Eternal God is such as to communicate Himself; co-eternal with His ultimate Being is His Word, which is His mind in self-expression. The form of that self-expression is the created universe, as the form of Shakespeare's self-expression is the scheme of words that constitutes each of his poems and plays. The divine and creative Word was not uttered once for all, but it receives perpetual utterance in the radiation of light, in the movements of the stars, in the development of life, in the reason and conscience of man. So soon as there is life, there is self-determined response to environment, though at first the part played by the "self" in this process is very small. Where it occurs, there is a transition from purely efficient to efficient *plus* final causation. Action is now governed in some measure by the apparent good. The good which appears, as being objectively given, is an activity of the divine Word—that self-expressed mind of God wherein man's mind gropingly finds itself, with many distortions and errors, but never without some reality of correspondence. This discovery or recognition shows itself in man as a more eager appetition of that good, and this responsive appetition is felt also to be divine and is called by Christians Holy Spirit. It was hardly recognised as distinct from the Word until the Word was uttered in a new fullness of expression, as Christians believe, in the historical Person, Jesus of Nazareth. That fuller objective self-manifestation of the divine called forth a new potency of responsive aspiration to which, as an experienced fact, was given the name Holy Spirit. This power of God within the soul, responding to God self-manifested in Jesus Christ, could afterwards be recognised in the responsive reaction of all life to the good wherever manifest.

But this response is not mechanically evoked; the degree or direction of it cannot be calculated in advance by reference only to the appeal offered to it. In this field it is not true that "action and reaction are equal and opposite". The living, self-determining organism is an uncertain entity until its response is made. Therefore life has taken many lines of development that lead nowhere, and living objects, from parasitic worms or beetles up (or down) to self-seeking men of high intelligence, seek their good—that is, their true selves—in what brings loss to others. Every time this happens it brings disappointment to God at work in the process of time; for God Himself, so far as His experience is temporal, has not absolute knowledge when the response that gives Him full sovereignty will be made; so that it is said "Of that day and of that hour knoweth no man, neither the Son" who is the divine Word, God self-manifested in the created process. But God is not only known as the Word who makes God manifest, nor as the Spirit who makes response to that manifestation, but as the Father, the fount of Deity and therein of all else, with whom a thousand years are as one day, and whose Love—that is, giving of self to rejoice in the self-gift which answers—is fulfilled in Word and Spirit, with all that in redemption and sanctification issues from the eternal creativity. This is not all that Christians have meant by the doctrine of the Triune God, but it is that part of it which coheres with our present line of enquiry.[1]

Does History then make any difference or not to the Eternal? In one sense, it manifestly does not. The question is framed in the language of succession. To make a difference is only possible in a literal sense where one phase succeeds another. And the Eternal is not successive. But in another sense History makes a great difference to the Eternal; for if there were no History, or if History were other than in fact it is, the Eternal would not be what the Eternal is. God the eternal is such as to sustain His own fullness of being, with the self-giving and the reality of victorious sacrifice which Religion apprehends as the heart of that fullness of being, through the historical process which supplies to these elements in His nature an opportunity of actualisation not otherwise conceivable. History does not make a difference to God in the sense of making Him different at one time from what He was at another; but it does make a difference to Him in the sense of being so vitally united to His eternal essence as its inevitable self-expression that if it were annihilated, or even changed, that would involve a difference in Him as compared with what, as author, over-ruler, and fulfiller of History, He is.

It may be legitimate to put this in the terms of traditional Christian belief. The Nativity, Death and Resurrection of Christ did not, according to that belief, make God other than He was before. They did, indeed, enable Him to treat mankind in a new way, and so in a real sense altered His active relationship to men;

[1] Cf. my sermon on "The Holy Spirit and the Blessed Trinity" in *Fellowship with God*, pp. 130-144; and the closing chapter of *Christus Veritas*.

There appears to be a difference in the New Testament between "Holy Spirit", to which reference is made above, and "The Holy Spirit"—the Divine "Person" who is the source of this responsive energy in the human soul. Unfortunately our versions do not observe this distinction.

manifestation of what human selfishness means for divine love rendered morally appropriate a new method of action on the part of the divine love. But the love itself was unchanged. This does not mean, however, that the Eternal Life of God was unconcerned with the historical life of Christ, which merely exhibited it. On the contrary, that historical life is so intimately one with the eternal which it makes manifest, that if it could be annihilated, the eternal life would be different in quality. It is not incidental to God's eternity that (if the Christian Gospel be true) He lived and suffered and triumphed in the process of time. If that happened, then His eternal being is such as to necessitate its happening, so that its not happening would prove His eternal being to be other than Christianity believes. The quality of God's eternal life is such that "it behoved the Christ to suffer"; and if either there were no History, or History contained no divine passion, that quality would be other than it is. *The eternal is the ground of the historical, and not* vice versa; *but the relation is necessary, not contingent—essential, not incidental.* The historical is evidence of the eternal, not only as a shadow is evidence of substance, but as a necessary self-expression of a Being whose essential activity is at once self-communication and self-discovery in that to which He communicates Himself.

To enter upon any discussion of the meaning of actual human history as known to us is to leave the field of necessary connexions for the contingent. For owing to the nature of spirit, contingency is itself a necessary characteristic of human history. But we can lay down certain principles even here. If our whole account of the nature of Value is true, or even only contains truth, then the meaning of History is found in the development of an ever wider fellowship of ever richer personalities. The goal of History, in short, is the Commonwealth of Value. From this standpoint the formation of the League of Nations marks an epoch of significance not only for our historical period but for History itself when viewed in relation to Eternity. And the difficulties of the enterprise are part of its significance. For those difficulties represent the claims of the several units to fullness of independent life within the fellowship. The goal is neither richness of individuality without recognition of the claims of fellowship, nor width of fellowship established between units that have little depth of individuality; the goal is individuality in fellowship where each term is heightened to the maximum. It is idle to speculate which of the two terms is the more important in principle; but it may well be held that we have now reached a stage in the development of warfare at which hostilities are so disastrous to all parties that the cause of national individuality can never be served by such national individualism as may involve war. Certainly in the last resort the two terms are necessary to one another. There can be no richness of individuality for men or for nations without fellowship, and there can be no fellowship apart from individuality nor depth of fellowship apart from rich variety of individuality.

But this History of nations is an affair of a few generations. Its whole drama is enacted upon a planet which is losing its power to sustain life. Astronomers seek to comfort us with the thought that for many millions of years life can continue, and there is plenty of time for our enterprise of progress. That thought brings comfort if the harvest of the world is to be gathered into some eternal store; but it is sheer lack of imagination to suppose that a vista of a million million years can give more significance than a week or a fortnight to our moral strivings, if at the end it is all to be as though we had never been at all. If that is the end for the race, and all its members pass out of existence, then it is in such a futility that the Eternal finds expression, and nothing can check the attribution of the futility to the Eternal there expressed. Yet what is the alternative? Mere prolongation of existence for individual spirits points either to an everlasting stagnation or to an unending restlessness; and neither is very satisfactory. What would give meaning to all the movement of History is the attainment of that synoptic vision of its process which at once appreciates the process as such and yet enables the mind to compass it instead of being immersed in it. Such a serene relationship to the occurrences of Time—entering into them with sympathy but yet detached from them because possessed of the principles (or the Spirit) which shape them—is perhaps one part of what has been called the Peace of God. The reality of that Peace, and its availability to finite spirits, would give to History a meaning; if there is no such condition, or if finite spirits cannot reach it, then History is indeed

> a tale
> Told by an idiot, full of sound and fury,
> Signifying nothing.[1]

Here we recall the intuition of Religion at its deepest that History moves to a climax which is historical because it occurs in, and crowns, the course of History, but which is in its own nature a transition to a new order of experience. That order is not one which has no relationship to the historical. The "things above" on which this hope would bid us "set our affection"[2] are none other than the things on earth which are "the fruit of the spirit".[3] "Life eternal"[4] is such that it is attainable before as well as after the catastrophe of death. Yet the order of experience which death makes possible is new, and unpredictable by those whose experience is of the historical order only. Therefore we are not only unable to anticipate the experience that awaits us, but are for that reason unable fully to understand or to justify the historical order itself. The historical order together with the climax which is a transition to something more and other than history is, on this view, one of those unities

[1] Shakespeare, *Macbeth*, Act V.
[2] Colossians iii. 1.
[3] Galatians v. 22.
[4] St. John xvii. 3.

where the principle of unity is in the whole, so that even what precedes is fully intelligible only when what follows has completely developed the ground of the necessity of every part. This type of unity, as we have seen, is perfectly familiar in every good poem or drama. From the standpoint of the end, necessity governs the whole; from any earlier standpoint, there is contingency and indeterminacy. We are living out such a drama—the drama of which the plot is the creation of finite spirits by divine love, and the fashioning of their initially selfish individualities into the Commonwealth of Value. *The end is not predictable from the beginning; and the beginning can only be understood in the light of the end. Consequently our apprehension of the Meaning of History is very meagre. But we apprehend these two points. It can only have meaning at all if Eternal Life is a reality; and the meaning then is one which we do not so much discover as actually make.* For human History is nothing other than ourselves; and we make its meaning by living out its process in the power, already available to us, of the Eternal Life which is at once the source of that meaning and its culmination.

LECTURE XVIII

MORAL AND RELIGIOUS CONDITIONS OF ETERNAL LIFE

THE moral and spiritual life of man imperatively demands that allowance should be made for its distinctive quality in any estimate of the nature of ultimate reality. This life—so alien in many respects from the processes of nature in all other known departments—calls for explanation. The ultimate reality must be such as to account for its occurrence. By this and other kindred reflections we were led to the assertion that the governing principle of reality is a living and righteous God. But the argument will not let us stop there; for man's moral and spiritual life is in this world a baffled and thwarted enterprise; and the scene of our endeavour is slowly becoming uninhabitable, so that even though men labour for a remote posterity, yet if this life only is permitted them, it will one day make no difference whether we have striven or not for noble causes and lofty ideals. An earth as cold as the moon will revolve about a dying sun. Duty and love will have lost their meaning. The President of the Immortals, if there be either immortals or president, will have finished his sport with man. And how shall the argument which posited the righteousness of that same Potentate allow us to rest in any such connexion? Moreover the worst has not been told. For we have seen that values even of past events may alter, and the value of a whole process depends upon the order of its episodes. A drama which starts in sunshine and ends in gloom has not the same quality in respect of optimism or pessimism as one that starts in gloom and ends in sunshine, though the average tone of the scenes taken separately may be identical; the drama with a descending scale, so to speak, conveys a sense of even deeper gloom than one that is in the bass register throughout. If at the end there is to be nothing but cold dead cosmos—which might as well be chaos—then, though their presence shines like a jewel in the prevailing gloom, yet it were more creditable to the Determiner of Destiny that virtue and love had never bloomed. That they should appear to be discarded makes the ultimate principle of reality more ruthlessly non-moral than if it had never given birth to them at all. On that hypothesis virtue itself is a blot on the escutcheon of the Ruler of the universe and heroism is His deepest shame.

Further, we have seen when considering the action of divine grace upon the soul that if its operation be limited to the space of this mortal life, it cannot escape censure for such favouritism as to deny the justice and the love of God.[1] And if divine Providence is exposed to such condemnation in its dealings with individuals, it is no more successful in its ordering of human history as a whole. That too ismeaningless "if in this life only we have hope".[2] Every consideration of serious importance intensifies the urgency of the moral demand for at least the possibility of life after the death of the body. Yet there has never been a period in which there was so little positive belief in this, or indeed so widespread an absence of concern for the whole subject. Probably this is due to the forms in which the idea has traditionally been presented rather than to any lack of compelling attraction in the idea itself or its intrinsic claims upon the attention of mankind; but it is also due to the triumphs of science which have made this world so intensely interesting.

It is, indeed, not easy to estimate the place which the idea of Immortality now holds in the actual religion of English people. Certainly it is nothing like so prominent as it has been in most previous ages of Christian history. And so far as it plays a part, it is a very different

[1] Lecture XV. [2] See 1 Corinthians xv. 19 and Lecture XVI.

part. Here as in other departments of life we find ourselves at the end of a period of reaction from the Middle Ages. The mediaeval scheme is entirely intelligible in its broad outlines. Universal immortality is assumed; for those who are beyond pardon there is Hell; for those who are pardonable, Purgatory; for those whose pardon is accomplished, Paradise. And alongside of these, for the unawakened soul there is Limbo. The scheme presents certain administrative difficulties. It involves, in practice, the drawing of a sharp line between the awakened and the unawakened soul, and again between the pardonable and the unpardonable. But unless it be held—as in fact I find myself driven to hold—that these difficulties are insoluble in principle, it may be urged that they are soluble to omniscience, which, *ex hypothesi*, is available for the purpose.

There are many of us, however, to whom the difficulty mentioned is so overwhelming as to make the whole scheme unreal, however water-tight it may be dialectically. And I have not hesitated to speak of it in terms which indicate that sense of unreality. For the human soul is at once too delicately complex, and too closely unified, to be dealt with by any method of classification into mutually exclusive groups. And how can there be Paradise for any while there is Hell, conceived as unending torment, for some? Each supposedly damned soul was born into the world as a mother's child, and Paradise cannot be Paradise for her if her child is in such a Hell. The scheme is unworkable in practice even by omniscience, and moreover it offends against the deepest Christian sentiments.

But this is a very modern reaction to it. What happened at the Reformation was entirely different. The doctrine of Purgatory was the focus of many grave abuses—sales of Indulgences and the like. These called for remedy, and thus set moving the normal method of the Reformers—the method of referring whatever was found to call for remedy to the touchstone of Scripture.

And Scripture was thought to supply no basis for a doctrine of Purgatory. So the doctrine was not freed from its abuses but was eliminated, and the Protestant world was left with the stark alternatives of Heaven and Hell.

Now the mediaeval scheme, being easily intelligible as a theory, however difficult in practice, had great homiletic value. It presented vividly to the imagination the vitally important truth of the "abiding consequences" of our actions and of the characters that we form. And this homiletic value was if anything increased at first through the simplification effected by the Reformers. There, plain before all men, was the terrible alternative. Only by faith in Christ could a man be delivered from certain torment in Hell to the unending bliss of Heaven; but by that faith he could have assurance, full and complete, of his deliverance; and that faith would be fruitful in his life and character.

But there was much to set upon the other side. The new form of the scheme gave a new prominence to Hell, and whereas the popular mind in the Middle Ages was mainly concerned with Purgatory and with ways of shortening or mitigating its cleansing pains, it was now Hell that alone supplied the deterrent influence arising from belief in a future life. And this, while it lasted, reacted on the conception of God. For, in the long run, punishment which is unending is plainly retributive only; it may have a deterrent use while this life lasts, but from the Day of Judgement onwards it would lose that quality; and it obviously has no reformative aim. Now it requires much ingenuity to save from the charge of vindictiveness a character which inflicts forever a punishment which can be no other than retributive. Certainly the popular conception of God in many Protestant circles became almost purely vindictive. We can read in the protests of such writers as Shelley and Byron what sort of picture of God had been impressed on their imaginations.

Is there a God? Ay, an almighty God,
And vengeful as almighty. Once His voice
Was heard on earth; earth shuddered at the sound;
The fiery-visaged firmament expressed
Abhorrence, and the grave of Nature yawned
To swallow all the dauntless and the good
That dared to hurl defiance at His throne
Girt as it was with power.[1]

No doubt Shelley was in violent reaction, and misrepresented by exaggeration what he had been taught, in addition to using the irony of indignation in order to satirize it. Yet a caricature depends for its force on maintaining some resemblance to what it ridicules. And there are sermons of the eighteenth century which go far to justify the poet's indignant contempt.

But such conceptions could not permanently survive in the minds of people who read the Gospels. Steadily the conviction gained ground that if God is rightly conceived as the Father of Jesus Christ, in whom His character is disclosed, He cannot be conceived as inflicting on any soul that He has made unending torment. So Hell has in effect been banished from popular belief; and as Purgatory had been banished long before, we are left with a very widespread sentimental notion that all persons who die are forthwith in Paradise or Heaven. And this seems to involve a conception of God as so genially tolerant as to be morally indifferent, and converts the belief in immortality from a moral stimulant to a moral narcotic. There is a very strong case for thinking out the whole subject again in as complete independence as possible alike of mediaeval and of Protestant traditions. The reaction from the Middle Ages here as elsewhere has worked itself out.

It has often been pointed out that in the religious experience of Israel the hope of immortality is of late origin. In the earlier times there was an expectation of a shadowy existence in Sheol; but it was not a hope. "O spare me a little that I may recover my strength, before

[1] Shelley, *Queen Mab.*

I go hence and be no more seen" is a prayer as far removed as possible from either the later Jewish or the Christian faith in the life to come. The hope of immortality as we understand it only dawned when faith in God as One and as Righteous was already firmly established. Those who believe in the providential guidance of Israel's spiritual growth will at once seek a divine purpose in this order of development; but those who start with no such presupposition may quite well trace a value in it which has permanent importance.

The great aim of all true religion is to transfer the centre of interest and concern from self to God. Until the doctrine of God in its main elements is really established, it would be definitely dangerous to reach a developed doctrine of immortality. Even when the doctrine of God is established in its Christian form, the doctrine of immortality can still, as experience abundantly shows, perpetuate self-centredness in the spiritual life. If my main concern in relation to things eternal is to be with the question what is going to become of *me*, it might be better that I should have no hope of immortality at all, so that at least as I look forward into the vista of the ages my Self should not be a possible object of primary interest.

For as in order of historical development, so also in order of spiritual value, the hope of immortality is strictly dependent on and subordinate to faith in God. If God is righteous—still more, if God is Love—immortality follows as a consequence. He made me; He loves me; He will not let me perish, so long as there is in me anything that He can love. And that is a wholesome reflection for me if, but only if, the result is that I give greater glory to God in the first place, and take comfort to myself only, if at all, in the second place. I wish to stress this heavily. *Except as an implicate in the righteousness and love of God, immortality is not a religious interest at all.* It has an interest for us as beings who cling to life, but there is nothing religious about that. It has an interest for us as social beings who love our friends and desire to meet again those who have died before us; that is an interest capable of religious value, but even this is not religious in itself. No; the centre of all true religious interest is God, and self comes into it not as a primary concern which God must serve, but as that one thing which each can offer for the glory of God. And if it were so, that His Glory could best be served by my annihilation—so be it.

But in fact God is known to us through His dealings with us. And if He left us to perish with hopes frustrated and purposes unaccomplished, He could scarcely be—certainly we could not know Him to be—perfect love. Thus the hope of immortality is of quite primary importance when regarded both doctrinally and emotionally as a part of, because a necessary consequence of, faith in God. There is here a stupendous paradox; but it is the paradox which is characteristic of all true religion. We must spiritually renounce all other loves for love of God or at least so hold them in subordination to this that we are ready to forgo them for its sake; yet when we find God, or, rather, when we know ourselves as found of Him, we find in and with Him all the loves which for His sake we had forgone. If my desire is first for future life for myself, or even first for reunion with those whom I have loved and lost, then the doctrine of immortality may do me positive harm by fixing me in that self-concern or in concern for my own joy in my friends. But if my desire is first for God's glory, and for myself that I may be used to promote it, then the doctrine of immortality will give me new heart in the assurance that what here must be a very imperfect service may be made perfect hereafter, that my love of friends may be one more manifestation of the overflowing Love Divine, and that God may be seen as perfect Love in the eternal fellowship of love to which He calls us.

For these reasons it seems to me, so far as I can judge, positively undesirable that there should be experimental proof of man's survival of death. For this would bring the hope of immortality into the area of purely intellectual apprehension. It might or might not encourage the belief that God exists; it would certainly, as I think, make very much harder the essential business of faith, which is the transference of the centre of interest and concern from self to God. If such knowledge comes, it must be accepted, and we must try to use it for good and not for evil. And I could never urge the cessation of enquiry in any direction; I cannot ask that so-called Psychical Research should cease. But I confess I hope that such research will continue to issue in such dubious results as are all that I am able to trace to it.

When we turn from the relation of this doctrine to Religion and consider its relation to Ethics we are confronted with a different but, as it were, parallel paradox. The expectation of rewards and punishments in a future life has certainly played a considerable part in disciplining the wayward wills of men. And of this as of other discipline it is true that there may grow up under it a habit of mind which afterwards persists independently of it. But so far as conduct is governed by hope of rewards or fear of punishments as commonly understood, it is less than fully moral. We are probably agreed in rejecting the extreme austerity of the doctrine often, though unfairly, attributed to Kant,[1] that the presence of pleasure in association with an action is enough to destroy its moral character; but even more probably we shall agree that if an act is done for the sake of resultant pleasure or profit of the agent, so that apart from that pleasure or profit it would not be done, it is not a truly moral act. Consequently the ethical utility of Heaven and Hell, conceived as reward and punishment, is disciplinary and preparatory only. So far as true moral character is established, whether with or without their

[1] Cf Webb, *Kant's Philosophy of Religion*, pp. 96-99. I owe the reference to Canon Quick.

aid in the process, it becomes independent of their support and will only be injured by reference to them.

Moreover, the utility of Hell, so conceived, is very early exhausted, even if it be not from the outset overweighed by disadvantages. For in Ethics as in Religion the fundamental aim is to remove Self from the centre of interest and concern. But fear is the most completely self-centred of all emotions, and to curb irregularity of conduct by constant use of fear may easily make this aim harder of attainment than it was at the outset. It is probably good for most people to have an occasional shock of fright with reference to their shortcomings; but there is no doubt that to live under the constant pressure of fear —in the sense of anxiety concerning one's self—is deeply demoralising.

It is notorious that Kant, while excluding hope of profit from the motives of a truly moral act, yet found himself bound to postulate immortality as a means of securing that adjustment of goodness and happiness which he considered Reason to demand. I believe this line of argument to be substantially sound. But if it is, then we find that the hope of immortality is wholesome as an implicate in an independently established morality, though if introduced earlier it may hinder as much as help the establishment of that morality, just as it has high value as an implicate in faith in God, though if introduced earlier it may hinder as much as help the establishment of such faith.

In the light of such considerations we may proceed to form some estimate of that doctrine of the future life which properly belongs to our own religious tradition. This will involve our first disentangling the authentic teaching of the classical Scriptures from accretions which very quickly began to obscure this. We shall not assume that whatever those Scriptures teach must be true; that is a question for the theologian of Christianity as a positive religion. But the deliverances of the classical period of Christianity constitute important data for Natural Theology. The authentic Christian doctrine has three special characteristics:

(*a*) It is a doctrine, not of Immortality, but of Resurrection.
(*b*) It regards this Resurrection as an act and gift of God, not an inherent right of the human soul as such.
(*c*) It is not so much a doctrine of rewards and punishments, as the proclamation of the inherent joy of love and the inherent misery of selfishness.

(*a*) The Christian doctrine is a doctrine not of Immortality but of Resurrection. The difference is profound. The method of all non-Christian systems is to seek an escape from the evils and misery of life. Christianity seeks no escape, but accepts these at their worst, and makes them the material of its triumphant joy. That is the special significance in this connexion of the Cross and Resurrection of Jesus Christ. Stoics teach an indifference to death; the Gospel teaches victory over it. Richard Lewis Nettleship said our aim should be to reach a frame of mind in which we should pass through the episode of physical death without being so much as aware of it.[1] That is a splendid utterance; and yet it implies a detachment from wholesome interests and from the intercourse of friends which is a little inhuman. Surely it is true that death is a fearful calamity—in itself; and as such the Gospel accepts it; there is no minimizing of its terrors. Only its sting—its very real sting—is drawn; only its victory—its very real victory—is converted into the triumph of its victim. It is one thing to say that there is no real tragedy in the normal course of human life; it is quite another thing to acknowledge the tragedy and then to claim that it is transmuted into glory.

We lose very much if we equate with a doctrine of mere survival this hope of transformation, of resurrec-

[1] *Philosophical Remains*, p. 93.

tion whole and entire in all that may pertain to fullness of life, into a new order of being. Incidentally this glorious hope coheres with a totally different conception of the relation of Time or History to Eternity; for it both clothes History with an eternal significance, and at the same time points to a conception of Eternity as something much more than the totality of Time; and Time becomes not so much the "moving image of Eternity" as a subordinate and essentially preparatory moment in the eternal Reality, in the manner that was outlined in the previous Lecture.

(*b*) The Christian conception of the life to come as a gift of God has affinities with the Platonic doctrine of Immortality. Plato had sought to demonstrate the inherent immortality of the individual soul. In the *Phaedo* he fashioned an argument which seems for the moment to have satisfied him. But in fact it is invalid. What Plato proves in the *Phaedo* is that the soul cannot both be, and be dead; he does not prove that it cannot pass out of existence altogether.[1] In the *Republic* he advances an argument of which the minor premise seems to be simply untrue. He says that what perishes does so by its own defect; but the essential disease of the soul—injustice—does not cause, or tend towards, the decay of the soul; therefore the soul is imperishable.[2] But there is every reason to deny the second proposition. When once the essential nature of the soul as self-motion is established, it is at least open to question whether injustice is not a negation of that quality. No doubt the wicked man may display great activity; so may metal filings in the proximity of a magnet; that does not mean that they are endowed with self-motion.

It is in the *Phaedrus* that Plato first reaches the clear conception of the soul as characterised essentially by self-motion, and argues from this its indestructibility.[3] But not each individual soul is completely self-moved, and the argument, supposing it to be valid, as I think

[1] *Phaedo*, 103 B-106 E. [2] *Republic*, 608 D-611 B. [3] *Phaedrus*, 245 C-E.

it is, only establishes the indestructibility of the spiritual principle in the universe, not the immortality of each individual soul. Plato seems to have accepted that result, for in the *Timaeus* he declares that only God is immortal in His own right, and that He of His bounty bestows on individual souls an immortality which is not theirs by nature.[1]

That this is the prevailing doctrine of the New Testament seems to me beyond question as soon as we approach its books free from the Hellenistic assumption that each soul is inherently immortal in virtue of its nature as soul. That is a view which is increasingly hard to reconcile with psychology. I do not claim that in the New Testament there is a single doctrine everywhere accepted; on the contrary it seems to me that here and there a relapse into the Hellenistic point of view may be detected. But its prevailing doctrine, as I think, is that God alone is immortal, being in His own Nature eternal; and that He offers immortality to men not universally but conditionally. Certainly we come very near to a direct assertion of the first part of this position in the description of God as "the blessed and only Potentate, the King of them that reign as kings, and Lord of them that rule as lords, who only hath immortality" (1 Tim. vi. 16). The only approach to an argument for a future life of which Jesus Himself makes use is based on the relationship of God to the soul; "He is not the God of the dead, but of the living: for all live unto Him" (Luke xx. 38). And in close connexion with this saying in the Lucan version are the words, "they that are accounted worthy to attain to that world and the resurrection from the dead" (Luke xx. 35). It is in consonance with this that the Resurrection of Jesus Christ is constantly spoken of throughout the New Testament as the act of God Himself. No doubt St. Paul explicitly states that "We must all be made manifest

[1] *Timaeus*, 41 A, B. But in the *Laws* it is still held that each soul is immortal: *e.g.* 959 b.

before the judgement seat of Christ" (2 Cor. v. 10), but that settles nothing, unless we make, with some followers of "psychical research", the entirely unwarrantable assumption that the survival of physical death is the same thing as immortality.[1] Quite clearly it is not; for a man might survive the death of his body only to enter then upon a process of slow or rapid annihilation. And St. Paul elsewhere declares that he follows the Christian scale of virtues "if that by any means I might attain to the resurrection of the dead" (Phil. iii. 3).

Are there not, however, many passages which speak of the endless torment of the lost? No; as far as my knowledge goes there is none at all. There are sayings which speak of being cast into undying fire. But if we do not approach these with the presupposition that what is thus cast in is indestructible, we shall get the impression, not that it will burn for ever, but that it will be destroyed. And so far as the difficulty is connected with the terms "eternal" or "everlasting", as in Matt. xxvi. 46 ("eternal punishment") it must be remembered that the Greek word used is *αἰώνιος*, which has primary reference to the quality of the age to come and not to its infinity. The word that strictly means "eternal" is not frequent in the New Testament, but it does occur, so that we must not treat the commoner word as though it alone had been available, and when a vital issue turns on the distinction it is fair to lay some stress upon it. And after all, annihilation is an everlasting punishment though it is not unending torment.

But the stress in the New Testament is all laid upon the quality of the life to come and the conditions of inheriting eternal life. It does not call men to a mere survival of death while they remain very much what they were before, but to a resurrection to a new order of being, of which the chief characteristic is fellowship with God. Consequently the quality of the life to which

[1] But it may be a "lapse into Hellenism".

we are called is determined by the Christian doctrine of God.

What is abundantly clear throughout the New Testament is its solemn insistence upon what Baron von Hügel spoke of as "abiding consequences". Language is strained and all the imagery of apocalypse employed to enforce the truth that a child's choice between right and wrong matters more than the courses of the stars. Whatever is done bears fruit for ever; whatever a man does, to all eternity he is the man who did that. Moreover, evil-doing entails for the evil-doer calamity hereafter if not also here, while for him who gives himself to the will of God there is stored up joy unspeakable.

Further, there can be no question that Christ was prepared to use a certain appeal to self-interest to reinforce the claims of righteousness: "It is good for thee to enter into life with one eye rather than having two eyes to be cast into the hell of fire" (Matt. xviii. 8). But these passages are mostly connected with cases where loyalty to righteousness involves some great sacrifice or self-mortification; they are not so much direct appeals to self-interest as counter-weights to the self-interest that might hinder the sacrifice or mortification required. And the positive invitation to discipleship is never based on self-interest. He never says, "If any man will come after Me, I will deliver him from the pains of hell and give him the joys of heaven". He calls men to take up their cross and share His sacrifice. To those who are weary and heavy laden there is the promise of rest; but the general invitation is to heroic enterprise involving readiness for the completest self-sacrifice, and concern for the mere saving of the soul is condemned as a sure way of losing it.[1]

The Gospel is a call to fellowship with Christ, in whom it bids us see the eternal God. The call is to fellowship with Love, complete and perfect in its self-giving. How weak is the lure which this offers to our

[1] St. Mark viii. 35.

selfish instincts! There is in the Gospel a warning that the way of self-will leads to destruction, so that prudence itself counsels avoidance of it. But when we turn to seek another way there is none that commends itself to prudence only. For the reward that is offered is one that a selfish man would not enjoy. Heaven, which is fellowship with God, is only joy for those to whom love is the supreme treasure. Indeed, objectively regarded, Heaven and Hell may well be identical. Each is the realisation that Man is utterly subject to the purpose of Another—of God who is Love. To the godly and unselfish soul that is joy unspeakable; to the selfish soul it is a misery against which he rebels in vain. Heaven and Hell are the two extreme terms of our possible reactions to the Gospel of the Love of God. "This is the judgement, that the light is come into the world, and men loved the darkness rather than the light" (John iii. 19). "This is life eternal, that they should know thee the only true God, and him whom thou didst send, Jesus, as Christ" (John xvii. 3).

The Natural Theologian is not directly concerned with the claim made by Christians that in Jesus of Nazareth God has fully revealed His character. But he is very much concerned to consider with what conception of the future life that claim coheres, and how this is related to his general conclusions. Before we attempt any summary exposition of our results in this connexion it will be convenient to take up here the question how far our understanding of human nature has indicated any possibility that the self can survive physical death. That the moral and spiritual interests of man are bound up with such survival we have already seen. And if eternal life is always the gift of God and neither a natural property of human nature nor a necessary consequence of a certain degree of moral achievement, the believer in God might be content to refer the question of possibility to the divine omnipotence. But a theory which calls for such special and peculiar divine action as may reasonably be called miracle at a point where without such action the theory must be utterly discredited is on very precarious ground. If God has created beings of such sort that their destiny can only be fulfilled in eternity, it is likely that their nature gives evidence of their capacity to survive an episode to which every one of them must come.

We turn back once more to the characteristic of mind which first and most completely distinguishes it from whatever does not share its nature. This is its formation of "free ideas" whereby it detaches itself from the course of the natural process and enters upon a realm of its own, where its conduct is determined, not by the impulsion of force, but by the apparent good. *The mind of a human being increasingly organises itself and its own world apart from the processes which, for the most part, control the body within which, and (at first) as a function of which, the mind has come into being. As mind increasingly takes control of the organism, so it becomes increasingly independent of the organism as physiologically conceived.* A man may be so absorbed in thought as to become insensitive to occurrences that would usually occasion severe pain. In some such cases a degree of detachment is achieved which would have antecedently been pronounced by fully competent judges to be impossible. The greater the capacity for concentration of attention, the more complete does this detachment become; but every person who is ever conscious of obligation illustrates the vital principle of it. For obligation is not a calculation of the interests of the organism and of the way to serve these; it is an appreciation of value so distinct as to demand the sacrifice of all other interests for its sake. The mind which has achieved that is detached from "the whole might of nature". Duty and freedom have visited it together, for these are, as Kant perceived, inseparably correlated with one another.

But free ideas are not ideas which have no counterpart in physical experience. They have their origin in that experience. The spiritually minded man does not differ from the materially minded man chiefly in thinking about different things, but in thinking about the same things differently. It is possible to think materially about God, and spiritually about food. Hence the possibility of superstitions like that of Loretto on the one hand and of true mysteries like that of the Eucharist on the other. Consequently the ideal attainment of human nature would be a lifting of the physiological organism itself to the status of a free vehicle of the completely spiritual mind. But short of that there is at least indicated the possibility of life for the mind in independence of the physiological functions of the organism. Man is not in his own nature immortal, but he is *capax immortalitatis*.

If, with this background to our enquiry, we try to bring together the various indications which our argument has supplied, we find it possible to give some definite shape to the resultant conception of the future life.

God has created us as children of His love, able to understand that love in some degree and to respond to it. In the psycho-physical organism of human personality there is the possibility for a development of the spiritual elements, in response to and communion with the eternal God, which makes these capable of receiving from God the gift of His own immortality. Unless there has been such degeneration that only animal life continues to exist, it must be presumed that this possibility remains; and as it is hardly conceivable that any human being descends altogether to the level of the animal during this mortal life, it is further to be presumed that every personality survives bodily death. But that is not the same as to attain to immortality. And here we are confronted with a dilemma, which we must expect to remain insoluble so long as we have available only those data which are afforded by experience on this side of death. On the one hand is the supreme significance of free human personality, that is of will as determined by its own apparent good, which seems to involve the possibility for every soul that it may utterly and finally reject the love of God; and this must involve it in perdition. God must assuredly abolish sin; and if the sinner so sinks himself in his sin as to become truly identified with it, God must destroy him also. And this destruction is no painless swooning out of existence. The complacent sinner need not hope for that. Evil is a principle of division. The soul which is altogether evil would be one which cannot find itself even in its own nature; it is torn with an agony of self-diremption and perishes in a torture of moral insanity. That possibility remains for man as a free personality. On the other hand this result is failure on the part of God; for though He asserts His supremacy by destruction of the wicked, yet such victory is in fact defeat. For He has no pleasure in the death of him that dieth. The love which expressed itself in our creation can find no satisfaction in our annihilation, and we are prompted by faith in God's almighty love to believe, not in the total destruction of the wicked, but rather in some

> sad obscure sequestered state
> Where God unmakes but to remake the soul
> He else first made in vain; which must not be.[1]

As I have said, I do not think the dilemma can be resolved by us here on earth. But while I am now by no means confident, I will offer what slender hope of a solution to the difficulty I am able to entertain.

There is one condition on which our conduct can be both free and externally determined. It is found wherever a man acts in a certain way in order to give pleasure to one whom he loves. Such acts are free in the fullest degree; yet their content is wholly determined by the pleasure of the person loved. Above all do we feel free when our love goes out in answer to love shown to us.

[1] The Pope in Browning's *The Ring and the Book.*

Now the Grace of God is His love made known and active upon and within us; and our response to it is both entirely free and entirely due to the activity of His love towards us. All that we could contribute of our own would be the resistance of our self-will. It is just this which love breaks down, and in so doing does not override our freedom but rather calls it into exercise. There is, therefore, no necessary contradiction in principle between asserting the full measure of human freedom and believing that in the end the Grace of God will win its way with every human heart.

But this must be interpreted in the light of a doctrine of "abiding consequences", to use once more von Hügel's favourite phrase. Every consideration of reason and of justice requires this. Whenever I act, however light-heartedly, to the end of all the ages I am the person who then acted thus. Nothing can alter that fact; and while its value can be altered, it can never be the same as the value of some other action. Reason, with its insistence on coherence, allows no escape here. If I allow myself to become set in self-centredness the love of God can only reach me through the pain that causes or results from the break-up of that self-centredness; and when it has found me, and stirred my penitence, and won me to forgiveness, I am still the forgiven sinner, not the always loyal child of God. And this general truth has application to every act of moral choice.

Justice makes the same demand. It is not reasonable that if a man lives like a devil he should be permitted to die like a dog. Survival of physical death would be required if only to ensure that spiritual death were other than merely animal decease. And if we refuse to believe that God ever so far fails as to be under moral necessity to extinguish the light of spiritual life which He has kindled, yet by one means or another the soul must be led to appreciate the sinfulness of its sin as the only condition of really transforming its value by making it the occasion for penitence and for the appropriation of the redemption offered by divine Love.

Again, because God is Love, the universe is so ordered that self-seeking issues in calamity. Thus we are warned that even when judged from its own standpoint self-seeking is unprofitable. But while mercy in this way gives to selfishness the only warning it is capable of heeding, there is no way offered of avoiding the calamity while the selfishness remains. The fear of future pain or of destruction may stimulate a man for his own self's sake to seek salvation; but the only salvation that exists or can exist is one that he can never find while he seeks it for his own self's sake. The warning is a warning that while he remains the sort of man he is, there is no hope for him; it is a call, not merely to a grudging change of conduct for fear of worse or hope of better; it is a call to a change of heart which can only exist so far as it is not grudging but willing. Thus it is a call for surrender to that Grace of God which alone can effect such a change of heart. It is Love that keeps aflame the hell of fire to warn us that in selfishness there is no satisfaction even for self; and Love then calls the soul which heeds that warning to submit itself to the moulding influences of Love by which it may be transformed; and the promise of a joy which only those who are transformed into the likeness of Love can know, while to others it is the very misery from which they seek deliverance.

On such conditions it is possible to hold without demoralising consequences the hope which alone coheres with the faith in Almighty Love—the hope that in eternity every soul which God has made shall thank Him for every tittle of its experience. Sufferers and sinners as we are, at least we are at liberty to hope that we shall one day recognise in our suffering and even in our sin some further occasion for the glory of that divine love, which enables those who suffer to make their pains the means to self-conquest and makes of sin the occasion of its own self-sacrifice. At long last, we may hope, every sinner—even Judas Iscariot and every traitor with him—shall be so purged of self-concern by the very shame which his offence has caused to that same self-concern, that he in utter humility will thank God that his vileness has become a further occasion of the divine triumph.[1] And if in entertaining such a hope we are passing beyond what any argument can be said to warrant, at least in such a view as has been outlined there is neither the demoralising influence of a shallow optimism which says, "Never mind; it will all come right in the end", nor the equally demoralising influence of a terrorism which stereotypes self-centredness by undue excitation of fear. There is an appeal to self-concern in those who can heed no other, but it is an appeal to leave all self-concern behind. Again there is no promise for the future which can encourage any soul to become forgetful of God, for the promise is of fellowship with God, and therein, but only therein, of fellowship also with those whom we have loved. It is an austere doctrine, more full of the exigency than of the consolations of religion, though it offers these also in gracious abundance to all who submit to its demands, for to be drawn into fellowship with God is to find that the Communion of Saints is a reality. And the core of the doctrine is this: Man is not immortal by nature or of right; but he is capable of immortality and there is offered to him resurrection from the dead and life eternal if he will receive it from God and on God's terms. There is nothing arbitrary in that offer or in those terms, for God is perfect Wisdom and perfect Love. But Man, the creature and helpless sinner, cannot attain to eternal life unless he gives himself to God, the Creator, Redeemer, Sanctifier, and receives from Him both worthiness for life eternal and with that worthiness eternal life—for indeed that worthiness and that life are not two things, but one.

[1] Cf. Dante, *Paradiso*, ix. 103-105.

LECTURE XIX

THE SACRAMENTAL UNIVERSE

OUR argument has led us to the belief in a living God, who, because He is such, is transcendent over the universe, which owes its origin to His creative act and which He sustains by His immanence within it. The created universe, at least as known to us, is historical; it is marked at every point by successiveness or process. That process is traced out by the sciences of astronomy, geology and biology. But the data for a comprehensive science of the universe are not available to us. We have no knowledge of life in any portion of it except upon our own planet. The conditions necessary for the support of life as we know it do not certainly exist anywhere else, and the supposition that they occur belongs to speculation if not to guess-work. It is true that such conditions may exist elsewhere; it is also true that life in the general sense of organic responsiveness in physical objects may occur in forms quite unknown to us and unimaginable by us. Yet our ignorance on these points need not lead us to hesitate in attributing to life a great place among the factors determining our estimate of the Universe. It is the quality of life, not the extent of its diffusion in space, which endows it with importance for the philosopher. Even more true is this concerning mind. It is a late-comer in the historical process, as far as we know. When it comes it is at first so rudimentary, and of so little influence on the conduct of the organism in which it is found, that its existence may be plausibly denied or its significance dismissed by the process of dubbing it epiphenomenal. Yet so soon as there is an entity which has even once been determined in its conduct, not by the impulsion of efficient causation but by the lure of apparent good, a new principle, utterly incapable of reduction to efficient causation, has made its appearance, and any coherent account of the universe must allow for it. But to do this is at once to pass from a materialistic to a spiritual interpretation of the universe. For if among the principles found to be operative in it is determination by good, no limit can be set *a priori* to the application of this. Indeed, as we have seen, it becomes a necessity of reason to test the hypothesis that this is itself the supreme principle of reality.

A great part of these Lectures has been concerned with one method of testing that hypothesis, namely the attempt to see what follows from its adoption. In this attempt we have drawn upon the tradition and experience of religion, and more especially of the Christian religion, as a main source of our data. But it is at once evident that the general outline of the structure of the universe, as presented by science to-day, is far more congenial to the theistic hypothesis, as we have been considering it, than were the scientific theories prevalent in the eighteenth and nineteenth centuries. That remains true even though we go on to admit that in some respects those earlier theories were influenced by ideas drawn from religious sources to a greater extent than the scientific theories of our own time. Truth is one, and the progress towards truth in religion and in science follows converging lines. We serve truth as a whole most effectively, not when we seek to impose religious ideas upon science, nor when we seek to impose scientific ideas upon religion, but when studying both religion and the physical world with open and unprejudiced minds we seek to read their lesson.

Broadly speaking, the modern scientific view affords an apprehension of the world as existing in a series of strata, of such sort that the lower is necessary to the actuality of the higher but only finds its own fullness of being when thus used by the higher as its means of self-actualisation. Without the mechanical basis in matter, there could be no life of the kind that we know. Without living matter—bodily organisms—mind, as we know it, does not arise. Without animal mind (seeking means to an end presented as good) there could be no spirit such as we know (choosing between ends by reference to an ideal standard of good).[1] Now such a scheme can be regarded from two points of view; but whichever is adopted, care must be taken to avoid obliterating what is evident from the other. We may begin at the lower end of the series, and then there is no doubt about the reality of the material world. But the fact that this is real, and is the necessary basis of the world of life and mind and spirit as known to us, must not lead us to the supposition that there is nothing in these which is not observable in the material world as such. In the last resort it is, no doubt, true that there is only one world, and each department in isolation is an abstraction. We can say if we like that there is only one substance, and that the different sciences study not different substances, but different modes of action and reaction on the part of the same substance. But then we must be careful not to say that, because the actions and reactions studied in physics and chemistry are certainly real, therefore those studied in biology, in aesthetics, in ethics, in theology, are either unreal or else are only complicated forms of the other group.

If we begin at the other end, the temptation to bias is reversed. Because the actuality of the spiritual is assumed, the equal actuality of the physical tends to be doubted or denied. Now there is a sense in which a doctrine of Degrees of Reality may be true and important; but in that sense this doctrine does not affirm that some things more genuinely exist than others. Between bare existence and bare non-existence there is no middle term; any alleged entity either exists or it

[1] I have outlined this view in the first chapter of *Christus Veritas*; there is a fuller statement of it in L. S. Thornton's *The Incarnate Lord* specially in chapter ii.

does not. If it exists, a question may be raised concerning the manner of its existence, and concerning the extent to which the ultimate principle of reality is expressed in, or qualified by, its existence. Thus I am prepared to affirm that in this year 1934 "the present King of France" does not exist. Some contemporary logicians, including Lord Russell if I understand him rightly, say that "the present King of France" has being but not existence. That seems to me an unnecessary refinement, which only confuses the issue unless it be held that every thought which can be framed without internal contradiction is balanced by somewhat possessed of Being, whatever that may be. This would lead us in the direction of an Idealism even more remote than are most varieties of that philosophical tradition from the position which these Lectures have sought to vindicate. But though "the present King of France" has no existence, and "the King of France reigning in 1934" never will have existence,[1] Shakespeare's Ariel has existence—the existence of a poetic phantasy; and the atoms of hydrogen have existence—the existence of physical actuality; and "the present King of England" has existence, the existence of historical actuality. Now Shakespeare's Ariel, possessing existence as a phantasy, possesses actuality also in a secondary degree. He is not, so to speak, a primary entity, like atoms, or animals, or individual persons, or nations; he exists in imagination only. As imaginary, he is actual; but what is meant by an actual man is one who exists, not only in the thought or imagination of other men, but in himself and for himself, so that if all else were abolished he would still exist, indefinitely modified but subsistent; whereas if Shakespeare and all his readers were abolished, Ariel would simply not exist at all.

It is with actualities—primary existents—that philosophy or metaphysics, the science of the real as

[1] Unless indeed he obtains through Lord Russell's speculations an existence similar to that which Ariel obtains through Shakespeare's creative imagination.

such,[1] is concerned. It does well to attend to such secondary actualities as Ariel, because the genius of a great poet partly consists in the penetration of his insight, and his imagination, though in one sense truly creative, yet draws its material from what it perceives in the world about it. A view of reality to which Ariel is merely irrelevant seems to involve a view of Shakespeare as partly lunatic; and that is strong evidence against it. But while we call on the creations of poets for illumination and suggestion, our concern as philosophers is with primary actualities. Among these there may be degrees of reality if by that is meant that they represent, or express, the ultimate principle of Reality with varying degrees of completeness. But all truly exist. And to deny the real existence of matter is as fatal to a truly spiritual conception of spirit as is materialism, or the denial of all spiritual actuality. *For as it is true that matter is the necessary condition for the actuality of life and this also of spirit, so also is it true that, in our experience at least, spirit arises within and as part of an organism which is also material, and expresses its spirituality, not by ignoring matter but by controlling it.*

It must be admitted that the testimony of the great religions is not unanimous on this point. The religions of the East, and conspicuously of India, seek to affirm the supremacy of the spiritual by the denial of reality to the material; but the result is, in fact, a materialistic doctrine of the soul, and the invasion of religion itself by materialism in the form of sensuality. The latter is not denied as regards popular Hinduism. It is not so widely recognised that the doctrine of Karma is essentially materialistic. But it is hard to acquit of that charge a doctrine which attributes continuity of moral being, and liability to the penal consequences of acts done in a former existence, to a soul-substance which has no persistent self-consciousness. By such a theory the moral regulation of the universe is reduced from action according to good

[1] ἐπιστήμη ἣ θεωρεῖ τὸ ὂν ᾗ ὄν.—Aristotle, *Metaphysics*, 1003 a 21.

conceived as, in its fullness, a personal relationship, to the plane of efficient causation, which is the plane of the material *par excellence*. For it would be no unfair description of the material world to speak of it as, in itself, the sphere of efficient causation, while the distinctive feature of life, more profoundly of mind, and essentially of spirit, is determination not by any impulsion of force but by the attraction of, and responsiveness to, apparent good.

It may safely be said that one ground for the hope of Christianity that it may make good its claim to be the true faith lies in the fact that it is the most avowedly materialist of all the great religions. It affords an expectation that it may be able to control the material, precisely because it does not ignore it or deny it, but roundly asserts alike the reality of matter and its subordination. Its own most central saying is: "The Word was made flesh", where the last term was, no doubt, chosen because of its specially materialistic associations. By the very nature of its central doctrine Christianity is committed to a belief in the ultimate significance of the historical process, and in the reality of matter and its place in the divine scheme.

Now if spirit is real in our experience at all, it is real by the effectiveness of the control which it exercises. This is true of each higher grade as it supervenes upon that lower grade which supplies the indispensible condition of its actualisation. The higher can only exist by means of the lower; but, far from being controlled by that lower, takes control of it. The life of the plant subsists by means of chemical energy absorbed from the soil, but turns this to its own functions. In the animal organism much that occurs belongs to the realms of physics and chemistry; the vegetable principle is also active; but the organism as a whole is animal, and the principle of life at the animal grade takes charge of these other processes, neither dispensing with them nor superseding them, but making them subordinate to its own proper functions. So it is, once more, with the human being; the organism that is called a man obeys the laws of physics and chemistry and is fitly studied by biology, zoology and physiology; yet its organic principle of unity—what Thornton calls its *highest law of being*[1]—is spiritual. It may be true of any—or every—particular man that in fact he behaves for the most part exactly as he would if he had no spiritual capacity. But even when this is true of his acts, it is not true of his action in doing them. When a being capable of spiritual discrimination blindly obeys an appetite, this is not, as moral conduct, identical with obedience to the same appetite on the part of an animal which has no power of spiritual discrimination. In the animal it is natural, even when to human taste it is distressing; in the man it is evidence of defect when it is not proof of depravity. In that distinction is implicit the naturally controlling efficacy of spirit wherever it is present at all.

From this it follows that *in so far as the universe is a single system, its "highest principle of unity" must be sought in spirit.* This is not merely an affirmation that in the hierarchy of modes of being the spiritual is to be recognised as having some pre-eminence of honour. It is a claim that where spirit exists it exercises control, so that if, as we have tried to establish, there are not only sporadic spirits active by means of particular organisms, but the whole cosmic system exists by the will of a Creative Spirit, then in all things that Creative Spirit exercises control, and all other entities are truly intelligible and explicable only by reference to Him. He is *παντοκράτωρ*. The whole universe is the expression of His will. But if we go so far as this we must go further. For we have seen that History is not adequately represented as "the moving image of eternity". The Eternal is self-expressed in History; but this act of self-expression is not epiphenomenal to the Eternal—a mere by-product of its own unmoved perfection. The

[1] *Op. cit.* p. 37 and then *passim.*

Eternal fulfils itself in its historical self-expression, so that if this were abolished, it would in its own nature be other than it is. The relation is not one of complete, or approximately complete, reciprocity; yet it is not one of subservience on the one side and detachment on the other. In terms of dependence for actual existence there is complete disparity, for the historical depends on the eternal for its very existence, and the eternal does not, *for its existence*, in the smallest degree depend on the historical. But the values found in the historical, and pre-eminently those found in that sphere by Christianity, are such as belong essentially to the eternal. If the eternal is indifferent to these, a cleavage of the totality of things is effected so complete as to make the world unintelligible. The historical is of significance and importance to the eternal inasmuch as the eternal is such as to create it, so that if it were not created that would prove the eternal to be other than, in the light of its creativity, it is known to be. The relationship is one which we can only hope to understand in part, and then only if we take alternately the two standpoints so far as we are able. Here is the world, existing as a historical process. Both general consideration of Process as such, and observation of this actual process in particular, point to an eternal ground of the process as its only possible explanation. This ground, we have found, must be spiritual; in all positive content of the term "personal" it must be personal; it must be the living God. Upon God the world depends for its existence; in no sense does God depend upon the world for His existence. But when we turn to the nature of the world as we know it, with its aspirations and heroisms, its beauty and its love, we must needs say that these have value for God as the only alternative to saying that God is inadequate, even inferior, to the world which has proceeded from His creative act; and if it were true that the world, though dependent on Him for its existence, was superior to Him in its nature, it would follow that the principle introduced as explanation of the world (the eternal or God) accounts for it only by some form of efficient causation; and this can never account for that determination by good which we know to exist. In other words, the explanatory principle would cease to explain. But if God made the world, being determined thereto by good (which is His own nature, so that for Him self-determination and determination by the good are identical), then He must prize what is good in it; its beauty and its love must be dear to Him; so that the spiritual richness of His eternal being is in some measure constituted by the moral achievements of His temporal creatures. To put the matter once more in the terms of Christian belief; the death and resurrection of Christ did not cause God to be after their occurrence what He was not before, but neither are those events without meaning and value for His eternal being. On the contrary, His eternal being, in being what it is, requires self-expression in those events, and while the events make no difference in the quality of love which is expressed in them, yet the activity of the expression is a part of the fullness of the eternal love. Thus we may truly say that the glory of God is not only revealed in, but actually in part consists in, the death and resurrection of Christ. This is the more true if the Christian interpretation of the events be adopted, but it is also true on a purely humanitarian hypothesis; and it is true concerning the death even if the historical resurrection be doubted or denied, though of course the significance of the one event alone is not the same as that of the two together.

It is clear that, as in Lecture XVII, we are trying to frame a conception which is not identical with any of the commonly offered suggestions concerning the relation of the eternal and the historical, and are now extending its application so as to include the relation of the spiritual and material. It is not simply the relation of ground and consequent, nor of cause and effect, nor of thought and expression, nor of purpose and instrument, nor of end and means; but it is all of these at once. We need for it another name; and there is in some religious traditions an element which is, in the belief of adherents of those religions, so close akin to what we want that we may most suitably call this conception of the relation of the eternal to history, of spirit to matter, the sacramental conception.

No doubt the term "sacrament" covers a wide diversity of meaning; but there is always a central core which is found in all interpretations of supposed sacraments. If we attend to this, and to some at least of the diverse views which it holds together by their relationship to itself, we may find that we have in familiar religious experience exactly what is wanted as a clue to our metaphysical problem. The interpretation of sacraments is notoriously a focus of contention among rival schools of theology. But we are only concerned with two points, on one of which there is no disagreement, and the other of which is supremely valued by those who find most value in sacraments. The first is that, within the sacramental scheme or order, the outward and visible sign is a necessary means for conveyance of the inward and spiritual grace, but has its whole significance in that function. It is not maintained that the spiritual grace cannot be imparted in any other way; but it is universally agreed that when it is otherwise conveyed—as for example through instruction, through personal influence, or through mystic rapture—there is no sacrament. What in that case is the special importance of sacraments is a question for the dogmatic rather than for the natural theologian. But the use of sacramental rites is a common feature of human religion; it is especially prominent in Christianity; and, whatever may be thought about the comparative merits of sacramental and non-sacramental religion, it is agreed that if there is to be a sacrament there must be the material sign. We are confronted therefore with this fact: in many forms of religion, and conspicuously in the most extensive tradition of Christianity, prominence is given to rites in which the spiritual and the material are intimately intertwined. That proves nothing; but for those who on other grounds expect to find in religion guidance for the ultimate interpretation of reality it is suggestive.

Further, among those traditions which give most prominence to sacraments in the ordering of religious practice, the sacramental rite is regarded as effectual *ex opere operato*. This is said, of course, not by way of contrast with the doctrine that the benefit of the sacrament is received by faith alone, for in one form or another this is again common ground;[1] it is said in contrast with any notion that the sacrament is effective *ex opere operantis* or through the personality of the administrant, though it is required that he have the intention to "do what the Church does".

There is here an assertion—not indeed of identity, as that word is commonly understood—but of the unity of matter and spirit which is even more suggestive than the intimate relationship between them which is asserted by all use of sacraments whatsoever. But those who have clung to this conception as an interpretation of sacramental experience as an element of worship have seldom used it as a clue to the general interpretation of the universe. It is precisely this that we desire to suggest, always bearing in mind the constant and irreducible difference between man's utilisation of existent matter and God's creation of matter *ab initio*.

A sacrament, regarded as effective *ex opere operato* in

[1] The Roman Catholic doctrine is that grace is conveyed to those who put no bar to its entry—*non ponentibus obicem* (Tridentine Canon VI). Impenitence, lack of faith or uncharity would be such a bar. Other traditions hold that a positive appropriation by faith is requisite; but many among these latter would also hold that a general devout intention and reliance upon the promise of Christ qualify the worshipper to receive grace, apart from any distinct consciousness of reception in the moment of the sacramental act. The difference between Roman Catholic and Evangelical teaching at this point is therefore far less than is often supposed. The former says: the sacramental act is effective for you unless you hinder it by (*e.g.*) lack of faith; the latter says, if you have faith, the sacramental act is effective for you, while, if you have none, it is not.

the sense explained, is not regarded as only or chiefly a stimulus to a psychological process issuing in some spiritual apprehension; it is this, but it is also an actual conveyance of spiritual meaning and power by a material process. We find a real analogy to this in the familiar use of written or spoken language, when this takes the form of poetry. A word is in itself only a noise or a set of marks on paper. But by a social convention it is secured that, when one man speaks or writes a word, another apprehends his meaning. In so far as the word only denotes some object, this is an instance of sheer occasionalism operating by means of a convention. The meaning here is not *in* the word at all. It is first in the mind of the speaker, and then, on the occasion of his utterance, it is also in the mind of the hearer. But when a poet takes words as his instruments, that account of the matter becomes inadequate. The very sound of the words is now part of the meaning; that meaning can never be apprehended or recovered except by re-hearing physically or in imagination the actual sound of the words. It is not the sound apart from the meaning which exercises the magic spell; it would not exercise any such spell upon a person ignorant of the language used. Nor is it the meaning apart from the sound, for that simply does not exist; in the divorce of one from the other the meaning vanishes away. It exists as significant form or sound. Here we are near to a sacrament; but the sound that is thus filled with spiritual quality remains (for the physicist) no more than a movement of inorganic particles. The conferring of spiritual quality upon inorganic matter, of which the bare possibility is sometimes denied, is one of the commonest experiences of life; the phrase is almost a definition of Art.

But to convey meaning is not to convey the self. A sacrament is something more than a divine poem, because it conveys (as is believed by those who make use of it) not only God's meaning to the mind, but God Himself to the whole person of the worshipper. No doubt it is "Grace" which is commonly spoken of as thus conveyed; but Grace is not something other than God, imparted by Him; it is the very Love of God (which is Himself) approaching and seeking entry to the soul of man. How can this intimately spiritual process be mediated by a material rite *ex opere operato*? We here come to a point where the sacraments of religion are unique. The finite spirit can impart his thought through a physical, even an inorganic, medium; he cannot so impart himself. But the divine spirit can so impart Himself, because He is the omnipresent. All things are present to Him, and are what they are by His creative will. In and through all of them He is accessible; there is therefore no contradiction in the supposition that in and through certain physical elements, by methods which He has chosen because of their appropriateness to our psycho-physical nature, He renders Himself in a peculiar degree accessible to those who seek Him through such media. Whether in fact He does this, only specific experience can decide—not, indeed, the momentary experience of the individual worshipper, but the whole experience of the adherents of a religion which finds in sacramental worship its focal points.

We are not now concerned to justify the religious use of sacraments, still less the particular sacraments of any positive religion, but only to vindicate the principle on which belief in sacraments reposes, in order that we may be secure in using it as a clue to the understanding of the relation of spirit to matter in the universe. From two sides there is a constant pressure to separate these two as widely as possible. From the scientific side pressure is exerted by the proper and necessary insistence that physical phenomena shall be accounted for in physical categories, and that reference to spirit—to determination by the good rather than by efficient causes—shall be excluded from physical enquiry. If this demand of the scientist be pushed to the uttermost, spirit is made to appear an alien sojourner in this material world, and its connexion with its physical counterpart is a mystery not only unsolved but demonstrably insoluble. From the religious side there is constant pressure to keep the spiritual free from what is felt to be the contamination of the material world, which is regarded as in some way gross and unworthy. Because the life of the spirit is characterised by determination by the good, the physical world of mechanical forces and chemical compounds is regarded as merely alien from it. But this results, as logic would lead us to anticipate and history proves to be the fact, in leaving the physical to go its own way unchecked by spirit, so that the vaunted spiritual exaltation has its counterpart in bodily immorality. In either case the unity of man's life is broken; the material world, with all man's economic activity, becomes a happy hunting-ground for uncurbed acquisitiveness, and religion becomes a refined occupation for the leisure of the mystical. *It is in the sacramental view of the universe, both of its material and of its spiritual elements, that there is given hope of making human both politics and economics and of making effectual both faith and love.*

It is to such a view that our whole course of enquiry has been leading us; and it is such a view which affords the strongest hope for the continuance in reality and power of religious faith and practice.

(1) In the view which we have outlined, the transition from the material to the spiritual is no more sudden and abrupt than other transitions in the course of cosmic history. Perhaps the inorganic is potentially spiritual; but if it is purely inorganic, it is determined wholly from without, contributing to its own reaction only inertia. At a certain stage of complexity of organisation, elementary consciousness shows itself in the fact of self-motion. Already the basis of spiritual life is present; for already there is in some measure determination by the good. At first this "good" is fixed. There are not yet

"free ideas" by means of which the fully mental organism exercises comparison of one good with another. But it is impossible to say of any organism capable of either desire or affection that at some one point the stage of "free ideas" is reached. In the psycho-physical organism of man that stage is already established. Man can form ideas drawn from his experience, and attend to them in detachment from the experience which gave rise to them. He can unite them in new combinations of which experience gives no illustration. He can work upon his environment to ensure that it shall in future afford illustrations of those combinations of elements which hitherto have existed only in his thought. He can compare the good offered by circumstance with a good apprehended only in idea, and can deliberately forgo the former in hope of thereby making actual the latter. All this is very far from the reaction of mere inertia, or of the most elementary stages of life. Yet it is one with them, and they are to be understood as potentialities of this which has proceeded from them. The magnitude of the difference is both evident and important; but the continuity need not be denied on that account. As the flower turns to the sun, or the dog to his master, so the soul turns to God. *My consciousness is not something else within the entire organism which is myself, taking note of the relations of that organism to its environment; my consciousness is itself that organism, being not only physical but psycho-physical, as related to its environment, namely to the universe of which it is a part, though as the spiritual elements in the organism become predominant, the concomitant physical relations become relatively less important and may finally drop away.*

(2) There is reason to think that this conception of the intimate unity of spirit and matter affords the chief hope of securing for the spiritual an effective control over matter throughout any period now worth considering. This may surprise those who recognise it as closely akin to the so-called Dialectical Materialism of Marx,

Engels and Lenin. But a close examination of this Dialectical Materialism, strongly distinguished as it is by its upholders from Mechanistic Materialism, suggests that its own dialectic will destroy its character as materialist, except in so far as it is opposed to the idealistic view of matter as existing only "for mind". Dialectical Materialism so-called, asserts the temporal priority of matter, as we have been led to do; it regards mind as appearing within matter, as we have done; it asserts that mind, so appearing, acts by its own principles, which are not reducible to the categories of physics and chemistry; while mind is regarded as originating in, and out of, what is material, it is not itself regarded as identical with matter. What is postulated by this view is not an identity of mind and matter, but a unity of mind and matter; to present mind and matter as identical is condemned as Mechanistic Materialism.

But so soon as the distinctive nature of mind is admitted, nothing can check its predominance, just because it is moved from within by appreciation of apparent good (its own self or kin presented to it from without) and not only from without by conquest of its inertia. There are those who seek to represent matter itself as *quasi* spiritual, using for this purpose the notion expressed by Smuts as follows:

"The old, contradictory notion of dead matter as the vehicle of life must disappear in the light of our new knowledge. The difference between matter and life is no longer measured by the distance between an absolute passivity on the one hand and activity on the other—a distance so great as to constitute an impassable gulf in thought. The difference between them is merely a difference in the character of their activities. So far from matter being pure inertia or passivity, it is in reality a mass of seething, palpitating energies and activities. Its very dead weight simply means the push of inner activities. Its inertia, which is apparently its most distinctive quality, and has been consecrated by Newton in his first Law, has received its deathblow at the hands of Einstein. From the new point of view the inertia of matter is simply the result of the movements of

Nature's internal energies: its apparent passivity is merely the other side of its real activity".[1]

To interpret matter as more akin to life and mind than it had been recognised to be, certainly does not strengthen the case for materialism as a philosophy which denies the independence or the supremacy of mind. But it is hardly conceivable that the revision of Physics will go so far as to assert that the vagaries of electrons are due to appreciation of apparent good on the part of the electrons, or in other words to their own choice. Till that assertion is made, the essential difference between mind and matter remains. It may be a difference of mode in the activity of one entity; indeed that view seems more probable than one which asserts either the existence of a "mind-stuff" or the activity of thought apart from anything which thinks. But the difference remains—the difference between action in response to stimuli without any contribution except inertia, and action initiated by appetitive appreciation of presented or imagined good.

We have seen reason to hold, first, that experience manifestly contains instances of such determination by good; *κινεῖ ὡς ἐρώμενον*—"It initiates movement as does an object of desire"—is a perfectly familiar fact of experience. We have further seen reason to hold that when once the actual operation of this principle in experience has been recognised, it is impossible to prevent its attaining, hypothetically at least, the status of a pretender to the supreme place in the universe. From Plato's assertion that the Idea of Good is the source alike of existence and of knowledge, or (as some modern philosophers would prefer to say) of both the objective and the subjective elements in experience, to the Hebrew doctrine of creation by the living God, and the Christian incorporation of both in the doctrine of the Divine Trinity, we find the successful claim of this principle to be regarded as supplying the ultimate

[1] J. C. Smuts, *Holism and Evolution*, p. 51.

explanation of the universe. If Materialism once becomes Dialectical, it is doomed as Materialism; its own dialectic will transform it into Theism.

But not into Idealism, which we regard as an error due to the effort to construct philosophy as a theory of cognition rather than as a theory of living experience. No doubt it is true that a study of knowledge in isolation easily leads to Idealism; for what is then studied is the relation of the apprehending mind to its own activity of apprehension. The starting-point is the mind and its thoughts or ideas. The inference to Idealism is most nearly inevitable when the ideas in question are the elaborate intellectual constructions of modern science, which it is impossible to verify by direct experience. But such isolated departmental enquiries do not represent the impact of the data of experience as a whole upon the enquiring mind. So soon as the whole range of living experience is allowed to exercise its influence upon the theory which is to articulate it, mind is seen as above all an element in the cosmos distinguished by its capacity to apprehend and progressively to understand the process within which, and out of which, it arises. In the phrase of Whitehead already quoted, "consciousness presupposes experience, and not experience consciousness".[1] But if the Process of the cosmos produces beings capable of understanding and evaluating the cosmos, that tells us, as has been repeatedly urged, a great deal about the process itself. The more deeply mind is seen to be rooted in nature —in matter if you like—the more manifestly is it impossible to account for nature or matter in any other terms than those of mind; and so soon as that enterprise is attempted, mind increasingly discloses itself as qualified to be the ultimate ground of all things.[2] But we must not, in our concern for the conclusion, ignore the course of argument which leads us to this result; it is an argument based on investigation of nature regarded

[1] *Process and Reality*, p. 68; cf. *supra*, p. 112.

[2] Cf. Lecture X.

at first as material. *We reach a conviction of the independence and the supremacy of mind or spirit; we do not reach a conviction of the non-existence of matter. On the contrary, it is from an assertion of the reality of matter that we reach our conviction of the supremacy of spirit.* It is from the strong assertion of both convictions together—of the reality of matter and of the supremacy of spirit—that we are led to enquire whether there is any further illumination to be gained by consideration of that element in some religions wherein the material and the spiritual are inseparably conjoined.

Now a sacrament, as understood by those who prize sacraments most highly, is an instance of a very definite and special relationship of spirit and matter. We have already distinguished it from mere conventional symbolism such as we find in ordinary speech or (more accurately) in nomenclature. We have also pointed to the less marked distinction which separates it from the "essential symbolism" of poetry.[1] It is a spiritual utilisation of a material object whereby a spiritual result is effected. Its operation is not independent of symbolism or of the psychological processes set in motion by symbols; but its operation and effectiveness does not consist in these. Indeed many of those who set special store by the sacramental mode of worship value it because of their belief that the efficacy of the sacramental rite is totally independent of any conscious apprehension or other form of spiritual experience at that time. When faith exists as a struggle to believe in spite of empirical and temperamental pressure to unbelief, when the whole life of feeling is dead, when nothing is left but stark loyalty to God as He is dimly and waveringly apprehended to be—then the sheer objectivity, even the express materialism, of a sacrament gives it a value that nothing else can have. And when faith revives its ardour, and feeling is once more aglow, when the activity of prayers spoken and praises sung is

[1] See above, p. 484, and my *Mens Creatrix*, pp. 129-134.

again a natural expression of devotion, the rite which is believed to have retained its efficacy when all else failed becomes a focus of grateful adoration to the God who therein offered grace—that is, His love in action—to a soul that could receive Him in no other way. All turns, of course, on the conviction that in the sacrament God acts, fulfilling His own promise. This distinguishes the sacrament from magic, of which the essence is that man through the rite puts compulsion on the god, while it also endows the sacrament with the virtue and potency which magic falsely claims to offer.

In the sacrament then the order of thought is spirit first and spirit last, with matter as the effectual expression or symbolic instrument of spirit. That is the formula which we suggest as an articulation of the essential relations of spirit and matter in the universe. Our enquiry starts from matter, or at least from physical process. But that process produces centres of spiritual life, which, once manifested, displays its true nature as logical *prius* as well as temporal resultant. Consequently we reach, from the consideration of the world as apprehended, and without any reference to the data of distinctive religious experience, the scheme familiar in the religious interpretation of the world: (*a*) God, supreme, and perfectly free to express Himself according to His own nature of perfect spirit; (*b*) the world, at first in its crudest material form of inorganic matter—or at least of matter not yet perceptibly or effectively organic; then organic matter exhibiting the activities of life; then mind directing vital activities by selection of appropriate means to an end fixed by its correspondence to the nature and needs of the organism; then mind forming free ideas, and thus becoming capable of self-determination in accordance with apparent good, making selection among ends presented by outward experience and ends held in thought and imagination as true ideals or principles of conduct; (*c*) the world, thus understood as a sphere of finite spirits self-expressed through their own physical organisms, now transformed into the Kingdom of God by the uniting of finite spirits in a fellowship which reproduces in the creature the love which is the essential being of the Creator. Thus we pass from God through the world of process and history to God. But God is God in the activity which sustains the process and directs the history. If He did not create He would still exist, for He is not dependent for existence on His creation. But if He did not create, He would not be what He is, for He is Creator.

Thus the view of the universe which I have called sacramental asserts the supremacy and absolute freedom of God; the reality of the physical world and its process as His creation; the vital significance of the material and temporal world to the eternal Spirit; and the spiritual issue of the process in a fellowship of the finite and time-enduring spirits in the infinite and eternal Spirit. Matter exists in full reality but at a secondary level. It is created by spirit—the Divine Spirit—to be the vehicle of spirit and the sphere of spirit's self-realisation in and through the activity of controlling it.

This conception does not only mean that a mind of sufficient insight can detect the activity of God in all that happens if it be seen in its true context and perspective, so that the sublimity of nature is an expression of the divine majesty, and its beauty of the divine artistry, and love's sacrifice (wherever it be offered) of the divine heroism. That is true and precious. But more than this is involved. The world, which is the self-expressive utterance of the Divine Word, becomes itself a true revelation, in which (as we saw[1]) what comes is not truth concerning God, but God Himself. This (as we also saw[2]) does not exclude the possibility of special revelations; rather it is the condition of that possibility. The spiritually sensitive mind can be in personal communion with God, in, and by means of, all its experience. It is probable that no adequately sensitive mind exists,

[1] See p. 306. [2] *Ibid.* 306.

and that all must deepen their insight by periods of adoring contemplation, which alternate with periods of activity inspired and guided by what is then apprehended. But the goal is to fuse action and worship into the continuous life of worshipful service; in the holy city which came down from God out of heaven the seer beheld no place of worship because the divine presence pervaded all its life.[1]

The significance of this conception from the side of the historical process we have tried already to adumbrate.[2] We must also attempt to grasp its significance, in what restricted fashion we may, from the side of the eternal and divine. One aspect at least of the Divine Glory is the triumphant self-sacrifice of love. This is God's very being—not perhaps its entirety, but truly a part of its essence. That fact determines the dominant issue of history, which is the prevailing and increasing supremacy of love in all its forms over self-centredness in all its forms—a supremacy both won and sustained by love's own method of self-sacrifice. This is the divine glory whereof the heaven and the earth are full. If heaven and earth did not contain this, it could not be the glory of God who is creator of earth and heaven. It is in and through being such as we find Him in the course of history at its greatest moments to be, that He is eternally love and joy and peace. Even to the eternal life of God His created universe is sacramental of Himself. If He had no creatures to redeem, or if He had not redeemed them, He would not be what He is. Neither does His historical achievement *make* Him eternally Redeemer, nor does His eternal redemptive love simply express itself in history while remaining unaffected. But each is what it is in and through the other, like spirit and matter in a sacramental rite, yet so that the eternal and spiritual is first and last, with the historical and material as its medium of self-actualisation.

The thought seems tangled. Yet I believe that is only

[1] Revelation xxi. 22. [2] In Lecture XVII.

because we are attempting the inevitable, yet impossible task of expressing in conceptual terms what is nothing less than life itself. Let us take an analogy from an enquiry apparently remote. The question has lately been revived whether thought most fitly precedes action, to determine its direction, or follows it, to account for what has occurred. If our whole position is sound we shall repudiate the implied dilemma. Thought and action, if separated from one another, are abstractions and falsifications; the real fact is active rational life; and this is best expressed in rational activity, where thought and conduct are inextricably united. The man of trained and disciplined mind spontaneously acts in relation to an emergency in a manner quite different from that adopted by the thoughtless or undisciplined man. He may not consciously think for a single moment about the situation; perhaps there is not time for thought; yet his action is rational, and he can, if desired, afterwards articulate its principles. Here the logical, if not also the temporal, order is thought first and thought last with physical movement as its mode not only of expression but of self-actualisation. This complete integration is not always attained; when it is lacking, the question whether thought or conduct takes precedence must be settled by circumstance. But action without understanding is likely to be misguided, and abstract thought in detachment from the detail of the concrete situation is sure to be misleading. Thought is most of all itself in and through the process of determining rational action in face of the complexity of a given situation.

So God, who is spirit, is His eternal self in and through the historical process of creating a world and winning it to union with Himself. His creation is sacramental of Himself to His creatures; but in effectively fulfilling that function it becomes sacramental of Him to Himself—the means whereby He is eternally that which eternally He is.

LECTURE XX

THE HUNGER OF NATURAL RELIGION

At the outset of our enquiry we laid it down[1] that if Natural Theology is to be in any true sense scientific, it must regard as part of its data the content of the positive religions. It will accept no proposition on authority, however august the authority may be; but it will take note of the beliefs held by adherents of the positive religions, and especially by founders and leaders of those religions, as supplying evidence of what human religion actually is. We proceeded to outline the practical problem of Natural Religion or Theology, which arises from the inevitable and essentially wholesome tension that exists between the religious and the scientific habit of mind.[2] If the Natural Theologian is to know in any real sense the subject-matter of his study, he must know it from within by personal experience; that is, he must know it as a worshipper. Otherwise he will resemble a blind man who writes criticisms of the Royal Academy's Exhibition. But to worship is to surrender all faculties to the object of worship; it is totally incompatible with critical enquiry into the being and attributes of the object of worship. Yet critical enquiry is the essence of Natural Theology. The only solution seemed to lie in a deliberate alternation of interest, which is made possible for those who believe in God as the Creator, or even as the Immanent Principle, of the Universe; because for them even critical enquiry is enquiry into the ways and works of God, and surrender to God is surrender to Him whose activities they are studying in their scientific pursuits. Thus for them the alternation is at least within the life of

[1] Lecture I. [2] Lecture II.

religion itself and is not an alternation between religion and something else. For the fullest practice of some religions, and notably of the Christian religion, the two sides must be held together as closely as possible. An uncritical surrender will involve an unsanctified intellect; while an unsurrendered criticism will be incapable of worship. What is called for is the free movement of the mind within an environment that stimulates and supports and corresponds to its aspiration towards worship.

Having thus stated the method of enquiry and the outline of the problem, we considered various classical schemes offered by modern philosophers, and found reason to reject them all.[1] We found the source of their inadequacy to be an exclusive, or at best exaggerated, concentration of attention upon problems of cognition, resulting in an altogether undue exaltation of intellectual processes as the sole means of truly apprehending the world. This had led both to the mistaken idea that mathematics supplies the norm of real knowledge and to the whole set of errors associated with the term Idealism. In repudiating these we were led to a conception of thought as essentially dynamic, and consequently to the belief that the history of thought is itself the true discipline of the mind.[2] Following the dialectical implications of that belief, we endeavoured to sketch in outline the world as apprehended, and to determine the place of mind in relation to it.[3] We accepted the view presented alike by common sense and by modern science that the universe existed long before there were within it minds to apprehend it; that thought is in its historical origin a function of the physiological organism; and that, in Whitehead's words, "consciousness presupposes experience, not experience consciousness".

[1] Lecture III.

[2] Lecture IV. It is always to be remembered that Kant went far to supply what was needed when he added the *Critique of Practical Reason* and the *Critique of Judgment* to the *Critique of Pure Reason*.

[3] Lecture V.

Our starting-point is therefore, as has been stated,[1] nearer to Materialism than to Idealism. It is indeed closely allied to that Dialectical Materialism which Marx and Lenin adopted as the philosophical basis of Communism. This Dialectical Materialism is avowedly drawn from Hegel by a conscious inversion of the logical Dialectic which was his chief contribution to philosophical method. But Marx and Lenin, though insisting on the contrast between Dialectical and Mechanistic Materialism, and on the distinct reality of mind and its own processes, yet limit the activity of mind to reaction, according to those processes, to situations presented by the material order, so that mind is always secondary and dependent. We found on the contrary that the distinguishing feature of mind is its capacity for free ideas, and for directing its attention to those ideas apart from any material occasion for doing so.

Because of our insistence upon this point our method might fitly be named Dialectical Realism. For starting with a realist view of the physical universe we were led to consideration of the fact that the world-process gives rise to minds, which themselves are capable of free ideas; and this in turn led us forward to a position which in its positive content is almost identical with such an Idealism as that of Edward Caird or of Bernard Bosanquet, apart from the method of arriving at it. For after repudiating the priority of mind *qua* knowing subject as a precondition of the actuality of the objective world, we were led to reaffirm the priority of mind *qua* purposive as the only condition of the intelligibility of that same objective world.[2] Thus Realism becomes a basis for a spiritual interpretation of the universe, and the Materialism of our empirical starting-point is balanced by the uncompromising Theism of our conclusion.

It is the occurrence of Mind at all as an episode in the

[1] P. 198. [2] Lecture X.

objective world-process which supplies to our Realism its dialectical impulse and leads to a theistic interpretation of it. But this result is rendered the more inevitable by consideration of the most characteristic activities of mind—its search for Truth, its creation and appreciation of Beauty, its consciousness of obligation. Each of these is found to reinforce the dialectical argument that carries us from bare existence to the living God.[1] Still more is this secured by the freedom of mind over against "the whole might of Nature",[2] and its mastery of Time—a mastery achieved in principle by man, yet never so established as to make him completely, in this life at least, a partner in God's Eternity.[3]

It is in this realm of Truth, Beauty and Goodness, of Freedom and Eternity, that the life of religion has its being. Our task in this closing Lecture is to consider whether there is any consummation to which our consideration of that life of religion points, and whether the indications provided offer any clear outline of such a consummation. We have seen that because our argument leads us to belief in a living God, it also of necessity leads to the possibility, and even to the high probability, of specific acts of divine self-revelation.[4] We considered the mode of such revelation and the relation of the spiritual authority grounded in it to the autonomy of the spiritual life and the individuality of religious experience.[5] We saw that the mode of revelation congruous with all that we had learnt concerning God consisted in a coincidence of divinely guided events with minds divinely illuminated to apprehend those events, so that there would be no "revealed truths", but there would be "truths of revelation". The essential revelation is an act of God apprehended in a complete living experience, in which subjective and objective factors are both active; it is not capable of isolation from that experience, and is only renewed so

[1] Lectures VI and VII. [2] Lecture VIII. [3] Lecture IX.
[4] Lecture XI. [5] Lectures XII and XIII.

far as the experience itself is recovered or renewed. Sacred writings and authoritative formulae are not themselves the substance or reality of revelation. That is always the living God Himself, and nothing less or other. But sacred writings and authoritative formulae may contain the record of the divine act which actually is the revelation, and point the way to recovery or renewal of the experience in which it is apprehended. Thus for a Christian the Nicene Creed is not an object of faith, but a formulation of a faith of which the object is God revealed in Christ. Nor is the Creed itself a revelation. It is a formulation of inferences drawn from revelation. The revelation (on this view) is Christ Himself as apprehended by minds spiritually enlightened to that end. Therefore no creed is in principle irreformable even though we may believe with confidence that every new enquiry will lead in the long run to the reaffirmation of the creeds which have won acceptance in the past. There is no disloyalty to an acknowledged revelation in the enquiry whether its contents may not be more accurately, or more usefully, formulated than hitherto. The revelation is received in a living experience; all doctrines are inferences drawn from that revelation in the context provided by the rest of experience; and their spiritual value is not in themselves; it is in the directions which they offer for recovering the experience from which they spring.

At this point, however, the even movement of our argument was disturbed, as the movement of any Theistic argument is bound to be disturbed, by the recognition of Evil as an overshadowing fact in the world as known to us.

Our earlier consideration of Freedom[1] had led us to the conception of it as determination by "apparent good"—good being understood as that in which the mind (or at a lower stage the organism) finds that which in one way or another is akin to or harmonises with

[1] In Lecture IX.

itself. At the animal level, if we rightly estimate it, there is scarcely more than appetition; but the principle of determination is even then different from that of efficient causation as ordinarily understood. As consciousness develops into mind with its free ideas, choice becomes possible, not only as between means to a fixed end (such as the satisfaction of an appetite) but between alternative and incompatible ends (as between duty and pleasure). Only at this stage is there real freedom; and that freedom is not any kind of indeterminacy, but is self-determination in accordance with apparent good. That the finite mind, rooted as it is in a physiological organism, should at first find its apparent good in what gratifies itself and brings comfort to the organism is "too probable not to happen", though not strictly necessary; for it is possible without contradiction to conceive a mind which from the outset chose the general good as its own. Inasmuch as finitude does not necessarily involve self-centredness, it cannot be said that the very principle of the actual creation involved sin; on the other hand, inasmuch as it was "too probable not to happen", we must admit, or rather affirm, that God accepted the occurrence of evil as a consequence of the principle of creation which He adopted and that therefore its occurrence falls within, and not outside, the divine plan. No doubt the evil is in a most true sense contrary to God's will; for it is the taking by a finite will of its own way in preference to God's. Yet it must be regarded as falling within the divine purpose that finite spirits should make choices contrary to that purpose. No man who chooses evil can justly plead—"God willed me so to choose", for the essence of his evil choice is that it is a rejection of God's will for him. But he can plead, and his moral health depends upon his recognising, that God has made him and all men such that if they follow their own apparent good without reference to God, they will act contrary to God's will and to their own real good. This is, we have suggested, the vital truth and importance of Original Sin.[1]

This situation presents a whole complex of problems; but as usual they can be classified under the two heads—the theoretical and the practical; the two groups of problems, however, vitally affect each other. The theoretical group is concerned with the point at which the self-centredness of the finite being begins to constitute evil. Is it already evil at the level of the purely physiological organism? Is it, for example, a real evil that animals should prey upon each other? Or does it only begin to be evil where there is at least some consciousness of alternative ends—so that there is a rudimentary recognition of Good and Evil as principles? Most of us will hold that the suffering of the animal world is evil, though whether it implies the presence of even potentially moral evil is debatable. Certainly it is at this level that the occurrence of evil is, on a theistic hypothesis, most difficult to explain. We can offer some explanation of evil at the human level, whether or not it seems to be adequate. But unless or until we can either enter more fully into the consciousness of animals, or else trace more surely the continuity of life from the animal to the human level, it seems impossible to see how the Divine Goodness can make of animal suffering a means to its own self-expression. If indeed there be close continuity between the evolutionary stages, it may be possible to show that the conditions which involve animal suffering are those which also at the human level give occasion for such virtues as fortitude, so that the justification of human suffering may be held to cover also by implication the suffering of animals. Apart from that hope, the utmost open to us is to say that, according to all the evidence, the life of the animal creation is on the whole happy, and that for creatures who live in the present, even great pain at one time would not dim the pleasure felt at another time. On balance, animal life is good.

[1] Lecture XIV.

That is something; but it does not wholly satisfy the demands of a conviction that the world is the creation of Almighty Goodness. That conviction impels us to enquire, not whether the world, or any part of it, is good on the whole, but why there should be in it any evil at all. The fact that this question arises below the human level, and arises there in its most unanswerable form, has driven some to the speculation of a "Fall" before the Creation, or of a "World-Soul" which has "fallen", or (by a special application of Berkeleyan principles) of an infection in the world due to the fallen state of the human minds whose perception of it is the ground of its being. But none of these really helps us. It is still true that the thing has happened, and is real, in God's world. To attribute it, by whatever device, to the "free" action of a spiritual being does not solve the problem unless we regard "free will" as an absolute source of initiation; and that leads to a dualism which doctrinally is heresy and philosophically is nonsense. Why did this will choose evil? If for no reason, the moral life is reduced to chance and destroyed. If for some reason, then we must ask why it was so constituted as to find that reason persuasive. Here is our dilemma: freedom, if it means indeterminacy, reduces life to chance and chaos, and thus abolishes the foundations of morality; freedom, if it means self-determination, leads to the question why is the self such as to determine itself thus?—and the answer must be sought in the purpose of the Creator. Shelve the responsibility for human evil on to Satan if you will; personally I believe he exists and that a large share of that responsibility belongs to him and to subordinate evil spirits. But still you have not escaped the ultimate attribution of evil to the purpose of God, unless you so interpret the freedom of Satan as to make nonsense of him and of all that his existence might help us to understand. We have still to ask, Why is the devil wicked?[1]

[1] Of course he cannot be *purely* evil; such a being could not exist.

If there is to be any solution of this whole problem for our minds it must be sought at the level of our own experience. Whatever considerations we find to help us there may be capable of application to the stages which precede and condition the human. We have offered the only suggestion that seemed capable of accounting for the facts. We have now to ask on what conditions it may be capable of also explaining them as falling within the purpose of a God unlimited in goodness and in power. Our suggestion was as follows.[1] There is throughout the world a system of interrelations, such that each separate entity affects, and is affected by, all other things. To each entity, therefore, every other entity makes a difference. As consciousness arises, this is one of the facts of which it becomes aware, and one of the main factors determining its guidance of its own organism in each case. So far, this addition of consciousness to the scheme of things only makes more harmonious the interrelations which it observes, by securing a more perfect adaptability of reaction on the part of the organism. But when consciousness is developed to the stage fitly called "mind", it discovers in the relations between its organism and the environment an object of distinct contemplation. Mind is now no longer an observer of a given system of relations, within which it secures a more harmonious adjustment; but by use of its capacity for free ideas, it conceives situations for its organism which do not exist, and directs the energies of the organism towards bringing these into existence. Thus are initiated moral action and responsibility, art, science and every form of deliberate progress. In principle, the mind could, from the outset, devote itself and its great capacity for free ideas to the yet greater perfection of adjustment within the system of interrelations which it finds. But its range at first is very narrow, even as compared with that extremely limited scope which it has in ourselves. It is to be expected that

[1] See Lectures XIV. and XV.

it should start, not with the system as a whole, but with the organism in which it is found, and serve the comfort and convenience of that organism. Its vision, which it seeks to actualise, is not that of a perfect fellowship, but that of its own organism more powerful, more effective in satisfaction of its desires. Thus the whole process of consciously guided action begins in self-centredness. Will, so soon as it appears, is distorted from what alone would bring peace to itself or harmony to the society of wills. It is ego-centric—and so are its fellows in that society. Even their co-operation is prompted in part by antagonism against others like themselves. Hence civilisation and culture—which might be, and aspire to be, the expression of the Commonwealth of Value—are in actual fact riddled with selfishness and enmity; love and beauty are stained with lust; and "all our righteousnesses are as filthy rags".

This is the source of the paradox of man's moral and spiritual life. Its corruption has its seat in the highest part of his nature, the part that controls the whole, the "principle of unity" in the complex organism of his personality. By the interaction of all the several self-centred wills the vast fabric of human evil is built up; but the source of that evil is also the only source in himself of man's highest hope and highest achievement. Consequently he can never either grow, or lift himself, out of this entanglement of sin. Most truly he is "born in sin" and is a "child of wrath". His science, which calls in its own interest for the widest fellowship of co-operation, he uses in the service of his enmities and so destroys the basis of that fellowship. His civilisation, which creates the State as a controller of force in the service of law in order to prevent the lawless use of force, becomes corrupt through the need to exercise force at all (which is always, as far as it goes, a confession of love's failure when it is not a repudiation of love), so that the State itself is continually guilty, as always in entry as a sovereign into war,[1] of treason to its own function.

Yet these fruits of man's self-consciousness, his science and his politics, in spite of all the corruption in them which flows from the corruption of their source, are necessary, and even good. The man who thinks he has found some higher principle of life—perhaps a divine revelation—cannot ignore them or repudiate them. They are the very arena wherein the divine purpose for him is to be fulfilled. And if he is to act in and through them, it must be according to the law of their actual being, even though this expresses their corruption as well as their true substance. Of course he must do this always with an eye to that true substance and using the laws of the actual as means to its transformation to the ideal. In this he must be ready for sacrifice, and must involve himself in ruin at the hands of the actual rather than abandon his service of the ideal; but he must not live in the actual as though it were already the ideal, for by such heroic but unpractical service of the ideal, the ideal is discredited rather than promoted. Neither by monasticism alone, wherein men seek to withdraw from the contamination of the world, nor by quixotic idealism alone, wherein men assume the actuality of the yet unrealised ideal, is the transformation of actual to ideal forwarded, though some have a special individual vocation to each of these forms of testimony to the ideal; but mostly the transformation is to be effected by those who, being in their own minds conformed to the ideal, act upon the actual according to its capacity of response. No doubt it often has a higher capacity of response than the cynic supposes, and the moral idealist is often tempted to cynicism by his very consciousness of the gulf between the ideal and the actual; but the fact that the principle may be misapplied does not make it unsound in itself.

[1] See the chapter on "The State in its External Relations" (also printed separately) in my *Christianity and the State.*

> The common problem, yours, mine, everyone's,
> Is not to fancy what were fair in life
> Provided it could be—but, finding first
> What may be, then find how to make it fair
> Up to our means: a very different thing!
> No abstract intellectual plan of life
> Quite irrespective of life's plainest laws,
> But one, a man, who is man and nothing more,
> May lead within a world which (by your leave)
> Is Rome or London, not Fool paradise.[1]

To which I only add that the idealist must be careful not to carry the actual through the next stage of its journey towards the ideal by methods which make further advance beyond that stage impossible.

But who is this moral idealist? And how did he come by his ideals? He is himself a product of the noble but corrupt actuality that he would transform. He has had, perhaps, some more penetrating glimpse than others into the nobility which is its true substance—the thing that it can be if all its parts fulfil their function as the parts that they are. But the corruption that is in it is also in him. His very project of reform, so far as it is his, has about it a priggish air, which may mean that despite his deeper insight he is in will more self-centred than those whom he seeks to transform.[2]

The apparent hopelessness of the practical problem so presented is vitally relevant to the theoretical enquiry. The whole theistic scheme is condemned unless it can provide from its own principles, or at least in accordance with them, a solution in outline of the problem of evil. Our account of evil, as we know it in ourselves, has traced it to the very existence of finite spirits. It may be that evil can be justified, that is—understood as a possible element within the purpose of a Creator who is wholly good—if these finite spirits are being fashioned into a fellowship of mutual love. For such a fellowship is realisation of the essential principle of good in its highest form, because in it each mind is

[1] Browning, *Bishop Blougram's Apology*.

[2] S. Matthew xxiii. 15.

finding itself in its object in the fullest sense. For an end so superlatively excellent, the evil incidental to the finitude which is its indispensable condition would not be too great a price to pay. With such a hope before us we, like St. Paul, may "reckon that the sufferings of this present time are not worthy to be compared with the glory that shall be revealed to us-ward".[1] And with that, perhaps, we could be content, if only the hope were sure. But this is, after all, an external justification of evil; for us with our limited capacities it is often as much as we can hope for that the price we pay for the satisfaction of our aspirations should not be excessive. But if the price is to be regarded as in any sense at all a deduction from the total good, it seems out of place in the designs of the Creator of all things. What is wanted is some ground for belief that the occurrence of the evil is an actual element in the total good. The point has been so well expressed by Bosanquet that I will quote his words. First he states a principle substantially identical with that which I have attempted to set forth above:[2]

> "It is not an imperfection in the supreme being, but an essential condition of his completeness, that his nature, summing up that of Reality, should go out into its other to seek the completion which in this case alone is absolutely found. The "other" in question can only be finite experience; and it is in and because of this, and qualified by it, that the Divine nature maintains its infinity. And, therefore, it may be said that the general form of self-sacrifice—the fundamental logical structure of Reality—is to be found here also, as everywhere. Not, of course, that the infinite being can lose and regain its perfection, but that the burden of the finite is inherently a part or rather an instrument of the self-completion of the infinite. The view is familiar. I can only plead that it loses all point if it is not taken in bitter earnest."[3]

This is followed by the claim that evil, at least in the form of pain, can be so confronted by him who experiences it that the whole is not a mere preponderance of satisfaction, but an enriched personality for which the

[1] Romans viii., 18

[2] In Lectures XVII. and XIX.

[3] Bosanquet, *The Principle of Individuality and Value*, pp. 243-244.

evil moment has made an indispensable contribution to the enrichment.

"The question cannot surely be how many moments of pain you have experienced, and whether you have had enough moments of pleasure, allowing for the intensities on each side, to outweigh them, but whether the experience has done its work, and returned you to yourself a complete or at least a completer being. So, it would seem, the problem should be stated about the universe. Not, if we could reckon up moments of equal pleasure and pain (to simplify the question by reducing it to a matter of counting), which of the two classes would be found to outnumber the other, but rather, is there reason for thinking that pain and finiteness are elements, playing a definite part in the whole, such that its completeness depends upon containing them?[1] . . .

"If our enquiry presses behind the details of the "scheme of salvation" and we ask, "But was the Fall itself a part of the scheme of salvation, and is a world with sin and atonement a better world than one without them?" . . . it would seem that for a Christianity which has the courage of its opinions the idea of victory involves the idea of the Fall, and the answer would be that the scheme of salvation, involving finiteness and sin, was essential to the nature of God and the perfection of the universe".[2]

That is our own contention. But to make it good, we must be able to show that the various forms of evil at least can be thus subordinated to a good which makes them contributors to its own excellence.[3] How far can this, in fact, be shown?

Evil is of three main kinds—Error, Suffering and Sin, and to a very great extent the two former are due to the last. But this does not remove the question whether suffering, even when caused by sin, can be an element in the fulfilment of the divine purpose. I do not propose at this stage to discuss the possible uses of suffering in detail. It is enough to say that it is the indispensable condition of fortitude, and that it is the most potent stimulus and bond of sympathy. Perhaps

[1] Bosanquet, *The Principle of Individuality and Value*, p. 245.

[2] *Ibid.* p. 254.

[3] I have attempted this at greater length in the chapter on 'The Problem of Evil' in *Mens Creatrix*.

if we were not so self-centred we should find in joy as strong a stimulus to sympathy as in pain or sorrow; it is certain that in fact we do not find it so.

> Mankind forsooth!
> Who sympathises with their general joy
> Foolish as undeserved? But pain—see God's
> Wisdom at work! . . .
> That brings flesh
> Triumphant from the bar whereto arraigned
> Soul quakes with reason. In the eye of God
> Pain may have purpose and be justified.
> Man's sense avails to only see, in pain,
> A hateful chance no man but would avert
> Or, failing, needs must pity.[1]

And in that pity, we must believe, is the purpose that God sees. Moreover, if it be argued that this is an accidental vindication, because we might have been so made as to be roused to sympathy by other means, at least it is true that without suffering there could be no fortitude; and the admiration of the natural human heart is ready to testify that a world with pain and fortitude is better, because nobler, than a world with neither.

When we turn to Sin, of which the essence is self-centredness, we note that the pre-condition of a fellowship of finite spirits united in mutual love is the existence of finite spirits; we saw that the creation of finite spirits did not necessitate their self-centredness, but rendered it so overwhelmingly probable that its occurrence must have been accepted as part of the whole plan. Can we understand this? We are in the realm of value-judgements, where, because the essence of those judgements is the discovery by mind of what answers to itself, we are subject to the varieties of individual temperament and character. But for myself I can confidently apply here the argument used concerning suffering. When love by its own sacrifice has converted self-centredness into love, there is an excellence, alike in the process and

[1] Browning, Mihrab Shah (in "Ferishtah's Fancies").

in the result, so great as to justify the self-centredness and all the welter of evil flowing from it. Even if we cannot say, as, for myself, I should not hesitate to say, that a sinful world redeemed by such a sacrifice as the Crucifixion of Christ, when interpreted as Christians interpret it,[1] is better than a world that had never sinned, at least we can and must say that it has a special excellence so great that the universe as a whole would be the poorer for lack of it. And this may be the nearest that we can come to the truth in the matter:

For God has other words for other worlds
But for this world, the Word of God is Christ...
So that for ever since, in minds of men
By some true instinct this life has survived
In a religious immemorial light,
Pre-eminent in one thing most of all;
The Man of Sorrows;—and the Cross of Christ
Is more to us than all His miracles.[2]

But to show that evil is capable of justification is not to show that it is justified; and nothing less than this is required. If evil were only a possibility, a possible justification might suffice. But evil is actual, and only an actual justification is relevant. God has so made the world that evil has occurred in it; then either He must subordinate that evil to a good enhanced by its occurrence, or else He is not God as we have learnt to understand that Name. Can it be said that, as He created it liable to evil, so also He created it such as to overcome the evil and transmute it into a subordinate element in perfect good?

The evil, we have seen, is a corruption of what can be, and partly is, good. There is selfishness in the world, but also love. There is greed in the world, but also self-discipline. There is avarice in the world, but also generosity. Actual human history and civilisation are carried forward and moulded by each of these. As Plato showed in the *Republic*, society with its conventions

[1] I have tried to express this in my own way in the chapter on that Atonement in *Christus Veritas*.

[2] Mrs. Hamilton King, *The Disciples*.

would indeed arise if men were purely selfish, for the misery of internecine competition would make them form a social contract "neither to commit nor to suffer injustice"; but society would also arise if men were purely unselfish, because they have different aptitudes and need one another for the enrichment of life. Actual society rests upon both principles at once; and moral progress consists in the increasing predominance of the "rational" element which seeks the common good over the element of pride which seeks individual advantage or pre-eminence. This progress is stimulated and maintained by both elements. Selfishness or Pride finds that it gains by methods of co-operation; and the rational element finds good in the fellowship of co-operation for its own sake. So, for both reasons, co-operation is developed. But the full joy of spiritual fellowship, which comes when each wholly trusts himself to others and all suspicions and anxieties are over, can never be fully known by any one whose motive for co-operation is still partly self-regarding in the evil sense, that is to say in the sense, not of regard for the self as one member of the community whose rights have an equal claim with those of others, but a regard for the self as "my" self, whose claims, even though only equal in principle to those of others, are yet of special and distinctive concern to "me". That motive will prohibit the self-abandonment which is the essence of that joy. Consequently the motive of love can never operate in full power so long as the motive of self-interest is active at all; for the fullness of its joy will remain unknown; while on the other side the self-regarding motive can only be extirpated in the abandonment of love, for indeed that abandonment and that extirpation are one thing. The entanglement is complete, and our whole theory is throttled by it. For we can only understand the world if it be the Creation of a God who is unlimited alike in goodness and in power; the world can only be that, if the evil which it undoubtedly contains is being transmuted into a constituent element of perfect good; but this can only be, if selfishness is so giving place to love that at last it will be altogether swallowed by love. And this, it seems, can never happen. The mere presence of selfishness in a soul is sufficient to prevent its love from growing to that perfection which would enable it to swallow up selfishness. The only road of human progress is barred. However far civilisation advances, it will still contain the self-regarding motive; and at any moment this may corrupt the whole to any degree. Some individual, or group or nation may acquire some means of power which makes them independent of all others and able to impose their will upon all others. If the measure of fellowship achieved has rested in any degree upon self-regard, such as fear of disaster if the fellowship be broken (as the League of Nations in some degree rests viciously and precariously on the fear of war) it is unlikely that such fellowship will survive the temptations which possession of this power implies. Only in genuine mutual love is there release from the evils of the world; and though men move in that direction, yet they are impelled partly by motives which will for ever prevent the approximation from culminating in identity. Communism seeks to create by force a world of mutual co-operation, believing that those who grow up in such a world will be freed from acquisitiveness and self-concern. But the effect will only be to direct these motives upon other objects than wealth, such as honour and influence. And the initial trust in force, which is always an appeal to self-concern, will stimulate the sentiment which it aims at destroying. Man cannot meet his own deepest need, nor find for himself release from his profoundest trouble. What he needs is not progress, but redemption. If the Kingdom of God is to come on earth, it must be because God first comes on earth Himself.

But is He not there already? Is not the world His creature? Is not His purpose its governing principle? Yes: all that is true. But since life in man, if at no earlier stage, has pursued an apparent good which is not its real good, it does not possess within itself the power to redirect its course. And if man cannot generate from within himself the means of his deliverance, that deliverance must come from without or not at all. Natural Theology cannot say whether in fact it has been offered; but it can enquire into the conditions to be fulfilled by any Gospel that promises deliverance. It can diagnose the disease and indicate the functions of the remedy.

The seat of the trouble is that freedom which consists in determination by "apparent good".[1] It is no mere question of animal impulses surviving into a stage where reason should take control but is not yet strong enough to do so. It is a corruption of that spiritual principle itself, whereby man chooses between ends. It is his glory that he is determined not by his own convenience, or interest, or pleasure, but by what he judges to be objectively good—the true counterpart of his real mind. This is his apparent good. But because he is self-centred he judges amiss, and what appears to his mind as good is not really good. For while a man's conduct is determined by his apparent good, his apparent good is determined by his character. Being such as he is, he judges to be good, and therefore pursues as good, what is not truly good. This is the ignorance which Socrates truly said was the essence of vice. But it is not a process of false argument; nor can it be removed, except in very small degree, by true argument. It is the judgement, not of intellect but of the whole personality—as every value judgement always is. But this does not mean that "character" and "apparent good", because mutually determining each other, are for ever unalterable. One main aim of education is to alter them. How, then, does the alteration come?

The appreciation of beauty offers our clearest illustration. I look back with some astonishment to a time

[1] See Lectures IX. and XV.

when I admired Doré's pictures more than Rembrandt's, and enjoyed Spohr's music more than Bach's. The cruder artists had an appeal to my primitive taste which was lacking in the others. But I submitted to authority enough to look at pictures and listen to compositions which others told me were good as well as those which appeared good to me. Imperceptibly a change took place. By intercourse with the better art I became sensitive to it and appreciative of it, and in the process lost most of my liking for the cruder and more sentimental expression. The real good began to appear good by the transformation of my taste under its influence.

Something similar happens to our moral judgements. We tend at first to admire rather self-conscious and strutting heroes, because that is the kind of heroism to which we ourselves aspire. It is our apparent good. And for a time such an ideal may satisfy. Then one day we see Bombastes Furioso confronted by some great gentleman, and the bubble is pricked. There is the latent capacity to admire true goodness and greatness, if only it be presented in a form that we can really see. In its most obvious sense, there is no truth whatever in the oft-repeated line—

> We needs must love the highest when we see it.

We quite easily hate it.[1] That saying is only true if "seeing" be interpreted in an almost mystical sense as "seeing it for what it is". If that is to happen, "the highest" must be presented in a form adapted to our capacity to see.

Broadly speaking it is true that the essence of all education, intellectual, moral and spiritual, is the intercourse of the less with the more matured mind or spirit. This may take place through the medium of books or works of art, or through direct personal communica-

[1] "Now have they both seen and hated both me and my Father."—St John xv. 24.

tions. All that is studied under the repulsive name of pedagogics is (so far as it is truly educational at all) a means of facilitating that intercourse. Moreover we do not live at one level. We have better and worse moments. Our growth in spirit very greatly depends upon the use which we make of our better moments. If at times when we are most capable of appreciating the really good—when the true good in some respect is also for us the apparent good—we give to it our attention and (so far as it is yet quickened in that direction) our affection also, the influence of such nourishment of the mind leads it to turn with distaste from what had appealed to it in its less exalted mood, and to become capable of an ever fuller appreciation of true good as it grows to spiritual maturity. In this process of growth there is, as we saw,[1] a steadily increasing detachment from self-centredness. The subjective element in the judgement of value is still present, but exerts less constraint. We pass to a more and more objective habit of mind.

This point is of importance both for theory and for practice. The organism, at the animal stage, seeks to adjust itself to its environment so as to secure pleasure, comfort and the satisfaction of appetite. In a certain sense it might be held that already in this adjustment there is Good or positive value. We have seen reason for holding that confusion is avoided if the use of those terms is postponed until the stage of self-conscious reflection is reached.[2] Between these two occurs the stage which Bergson regards as most decisive, where the organism, instead of adjusting itself to its environment, adjusts the environment to itself. Here the possibilities are indefinitely more numerous and there arises need for selection; this of itself involves the choice between aims or ends, which is at the same time made possible by the capacity for free ideas. That capacity, with the selection between ends which it facilitates,

[1] Lecture XV. [2] See Appendix A, pp. 162-165.

and to cope with which, presumably, it arises, marks the transition to a definitely moral and spiritual stage. If the end is fixed, and choice is only between a variety of means to it, there may be cleverness or stupidity, but no moral quality. So soon as the mind is able to entertain the idea of different ends, and proceeds to choose between them, it becomes a subject of moral predicates in accordance with its choice. But these predicates are determined, not by the degree of satisfaction received from the selected end, but by the quality of the end in which satisfaction is sought. Consequently we have here a different kind of judgement concerning the mutual adjustment of subject and environment from that which is found at the animal stage; and there is convenience in keeping the words Value and Good for this stage, of which the characteristic is that in it we have passed from the subjective judgement "This pleases me" to the objective judgement "I find this good".

We do not thus escape from subjectivism all at once or completely. For to say "I find this good" is to say "My mind finds here the principle of its own being". Of course this does not mean that my mind finds only an expression of that principle similar to its own; if that were so, there would be "liking" but no admiration. What the mind seeks in Truth and Beauty and Goodness or Love is a more perfect expression of the principle of its being than it can be, or provide, in itself. So far there is truth in Emerson's dictum, "I the imperfect adore my own perfect".[1] But the hierarchy of values depends, in part at least, upon the relative importance of the subjective reference in each value-judgement. At the lower level, self or the subject plays a great part. Where a man chooses comfort as his "good" he is in fact choosing to remain at the animal level when he has capacity for more. Where acquisition of wealth is taken as a chief good, we have left the animal level, but

[1] Essay on *The Over Soul*: last paragraph.

reference is still predominantly to the self; for the desire to create wealth for others to possess and enjoy is not acquisitiveness, and the aim here sought is not really acquisition of wealth but the benefit of friends procured thereby. All such self-centred value judgements are non-social in essence and anti-social in effect; for they bring men into rivalry and enmity with one another.

When we pass to the goods which are appreciated and enjoyed through the distinctively human faculties —of which Knowledge, Beauty and Love are the obvious illustrations—we come to a stage where the subjective reference falls into the background, and the goods are social in the sense that enjoyment of them by one prompts rather than hinders a similar enjoyment on the part of others. The scholar does not exhaust the stock of knowledge so that others must be ignorant that he may know; the poet does not suck the beauty from the sunset; the loyal friend or disciple does not make love more difficult for his fellows. These goods are multiplied by being possessed. And they are truly possessed only in so far as they become the possessors. The man who would see Truth must yield his mind to the facts; the man who would enjoy Beauty must surrender his soul to its spell; the man who would love must give his very self, for that is what love is. At every point therefore the aspiration towards these forms of good requires a denial of self, and in the measure of its attainment passes over into worship, of which the meaning is total self-giving and self-submission to the Object of worship. This then, it seems, is man's true good—to worship. Only so can he be set in his true place within the Commonwealth of Value and find his own peace in rendering within that Commonwealth the special service for which his divine-created qualities fit him.

But how is he to do it? Natural Theology can tell him that the higher goods are those which call for most self-denial in the search for them—not denial of pleasures or other interests, though that is likely to be involved, but precisely of self as a subject of rights, claims, and interests. But if he asks how, being self-centred, he is to accomplish this, its answer is meagre. It bids him find what higher values have appeal for him, and first give himself to those; it may be that, drawn out of himself on that side, he will find himself able to respond more freely on others also. He may by such means be carried a short way or a long way, but his full deliverance by such means remains impossible; for that can only come with worship, and none of these various "goods" is by itself an object worthy or able to win that absolute submission. And Natural Theology cannot win him to worship. It may assure him that there is a God who both claims and deserves his worship; it may bid him to seek that God and the way to worship Him; but it cannot confront him with the God whom it describes. It can only discuss God; it cannot reveal Him. And for this reason its whole fabric of thought is liable to be laid in ruins by devastating doubt. For the existence of God is fully credible only if evil is being transmuted into good; and that cannot—demonstrably cannot—finally be accomplished unless God the Supreme Good becomes the apparent good to every man. Nothing else can destroy self-centredness, because in all value-judgements other than that expressed in worship the element of self-centredness remains. While it is there, it is a focus of possible temptation which may become a seed-plot of havoc laying waste the fairest spiritual achievements. Therefore Natural Theology, which is indispensable as a source of interpretation and as a purge of superstition even for those who have received a true revelation, yet if left to itself, ends in a hunger which it cannot satisfy, and yet of which it must perish if no satisfaction is forthcoming.

How is the Supreme Good to be my apparent good in such wise as to win from me the submission of my conscience, the subjection of my will, the adoration of my heart—in one word, my worship? Not by argument, for my mind must be critical towards that, and even when convinced could not control my heart; not by force, for my conscience must resist that; not by bribery, for my will cannot be bound by that. The Supreme Good can only be my apparent good and so dominate my Self if it both is, and, in a form quickening my sympathy, manifestly displays itself as, utterly selfless love. In order to evoke the full sympathy of human personalities, the form of its self-manifestation must be a human personality, subject to all human limitations, yet never yielding to the temptation arising from its finitude to prefer its own interests to that universal good which is the will of God—in other words, a finite self whose apparent good is the real good. Moreover, this manifestation must not be a single episode, but the opening of a way to communion with the eternal God, so that as we nourish our minds with the story of the manifestation they are in fact becoming increasingly possessed by the universal and eternal Spirit. Granted that divine self-revelation, the world may be intelligible; without that, the arch falls for lack of its keystone and the gulf between mind and the universe in which it appears remains unbridged. The fear lest that be so is the burden with which mankind is heavy laden; the task of lifting themselves from their own self-centredness is that whereat men vainly labour on pain of else becoming lower than the brutes. Natural Theology ends in a hunger for that Divine Revelation which it began by excluding from its purview. Rightly sifting with relentless criticism every argument, it knows what manner of Voice that must be which shall promise relief to mankind; but the Voice is not its own, nor can it judge the message that is spoken. "Come unto me . . . and I will give you rest"; it is not Philosophy that can estimate the right of the Speaker to issue that invitation or to make that promise; that right can be proved or disproved only by the experiment of life.

SUBJECT INDEX

[See following Index for Proper Names]

INDEX OF PROPER NAMES

SCIENTISTS

Astronomers

Biologists

Physicists

STATESMEN, SEERS AND SAGES

THE END

PRINTED IN GREAT BRITAIN BY
BILLING AND SONS LTD.
GUILDFORD AND LONDON
H9266